Keep this book. You will
need it and use it throughout
your career.

MANAGEMENT of FOOD and BEVERAGE OPERATIONS

Second Edition

Educational Institute Books

MANAGEMENT OF FOOD and BEVERAGE OPERATIONS

Second Edition

Jack D. Ninemeier, Ph.D., CHA

EDUCATIONAL INSTITUTE
American Hotel & Motel Association

Disclaimer

This publication is designed to provide accurate and authoritative information in regard to the subject matter covered. It is sold with the understanding that the publisher is not engaged in rendering legal, accounting, or other professional service. If legal advice or other expert assistance is required, the services of a competent professional person should be sought.

—From the Declaration of Principles jointly adopted by the American Bar Association and a Committee of Publishers and Associations

The author, Jack D. Ninemeier, is solely responsible for the contents of this publication. All views expressed herein are solely those of the author and do not necessarily reflect the views of the Educational Institute of the American Hotel & Motel Association (the Institute) or the American Hotel & Motel Association (AH&MA).

Nothing contained in this publication shall constitute a standard, an endorsement, or a recommendation of the Institute or AH&MA. The Institute and AH&MA disclaim any liability with respect to the use of any information, procedure, or product, or reliance thereon by any member of the hospitality industry.

Library of Congress Cataloging-in-Publication Data
Ninemeier, Jack D.
  Management of food and beverage operations / Jack D. Ninemeier.—
  2nd ed.
    p. cm.
  Rev. ed. of: Principles of food and beverage operations. 1984.
  Includes index.
  ISBN 0-86612-057-2
  ISBN 0-86612-100-5 (pbk.)
  1. Food service management. 2. Restaurant management.
3. Bartending. I. Ninemeier, Jack D. Principles of food and
beverage operations. II. Title.
TX911.3.M27N55 1991
647.95'068—dc20   90–36083
                                                      CIP

Editor: Jim Purvis
Cartoonist: Tim Hurst

Contents

Preface

It seems like only yesterday that the first edition of this book was written. Since that time, much has happened in the food service industry. A renewed focus on guest relations, marketing, technology, and the increased need to operate efficiently and professionally are among the many trends that have changed the industry and that will continue to confront it in the 1990s.

The primary goals of the book remain the same:

- To provide an up-to-date introduction for those who are considering a management career in commercial or institutional food service

- To reinforce basic knowledge and provide fresh perspectives for those currently managing food service operations

- To provide a source of information useful in food and beverage training programs

Part I is an introduction to the food service industry and to the art and science of managing. Food service marketing is also covered in Part I. Part II addresses menu management—nutrition concerns; planning, designing, and evaluating menus; and menu costs and pricing strategies. Part III deals with production, service, sanitation, and safety issues. Facility design and equipment, accounting, and food service automation make up Part IV.

In one sense it has been difficult to write this book; there is a constant challenge to capture all of the most important information about our complex industry and present it in a way that is easily understood. However, the task has been made immeasurably easier by content specialists and editorial staff at the Educational Institute. A special thank you is extended to Jim Purvis, editor of this book, who pointed out inconsistencies, eliminated redundancies, and made clear that which was unclear.

It is appropriate to remember those serving on the Review Committee for the first edition; most of their ideas, which helped form the foundation for the first book, are still present in the second: Richard A. Bruner, The University Club, East Lansing, Michigan; John D. Correll, Pizzuti's, Canton, Michigan; Michael E. Hurst, Fifteenth Street Fisheries, Fort Lauderdale, Florida (who in 1990 became president of the National Restaurant Association); Angelos Vlahakis, School of Hotel, Restaurant and Institutional Management, Michigan State University; and Ferdinand Wieland, CHA, CFBE, Hotel duPont, Wilmington, Delaware.

The second edition has been strengthened and enriched with subject-matter input from a new Review Committee: Norman Crawford, Sous Chef, Sparrow Hospital, Lansing, Michigan; George Fritz, CHA, Visiting Lecturer, Michigan State University; Robert Garlough, CEC, CCE, AAC, Director, Grand Rapids Junior College, Grand Rapids, Michigan; Jim Masceri, Owner, Bogie's Cafe, Okemos, Michigan; Dennis Panagopoulos, CFBE, Director of F&B, Muskegon Harbor Hilton, Muskegon, Michigan; Peter Wells, Instructor, Seneca College of Applied Arts &

Technology, Kings City, Ontario; and Arlea Williams, CHA, Instructor, The Educational Institute, East Lansing, Michigan.

Additionally, the countless professionals with whom I have come in contact during years of study, writing, research, teaching, consulting, and reading deserve a special—albeit anonymous—mention.

Since the time of the first edition, the food service industry has lost a most intelligent, creative, and professional individual. Mr. Rudy Mazzonelli was a long-time member of the American Hotel & Motel Association's Food and Beverage Committee and made innumerable formal and informal suggestions to improve the first edition and other early food service textbooks developed by the Institute. Rudy personally taught this writer many of the concepts that are now incorporated into lecture notes and publications.

The first edition of this book was dedicated to Mr. E. Ray Swan, President and Chief Executive Officer, Educational Institute of the American Hotel & Motel Association. His personal inspiration has continued over the years and the leadership he has brought to the Educational Institute will leave a permanent impact on the quality of educational opportunities available to the hospitality industry and academia worldwide. It is indeed an honor to dedicate this second edition to this creative leader and friend.

Jack D. Ninemeier
East Lansing, Michigan

Part I

Introduction

Chapter Outline

Food Service Origins
    Hotel Restaurants
        Inns in Ancient Times
        The Roman Catholic Church
        English Inns
        American Inns
        Hotels in the Twentieth Century
    Freestanding Restaurants
        Early Restaurants
        First U.S. Restaurant
        Chain Restaurants
        Drive-In Restaurants
        Fast-Food Franchise Operations
        Today's Food Service Innovations
    Food Service in Institutions
        Businesses
        Hospitals
        Schools
Commercial vs. Institutional Food Service Operations
    Commercial Operations
        Independents
        Chain Restaurants
        Franchises
    Institutional Operations
        Management Companies
Types of Food Service Facilities
    Commercial Facilities
        Freestanding Eating and Drinking Places
        Hotel Food Service Facilities
    Institutional Facilities
        Businesses
        Hospitals and Nursing Homes
        Schools
        Leisure Operations
        Transportation Companies
        Others

1

The Food Service Industry

WHEN YOU HEAR the term "food service," do you picture a dining room with starched white tablecloths in an expensive restaurant, a truck stop on a busy interstate, a fast-food outlet in the suburbs, or a concession operation in a professional sports arena? How about dietary services in schools, colleges, hospitals, nursing homes, and other institutions? And are you aware that military food service facilities and country clubs are also part of the food service industry? As you can see, the food service industry is vast, encompassing every type of food service operation that provides meals to people away from their homes.

The food service industry can be divided into two basic segments: commercial and institutional operations. Commercial operations seek to maximize profits. Examples of commercial operations include freestanding restaurants, hotel dining rooms, coffee shops, fast-food restaurants, and ice cream stands. Institutional food service operations exist in properties for whom providing food and beverage service is not the primary mission. Usually, but not always, institutional food service operatons seek to minimize expenses while paying special attention to providing nutritious meals. Examples of institutions that provide food services include schools, health care facilities, businesses, prisons, military installations, and leisure operations such as sports arenas and movie theaters.

Exhibit 1.1 recaps sales, food and beverage purchases, and growth information for the food service industry for the years 1986–1988. Note that, in 1988, total market sales were over $250 billion.

Another way to get an idea of the industry's scope is to look at the food service giants. Exhibit 1.2 shows the 25 largest food service companies in 1989. There may be some surprises for you on the list. Exhibit 1.3 lists basic information about the 25 largest independent restaurant operations in 1989. It's hard to imagine an independent restaurant grossing $31.5 million in one year, but that's what The Hilltop Steak House in Massachusetts did.

This chapter examines the origins of food service and some of the most important elements in the organization of food service operations of all types. If you are considering a career in food service, this information may be of great interest as you make a vocational decision. If you are already working in food service, the information may help you plan and develop your career.

Food Service Origins

In this section we will take a brief look at the origins of hotel restaurants, freestanding restaurants, and food service in institutions.

3

Exhibit 1.1 Food Service Industry Summary

FOOD SERVICE INDUSTRY SUMMARY	1987 Units	1987 Sales ($000,000)	1987 Purchases ($000,000)	1987 vs 1986 % Sales Growth Nominal	Real	1988 Sales ($000,000)	1988 Purchases ($000,000)	1988 vs 1987 % Sales Growth Nominal	Real	1993 Projected Sales ($000,000)	1988–1992 Projected % Compound Annual Sales Growth Nominal	Real
TOTAL MARKET	634,435	235,605	90,756	7.8	3.7	250,712	96,463	6.4	2.3	341,054	6.3	2.1
Commercial/Contract/Vending	488,600	199,350	72,824	8.3	4.1	212,802	77,705	6.7	2.6	293,518	6.6	2.3
Institutional/Internal	143,515	33,511	16,560	5.2	1.2	35,056	17,331	4.6	0.6	43,851	4.6	0.4
Military	3,320	2,744	1,372	4.4	0.4	2,854	1,427	4.0	0.0	3,685	5.2	1.0
MAJOR MARKET SEGMENTS:												
Eating & Drinking Places	336,400	137,106	47,290	9.4	5.2	146,221	50,341	6.6	2.5	200,938	6.6	2.3
Eating Places	303,800	125,730	43,308	10.1	9.7	135,009	46,417	7.4	3.3	187,165	6.8	2.4
Limited-Menu Restaurants	145,000	54,976	17,042	14.0	9.6	60,426	18,732	8.3	4.1	88,158	7.8	3.5
Full-Menu Restaurants	149,000	65,294	24,159	7.0	2.9	68,764	25,443	4.9	0.8	90,998	5.8	1.5
Retail	92,600	12,215	4,611	7.1	3.0	12,956	4,888	6.1	1.9	18,164	7.0	2.7
Hotel/Motel	25,600	12,050	3,704	2.2	(1.7)	12,598	3,873	4.5	0.5	16,642	5.7	1.5
Leisure	25,000	6,228	2,180	6.0	2.0	6,801	2,380	9.2	4.9	9,921	7.8	3.5
Business & Industry	16,000	14,065	7,033	6.0	1.9	15,140	7,570	7.6	3.4	20,534	6.3	2.0
Health Care	32,635	13,783	6,892	4.6	0.6	14,416	7,208	4.6	0.5	18,631	5.3	1.0
Student	92,350	18,840	9,050	5.2	1.2	19,741	9,490	4.8	0.8	25,119	4.9	0.7
Vending	9,000	13,264	5,969	5.8	1.8	14,140	6,363	6.6	2.4	18,712	5.8	1.5
Airline	30	3,244	1,622	13.1	8.8	3,610	1,805	11.3	6.9	5,526	8.9	4.5

NOTE: Sales estimates for Business & Industry, Health Care, Student, Vending, and Airline markets have been adjusted to reflect equivalent consumer expenditures, i.e., in non-commercial operations where a food sale, per se, does not take place. Other primarily institutional segments such as penal facilities, religious orders, cargo lines, etc., are included in institutional/internal feeding totals.

Purchases include all food, alcoholic, and non-alcoholic beverages. Alcoholic beverages have been excluded in Business & Industry, Health Care, Student, and Airline markets only. Limited-menu and full-menu restaurant sales are included in eating place sales. Eating place sales are included in eating and drinking place sales and should not be added with other major market segments to arrive at total market sales.

Source: Reprinted with permission of Restaurant Business Magazine.

Exhibit 1.2 Food Service Industry Giants

Rank '89 ('88)	Organization Segment	'88 sales/ ('87 sales) in $ millions	% change sales	'88 units/ ('87 units)	% change units
1 (1)	McDonald's Corp. Fast-food (hamburgers)	16,100.0 (14,330.4)	12.3	10,513 (9,911)	6.1
2 (A)	Burger King Corp. Fast-food (hamburgers)	5,400.0 (5,000.0**)	8.0	5,793 (5,179)	11.9
3 (A)	Kentucky Fried Chicken Fast-food (chicken)	5,000.0 (4,100.0)	22.0	7,761 (7,522)	3.2
4 (A)	Pizza Hut Fast-food (pizza)	3,390.0 (A)	—	6,662 (A)	—
5 (A)	Marriott Food Service Mgmt. Contract management	3,353.4†* (A)	—	2,300* (A)	—
6 (5)	U.S. Dept. of Agriculture Food & Nutrition Service Government institutions	3,035.8† (3,095.4†)	−1.9	89,791 (90,180)	−0.4
7 (6)	Wendy's International Inc. Fast-food (hamburgers)	2,902.0 (2,870.0)	1.1	3,762 (3,816)	−1.4
8 (A)	Hardee's Inc. Fast-food (hamburgers)	2,733.3* (2,418.9)*	13.0	3,100 (2,959)	4.8
9 (7)	ARA Services, Inc. Contract management	2,350.0 (2,144.0ᴿ)	9.6	2,500 (3,842)	−34.9
10 (10)	Domino's Pizza Inc. Fast-food (pizza)	2,300.0 (1,980.0)	16.2	4,943 (4,279)	15.5
11 (A)	Dairy Queen Fast-food (sweets)	2,067.0 (1,900.0)	8.8	5,122 (5,005)	2.3
12 (A)	Taco Bell Fast-food (Mexican)	1,630.0 (1,500.0)	8.7	2,930 (2,712)	8.0
13 (14)	The Sheraton Corp. Lodging	1,600.0 (1,391.2)	15.0	1,750 (1,555)	12.5
14 (32)	U.S. Army Troop Support Agency Military	1,332.8† (1,310.4†)	1.7	995 (1,074)	−7.4
15 (13)	Denny's Inc. Full service (family dining)	1,300.0 (1,251.0)	3.9	1,299 (1,221)	6.4
16 (A)	Red Lobster Full service (seafood)	1,300.0** (977.0)	33.1	512 (410)	24.9
17 (A)	Canteen Corp. Contract management	1,288.8 (A)	—	1,883 (A)	—
18 (A)	Marriott Lodging Division Lodging	1,218.3* (A)	—	585* (A)	—
19 (20)	Arby's, Inc. Fast-food (sandwiches)	1,160.0 (980.0)	18.4	2,049 (1,973)	3.9
20 (21)	Hilton Hotel Corp. Lodging	1,054.0 (970.0)	8.7	1,185* (1,185)	—
21 (19)	Service America Corp. Contract management	1,001.0** (1,030.0**)	−2.8	2,000ᴮ (11,000**)	—

(continued)

Exhibit 1.2 *(continued)*

Rank '89 ('88)	Organization Segment	'88 sales/ ('87 sales) in $ millions	% change sales	'88 units/ ('87 units)	% change units
22 (46)	**Big Boy** Full service (family dining)	944.0** (A)	—	912 (A)	—
23 (30)	**Little Caesars Pizza** Fast-food (pizza)	908.0 (A)	25.2	2,180 (1,820)	19.8
24 (24)	**U.S. Navy Food Service Systems Office** Military	896.0†** (810.0†)	10.6	684 (684)	—
25 (A)	**Shoney's Restaurants** Full service (family dining)	864.1 (718.6)	20.2	636 (614)	3.6

*R&I estimate; **company est; †commercial equiv.; (A) no comparison with '88 data possible; (B) adjusted method in reporting figures; (C) franchisee sales est.; (R) revised.

Source: *Restaurants & Institutions,* July 10, 1989, pp. 73–79.

Hotel Restaurants

Inns in Ancient Times. Food service operations as we know them today in hotels and motels evolved from early inns and other rest shelters for travelers. Just like travelers today, travelers in ancient times needed "bed and board." Along with sleeping accommodations and food, many inns also provided alcoholic beverages and entertainment for their guests. Innkeepers prepared meals from whatever food was available. There was usually plenty of wine and beer, plus cheese, vegetables, and a variety of cakes and buns. Meat, if available, included goat, pork, lamb, and fish. By the time of the Roman Empire, inns were commonplace.

The Roman Catholic Church. In the Middle Ages the Roman Catholic Church maintained hospices (a type of inn), monasteries, and other religious houses which were rest areas for travelers. One religious order, The Knights of Saint John of Jerusalem (founded in 1048), established many cathedrals and monasteries to protect pilgrims traveling to and from Jerusalem.[1] In effect, the church operated the first hotel chain.

English Inns. In England there were a few inns or "ale houses" that rented rooms as early as 1400. They were located in large towns, at major crossroads, at ferry landings, and along well-traveled roads. Whether travel was by foot, horseback, stagecoach, or canal boat, travelers had to rest and eat. Inns provided necessary services for these travelers. Some inns were actually private homes with one or two extra bedrooms. Others were large buildings with as many as 20 or 30 rooms.

American Inns. The evolution of inns and taverns in the United States was similar to the English pattern. While the food was often simple, it was plentiful; beer and rum were usually served also.[2] A tavern known as Cole's Ordinary was opened in Boston in 1634 by Samuel Cole. Cole's Ordinary was the first tavern in Boston and probably the first in the American colonies. In America, as elsewhere, lodging and food service accommodations followed travel routes.

Exhibit 1.3 Top 25 Independent Restaurants in Sales—1989

'89 Rank	'88 Rank	Restaurant/city/owner	Sales	Opened	Seats	People served/year
1	1	**The Hilltop Steak House** Saugus, Mass. Frank Giuffrida & Jack Swansburg	$31.500MM	1951	1,300	2,380,000
2	2	**Tavern on the Green** New York Warner LeRoy	25.900	1976	1,197	625,000
3	6	**Smith & Wollensky** New York Alan Stillman	16.500	1977	420	370,000
4	4	**Phillips Harborplace** Baltimore Brice, Shirley, Steven & Olivia Phillips & Paul Wall	14.960	1982	700	540,000
5	5	**Anthony's Pier 4** Boston Anthony Athanas & Family	14.800*	1963	650	650,000*
6	7	**The Manor** West Orange, N.J. Harry Knowles & Family	14.500**	1957	1,500	425,000
7	—	**Legal Sea Foods** Boston (Park Plaza) Dan, Mary & John Hountalas	14.200	1980	292	585,000**
8	8	**The Four Seasons** New York Paul Kovi & Tom Margittai	14.200*	1959	400	188,000*
9	17	**The Kapok Tree** Clearwater, Fla. Aaron R. Fodiman & Murray Steinfeld	12.726	1957	1,750	1,000,480
10	9	**Zehnders of Frankenmuth** Frankenmuth, Mich. Edwin L. Zehnder	12.555	1856	1,300	1,000,010
11	12	**Scoma's Restaurant** San Francisco Al Scoma	12.121	1965	300	528,394
12	10	**Spenger's Fish Grotto** Berkeley, Calif. Frank L. Spenger & Frank Spenger Jr.	12.000	1890	700	910,000
13	3	**The '21' Club** New York Knoll Int'l Holdings (Marshall Cogan)	12.000	1923	650	200,000
14	—	**The Waterfront** Covington, Ky. J. Ruby, P. Rose, B. Esiason & C. Collinsworth	11.028	1986	290	220,000
15	11	**Old San Francisco Steakhouse** Dallas Henry Reed & Partners	11.000**	1974	750	504,000
16	14	**Shooters on the Water** Fort Lauderdale, Fla. R. Moreau, A. Lahaye, M. Burge & R. Maranda	10.850	1982	340	620,500
17	15	**The Water Club** New York Michael D. O'Keeffe	10.700*	1982	250	150,000
18	16	**Old Original Bookbinders** Philadelphia John & Albert Taxin	10.500**	1865	800	264,000
19	18	**Le Cirque** New York Sirio Maccioni	10.000**	1974	125	145,000
20	36	**Bob Chinn's Crab House** Wheeling, Ill. Robert & Marilyn Chinn	9.595	1982	630	515,000
21	—	**The Cheesecake Factory** Marina del Rey, Calif. David Overton	9.440	1983	250	790,000

(continued)

Exhibit 1.3 *(continued)*

'89 Rank	'88 Rank	Restaurant/city/owner	Sales	Opened	Seats	People served/year
22	19	**Jimmy's Harborside** Boston Charles J. Doulos	9.400	1924	460	345,000
23	23	**Joe's Stone Crab** Miami Beach, Fla. JoAnn Sawitz-Bass	9.398	1913	380	330,000
24	13	**The Russian Tea Room** New York Faith Stewart-Gordon	9.340	1926	325	300,000
25	20	**The Hard Rock Cafe** New York Mecca Plc.	9.320	1984	250	711,228
R&I estimate **owner estimate						

Source: *Restaurants & Institutions,* March 6, 1989, pp. 48.

Hotels in the Twentieth Century. During the early 1900s, large modern hotels were constructed in nearly every large city in the United States.[3] These hotels became very popular with travelers. Community events and special occasions often centered on the hotel and its food and beverage operation.

In the 1950s there was a perceived decline in the quality of hotel food and beverage operations in some lodging properties. The mid-seventies saw a rebirth in the purpose and quality of hotel food service operations. Today, hotel restaurants are an integral part of the profit plan at many properties. Prime hotel space such as the lobby/atrium is often allocated to food and beverage outlets. Experienced chefs, highest quality food and beverage products and services, and extravagant community promotions have helped to create a new, positive image for hotel food and beverage operations.

Freestanding Restaurants

Early Restaurants. An early form of restaurant, the coffeehouse, appeared in England in the mid-1600s. By the early eighteenth century, there were approximately 3,000 coffeehouses in London.

Restaurants as we know them today began in 1765 in Paris, France. There is an interesting story about the proprietor of, perhaps, the first public restaurant. Before 1765, public food services were offered by inns and catering operations. The caterers, called "traiteurs," formed a guild (union) with limited membership. When a soup vendor created a soup made of sheep's feet and white wine sauce, he was brought to court by the guild because of alleged competition. However, the court ruled that this specialty dish did not compete with any dish prepared by the guild, and the vendor was allowed to continue. The soup vendor merchandised the soup as *"le restaurant divin"*—the divine restorative (this gave us the word "restaurant"). Because of the publicity, the vendor's soup kitchen became famous and even the king of France wanted to taste the specialty which created the public commotion.[4]

First U.S. Restaurant. In the United States, credit for the first restaurant is generally given to Delmonico's, established in New York City in 1827. The Delmonico family operated nine restaurants until 1923. These restaurants were known for lavish banquets and extensive menus (371 dishes could be ordered). Relatively few cities could support restaurants like Delmonico's, which offered high cuisine at high prices. Then, as now, the vast majority of American eating places offered simpler, less expensive food items for their guests.

Chain Restaurants. The first big chain restaurant operator was Fred Harvey; by 1912, his company operated a dozen large hotels, 65 railway restaurants, and 60 dining cars. John R. Thompson was another early chain operator. By 1926, he controlled 126 self-service restaurants in the Midwest and the South.[5]

Chain restaurants that are generally known today include specialty operations like Houlihan's and Bennigan's, and cafeteria chains—Furr's in the Southwest and Bishop's in the Midwest.

Drive-In Restaurants. By the 1920s, there were enough automobiles in the United States to support a new type of food service facility: the drive-in restaurant. People could eat in their cars with curb service provided by carhops. In the 1960s, this innovation was largely replaced with indoor fast-food franchise operations.

Fast-Food Franchise Operations. Nothing has had a greater impact on the food service industry than fast-food franchise operations. Fast-food franchising dates back to at least the 1920s and 1930s when A&W Root Beer and Howard Johnson's franchised some of their units.[6]

Many of the more familiar fast-food names appear in Exhibit 1.2. Sandwiches—primarily hamburgers—rule the fast-food segment of the industry. Hamburgers can be traced back to medieval times, but they were first served on a bun at the St. Louis World's Fair in 1904. Today many fast-food restaurants feature chicken or seafood, but the hamburger is still "king." Fast-food chain restaurants such as McDonald's, Wendy's, Burger King, and Kentucky Fried Chicken are familiar to millions throughout the world.

Today's Food Service Innovations. Drive-throughs are now part of many fast-food operations. Some drive-throughs accommodate two automobiles at the same time. "Food courts" in shopping malls provide shoppers with many different types of food choices in one convenient location. People who want food and conversation while doing their laundry can go to "laundro-bars"—operations with a Laundromat and food and beverage service (including alcoholic beverages) all under one roof. An increasing number of grocery and convenience stores devote a significant amount of space to "help yourself" salads, sandwiches, snacks, and other items that can be taken out or, sometimes, consumed on-site in sit-down or stand-up locations. Fast-food operations, once found only in freestanding buildings, are now occupying space in hotels, department stores, airline terminals, military installations, health care facilities, schools and colleges, and elsewhere.

Fax machines are adding a new wrinkle to ordering food. A fax machine scans a document and transmits it electronically to a receiving fax machine. The process typically takes less than 30 seconds per page. Busy executives and others with

Hamburgers can be traced back to medieval times.

access to fax machines can use them to transmit take-out orders to the restaurant; their orders can be prepared as they are traveling to the restaurant to pick them up. Many restaurants are joining what some call the "fax food revolution." Maxine's Seafood Cafe in Hollywood, California, receives almost half of its take-out orders via fax machine. The Brasserie restaurant in New York City has created a "Le Fax Menu."[7]

The increasing popularity of home delivery is another trend some restaurants are taking advantage of. In some large cities, delivery services are available to take your order, go to the restaurant of your choice, and transport your order home to you. Some delivery services will even serve your meal and clean up afterwards. A small but growing number of restaurants are using overnight delivery services to mail food great distances—even across the country—to customers who telephone for long-distance take-out.

Food Service in Institutions

There are many types of institutional food service programs; to cover the origins of them all is beyond the scope of this book. However, three institutions especially important to the development of institutional food service should be mentioned here: businesses, hospitals, and schools.[8]

Businesses. Robert Owen has been called "the father of industrial catering." As a young mill-operator in Scotland, Owen was appalled by the exploitation of workers in the British textile industry. About 1815, as part of a general program to improve the working conditions of his employees, he established a large "eating room" for employees and their families. Owen's methods were so successful that they spread throughout the world.

In the United States the textile industry began to grow rapidly after the first cotton mills were established in the 1820s along the Merrimack River in Massachusetts. Along with the mills themselves, boarding houses were built nearby to house and feed the workers.

By the 1890s a number of factories, insurance companies, banks, and other businesses provided food service for employees. The Seaside Institute, The National Cash Register Company, Metropolitan Life, Prudential, and the New York and Chicago telephone companies are just a few of the businesses that opened table service or lunchroom facilities during this decade. Cafeteria service was not introduced to businesses until 1902 when a building housing a kitchen, two cafeterias, and recreational facilities was built for the Plymouth Cordage Company, Plymouth, Massachusetts. By 1905, some 50 U.S. businesses, mostly manufacturing plants, were providing food service for their employees.

World War I saw an increase in the number of businesses that offered food service to workers. As plants expanded and workers became scarce, providing food service was a means of attracting and keeping good workers. Cafeteria service became more popular, since large numbers of workers could be fed quickly, fewer people were needed to run a cafeteria, and workers could select the food they wanted at the prices they were willing to pay. By 1928, a study of 4,075 manufacturing plants revealed that 75% of the plants that employed 1,000 workers or more provided food service for workers.

World War II saw another leap in the number of businesses providing food service. By the end of the war, approximately one-third of all industrial workers were getting fed on the job.

Of course, many changes have occurred in business food service programs since 1945. The coffee break was introduced widely during World War II and is now a business standard; many businesses provide coffee throughout the working day for free or for a modest fee. It isn't just the industry giants who are providing food service these days; more and more small businesses are setting up food service programs for their employees to improve morale and productivity. Programs range from gourmet dining to food from vending machines. Meals can be prepared on-site or catered in. There is a new emphasis on nutrition; more and more business food service programs are providing nutritious menu alternatives and educating workers on the benefits of eating properly.

Hospitals. Crude hospitals were known in India and Egypt as early as 600 B.C. In early Greece and Rome the sick took refuge in temples; as with hospitals today, food was provided for patients. The first hospital was established in England in

A.D. 1004. The first hospital on the American continent was established in Mexico in 1524.

An emphasis on a therapeutic diet became important in hospitals only in the mid-1800s. It was during this period that an English nurse, Florence Nightingale, created the beginnings of modern hospital organization. She is considered the first modern hospital administrator and dietitian.

In early hospitals in the United States, food preparation was the responsibility of a cook, the head housekeeper, or the head nurse. As the relationship of nutrition to a patient's recovery and good health became recognized, doctors began to seek people in food service to assist in creating healthy diets for their patients. At an 1899 Home Economics Conference in Lake Placid, New York, the title of "dietitian" was selected for people who entered this new profession. In 1917 the American Dietetic Association was founded with 98 members; today the association boasts 50,000 members.

During the two world wars, trained dietitians were very successful at providing appropriate food for patients in military hospitals. During World War II, 1,998 dietitians served in the Armed Forces. Many dietitians saw service during the conflicts in Korea and Vietnam as well.

Menus offering patients a selection of menu items are the norm for most hospitals today. Centralized kitchens make food preparation more efficient. Many hospitals have cash cafeterias for employees and visitors. In some hospitals, management companies run the food service operation under the guidance of a dietitian (management companies will be discussed later in the chapter). Modern hospital food service programs feature extensive menus, high-quality food products, and modern preparation and service equipment. Many hospital food service programs are comparable in many ways with commercial food service operations. In fact, some hospital food service facilities compete with commercial operations by offering take-home food for employees.

Schools. Although schools were known in ancient times, there are few records of their methods of food service. The universities that began to be established in Europe during the twelfth century typically did not provide food service. Students boarded with residents of the local community and were responsible for their own meals. Students at Oxford (founded in England in the latter part of the twelfth century) and Cambridge (established in the thirteenth century) had living quarters on campus, but had to make their own meals with the help of their servants. Eventually, dining halls were established at these universities. In these halls, a very formal evening meal was provided.

English public schools for children such as Rugby, Eton, and Harrow evolved from religious institutions established during the Middle Ages. (Because of their character and approach to education, "public" schools in England are the equivalent of "private" schools in the United States.) These and other public schools were not known for their food service. Charles Dickens paints a bleak picture of public schools and the food they served in *Nicholas Nickleby* and other novels.

American schools were patterned after English schools. By 1776 ten universities were established in the American colonies. From the beginning, various forms of food service were provided at each university. School food services in elementary and secondary schools began in the mid-1800s and evolved into modern programs reaching millions of students daily during the school year. In 1935 Congress first made federal funds available to subsidize school food programs. Federal support programs have continued and expanded in the years since.

Early school food service at the university level tended to be table service; today cafeteria service is preferred by most universities, as well as by elementary and secondary schools. Food service in dormitories, student unions, and lunchrooms can be provided by the schools themselves or by management companies. Care is usually taken to provide well-balanced meals. Commercial food service operations have been built near college campuses for hundreds of years; a recent trend is for commercial operations, especially fast-food franchises, to appear on campus in student unions.[9]

Commercial vs. Institutional Food Service Operations

As previously mentioned, the food service industry can be divided into two basic segments: commercial or for-profit operations and institutional or non-profit operations. The task of separating operations into for-profit and non-profit categories is not as simple as it sounds. There are many for-profit management companies which operate food services in institutions. In these cases, while the institution itself does not seek to make a profit from the sale of food items, the company managing the food service program does.

Commercial Operations

Three basic commercial food service operations are independents, chain restaurants, and franchises.

Independents. An independent operation is owned by an owner or owners who have one or more properties that have no chain relationship—menus may not be identical among properties, food purchase specifications may differ, operating procedures are varied, etc.

A large number of restaurants that open are not in business five years later, so the statistics work against independent operators. New operators are lured into the restaurant business for many reasons. "People have to eat—why shouldn't they eat at my place?" is a thought that has launched many restaurants. New entrepreneurs are further encouraged because many restaurants require relatively little capital to get started. Land, facilities, and equipment can be leased, and the minimal amount of inventory needed to open a restaurant can often be purchased on several weeks' credit.

In an industry increasingly dominated by chain restaurants and franchise operations, is there still a place for an independent operator? The answer is "yes." Entrepreneurs who can spot a market whose wants and needs are not currently being met may be able to capture that market and prosper—if they provide value and good service to guests.

Chain Restaurants. Chain restaurants are restaurants that are part of a multi-unit organization. They often share the same menu, purchase supplies and equipment cooperatively, and follow operating procedures that have been standardized for every restaurant in the chain. A chain restaurant may be owned by a parent company, a franchise company, or by a private owner or owners. Some chains are operated by a management company. There are many chain restaurants in the food service industry and their variety and numbers continue to grow (see Exhibit 1.4).

Some people incorrectly believe that a chain and a franchise operation are the same; they are not. While a franchise property is affiliated with a chain, a chain property is not necessarily a franchise.

Advantages. What are the advantages of restaurant chains? Large chains can readily acquire cash, credit, and long-term leases on land and buildings. This is not as feasible for many independent properties. Chains can afford to make more mistakes than independent operators can. Related to this is the ability of a chain to experiment with different menus, themes, designs, and operating procedures. After it discovers the correct "mix," the chain can develop a package for use by all its properties. The independent operator has limited opportunities to undertake extensive experimentation.

Restaurant chains also have a personnel advantage. Chains can afford staff specialists who are experts in finance, construction, operations, and recipe development. Independent operators must handle most, if not all, of these responsibilities.

Chains have another advantage from a control perspective. They are able to generate internal financial information that can be used as a basis of comparison among properties. Independent operators usually know how well their restaurants *are* doing, but are frequently unaware of how well their restaurants *should* be doing. A restaurant chain operating many properties within a certain geographic area can more easily generate information that can be used to set sales goals, as well as identify problems in specific properties.

Disadvantages. There are also disadvantages to restaurant chains. It can be difficult for chains to keep up with changing markets and economic conditions. As chains grow, a bureaucracy involving a large amount of paperwork, rules, and procedures can slow them down. Top management may lose the motivation to keep up, and what is best for the company might not always receive the highest priority.

Franchises. Franchises are a special category of chain operations. With a franchise, the franchisee (the owner of the franchise property) pays fees to use the name, building design, and business methods of the franchisor (the franchise company). Furthermore, the franchisee must agree to maintain the franchisor's business and quality standards. The franchisor expands the franchise chain by signing up franchisees. Franchisees are often local businesspeople with investment funds. However, large companies seeking investment options may also purchase a franchise.

The franchisee is usually responsible for generating funds to start the business. In addition to initial franchise fees, the franchisee may be required to pay (1) royalty fees assessed on the basis of a specified percentage of sales or other factors; and (2) advertising costs, sign rental fees, and other costs such as stationery and food products. (It may be against the law to stipulate, as part of the franchise agreement, that the franchisee must buy products of any kind from the franchisor).

Exhibit 1.4 Fast-Growing Restaurant Chains

TOP 50 GROWTH CHAINS
RANKED BY PERCENTAGE INCREASE IN SALES AND UNITS

Sales Rank	Chain	U.S. System Sales (000) 1988	U.S. System Sales (000) 1987	% Sales Change 1987–88	Avg. Unit Volume (000) 1988	U.S. System Units 1988	U.S. System Units 1987	% Unit Change 1987–88	Unit Rank
1	RALLY'S	$48,000*	$25,000*	92.0%	$600	112	46	143.5%	1
2	OLIVE GARDEN	244,000	137,000	78.1	2,500	125	70	78.6	3
3	TCBY	210,000	121,200	73.3	224	1,175	822	42.9	5
4	EL POLLO LOCO	120,900	75,000	61.2	1,100	149	83	79.5	2
5	OLD COUNTRY BUFFET	71,751	47,772	50.2	1,957	53	36	47.2	4
6	MRS. FIELDS	160,000*	110,000*	45.5	345	550	400	37.5	7
7	T.J. CINNAMONS	50,000	35,000	42.9	225	223	201	10.9	28
8	RUBY TUESDAY	128,000	94,500	35.4	1,800	80	63	27.0	12
9	PIZZERIA UNO	72,600*	54,300*	33.7	1,425	52	45	15.6	21
10	CRACKER BARREL	147,823	110,621	33.6	2,360	67	56	19.6	20
11	SBARRO	154,400	116,000	33.1	485	288	212	35.8	8
12	VIE DE FRANCE	32,500	24,600	32.1	600	56	54	3.7	47
13	CHILI'S	297,960	226,110	31.8	2,064	159	126	26.2	15
14	LE PEEP	32,000*	24,400*	31.1	540	67	48	39.6	6
15	WHATABURGER	272,000	210,000*	29.5	645	422	345	22.3	16
16	GOOD EARTH RESTAURANTS	66,000*	52,000*	26.9	2,000	33	26	26.9	13
17	RYAN'S FAMILY STEAK HOUSES	234,000	185,000	26.5	2,184	122	95	28.4	11
18	OLD SPAGHETTI WAREHOUSE	25,400	20,700	22.7	2,100	12	11	9.1	34
19	PIETRO'S	44,000*	36,000*	22.2	575	79	65	21.5	17
20	HOUSTON'S RESTAURANTS	69,557	57,019	22.0	4,067	18	16	12.5	26
21	BAKERS SQUARE	189,354	155,788	21.5	1,250	150	138	8.7	35
22	VALENTINO'S	34,000	28,000	21.4	950	40	30	33.3	10
23	ARK RESTAURANTS	37,853	31,394	20.6	2,000	19	15	26.7	14
24	L&N SEAFOOD GRILL	36,000	30,300	18.8	2,000	18	16	12.5	27
25	RED ROBIN	100,325	85,358*	17.5	2,134	47	45	4.4	46
26	BENIHANA OF TOKYO	84,000	71,600	17.3	1,750	47	44	6.8	39
27	SANDWICH CHEF	35,000	30,000*	16.7	210	175	200	(12.5)	50
28	TOGO'S	55,000	47,300	16.3	470	121	110	10.0	31
29	BLACK-EYED PEA	72,000*	62,000	16.1	1,350	55	48	14.6	23
30	SIRLOIN STOCKADE	52,305	45,149	15.8	770	67	64	4.7	45
31	OLGA'S KITCHEN	41,700	36,000*	15.8	900	51	38	34.2	9
32	JERRY'S SUBS & PIZZA	38,000	33,000	15.2	575	68	63	7.9	37
33	BLIMPIE	107,400	93,600	14.7	325	350	292	19.9	19
34	PICCADILLY CAFETERIAS	251,883	219,609	14.7	1,999	126	118	6.8	40
35	BOB EVANS FARMS	285,526	249,191	14.6	1,400	221	194	13.9	24
36	CHICK-FIL-A	232,189	202,724	14.5	622	386	363	6.3	41
37	GROUND ROUND	260,975	228,600	14.2	1,245	212	192	10.4	29
38	RALPH & KACOO'S	26,738	23,447	14.0	4,684	6	5	20.0	18
39	ORIG. GREAT AM. COOKIE	49,000	43,000	14.0	215	247	215	14.9	22
40	HUDDLE HOUSE	50,000	44,000	13.6	360	147	130	13.1	25
41	QUINCY'S FAMILY STEAK HOUSES	250,900	221,500	13.3	1,170	211	215	(1.9)	49
42	OLD SPAGHETTI FACTORY	36,900	32,600	13.2	1,600	23	21	9.5	33
43	LEVY RESTAURANTS	62,000*	55,000*	12.7	1,938**	32	29	10.3	30
44	PAPA GINO'S	132,000	117,500	12.3	650	207	192	7.8	38
45	RESTAURANTS UNLIMITED	56,000	50,000	12.0	2,900	19	18	5.6	43
46	HAPPY JOE'S PIZZA	28,283	25,304	11.8	362	78	78	0.0	48
47	TACO JOHN'S	116,000	104,000	11.5	273	448	424	5.7	42

(continued)

Exhibit 1.4 *(continued)*

Sales Rank	Chain	U.S. System Sales (000) 1988	U.S. System Sales (000) 1987	% Sales Change 1987–88	Avg. Unit Volume (000) 1988	U.S. System Units 1988	U.S. System Units 1987	% Unit Change 1987–88	Unit Rank
48	MARIE CALLENDER'S	245,000*	220,000*	11.4	2,000	148	135	9.6	32
49	CAROUSEL SNACK BARS	52,000*	46,800*	11.1	170	330	313	5.4	44
50	LUBY'S CAFETERIAS	264,000	239,000	10.5	2,360	117	108	8.3	36

*Technomic estimate   **RB estimate

Although many of the top restaurant chains have had to grow cautiously in the past few years, some of the small and midsize chains have posted impressive growth numbers. This exhibit ranks the top fifty chains in 1989 in terms of growth. Source: Reprinted with permission of Restaurant Business Magazine.

Advantages. The benefits of owning or managing a food service franchise typically include:

- Start-up assistance
- Company-sponsored training programs for management staff and training resource materials for employees
- National contributions toward local advertising campaigns
- Higher sales because of more extensive advertising, greater name recognition of the franchise chain, and the consistency of products and services among chain properties (guests know what to expect)
- Lower food costs due to volume purchasing by the chain
- Tested operating procedures which specify how things should be done

Many food service franchisors and franchisees have been tremendously successful. When franchisors are successful, they can command high fees and there may be long waiting lists to buy a franchise. Often, the franchisees are screened, and there may be little choice in the areas (territories) that are available for purchase.

Disadvantages. There are also disadvantages to owning or managing a food service franchise. The contract is generally very restrictive. The franchisee has little choice about the style of operation, the products served, services offered, and even methods of operation. The menu might be set, along with the decor, required furnishings, and production equipment. Since the franchise agreement is drawn up by the franchisor, the document generally favors the franchisor. The agreement may leave little to negotiate. This causes problems if there are disagreements between the two parties.[10]

Institutional Operations

Traditionally, institutional food service operations have focused on nutrition and other non-economic factors. Today, as pressures for cost containment accompany reduced income, there is a need to manage institutional food service operations as professional businesses. Sometimes this is done by the institutions themselves. Other institutions choose management companies to help them minimize costs.

Management Companies. An increasing number of institutions are using for-profit management companies or contract food services to operate their food service programs. There are many advantages to using management companies:

- Large nationwide management companies have greater resources to solve specific problems.

- Management companies can save money for institutions through effective negotiations with suppliers.

- Management companies can often operate institutional food service programs at a lower cost than the institutions can.

- Institution administrators, trained in areas other than food service operations, can delegate food service responsibilities to professional food service managers. (Large institutions often retain a "food service liaison" to represent them in the ongoing relationship with management company personnel.)

There are also potential disadvantages to using management companies:

- Some management companies may have too much control in matters that affect the public image of the institution, long-range operating plans, and other important issues.

- Some people may dislike having a profit-making business involved in the operation of a health care, educational, or other institutional food service program.

- There may be concerns that a management company will decrease food and beverage quality.

- The institutional operation may depend too much on the management company. What happens if the management company discontinues the contract? How long will it take to implement a self-operated program or find another management company?

- Although management companies are usually hired to reduce operating costs, higher operating costs are also possible when management companies are used.

Types of Food Service Facilities

There are many different types of commercial and institutional food service facilities in the food service industry.

Commercial Facilities

For the purposes of this text, we will divide commercial facilities into "freestanding eating and drinking places" and "hotel food service facilities."

Freestanding Eating and Drinking Places. Freestanding eating and drinking places can be independent properties, chain properties, or franchises. Types of freestanding eating and drinking places include:

- Full-menu restaurants and lunchrooms
- Limited-menu restaurants

- Public cafeterias
- Bars and taverns
- Ice cream and frozen yogurt stands
- Caterers

Full-menu restaurants and lunchrooms. These operations provide indoor and/or outdoor table service and a wide variety of menu items. They may be open for only one meal period or for 24 hours daily. Some offer a "California style" menu: items that are usually served for breakfast, lunch, or dinner are offered at all times. Many full-menu restaurants and lunchrooms serve alcoholic beverages. There are many examples of independent full-menu restaurants that are well-known locally; Denny's is an example of a full-menu nationwide chain restaurant.

Limited-menu restaurants. These operations have a limited variety of menu items. Typically, the guest walks up to a service counter or drives up to a service window, orders food, and carries it to a table if there is inside seating, or consumes the food in a car. Some limited-menu restaurants offer table service. Examples of limited-menu chain restaurants include Arby's and Pizza Hut.

Public cafeterias. These operations are often similar to full-menu restaurants and lunchrooms because they offer a wide variety of menu items, but table service may be limited.

Bars and taverns. These operations serve alcoholic beverages. Typically, limited or no food services are offered.

Ice cream and frozen yogurt stands. These operations offer primarily frozen dairy and related products.

Caterers. These operations prepare meals for large or small banquets and may provide food service in on- or off-site locations.

Hotel Food Service Facilities. In 1988, food sales were approximately 23.6% of total sales dollars generated by the U.S. lodging industry; beverage sales, 7.6%.[11] This suggests that hotel food and beverage facilities are much more than casual operations offered just for the convenience of guests. In fact, many hoteliers realize that food and beverage departments cannot generate required profits on the basis of sales to in-house guests only. Extensive patronage from the local community is often necessary for hotel food and beverage operations to realize economic goals.

Just as with freestanding eating and drinking places, there are many types of hotel food service facilities, such as coffee shops, family restaurants, specialty restaurants or gourmet rooms, and room service.

Trends. Trends in hotel food services include use of in-room bar (beverage dispensing) equipment, "take-up" (to the guestroom) deli-bar or other sandwich/snack services, and availability of pizza and beer through room service. Each of these services is designed to compete with food and beverage operations outside the hotel.

Institutional Facilities

Many institutional food service operations emphasize nutrition. People in some institutions receive 100% of their daily food intake at the institution, making it especially important to protect the health and well-being of those being served.

Trained dietitians are often retained on a full-time or consulting basis. In some cases dietitians actually manage the food service operation; in others they assist operating managers.

Institutions that provide food service include businesses, hospitals and nursing homes, schools, leisure operations, transportation companies, and others.

Businesses. Programs for businesses range from vended services in manufacturing plants to gourmet dining facilities in the executive dining rooms of large banks and insurance companies. Food service can be provided by contract food service companies or by the businesses themselves. Food service programs for employees can exist in almost any type of work situation. Sometimes programs are subsidized by employers who offer them as a fringe benefit to employees. Factories and construction sites may be served by mobile catering services—"meals on wheels"—and by street vendors who sell a variety of products—hot dogs, sandwiches, ice cream, etc.

Hospitals and Nursing Homes. Hospitals and nursing homes of all types make up an important part of the institutional food service market. Some of these institutions are privately owned; others are run by a government agency. Besides acute-care hospitals, where patients typically stay for only a short time, and nursing homes that provide permanent care for their residents, there are also homes for the blind, for orphans, and for mentally and physically handicapped people. Food service programs at these institutions can be self-operated or managed by for-profit companies.

Schools. Food service for schools—public and parochial elementary and secondary schools, and post-secondary schools (vocational schools, colleges, and universities)—can be provided by the schools themselves or by management companies.

Some public school systems in large cities serve hundreds of thousands of meals daily. Elementary and secondary schools may participate in the federally subsidized National School Lunch Program and other child nutrition programs. In addition to traditional school lunches, school food service programs may include school breakfasts, meals at community events, and senior citizen meals.

There are more than 2,800 accredited post-secondary schools in the United States. Approximately 1,500 of these schools have food service of some type under a contracted arrangement with a for-profit management company. Of the remaining 1,300 schools, 700 schools are large enough to have extensive food service programs for boarding students and others attending classes; 600 offer only vending machines or manual buffet food services.[12]

Leisure Operations. Food service in theme parks, sports arenas and stadiums, and race tracks is a large and exciting part of institutional food service. Leisure operations that provide food service also include drive-in movie theaters, bowling alleys, summer camps, and hunting lodges. These food service programs may be self-operated or operated by contract management companies.

Transportation Companies. Food services offered in transportation terminals and on airplanes, trains, and ships are included in this segment. These services may be provided by a for-profit management company or by the transportation company itself. Services range from vended operations to sandwich and short-order preparation to extravagant gourmet meals. Since the American public is traveling more, a corresponding increase in this market segment is expected.

Others. There are many other institutions which offer food service. Consider, for example, food service programs operated by prisons, religious organizations, and military installations. Cities may have athletic facilities and clubs (there are approximately 2,000 city clubs in the United States) that offer food service. There are also about 4,900 private country clubs that offer food service.

Endnotes

1. Donald E. Lundberg, *The Hotel and Restaurant Business*, 3d ed. (Boston, Mass.: CBI, 1979), p. 15.
2. Lundberg, p. 21.
3. Readers desiring more information should see Gerald W. Lattin, *The Lodging and Food Service Industry*, 3d ed. (East Lansing, Mich.: Educational Institute of the American Hotel & Motel Association, 1993).
4. H. Berberoglu, *The World of the Restaurateur* (Dubuque, Iowa: Kendall/Hunt, 1981), p. 29.
5. Lundberg, p. 203.
6. Lundberg, p. 297.
7. Michael L. Kasavana, "The FAX Food Revolution," *Restaurant Business*, March 20, 1990, pp. 60, 62.
8. Readers interested in more information about the history of institutional food services should see Bessie B. West and LeVelle Wood, *Foodservice in Institutions*, 6th ed. (New York: Macmillan, 1988).
9. Much of this section is based on material found in John W. Stokes, *Food Service in Industry and Institutions* (Dubuque, Iowa: Wm. C. Brown, 1960), pp. 1–15.
10. More information on franchise contracts can be found in Jack P. Jefferies, *Understanding Hospitality Law,* 3d ed. (East Lansing, Mich.: Educational Institute of the American Hotel & Motel Association, 1995), pp. 437–443.
11. *Trends in the Hotel Industry,* USA ed. (Houston, Texas: Pannell Kerr Forster, 1989), p. 32.
12. These statistics were supplied by the National Association of College and University Food Services, East Lansing, Mich., Michigan State University, 1988.

Key Terms

chain restaurant
commercial food service operation
franchise
independent
institutional food service operation

Discussion Questions

1. Restaurants as we know them today began in what city?

2. What was the name of the first restaurant established in the United States?

3. What are some of today's food service innovations?

4. Who had the responsibility for food preparation in early U.S. hospitals? Who typically has that responsibility today?

5. What are three basic types of commercial food service operations?

6. What are some of the advantages and disadvantages of chain restaurants? franchises?

7. What are the advantages and disadvantages of using a management company to run an institutional food service operation?

8. Freestanding eating and drinking places include what types of operations?

9. What types of institutions provide food service?

10. What are some trends in hotel food service?

Chapter Outline

People in Food Service
    Managers
        Line vs. Staff
    Production Personnel
        Chefs
        Cooks
        Assistant Cooks
        Pantry-Service Assistants
        Stewards
        Storeroom and Receiving Employees
        Bakers
    Service Personnel
        Dining Room Managers
        Hosts/Captains/Maître d's
        Food Servers
        Buspersons
        Bartenders
        Beverage Servers
        Cashiers/Checkers
        Other Service Personnel
Sample Organization Charts
Career Paths in Food Service
    Your Future in the Industry
        Perceptions of the Industry
        Salaries and Benefits
        Challenges and Opportunities

2

Organization of Food and Beverage Operations

THIS CHAPTER WILL focus on the organizational structures of food service operations. Organizations are created to achieve objectives, one or more of which is financial in nature. As mentioned in Chapter 1, commercial properties want to maximize profits; most institutional operations want to minimize expenses. An organization can have objectives in other areas as well. Food and beverage quality, guest counts, human relations, and employee training are examples.

The way an organization is structured affects its ability to achieve its objectives. If, for example, a supervisor must direct the work of too many employees, there is less likelihood that he or she can provide the individual attention necessary to foster effective interactions with employees, and human relations objectives might be unattainable.

All objectives of a food service operation must be considered as the organization is being developed. For example, if some of a hospital's objectives are to ensure that nutrition requirements are met in all meals, that proper nutrition education is given to all patients and residents, and that community outreach efforts in dietetic services are also provided, it's necessary that the organization create the employee positions to cover these responsibilities. Then people must be hired for these positions and trained.

An organization chart is a diagram showing the relationship among various employee positions in an operation. In this chapter we will review organization charts for various types of food service operations. First, however, let's take a look at food service positions and learn what production and service personnel do in their jobs.

People in Food Service

The food service industry is labor-intensive: a large number of people are required to do the work necessary to attain food service objectives. Technology has not been able to change this basic fact. There was experimentation with computerized kitchens as early as the 1960s, and while this effort yielded some automated and specialized equipment, no one has found a way to replace people with equipment to any significant degree in most food service operations. Many food service tasks have not changed in decades and are not expected to change radically through the end of this century.

The people in food service can be grouped into three general categories: managers, production personnel, and service personnel. For the sake of clarity, we will talk about some production and service managers along with the employees they manage. It should also be noted that the position titles cited in the following sections may vary from operation to operation, and not all of the positions described can be found in every operation.

Managers

In general, there are three levels of managers: top managers, middle managers, and supervisors. How top, middle, and supervisory levels are determined, and the typical duties for each level of management, will vary from property to property. Whether department heads are considered top or middle managers, for example, depends on the size of the organization they work for. Chefs are top managers in some operations, middle managers in others.

Top managers are concerned with long-term plans and goals. They focus more than other managers on the business environment in general. Top managers watch for environmental opportunities and threats such as changes in strategy by competitors, a sluggish economy, and so on.

Middle managers are in the middle of the chain of command. They are in key positions through which communication flows up and down the organization. They are concerned with shorter-term goals, and are typically less concerned with large, environmental issues. They supervise lower-level middle managers or supervisors.

Supervisors are sometimes referred to as "linking pins." They must represent higher levels of management to employees and, at the same time, transfer the wishes and concerns of employees upward. A supervisory position is the first level of management. Supervisors generally use their technical skills more than other managers, and are concerned with such short-term goals as preparing employee schedules and helping employees through the "rush" times that occur in almost every meal period.

Employees who exhibit superior knowledge and skills and who desire positions with more responsibility often become supervisors. It's a complex job—certainly not for everyone—but an interesting position to which an employee can aspire.

In large, multi-unit chain corporations, top management may begin with a board of directors elected by stockholders (see Exhibit 2.1). The board of directors is responsible for the long-range strategic planning of the corporation and for high-level evaluation and decision-making activities which affect current operations. The board may elect or appoint a chairperson of the board to coordinate the board's work. Many operations also retain a chief executive officer (CEO) who serves as an intermediary between the board of directors and lower-level managers. Sometimes one person holds the titles of chairperson of the board and chief executive officer. Very large organizations that own several food service companies—and, perhaps, business interests in non-food service areas as well—may have presidents to assume responsibility for specific companies. Each president may have regional vice

Exhibit 2.1 Top Managers in a Corporation

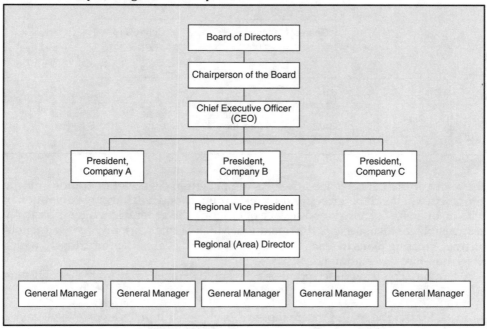

presidents who supervise regional or area directors. These directors oversee the work of general managers, who manage individual properties.

Even though it's contrary to the impressions of employees in specific food service properties, in large corporations it's common to refer to the general managers of restaurants or hotels as "middle management," not "top management." Exhibit 2.1 shows why this is so; general managers are relatively far down on the corporation's organization chart. However, at the property level, these same general managers are the property's top managers. (Large restaurant chain organizations frequently refer to the managers of their restaurants or units as "unit managers" rather than "general managers." Since the duties are virtually the same for both unit and general managers, we will use the term "general manager" throughout the chapter.)

Exhibit 2.2 shows top managers in a freestanding restaurant. The general manager oversees five department heads, as well as a controller who deals with the restaurant's finances. The chef is concerned with food production; the director of service has guest service responsibilities. The beverage director assumes responsibility for the beverage operation, the catering director manages tasks relating to banquets and other special functions, and the executive steward deals with purchasing and sanitation.

Exhibits 2.3 and 2.4 show, respectively, job descriptions for a restaurant manager and a hospital's equivalent of a restaurant manager—a director of dietetic services. These exhibits describe typical responsibilities of general managers and also

Exhibit 2.2 Top Managers in a Freestanding Restaurant

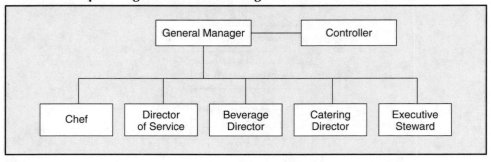

list many of their specific job tasks. As the person in charge of operations for the property (whether it be a freestanding restaurant, a food and beverage operation in a hotel, or an institutional food service operation), the general manager is basically responsible for all aspects of the operation. Much of this work involves setting objectives, creating plans to reach those objectives, and evaluating the extent to which objectives have been attained.

Exhibit 2.5 is a job description of a beverage manager. Beverage managers are typically considered middle management.

Line vs. Staff. Line managers are those who, along with their departments, have a direct impact on bringing in revenues for the property. Staff managers are those who provide support and advice to line managers. Staff managers and their departments do not have a direct impact on bringing in revenues. Examples of staff managers and specialists in food service operations include the following:

- *Human resources manager.* Large food service operations often have a human resources department with a staff of specialists supervised by a manager. Among other duties, the human resources manager recruits applicants for vacant positions, conducts preliminary employee selection activities, and makes hiring recommendations to line managers. The final hiring decisions rest with the line managers in the department that the employee will work in, not with the human resources manager.

- *Controller.* The controller is usually considered a staff manager. The controller typically reports to the general manager, but sometimes to area or regional directors above the general manager. Controllers and their staffs develop and help interpret financial statements so that line managers can make effective decisions. Controllers also help determine menu selling prices, audit guest checks and cash register sales tapes, and develop specialized records and reports for use by line managers.

- *Other staff specialists.* Large restaurant chains frequently have staffs of attorneys, real estate specialists, and construction experts at their headquarters to assist in the chain's expansion efforts. Many institutional food service operations have such staff specialists as dietitians or nutritionists who help design menus to ensure that nutrition requirements are met.

Exhibit 2.3 Job Description—Restaurant Manager

I. Basic Responsibilities

Responsible for meeting all budget goals; for ensuring that quality standards for food and beverage production and service to guests is constantly maintained; for meeting with clients and booking special catered events; for supervising, scheduling, and training the food and beverage controller and assistant manager; for delegating general management tasks to assistant manager; for verifying through analysis of source documents that all income due is collected from food and beverage sales; for designing/improving existing cash security and recordkeeping/accounting systems; for supervising department heads in absence of Assistant Restaurant Manager.

II. Specific Duties

  A. Develops, with department head assistance, operating budgets.

  B. Monitors budget to control expenses.

  C. Serves as restaurant contact for all advertising/marketing activities.

  D. Supervises, schedules, and trains Food and Beverage Controller and Assistant Restaurant Manager.

  E. Provides required information needed by the controller for payroll, tax, and financial statement purposes.

  F. Reviews all operating reports with department heads; conducts regular and ad hoc meetings to correct operating problems.

  G. Meets with clients; plans and prices special catered events.

  H. Designs and improves restaurant cash security and cash disbursements systems.

  I. Conducts cost reduction/minimization studies.

  J. Audits source documents to ensure that all monies due have been collected.

  K. Delegates miscellaneous administrative tasks to assistant managers.

  L. Serves as restaurant's contact with insurance agent, attorney, banker, and accountant.

  M. Works on special problems as assigned by owner.

  N. Reviews department reports; makes recommendations and follows up to ensure that all problems have been corrected.

  O. Is available to provide assistance as needed during busy periods.

III. Reports to

Owners.

IV. Supervises

Assistant Restaurant Manager, Food and Beverage Controller; department heads in absence of the Assistant Restaurant Manager.

V. Equipment Used

Must be able to operate all equipment in restaurant.

VI. Working Conditions

Works in all areas of restaurant; long hours, standing, and walking are routine components in the job.

VII. Other

Must know how to operate and do minor maintenance and repair work on all food production and service equipment and building heating, ventilating, air conditioning, plumbing, and electrical systems. Must be tactful and courteous in dealing with the public.

Exhibit 2.4 Job Description—Director of Dietetic Services

I. General Functions

The Director of Dietetic Services designated by Administration will be responsible for managing the total department. He or she will be responsible for maintaining functional relationships between Administration, Nursing Services, other departments and departmental staff of Dietetic Services. He or she will be responsible for implementing and maintaining a system of quality assurance. He or she will be responsible for developing and administering a policy and procedure manual for all Dietetic Services activities. He or she will prepare necessary financial and operational reports as required.

II. Specific Responsibilities

A. Develops departmental regulations in conformance with administrative policies and procedures and sets standards for the organization and supervision of Dietetic Services.

B. Meets at least weekly with Assistant Directors of Dietetic Services to determine standardization and management effectiveness.

C. Develops and administers a training program for management and supervisory personnel.

D. Develops policies and procedures governing the handling and storage of food and supplies and equipment.

E. Maintains financial records as required by Administration (monthly cost report).

F. Meets with staff to review progress and make future plans for Dietetic Services.

G. Monitors daily operations to ensure quality food service to patients, employees, and visitors.

H. Maintains safety and sanitation standards to ensure compliance with all regulatory agencies.

I. Prepares realistic budgets for each cost center. Monitors the budget for conformance. Takes necessary action when there is a deviation from the budget.

J. Reviews and evaluates the performance of supervisory staff.

K. Administers the preparation of job descriptions, scheduling manuals, and guide books covering all phases of the Dietetic Services operations.

L. Attends professional meetings and conferences to keep informed of current ideas and trends in the field of hospital food services.

M. Performs other related duties as requested by the Vice President of General Services.

III. Education

Director of Dietetic Services must have a minimum of a Bachelor of Science degree in Food Service Management, Nutrition, or Business Administration. A Master's degree is preferred.

IV. Experience

Director of Dietetic Services must have at least a minimum of five years' experience in all phases of hospital food service preparation and administration.

Courtesy of St. Lawrence Hospital, Lansing, Michigan

Production Personnel

Production employees are concerned primarily with food production and usually have little contact with guests. There are certain basic production tasks that must be assigned to employees regardless of a food service operation's type or size. Typical production personnel include:

- Chefs
- Cooks

Exhibit 2.5 Job Description—Beverage Manager

BEVERAGE MANAGER

OVERVIEW

The Beverage Manager is responsible to the Director/Manager of Restaurants or the Assistant Director/Manager of Food and Beverage for the successful and profitable management of the lounges and bars to maximize the profitability of the restaurants and of the hotel.

SPECIFIC RESPONSIBILITIES

Responsible for:

1. Maintaining warm, hospitable guest relations in all guest contacts.
2. Meeting or exceeding budgeted goals in sales and profits for the lounges and bars.
3. Developing accurate and aggressive long- and short-range financial objectives relating to liquor sales.
4. Operating within budgeted guidelines.
5. Facilitating highest-quality beverage and service related to the operation of the restaurants.
6. Maintaining Stouffer Hotel Company housekeeping and sanitation standards in lounges and bars.
7. Implementing corporate sales promotion programs and developing and implementing local sales promotions in the lounges and bars.
8. Knowing the competition and keeping current with industry trends.
9. Maintaining effective controls in the Beverage Department.
10. Implementing and supporting Stouffer Hotel Company policies and procedures.
11. Maintaining a high level of professional appearance, demeanor, ethics, and image of self and subordinates.
12. Sustaining professional development of self and subordinates.
13. Communicating effectively between departments and corporate office personnel within area of responsibility.
14. Operating in compliance with all local, state, and federal laws and government regulations.
15. Maintaining fair wage and salary administration in the department in accordance with corporate policy.
16. Assessing and reviewing the job performance of subordinates and maintaining personnel records of assigned employees as described in the Hotel Personnel Policy Manual.
17. Conducting and attending regular department meetings.
18. Directing and coordinating the activities of all assigned personnel and meeting department responsibilities.
19. Hiring, inducting, orienting, and training assigned personnel to meet department responsibilities.
20. Maintaining positive employee relations in a supportive environment.
21. Interfacing department and self with other departments of the hotel to ensure a harmonious working relationship.
22. Ensuring good safety practices of employees and guests throughout the hotel and assisting in the maintenance of proper emergency and security procedures.
23. Performing special projects as requested.

Courtesy of Stouffer Hotel Company

- Assistant cooks
- Pantry-service assistants
- Stewards
- Storeroom and receiving employees
- Bakers

Chefs. Executive chefs are managers in charge of production personnel in the kitchen. In large operations, an executive chef may perform managerial duties only, while other chefs assume production duties. In smaller operations, the executive or head chef (he or she may be the only chef) has both managerial and production duties. Executive chefs may plan menus with the restaurant manager, be responsible for recipe standardization and overall food quality, assist in development of food purchase specifications, prepare daily entrées, conduct studies resulting in "make-or-buy" and other decisions, plan and oversee special events, develop procedures for food production, and perform miscellaneous production tasks.

Executive chefs may directly supervise a number of different types of chefs, including sous chefs (the principal assistants to the executive chef) and chefs garde-manger (chefs in charge of cold food production).

Cooks. Cooks assist chefs and prepare soups, sauces, and food items to be sautéed, baked, poached, steamed, braised, roasted, grilled, broiled, or fried. They carve and cut meats and prepare cold meat and seafood salad plates, cold sandwiches, hors d'oeuvres, and canapés. Types of cooks include soup cook, sauce cook, fish cook, roast cook, pastry cook, relief cook, and so on.

Assistant Cooks. Assistant cooks help cooks prepare foods for cooking. They trim, peel, clean, grind, shape, mix, or portion foods before cooking and may do simple cooking under the instruction or guidance of cooks or chefs.

Pantry-Service Assistants. Pantry-service assistants supply dining room and banquet pantries with necessary items such as utensils, china, glassware, flatware, and other supplies. These employees may also prepare beverages and assist in serving food when required.

Stewards. Chief stewards are managers who typically oversee porters, dishwashing employees, and related personnel. A chief steward may also be in charge of purchasing at some operations.

Chief stewards and their staffs perform cleaning tasks to maintain a high level of cleanliness and sanitation. They may also scrape, wash, and store pots, pans, and other cooking utensils and equipment. Additional duties may include performing janitorial and special cleaning tasks in food and beverage areas and cleaning and storing china, glass, flatware, and related equipment according to acceptable sanitation procedures.

Storeroom and Receiving Employees. Storeroom employees assist in storing, checking, and dispensing storeroom supplies. Receiving clerks help suppliers unload food and other supplies and verify that the quality, size, and quantity of incoming products meet the property's specifications. They also check to make sure the prices of items ordered are correctly recorded on the suppliers' invoices.

Bakers. Bakers include senior bakers, bakers, and baker's assistants. Senior bakers are managers who specialize in all phases of bakery preparation and must be able to prepare a wide variety of bakery products following standard recipes. Bakers prepare less complex bakery products such as bread, rolls, pies, and plain cakes, and may assist senior bakers with other tasks. Baker's assistants help senior bakers and bakers prepare various bakery products.

Service Personnel

Service personnel have a great deal of contact with guests and perform a wide variety of functions and activities. Service personnel include:

- Dining room managers
- Hosts/captains/maître d's
- Food servers
- Buspersons
- Bartenders
- Service bartenders
- Beverage servers
- Cashiers/checkers

Dining Room Managers. At small properties, the dining room manager not only manages the dining room but often performs the duties of a host as well. At large properties, the dining room manager directly supervises an assistant, whose title may be assistant dining room manager, host, or something similar. The dining room manager helps his or her assistant greet guests and supervise other service employees. The dining room manager has many other duties as well. Typical examples are:

- Checking the physical condition of the dining room before it opens
- Checking the place settings on tables and the condition of the china, glassware, and flatware (at full-service operations)
- Making sure the menus are in good condition
- Noting the number of reservations that have been made
- If necessary, re-arranging tables to accommodate large guest groups
- Checking the schedule to make sure enough service personnel will be on hand
- Observing and, when necessary, recording the job performances of service employees
- Making sure that guests are satisfied and following up on any guest complaints
- Detecting dishonest servers and guests

- Taking appropriate action in case of an emergency or an accident

- Dealing with intoxicated or hard-to-handle guests in a discreet and appropriate manner

- Providing special services (within reason) to guests who request them

- Maintaining a pleasant atmosphere in the dining room

- Performing closing duties such as turning off lights and adjusting heat or air conditioning levels

- Providing reports and other data requested by upper management

Hosts/Captains/Maître d's. Hosts, called dining room captains or maître d's at some properties, directly supervise service employees. Hosts check all phases of dining room preparation; complete *mise en place*—a French term meaning "to put everything in place"; and discuss menu specials, expected regular guests, and anticipated total number of guests with servers and other service employees. During service the host may greet and help seat guests, present menus, and take guest orders. Other tasks can include serving wines, planning for and providing tableside preparation, helping servers when necessary, and preparing flaming desserts. The host may also offer after-dinner drinks and coffee to guests and present the check.

Food Servers. These employees serve food and beverages to guests. The skills food servers need depend on the operation. Guest service at a table service restaurant is different from guest service at a coffee shop. At an elegant restaurant, servers may need to know how to serve wine and flaming desserts; servers in diners may only need basic serving skills. Servers who work at an operation that uses electronic cash registers, precheck registers, and computer monitors will need to develop different skills than servers who work at an operation that uses a simple hand-written guest check system.

Buspersons. Typical responsibilities for buspersons include setting up tables with proper appointments and removing dirty dishes, linens, and so on from tables. They may also perform *mise en place* before the meal period begins and clean up afterwards.

Bartenders. Bartenders prepare mixed drinks and other alcoholic beverages and serve them directly to guests or to their servers. There are two basic types of bars: public bars and service bars. Bartenders working at public bars serve beverages directly to guests sitting or standing at the bar, or to servers who take the beverages to guests seated in the lounge. Bartenders working at service bars typically do not serve beverages directly to guests; they serve beverages to servers who present them to guests—usually guests in the dining room. Many bars are combination public/service bars.

Beverage Servers. Beverage servers provide food and beverage items to guests in lounge areas.

Cashiers/Checkers. These employees may take reservations, total the price of food and beverages on guest checks, and collect guest payments.

Exhibit 2.6 Organization Chart for a Small Restaurant

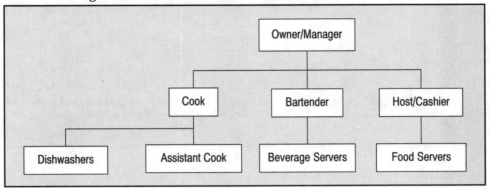

Other Service Personnel. Some operations use an expediter during busy periods to help production and service personnel communicate. This person, often a manager, controls the process of turning in orders and picking up food items. The expediter can monitor production times, resolve disputes about when an order came in, and coordinate the interaction among cooks and servers.

Another employee who may assist in the transfer of food from production employees to food servers is the food checker. This employee helps control product quality and costs by examining each tray before it goes into the dining area, checking food for appearance and portion size. Food checkers may also be an important part of the operation's sales income control system. The checker may collect a copy of the guest check and compare items on the check with those on the plate, for example. Today, there is a trend toward eliminating this position.

Sample Organization Charts

Of course, the sample organization charts presented earlier are not the only ways restaurants can be organized. The sample organization charts shown in this section can help you better understand where the personnel positions just discussed may fit into various types of organizations.

Exhibit 2.6 shows how simple the organization of a small food service operation can be. In this case, the restaurant manager is the owner. The cook, bartender, and host/cashier report directly to the owner/manager. A third level of the organization consists of an assistant cook and dishwashers (supervised by the cook), beverage servers (supervised by the bartender), and food servers (supervised by the host/cashier). Of course, every operation is different. The owner/manager of a similar operation could prefer a "flat" organization. In that case, every person, regardless of position, would be supervised directly by the owner/manager (see Exhibit 2.7).

As a food service organization becomes larger, more employees are needed. It's also necessary to make the work more specialized, so additional positions become necessary. Exhibit 2.8 shows a possible organization chart for a large restaurant. In this example, the general manager directly supervises two positions: the controller

Exhibit 2.7 Organization Chart for a Small Restaurant with a Flat Organization

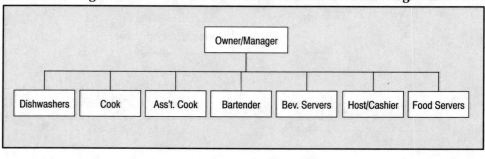

Exhibit 2.8 Organization Chart for a Large Restaurant

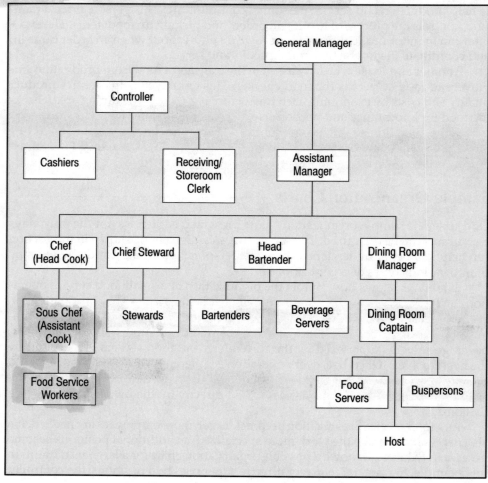

Exhibit 2.9 Organization Chart for a 200-Room Hotel

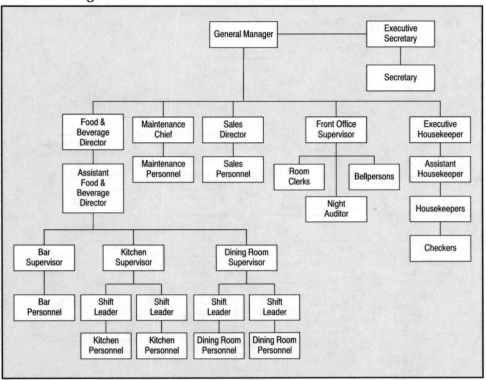

Courtesy of Mississippi Management, Inc., Jackson, Mississippi

(who is responsible for cashiers and a receiving/storeroom clerk) and the assistant manager (who directly supervises four department heads). The department head positions are the chef or head cook (responsible for food production), chief steward (responsible for purchasing and sanitation), head bartender (responsible for beverage production), and dining room manager (responsible for service). Each of these department heads supervises employees. Because of the increased number of levels, a greater amount of direction and communication is necessary in this operation than in the operations shown in Exhibits 2.6 and 2.7. The same needs—to purchase, prepare, and serve food and beverages, and to clean up—are necessary in all operations. The number of employees, the degrees of specialization, and the number of organizational levels make the difference between the organizational structures of small and large operations.

Exhibit 2.9 shows an abbreviated organization chart for a 200-room hotel. Note that the hotel's general manager supervises the food and beverage director who, in turn, supervises an assistant food and beverage director. The assistant food and beverage director manages the bar, kitchen, and dining room supervisors. The food and beverage director is on the same organizational level as the other department

Exhibit 2.10 Organization Chart for a Country Club

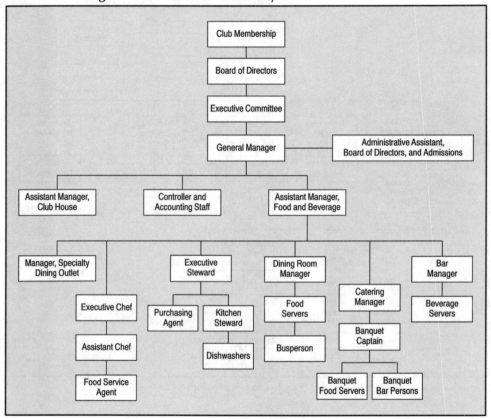

heads (maintenance chief, sales director, front office supervisor, and executive housekeeper).

The organization chart for a country club (see Exhibit 2.10) shows something not found in the organization charts we have seen previously: the members (guests) are in charge. At a typical country club, the club's members elect a board of directors, which appoints an executive committee. The executive committee hires and supervises the club's general manager. The assistant manager of the food and beverage department directly supervises the manager of the specialty dining outlet, executive chef, executive steward, dining room manager, catering manager, and bar manager.

Exhibit 2.11 shows a university residence hall's food service operation. The director, department of residence halls has overall responsibility for the residence halls, including their food service programs. The coordinator of food services for the university is in a staff or advisory relationship to the director. An area manager links the residence hall manager to the director. The residence hall manager (somewhat equivalent to a restaurant general manager) supervises the food service

Exhibit 2.11 Organization Chart for a University Food Service Operation

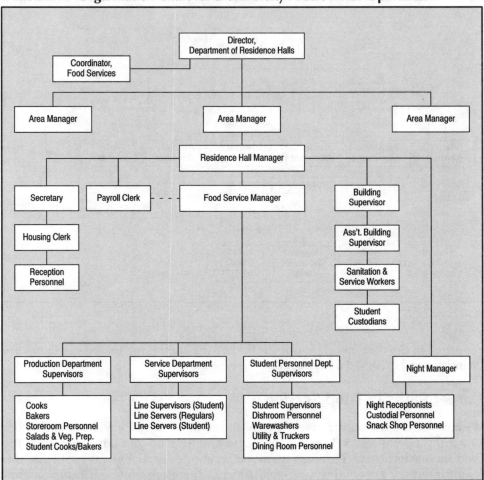

Courtesy of Michigan State University, East Lansing, Michigan

manager who, in turn, supervises personnel with responsibilities for production, service, and student employees. In some university organizations, the food service manager is responsible to the coordinator of food services. There are several residence halls, each of which is supported by an area manager and administrative personnel in the director's office. At a small college, the food service manager might undertake menu planning and purchasing in addition to coordinating all the activities required in the day-to-day operation of food services.

Exhibit 2.12 shows the organization of a hospital food service operation or dietetic department. Note that one assistant director coordinates production and special functions activities and supervises the lead or head cafeteria server. The second assistant director oversees the serving of food to patients and also

Exhibit 2.12 Organization Chart for a Hospital Food Service Operation

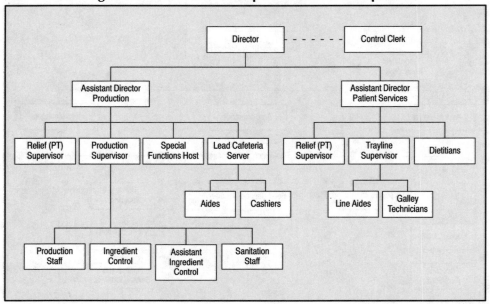

coordinates the therapeutic work performed by dietitians. In some health care facilities, food is served by nurses or their assistants.

Career Paths in Food Service

We have discussed many food service positions and how they relate to each other in various operations. Where do you begin and how do you advance within the food service industry? There are many career choices available. Everyone has different interests, knowledge, and abilities and, therefore, different career aspirations and opportunities.

One way to help get your career started is to obtain experience in the industry while you are a student. Not only will you learn things that can be useful later, you will also:

- Bring experiences to class that will help put facts in perspective

- Make contacts with people who can help you with employment after graduation

- Show that you are genuinely interested in making a career in the food service industry

If you are already a food service employee and want to know "Where can I go next?" you can look at your operation's organization chart for advancement opportunities. As you move up the organizational ladder, job requirements become greater and work tasks more challenging, but pay and benefits also generally increase.

Since there are no established, industry-suggested career advancement routes, where and how far you go depends on (1) what you want to do, (2) where you are now, (3) opportunities that evolve, and (4) your skills, abilities, attitudes, and interests.

The need for interpersonal skills is very important at all organizational levels. In the people business of food service, the ability to work with and through others will usually help you get ahead more quickly than just concentrating on technical skills.

Your Future in the Industry

In the 1990s, growth in the food service industry along with an expected labor shortage will yield a large number of job opportunities of all types and responsibility levels. If you want to get involved in this exciting industry, chances are very good that there will be a place for you.

Perceptions of the Industry. You should realize that there are many misconceptions about what work in the food service industry is like. For example, many students and teachers believe there is a significant emphasis on technology and marketing in lodging and fast-food restaurants and that there is less concern about these issues in independent and institutional food service operations. This is not true for many independents and institutional operations.

It's important for those considering a new—or different—career in food service to learn as much as possible about all positions being considered. Let's try to clarify some points. First of all, food service jobs can be hard, no matter what the position or organizational level. At lower organizational levels, jobs may be hard in a physical sense. At higher organizational levels the work is different, but still difficult—there are many important and far-reaching decisions that must be made. Work hours can be long for all food service employees and, at least in the commercial sector, many food service employees work when other people want to be entertained—evenings, weekends, and holidays. Institutional food service operations, which are often underrated by people aspiring to food service positions, usually count among their benefits more traditional work hours (at least for management staff). Weekends, holidays, and vacation times are also more likely to be free of responsibilities.

Some people may feel that, by definition, service positions are unattractive. There is no question that the food service industry involves serving guests, patients, residents, and others. If you think there is a negative image or lower social status attached to providing service to others, then a position in the food service industry may not be for you. On the other hand, the opportunity to help others is a drawing card for many people.

Salaries and Benefits. Wage and salary compensation and benefits for entry-level food service positions are often higher than minimum wage, especially in areas with labor shortages. The average entry-level salary for college and university food service graduates is generally higher than the entry-level salaries available to liberal arts and some business program graduates. However, as is true when deciding on any career, the question should not be, "What is the starting pay?" but rather, "What will I be receiving in compensation and benefits five years from now?"

When this question is asked, the food service industry is very competitive with other career alternatives. College graduates with five years of experience or less can be running multi-million dollar restaurant operations and earning a salary in excess of $35,000 a year, along with bonuses, stock options, and other benefits. Graduates starting in entrance position "fast track" operations (fast-food chains and other rapidly expanding companies) can easily become department heads earning very attractive salaries—perhaps with incentive plans to provide additional compensation. Benefit packages, including health care and retirement plans, are often competitive with benefit packages in other industries, and increasingly include tuition, vacation lodging, and meals-at-work reimbursements. Of course, salaries and benefits are influenced by company, region of the country, responsibilities of the position, experience, training, and related factors.

Another indirect benefit of working in the food service industry has to do with geography. Since food service operations are located everywhere, an employee's geographic preference is generally an easier objective to attain in the food service industry than in many other fields. Where do you want to live? Wherever it is, there are likely to be opportunities in the food service industry.

Challenges and Opportunities. Regardless of what segment of the industry you enter, the challenge of the job is a tremendous incentive. Do you want an opportunity to make decisions that will affect many people and many dollars over a long period of time? The example of a young person managing a multi-million dollar business has already been mentioned. The challenge and excitement of dealing with large numbers of employees and guests can also be cited.

How do you get involved in food service work? You might already be employed in a food service position. If so, you should talk with your immediate supervisor—if you haven't already—about professional development opportunities within your operation.

Maybe you are a college student who is already convinced that food service is for you. Where can you get more information? You should talk to your school faculty and placement officers and with managers in local properties about career opportunities.

If you are interested in the food service industry and are not a college student, contact a school or college in your area that offers a hospitality education program. You may be able to take courses or obtain placement advice from them. You can also study at home. The Educational Institute of the American Hotel & Motel Association offers courses that cover all major areas of hotel, motel, and food service operations. Designed so you can study at your own convenience, Educational Institute courses offer a planned, career-long program of professional growth and development.[1] You should also check with local hospitality operations about employment opportunities. Your primary objective should be to get your foot in the door. After that, there will be many career possibilities for you to consider as you gain experience and learn more about the industry.

Endnotes

1. For more information, contact the Educational Institute of the American Hotel & Motel Association, 1407 S. Harrison Road, P.O. Box 1240, East Lansing, MI 48826.

Key Terms

flat organization
line manager
mise en place
organization chart
public bar
service bar
staff personnel

Discussion Questions

1. People in food service can be grouped into what three general categories?

2. What are the chief concerns of top managers? middle managers? supervisors?

3. What is a typical way to organize top managers in a large corporation?

4. Restaurant or general managers typically perform what sorts of tasks?

5. What is the chief difference between line and staff managers?

6. A list of production personnel would include what types of employees?

7. What are typical duties of a host?

8. What is a flat organization?

9. What is the major difference between a country club organization and other types of organizations that provide food service?

10. What are some perceptions and misconceptions about the food service industry?

Chapter Outline

What Is Management?
    The Management Process
        Planning
        Organizing
        Coordinating
        Staffing
        Directing
        Controlling
        Evaluating
    Integrating the Process
Managerial Responsibilities and Relationships
    Primary Groups
        Guests
        Owners
        Managers
        Employees
    Secondary Groups
        Suppliers
        The Local Community
        Government Regulatory Agencies
The Importance of Hospitality

3

Fundamentals of Management

THIS CHAPTER EXAMINES the basics of management. First we will define management and take a look at the management process. Then we'll discuss the responsibilities managers have to guests, owners, employees, and others. The chapter closes with a discussion of the special importance the concept of hospitality has for food service managers.

What Is Management?

What is management? What does a manager do? Put simply, managing involves using what you've got—resources—to do what you want to do—attain organizational objectives.

There are many types of resources available to a food service manager, including:

- People
- Money
- Time
- Energy
- Products
- Equipment
- Procedures

All resources are in limited supply. You will never have enough people, money, time, etc., to do everything you would like to do. Your job as manager is to determine how best to use the limited resources available.

How do you do this? You do it by making decisions. A good manager is one who can allocate resources wisely and make good decisions when solving problems most critical to the operation. An ineffective manager is one who is unable to make the best allocation and problem-solving decisions.

The Management Process

One way to discuss management is to separate the management process into seven basic activities or tasks: planning, organizing, coordinating, staffing, directing, controlling, and evaluating (see Exhibit 3.1). You will be involved in all or most of these activities when you manage a food service operation.

Exhibit 3.1 The Management Process

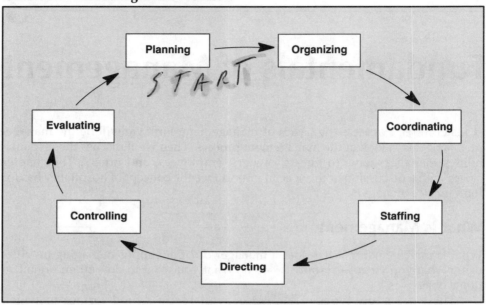

Planning. Planning is the management task of creating goals, objectives, and pro-grams of action to reach those goals and objectives. Goals and objectives indicate what you want to do; action plans tell how you propose to do it. Planning should be done before other management tasks are undertaken.

Every manager, regardless of position or type of food service organization, must plan. At the highest management levels, long-range planning is undertaken to develop strategies helpful in attaining long-term goals. At intermediate man-agement levels, operational plans are developed to attain short-term goals. At lower management levels, planning involves the day-to-day process of running the operation.

Let's look at how this might work at a large restaurant company with many units. At top management levels, the board of directors, chairperson of the board, and chief executive officer may establish long-term goals that may not be attained within two, three, five, or even twenty years. An example of such goals might be: "To be the number one restaurant chain in gross sales in the Midwest region within ten years." Intermediate levels of management—unit managers and department heads—focus on meeting a current budget and on short-term economic planning. At lower levels of management, supervisors cost next month's banquet, plan next week's labor schedule, or set goals that can be met within a short time period.

Whether the organization is a multi-unit chain or a single property, planning must start at the top. Only when top management establishes a definite course of action can managers at all organizational levels develop plans that fit into the orga-nization's long-range plans.

Other factors in effective planning include:

- *Information.* You must have access to complete information to plan effectively.

- *Communication.* Managers at all levels should communicate with each other when developing plans. For example, when a food and beverage director develops an operating budget, it is wise to get input from the chef and the beverage manager. Whenever possible, managers should also communicate with employees when making plans that affect them. Employees are more likely to follow plans they have helped develop. Such plans become "our plans," not "management's plans."

- *Flexibility.* Plans should be flexible. Some food service managers develop plans and then refuse to make changes even though conditions warrant them. One obvious example is the operating budget. What if sales volume is less than what was projected in the budget? Managers may have to make changes to lower costs and/or generate increased business.

- *Implementation.* Obviously, plans must be implemented to be effective. Sometimes a lot of time and discussion go into putting a plan together and the plan is never implemented or is only partially carried out. This is a waste of limited resources and is frustrating for staff members who provided input.

Managers should not plan only when they get around to it. Time should be set aside regularly for managers at each organizational level to establish objectives, create plans to attain them, and make revisions as necessary. If planning time is not set aside, the organization may drift into one crisis after another and managers may become "fire fighters," running from one unexpected problem to the next—problems that could have been avoided through effective planning.

Organizing. The management activity of organizing answers the question, "How can we best assemble and use our limited human resources to attain organizational objectives?" Organizing involves establishing the flow of authority and communication among people.

In any organization, care should be taken to make sure each employee has only one supervisor. If an employee has two bosses, problems can occur if conflicting orders are given.

The number of employees each supervisor manages should be carefully determined. The right number of employees for each supervisor depends on many variables: the supervisor's experience, the complexity of the work, the amount of supervision employees require, the frequency with which problems are liable to occur, the amount of help the supervisor can expect from higher-level managers, and other variables. What is important is that no supervisor be given more people than he or she can handle.

The authority to make decisions about using resources should be available at all levels. It is inefficient for a supervisor to have the responsibility to do something, but not have the authority necessary to get it done. Supervisors should not need to seek higher management approval for tasks that must be routinely done as part of the job.

Don't give a supervisor more people than he or she can handle.

Because an organization's structure evolves throughout the life of the business, many food service operations have organization charts that do not reflect current operating procedures. For example, an organization chart can indicate that the cook's supervisor is the chef when in fact the food and beverage director has assumed the responsibility for directing the cook. An organization chart should not be created, then forgotten. It should be regularly updated so that it gives a current and accurate picture of how the operation's human resources are organized.

Coordinating. Coordinating is the management task of assigning work and organizing people and resources to achieve the operation's objectives.

In many ways, coordinating depends on communication. There must be effective channels of communication to transmit messages up and down the organizational structure. It is also necessary for peers (those at the same organizational level) to communicate with each other. For example, you have probably heard the phrase "interdepartmental cooperation." This refers to the need for departments to work together to meet the goals of the whole organization. Achieving the organization's goals can happen only if there is open communication among department heads and other department managers.

Delegation is an important aspect of coordinating. Delegation means that authority can be "passed down" the organization. Ultimate responsibility, however, cannot be delegated. Perhaps a simple example will clarify this. The food and beverage department head is responsible to the hotel's general manager for all aspects of the food and beverage department's operating budget. He or she may delegate the authority to make some decisions about food and beverages to the head chef and the beverage manager, but the department head will still be responsible to the general manager for meeting budget goals.

Staffing. Staffing involves recruiting and hiring applicants.[1] The goal of staffing is to bring the best-qualified employees into the food service operation. At large properties, you may be asked to select from applicants screened by the human resources department; at smaller properties, the general manager may give you the total responsibility for finding, screening, and hiring applicants.

Application forms, selection tests, reference checks, and other screening devices should all be a part of the recruitment and selection process. Often, however, very little screening is done. When someone quits, the next person who walks through the door is hired. No wonder there are labor-related problems in the hospitality industry!

It's important to match the applicant to the vacant job rather than hiring someone and then asking what he or she can do. To do this, jobs must be defined in terms of the tasks to be performed. Job descriptions list required job tasks for each job and make the matching of applicants to jobs easier.

A second staffing tool, job specifications, lists the personal qualities necessary to perform jobs effectively. We all bring different amounts of knowledge, experience, and common sense to a job. A job specification indicates the personal attributes judged necessary for successful job performance.

All possible sources of job applicants should be considered. Human resources departments in large properties may recruit from within the organization. You can also ask currently employed staff members for suggestions, work with employment service agencies, and advertise.

Some managers think that the more applicants who apply, the more work it will take to sort them out, so they try to limit the number of applicants. From the perspective of the total organization, this is usually a poor strategy. The chance of finding the right person for the job increases if a large number of people are encouraged to apply.

Part of staffing is making sure new hires get off to a good start. An employee's early experiences on the job strongly affect his or her relationship with the organization. A well-planned employee orientation program is necessary to properly introduce new employees to supervisors, co-workers, and the organization in general.

Directing. Directing is a big part of most managers' jobs. Management is often defined as getting work done through other people. In the labor-intensive food service industry this is certainly true. Employees are absolutely critical to the success of every food service operation. All human beings are complex and at times difficult to understand. However, understanding the wants, needs, and expectations of your employees helps you direct them more effectively.

Directing includes supervising, scheduling, and disciplining employees. Supervising comprises all the ways you relate to your employees when work is being done. When supervising employees, you should know how to motivate, gain cooperation, give orders, and bring out the best in people. Ways to mesh organizational goals with the goals of employees become important. Employees can be motivated when their personal needs are addressed on the job. Whenever possible, employees should have input to decisions that affect them.

Scheduling employees effectively is very important. You must know exactly how much labor is needed, then be able to work within those parameters and treat all employees fairly.

Disciplining employees is a task many managers dread. However, it can be a positive experience if you keep in mind that discipline is not a form of punishment. Rather, discipline is a way to address and correct improper behavior and help employees become productive members of the organization. Discipline can consist of informal counseling sessions as well as more serious meetings between the manager, employee, and perhaps a higher-level manager or (in large organizations) someone from the human resources department. Written warnings and suspensions may be used in some situations. Following a formal, written disciplinary action program is the best way to protect yourself and your organization against charges of favoritism, discrimination, and unfair practices.

Directing people is complex and sometimes difficult. In many directing situations, it is useful to think about how you would like to be treated. Chances are, your employees share many of the same concerns you have.[2]

Controlling. There is no assurance that goals will be attained just because effective plans have been developed, resources organized, staff selected, and directions carried out. For this reason, you must develop and implement control systems.

Many food and beverage products pass through a food service operation. Therefore, control procedures for purchasing, receiving, storing, issuing, preparing, and serving products are necessary (these topics are discussed in detail in chapters 8, 9, and 10).

But control includes much more than just the physical tasks of locking storeroom doors, checking standard recipes, or weighing incoming products on a scale. The process of control actually begins with establishing a budget. A budget indicates expected sales and cost levels. You may look at your recent financial statements, especially income statements, or use statistics developed in-house as a base to project anticipated sales and expense levels. Once the budget is established, you must measure the extent to which budget goals are met. If the variance between expected results and actual results is excessive, corrective action must be taken and the results evaluated to assess whether the corrective action was effective.[3]

You should develop control systems that will alert you to problems on a timely basis. Obviously, it is not ideal to know many weeks after it started that a control problem exists. Food service managers often develop daily or weekly control procedures to supplement monthly budget information provided by their accountants or bookkeepers.

Be aware that controls must be worth more than their cost. For example, to use a system that costs $50 weekly to save $35 weekly is not a good idea. On the other hand, spending $500 for a piece of equipment that will save $50 a week is reasonable because the payback period is only ten weeks.

Evaluating. Evaluating is the management task of: (1) reviewing the operation's progress toward achieving overall organizational goals, (2) measuring employee performance, and (3) assessing the effectiveness of training programs. The constant question for managers must be, "How well are we doing?"

You must continually evaluate whether organizational goals are being attained because complacency can spell trouble for the future of the operation. If you are on target, you can move on to accomplish new goals. If goals are not being met,

Scheduling employees and speaking with suppliers who call in are just two of the many tasks food service managers must deal with every day.

the evaluation process served its purpose: it identified a problem. Awareness of a problem is the first step toward solving it.

Managers must also evaluate themselves. Some managers believe they always do a good job, so self-evaluation is unnecessary. Others believe they are doing the best possible job and cannot do any better—again evaluation is judged unnecessary. Both of these approaches are unproductive. Taking an honest look at their own performance from time to time can help managers improve their professional and interpersonal skills.

Evaluating is too important to be done "whenever there is time." Managers should regularly make time for this step in the management process.

Integrating the Process

In the previous section we discussed each activity in the management process separately. In the real world management activities are not so neatly categorized. Managers at all organizational levels perform many management activities each day, sometimes simultaneously. For example, during a typical day a food service manager might:

Exhibit 3.2 Managerial Performance

Primary Groups	Secondary Groups
Guests	Suppliers
Owners	The Local Community
Managers	Government Regulatory Agencies
Employees	

- Help plan next year's operating budget (planning, controlling)
- Deal with problems caused by improper delegation (coordinating)
- Work with a colleague in another department to plan an upcoming special event (planning, coordinating)
- Revise job descriptions and job specifications (organizing, staffing)
- Carry out routine supervisory activities (directing)
- Revise standard food and labor costs (controlling)
- Conduct employee performance reviews (evaluating)

As managers gain and learn from experience, they get better at performing all the various management activities and tasks that arise every day.

Managerial Responsibilities and Relationships

The people for whom you manage can be divided into two basic categories: primary groups and secondary groups (see Exhibit 3.2). The primary groups include guests, owners, managers, and employees. These are the people to whom you have the greatest and most direct responsibility. You have a more indirect responsibility to the secondary groups: suppliers, the local community, and government regulatory agencies.

Primary Groups

Guests. Guests make up the most important primary group. Without guests, no food service operation can survive.

Managing for guests is difficult because no two guests are the same. Each typically has a different reason for visiting your food service operation. Some may want a quick meal; others desire a leisurely dining experience. Some may want to escape from their day's activities, while others want to discuss a business deal. Special occasions, discovery of new places and new food items, and the opportunity to feel important are other reasons why guests may visit your property.

Managers manage for guests first by providing them with a clean, safe place to eat. Treating guests hospitably is also important (hospitality will be discussed in more detail later in the chapter). Then, managers must determine what guests want and need when they visit the operation. A fast-food giant like McDonald's has teams of researchers to help it discover what its guests want and need. An independent restaurant may use guest comment cards and surveys.

Once guest needs are determined, managers must try to meet them in order to build a loyal guest base and ensure the continued success of the operation. We will discuss guests, their needs, and ways to meet those needs in more detail in the next chapter.

Owners. Owners, of course, are vitally concerned with their operation. In a corporation, the owners are stockholders; in a partnership, the owners are two or more people with investment interests; in the case of a single owner, the owner is frequently the manager too.

What are the objectives of the owner(s)? Usually the primary objective is to maximize profits (in commercial operations) or to minimize expenses (in institutional operations). Owners may also have more personal objectives that involve ego needs or the desire for accomplishment.

Your primary responsibility to the owner(s) is to make the operation an economic success. The many factors that go into making an operation an economic success define the challenge of managing.

Managers. If you work at a large property, in the most immediate sense you probably manage for another manager—that is, your boss is a higher-level manager. Your responsibility is to fulfill your job responsibilities and perform other tasks as directed by your manager. He or she will be responsible for evaluating your performance. Sometimes it is easy to resent your boss or misunderstand his or her motives. Keep in mind that your boss probably shares many of your own concerns. He or she is also trying to satisfy performance requirements imposed by an owner or a higher-level manager, and fulfill personal needs and wants at the same time.

Employees. Managers not only manage employees, they manage *for* employees. Your decisions have an impact on making the operation a success, and a successful operation provides employees with a place to earn a living, make friends, and plan a future. In other words, as a manager you manage for the well-being of your employees as well as your own.

Secondary Groups

Suppliers. Your responsibilities to suppliers are to establish a reasonable working relationship and to be fair and ethical in all your dealings with them. Food service managers must guard against having an "I win—you lose" attitude with suppliers. This approach is, at best, shortsighted. Instead, a relationship stressing fairness and mutual satisfaction should be fostered. This can lead to trust, cooperation, and good service from suppliers.

There are at least two other reasons for maintaining a good relationship with suppliers: (1) suppliers and their employees are potential guests of your food service operation, and (2) they may discuss how they are treated at your operation with others who may be potential guests.

The Local Community. The community surrounding a food service operation is involved in an ongoing relationship with the operation. In many instances, entire sections of communities may be revitalized—or may deteriorate—due to the status of a nearby restaurant.

The following are some examples of common concerns a community may have that managers should be aware of:

- *Nuisance concerns.* Excessive noise and rowdy guests gathering in the parking lot are examples of nuisances to the community that managers should deal with.

- *Environmental concerns.* Managers should make sure their property's grounds are free from litter, and that no litter blows from the property onto neighboring properties. Using biodegradable supplies is another way a property can show its sensitivity to environmental concerns.

- *Entertainment concerns.* In operations that book singers, comedians, and other entertainment, managers should try whenever possible to provide entertainment that is desirable and appropriate to the community.

- *Civic concerns.* Managers can show their support for the local community by supporting charitable, educational, and other civic groups.

Our list of examples could continue but the message is clear: the food service operation is a "citizen" of the community, and managers must run the operation in a responsible manner if they want to enjoy the patronage and goodwill of community residents.

Government Regulatory Agencies. Government regulatory agencies collect taxes and other fees and ensure that applicable laws and regulations are followed. Concerns of government agencies include sanitation, safety, building codes, employees, and wage and hour insurance. Food service managers must understand the significant role of government regulatory agencies and manage their operations so that they comply with all applicable federal, state, and local laws.

The Importance of Hospitality

The food service industry is truly a "people business." Your job as a food service manager is not to unlock the door and wait for the cash register to ring. You must first provide products and services that guests will enjoy. You must then train and supervise your staff to provide these products and services in a hospitable way that will encourage guests to return.[4]

Hospitality—the cordial reception of guests—is easy to discuss, but frequently difficult to practice. Problems caused by lack of concern for guests are evident in too many food service operations.

Let's look at what can happen when an attitude of hospitality does not exist. Have you ever watched a television commercial that shows smiling employees at a fast-food restaurant inviting you to visit the property? What happens when you visit the restaurant and the employees do not act like the smiling, courteous employees pictured in the commercial? Don't you feel disappointed, even if only on a subconscious level? Contrast this example with a restaurant where friendly employees seem genuinely happy that you have chosen to visit their property.

Is the difference between friendly and unfriendly employees only a matter of personality? The ability to relate to people can be influenced by personality. However, it is also likely that friendly employees have a friendly manager who has a concern for guests and has promoted an attitude of hospitality in his or her employees. Even though they have a million other things to do, wise managers identify regular guests by name, remember the table they prefer, and provide any special attention that is practical. They set an example for their employees so their guests will have a positive experience.

Endnotes

1. For more information on labor laws and hiring practices, see David Wheelhouse, *Managing Human Resources in the Hospitality Industry* (East Lansing, Mich.: Educational Institute of the American Hotel & Motel Association, 1989).

2. For more information on directing employees, see Raphael R. Kavanaugh and Jack D. Ninemeier, *Supervision in the Hospitality Industry,* 2d ed. (East Lansing, Mich.: Educational Institute of the American Hotel & Motel Association, 1991), and Wheelhouse, *Managing Human Resources in the Hospitality Industry.*

3. For more information on food and beverage control, see Jack D. Ninemeier, *Planning and Control for Food and Beverage Operations,* 3d ed. (East Lansing, Mich.: Educational Institute of the American Hotel & Motel Association, 1995).

4. For details about guest relations programs, see *The Spirit of Hospitality* (East Lansing, Mich.: Educational Institute of the American Hotel & Motel Association, 1987). Seminar.

Key Terms

controlling
coordinating
directing
evaluating
hospitality

management
organizing
planning
staffing

Discussion Questions

1. What is the management process?

2. What resources does a food service manager have?

3. Why is it important to set aside time for planning?

4. What is the purpose of an organization chart?

5. Recruiting and hiring are part of which management activity or task?

6. Should a large number of people be encouraged to apply for a job opening?

7. Where does the process of controlling begin?

8. Managers' responsibilities extend to which primary groups?

9. How can a restaurant positively affect a community? How can it negatively affect the community?

10. What aspects of food service operations are regulated by government agencies?

Chapter Outline

4

Food and Beverage Marketing

FOOD AND BEVERAGE marketing is a complex and fascinating subject with many components. This chapter can only provide an introduction to marketing strategies and options. Feasibility studies will be discussed first, followed by a section covering ongoing marketing research. Marketing research should be conducted prior to the construction of a food service facility and continued throughout the life of the business. A marketing plan based on marketing research is covered next. The chapter concludes with a discussion of the three major tools used to reach a marketing plan's objectives: sales, advertising, and public relations and publicity.

Feasibility Studies

A feasibility study is generally conducted before a food service facility is constructed. Potential investors decide whether or not to finance the construction of a proposed facility—often referred to as a "project" at this stage—by evaluating the results of the feasibility study. The results of the study also guide the planners and architects of the project, and assist managers as they develop marketing plans and prepare initial operating budgets.[1]

Feasibility studies are generally prepared by organizations such as public accounting firms, real estate companies, or management consulting organizations that have been commissioned by the developers or potential owners. Although developers and potential owners may conduct feasibility studies themselves, an independent consultant usually conducts the study if outside financing is necessary.

While the scope of a feasibility study varies from project to project, the following functions are common to most studies:

- Identifying market area characteristics
- Evaluating the proposed site
- Analyzing the competition
- Estimating demand
- Projecting operating results

Identifying Market Area Characteristics

Market area characteristics include demographic information on potential guests in the general area of the proposed site. Useful demographic information on a potential guest includes age, sex, marital status, number of children, family income, type of employment, and location of residence. Other market area characteristics may include the area's volume of retail sales, the number and types of industrial and commercial businesses, the impact of tourism, and available transportation.

Generally, only those characteristics that relate to the success or failure of the project are presented in the study. However, while most feasibility studies present the same market area characteristics, the degree to which each is covered depends on that characteristic's perceived importance to the proposed facility.

In addition to presenting current market area statistics, a feasibility study analyzes positive and negative trends that may affect demand for the proposed facility. For example, the economic stability of the area's commercial and industrial enterprises has a direct bearing on the future success of the facility—especially if those enterprises are primary demand generators for the facility. Also, if the area surrounding the proposed site is experiencing an economic decline, the area's possible physical deterioration could make the project site an undesirable location.

Evaluating the Proposed Site

The site for a proposed food service facility is one of the most important variables determining the eventual success (or failure) of the operation. A restaurant that offers quality food and friendly service in an inviting atmosphere with beautiful decor will typically fail if it's in a poor location. On the other hand, a poor-quality restaurant may succeed *in the short run* if it's in a great location.

A feasibility study evaluates the project site and area by researching the number of people (1) in the surrounding metropolitan area, (2) living or working within walking distance, and (3) within easy driving distance. Other factors analyzed by the study include the availability and convenience of parking, traffic flow patterns, distances from exits off main highways, and the location of other attractions that draw guests such as shopping malls, banks, movie theaters, and other food service operations.

The study should also analyze the accessibility of the proposed site. Turning against oncoming traffic or having to cope with one-way streets may be bothersome, but not necessarily damaging to business. However, in a highly competitive market, restrictions on turns into and out of the site, as well as other accessibility inconveniences, may lower guest demand.

Analyzing the Competition

The competition analysis section of a feasibility study presents an inventory of all competing food and beverage facilities in the project's market area. Competition may consist of not only freestanding establishments, but also restaurants and meeting rooms located in office buildings, private clubs, and social and fraternal organizations.

Sometimes, the analysis of competition is confined to the immediate vicinity of the proposed site. However, when the facility is planned to have a special uniqueness, it's likely to attract guests from a wider area.

A feasibility study generally analyzes each competitor's:

- Location (proximity of competitors to the proposed site)

- Type of restaurant

- Source and volume of business

- Days and hours of operation

- Menu prices

- Check average

- Type of service

- Number of seats

- Availability of liquor service

- Entertainment

- Promotional efforts

- Chain affiliation

The feasibility study should also show how long each competitor has operated at its location, how busy each competitor is at various meal periods on different days of the week, and how current guests feel about the food and service provided by each establishment.

The competition analysis helps establish pre-opening marketing strategies for the proposed food service facility. For example, the results of a feasibility study can help determine:

- The type and volume of demand for both food and beverage service

- The adequacy with which the competition satisfies the current demand

- The strengths and limitations of the competition

- The points of difference that must be established between the proposed facility and the competition

The results of the competition analysis can also be useful in guiding the design of the proposed facility, planning the menu and the type of service, establishing prices, determining hours of operation, and developing advertising and promotion strategies.

Estimating Demand

Making an estimate of food and beverage demand begins with an analysis of the market area's restaurant and bar sales. This provides an overview of dining trends and market demands. Data for this analysis can be gathered by surveying potential guests about their restaurant, banquet, and meeting room needs.

Surveying can be accomplished by the feasibility study consultant through personal interviews or direct mail questionnaires. Potential guests are asked about their food preferences; how often they dine out; how far they are willing to travel when dining out; how much time they spend on breakfast, lunch, and dinner; and how much money they are willing to spend at a food service facility for each meal period.

Projecting Operating Results

Most feasibility studies project financial results for the first, second, and (sometimes) third year of operation. Potential investors need this information in order to decide whether to finance the facility's construction.

Generally, investors expect forecasts of food and beverage revenue and estimates of expenses for such categories as administration, labor, marketing, facility maintenance, energy costs, rent, insurance, and property taxes. While not all consultants use the same methods, nor give the same amount of detail, the feasibility study should clearly explain the basis of the estimate for each major revenue and each major expense category. Information from this section of a feasibility study often guides managers in planning the budget for the facility's first year of operation.

Studies Must Be Current

Feasibility studies are often conducted long before construction actually takes place. Given the dynamics of the economic environment, a feasibility study completed six months ago may not be of much value, unless the data the study's conclusions were based on has not significantly changed. Even then, it's often difficult to determine that the data has not changed without conducting further marketing research. The fact that feasibility studies can become dated so quickly emphasizes the need for food service facilities to conduct ongoing marketing research.

Ongoing Marketing Research

After a food service facility is constructed and in operation, ongoing marketing research must be conducted to ensure that the business meets the needs and wants of guests.[2] This type of research also provides the basis for developing an effective marketing plan. Ongoing marketing research typically includes a property analysis, a competition analysis, and a market analysis. (Combined, these analyses constitute a situation analysis.)

Property Analysis

A property analysis is a written, unbiased appraisal of a food service operation's production and service areas, products, and services. Such an analysis is used to assess the strengths and weaknesses of the operation. The building's exterior, the landscaping, and the property's sign should be included in the analysis. The facility should also be carefully evaluated in terms of traffic flow, accessibility, eye appeal, and compatibility with local surroundings.

The property analysis should also assess the operation in terms of the categories listed in the competition analysis section of the feasibility study: location, type of restaurant, source and volume of business, days and hours of operation, etc. Statistics on these categories will enable managers to make meaningful comparisons between the property and the competition.

However, a property analysis should be more than a simple checklist. It's important to think about the property from the guest's perspective. In other words, management should try to see the facility as guests see it. Friends of management and the staff can be invited as guests during selected meal periods to provide the kind of feedback that "insiders" may be incapable of providing.

Competition Analysis

While a property analysis is extremely important, it's equally necessary to be aware of what the competition is doing. A competition analysis should cover the same categories listed in the competition analysis section of the feasibility study.

However, while forms and checklists are useful for analyzing the competition, it's far more effective to actually experience what the competition has to offer. Food service managers and staff should visit competitor operations at a variety of times (breakfast, lunch, and dinner; slow and peak business periods; etc.) to get a complete picture of the service and atmosphere provided by competitors.

Market Analysis

A market analysis identifies the current markets served by the food service operation and examines marketplace factors and trends that provide opportunities or pose threats to the success of the operation. A market is a group of guests with similar needs, wants, backgrounds, incomes, buying habits, etc. Market analysis involves guest profile research and identification of marketplace factors and trends.

Guest Profile Research. Data on a guest's age, sex, frequency of visits to the property, and employment can be important in positioning or repositioning the food service operation. If guest research indicates that the operation draws businesspeople at lunch and families in the evening, for example, it makes it easier to plan menus that will appeal to each group. Similarly, if guest profile research shows that most lunch guests are businesswomen, the operation might want to appeal to that market with an eye-catching salad bar and specially priced small lunch portions for light eaters.

Guest profile information can be gathered by the manager, host, or food servers simply by talking with guests. Information can also be gathered by observing details such as briefcases that identify guests as businesspeople, shopping bags that identify guests as patrons of a nearby shopping mall, sports bags that identify guests as members of a local health club, etc.

Special promotions can also be used to obtain important guest profile information. For example, a special promotion could request business cards of guests as entry forms for a free meal drawing. One or more cards can be drawn on specified dates and each winner given a complimentary meal. This type of promotion is a cost-effective way of obtaining names, occupations, and telephone numbers of current guests.

Guest surveys, such as detailed questionnaires or short comment cards, can be excellent sources of information that may be valuable in menu planning and developing promotions for specific guest groups. Completed guest surveys may also aid management in making pricing decisions and provide clues about markets being missed.

The types of questions asked may vary with the meal period. For example, if the operation caters to businesspeople at lunch, the lunch survey could ask questions relating to favorite food selections, speed of service, access to fax machines, and other factors that would make the operation more attractive to the business community. Surveys also vary according to management's objectives. A questionnaire can focus on food preparation (such as the trend from fried foods to broiled and steamed items), or on the preferred type of service (buffet or table service).

To encourage guests to fill out questionnaires or comment cards, servers can draw attention to the form and tell guests that they will receive a bonus gift or discount coupon if the completed form is presented when making payment. Management can also provide conveniences to make filling out the form easier. These can include a complimentary pen or an envelope for the completed survey. Guests who have received less-than-perfect food and/or service may feel intimidated when turning in unflattering surveys to food servers. In these cases, an envelope helps deal with this problem and may be the key to obtaining more detailed responses from guests.

Marketplace Factors and Trends. A market analysis also identifies environmental opportunities and problems that can affect business. Changes in demographics; positive and negative events in the community, region, state, and nation; the cost and availability of energy; government regulation; and the cost of travel are just a few of the marketplace factors that can influence business volume and check averages. Statistics for projecting environmental effects on business can be found in census data, information from industrial commissions such as the state or city division of economic development, and industry reports. The marketplace analysis checklist in Exhibit 4.1 lists sources of information that managers can use to project environmental effects on business.

Food and beverage managers should be aware of current food trends and eating habits. Over the past several years, the trend has been away from heavy meals to lighter, healthier fare (salads, fresh fruits and vegetables, lean meats and fish, and so on). Industry magazines and academic publications offering information about food and beverage trends include: *Cornell Quarterly, FIU Hospitality Review, Food Management, Hotel & Motel Management, Hotel & Resort Industry, Lodging, Lodging Hospitality, Nation's Restaurant News, Restaurant Business, Restaurant Hospitality, Restaurants & Institutions,* and *Restaurants USA.*

The Marketing Plan

The marketing plan translates ongoing marketing research into strategies and tactics.[3] Creating a marketing plan involves selecting target markets, determining marketing objectives, creating action plans to meet those objectives, and monitoring and evaluating those plans to measure their success and help set new objectives.

Although many restaurateurs promote their restaurants as if they were a single business appealing to a single market, in reality most restaurants appeal to a number of markets. As mentioned previously, the guest mix at lunch may be very different from the guest mix at dinner. While this diversity should be kept in mind, it also should be remembered that it's impossible to be all things to all people. Restaurateurs should first identify which major markets their operation already appeals to, through guest surveys, comment cards, etc. They can then devote their

Exhibit 4.1 Sources of Information for Preparing a Marketplace Analysis

POPULATION AND DEMOGRAPHICS

Sales and Marketing Management
New York, NY
212/986-4800
> Ask for *Survey of Buying Power* ($65)

American Demographics Institute
Ithaca, New York
800/828-1133
> Members ($285/year dues) are allowed access to the Institute's vast statistical collection. Contact Donna Wenner.
> Statistical highlights are published in *American Demographics* ($48/year). Contact Michael Edmondson.

Donnelly Marketing Information Services
Stamford, CT
800/527-3647
> Current year estimates with five-year projections for population, income, and employment available by zip code and geographic areas. Report fees begin at $50.

Population Research Service
Austin, TX
512/837-0135
> *1987 Annual U.S. Summary Report* ($36) cites April 1987 population and growth estimates for 332 metropolitan areas as well as cities over 100,000 population.

Woods & Poole Economics Inc.
Washington, D.C.
202/332-7111
> Population statistics for 1970 to 2010 by age, race, and sex; income and employment by county, state, and metropolitan areas. Contact Sally Poole.

U.S. Bureau of Census
Population Information Division
301/763-5002

State Office of Demographics and Economic Analysis (sometimes called the Division of Research and Statistics)
Found in the governmental pages under the state name

INCOME

Sales and Marketing Management
American Demographics Institute
Donnelly Marketing Information Services

State Office of Demographics and Economic Analysis

U.S. Bureau of Census
Ed Welniak
301/763-5060

State Commerce and Economic Development Department
Division of Economic Development found (in telephone directory) in governmental pages under state name

EMPLOYMENT

Donnelly Marketing Information Services

Woods & Poole Economics Inc. (Sally Poole)

State Office of Demographics and Economic Analysis

U.S. Bureau of Census
Thomas Polumbo
301/763-2825

State Commerce Department
Division of Economic Development

U.S. Bureau of Labor Statistics
Labor Force Statistics Division
202/523-1944

RETAIL STATISTICS

Sales & Marketing Management
State Office of Demographics and Economic Analysis
State Commerce Department
Division of Economic Development

Donnelly Marketing Information Services
U.S. Bureau of Census
Ronald Piencykoski
301/763-5294

COMMERCIAL & INDUSTRIAL ACTIVITY

State Banking Department
See governmental pages of telephone directory under state name.

U.S. Treasury
Controller of the Currency, listed in governmental pages under "United States"

Chamber of Commerce (local)
State Department of Commerce

(continued)

Exhibit 4.1 *(continued)*

TOURISM	MARKET SUPPLY/DEMAND
State Highway Department	**Local Food Service Associations**
State Department of Transportation; Traffic and Safety Division; found in governmental pages under state name	**Convention and Visitors Bureau**
	DIRECT COMPETITION
Local Airport Authorities	**On-site inspections**
State Department of Transportation; Public Transportation Division; found in governmental pages under state name	**Directories** (chain, AAA, Mobil)
	Interviews with restaurant managers
Area Attractions	**POTENTIAL COMPETITION**
Area Hotels	**Building permits**
TRANSPORTATION	Local Department of Buildings found in governmental pages under County or State
State Highway Dept. (above)	**Project Status**
Local Airport Authority (above)	Local Department of Buildings in conjunction with local banks
Community Planning Agencies	**DEMAND**
Regional Office of Housing and Urban Development; Community Planning and Development Division; found in governmental pages under "United States"	**U.S. Department of Commerce directories**
	Local Chamber of Commerce statistics
AREA ATTRACTIONS	**Hotel sales tax figures** (if available)
Chamber of Commerce (local)	**Monthly and yearly food service reports**
Convention and Visitors Bureau	**Visitor and Convention Bureaus**
SITE ADAPTABILITY	**Local restaurant managers**
Community Planning Agencies (above)	

Source: Adapted from Kirby Payne, "How to Assess the Market for a Hotel," *Lodging*, November 1987, pp. 22–32. Used with permission.

marketing efforts to maintaining and increasing the number of guests from those markets before trying to pull in new markets.

Once target markets have been selected, the next step in developing a marketing plan is to establish specific marketing objectives. Ideally, there should be objectives for each market and each meal period. From these marketing objectives, specific sales objectives and quotas can be set. For best results, marketing objectives should be:

- *In writing.* Everyone has the same information when objectives are put in writing.

- *Understandable.* Objectives will not be reached unless managers and employees can understand them.

- *Realistic yet challenging.* Objectives should not be set so high that restaurant personnel give up before they start; conversely, objectives should not be set so low that they present no challenge.

- *Specific and measurable.* Objectives must be as specific and measurable as possible. For example, rather than have a marketing objective such as, "Increase lunch business," the objective should be stated as follows: "Increase lunch business during June by increasing the guest count by 5% and the average guest check by $2."

Once marketing objectives have been set, action plans with target dates must be created to reach them. Employees should be encouraged to contribute ideas to action plans. Action plans can be simple, perhaps involving only one employee, or relatively complicated, involving many employees. Action plan expenses must be included in the marketing budget. Responsibility for performing each action plan or seeing that it's carried out should be assigned to specific individuals. Assigning responsibility allows for easier accountability and monitoring.

The more carefully action plans are monitored and evaluated, the easier it will be to set future marketing objectives and action plans, because managers will learn what works and what doesn't work. Also, if action plans are monitored regularly, there may be time to take corrective action if a plan is not working. Evaluation and timely corrective actions may prevent costly mistakes and can lead to more effective marketing plans in the future.

The major tools used to reach marketing objectives are sales, advertising, and public relations and publicity.

Sales

Few marketing plan objectives can be reached without maintaining or increasing sales. Two broad categories of sales efforts are internal selling and external or personal selling. Internal selling focuses on increasing revenues from guests who are already coming to the restaurant. External selling is used by properties with large banquet facilities to find new sources of business.

Internal Selling

Internal selling can be defined as specific sales activities of employees in conjunction with an internal merchandising program to promote additional sales and guest satisfaction. Almost all employees can generate additional sales and repeat business through internal selling. Types of internal selling include suggestive selling, internal merchandising, and special promotions.

Suggestive selling occurs when food servers use suggestive selling techniques to sell such high-profit items as orange juice, appetizers, wine, and desserts. Food servers who aggressively sell high-profit items can have a significant effect on the operation's success. Suggestive selling will be discussed in more detail in Chapter 10.

Internal merchandising is the use of in-house signs, displays, and other promotional material to increase sales. In-house signs and displays include posters, table tent cards (see Exhibit 4.2), wine displays, and dessert carts. The power of suggestion can be overwhelming when a food server rolls a cart loaded with mouth-watering desserts directly to a guest's table.

Exhibit 4.2 Sample Tent Card

Courtesy of Days Inns of America, Inc.

Special promotions are limited only by your imagination (see Exhibit 4.3). As a food service manager, you can use special promotions for many purposes: increasing the public's awareness of your operation, attracting new guests, keeping regular guests happy, increasing business during slow periods, and spotlighting special events. Among the special promotions you can use are:

- Couponing
- Product sampling
- Contests
- Packages
- Premiums
- Gift certificates
- Discounting
- Bonus offers

Coupons are often printed with a special offer to attract potential guests. They can be given out personally, included in direct mail advertising, or printed in newspapers and magazines.

Exhibit 4.3 Special Promotional Materials

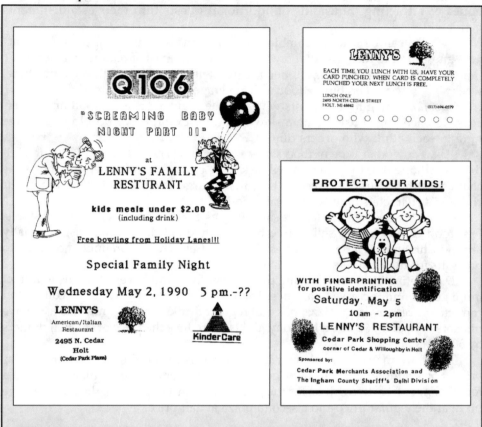

"Screaming Baby Night Part II" was the second such promotion sponsored jointly by Lenny's (a family restaurant), KinderCare (a local child care center), Q106 (a local radio station), and Holiday Lanes (a bowling alley). Parents who brought their kids to Lenny's on May 2 enjoyed their dinner in peace and quiet; the kids were fed and entertained in a separate room. The "Protect Your Kids!" promotion sought to bring guests to the restaurant by providing an extra service; representatives from the local county sheriff's department were there to fingerprint children as a safety measure. The "family" theme is continued with the Lenny's lunch card/coupon, which resembles the lunch cards children at many grade schools use. (Courtesy of Lenny's, Holt, Michigan)

Product sampling can acquaint guests with new food items. For example, after seating guests, you may pass around samples of an appetizer to interest them in ordering the appetizer from the menu.

A *contest* may prove cost-justifiable for your operation if it increases sales to offset the cost of prizes given to the contest winners. Dance or best-costume contests are typical examples of contests some food and beverage outlets use. Winners could receive a cash prize or a dinner for two.

Fast-food chains frequently have contests or games with large grand prizes in hopes of attracting thousands of additional guests into their establishments nationwide.

Packages can be used to combine several items at a discount price to attract new guests and to increase total revenue. Some examples of packages are dinner/theater packages combining dinner for two with two theater tickets, and hotel weekend packages combining food and beverages with hotel rooms.

Premiums are gifts for guests who pay the regular price for food and beverages. To encourage business on a slow night, for example, you could offer a free mug to each adult who orders dinner. Fast-food chains generally use premiums more than any other type of food service operation. They often offer gifts to children and hope that the children will ask their parents to take them to one of the chain's fast-food outlets to receive the gifts. A large soft-drink glass with popular children's characters on it is a typical premium.

Gift certificates are handled the same way as gift certificates sold in retail stores. Fast-food chains like to sell gift certificates in small denominations, especially around Christmas. These certificates allow children who are on limited budgets to buy gifts for their parents and relatives.

Discounting involves lowering the price of food and beverage items to attract more guests and increase total sales. There are a variety of ways to discount: you can offer $1 off any large pizza, price all regular drinks at $1.50 until 7:00 P.M., have pitchers of beer for $2.50 on Monday nights, or reduce the price of chicken dinners by 50%.

There are many ways to offer guests a *bonus* for buying an item at regular price. For example, you can offer guests three dinners at the regular price and a fourth dinner free, two drinks for the price of one on Thursday nights, or one large pizza at the regular price and a second pizza at half price.

External or Personal Selling

External or personal selling is a marketing technique that is not often used in the food service industry. Personal selling involves hiring salespeople to generate leads and make personal sales calls outside of the operation itself. The difference between personal selling and internal selling is that personal selling uses salespeople to sell outside groups on banquets and other large food and beverage functions, while internal selling uses employees to sell additional food and beverages to guests already at the property.

Only food service operations that have large banquet facilities are likely to use outside salespeople. Outside sales efforts are usually required to maximize banquet bookings and revenues. Banquet salespeople send out brochures, banquet menus, or letters about special packages to prospective groups and follow up these mailings with personal sales calls. They also handle group inquiries and personally discuss the details involved with banquets or meetings. Banquet salespeople work with the chef and other managers to design banquet menus and packages. Then they sell these menus and packages to help increase total revenues.

Advertising

Advertising is the second major tool managers use to reach marketing objectives. It's a less direct way of reaching guests than using internal and external selling. Managers use advertising to inform the public about their food service facility and persuade guests to visit it. Advertising comes in many forms and uses such media as outdoor signs, newspapers, magazines, radio, television, and direct mail. Each medium has advantages and disadvantages that you must evaluate to determine how to best use your property's advertising dollars.

When deciding which advertising medium to use, look for the medium whose target audiences most closely match your food service operation's target markets. Your operation's ongoing marketing research defines who your guests are and where they are located. Once the target markets are known, the medium that best reaches them at the lowest cost should be used for advertising. For example, if teenagers are an important market to your operation, a radio station that has a rock and roll format would be an effective medium.

Outdoor Signs

Outdoor advertising is used extensively by the food service industry. Such advertising tries to attract the attention of passersby by employing eye-catching, bold, and dynamic ads.

Two types of outdoor advertising are property signs and billboards. Property signs are used by food service managers to identify the property and attract guests. Billboards are used at roadside locations away from the property to attract guests.

Advantages of outdoor advertising include:

- *Low cost.* Property signs and billboards can be fairly expensive to produce, but once they have been produced, their rental or upkeep costs are relatively low. The cost per potential guest reached is very low.

- *Long life span.* Outdoor advertising can have a life span of anywhere between 30 days and several years.

- *Broad reach.* Property signs and billboard messages may reach hundreds or thousands of people each day.

There are disadvantages to outdoor advertising, including:

- *Limited message length.* Unlike media that can use lengthy copy or dialogue, property signs and billboards must be extremely brief. Because copy is so severely limited, you are only able to use outdoor advertising to make a few points. When people drive by a billboard at high speed, they have little time to read long copy and detailed information.

- *Waste coverage.* There is no audience selectivity with outdoor advertising. Thousands of people will see the sign who will have no interest or opportunity to visit the property. This means advertisers pay for coverage they don't need, since billboard fees are based in part on the amount of traffic that passes by.

Newspapers

Newspapers are used extensively by food service operations. Newspapers are located in every significant geographic market and reach almost every family in the country. For many families, the local newspaper is the only print medium purchased and read.

Advertising in newspapers is attractive for many reasons. The cost of placing an ad in a newspaper is low compared to other media. People of all ages, races, nationalities, occupations, classes, and income levels read newspapers. An independent food service facility such as a family restaurant can reach most families in the area through an ad in the local newspaper. Restaurant chains with several properties throughout the local area can get very effective coverage by advertising a common message and listing the address of each outlet.

Even though newspapers have a broad target market, they offer methods to target readership within the overall broad market. One method is flexible positioning. Newspapers are normally divided into several sections that appeal to various market segments. Many restaurants advertise in the entertainment section; food service facilities with businesspeople as a target market may advertise in the business section. Another way to target readership is to advertise in specific geographic editions of newspapers. The local newspaper of a large metropolitan area may have several geographic editions within its total circulation such as north-side, south-side, northwest, suburban, and statewide. A small restaurant on the north side of the city, for example, may find it cost effective to advertise only in the north-side edition of the city's newspaper.

Immediacy and flexibility are important advantages of newspaper advertising. If you decide to run an ad, you can place it in the local newspaper quickly; newspaper ads can be placed with one day's notice in many instances. Ads can run for a week, a month, several days in a row, once a week on a specified day, etc. Also, it's easy to cancel or repeat a newspaper ad.

There are also disadvantages to advertising in newspapers. Readers of newspapers typically skim through pages fairly rapidly and spend a short period of time reading the newspaper in total. Often, ads are merely glanced at or skipped entirely. Newspapers also become obsolete very fast. After they are read, they are rarely used for future reference and almost always are thrown away rather than passed on to others.

The usually poor quality of newsprint and the high speed of newspaper printing create reproduction problems. Food service managers that want to display mouth-watering menu items, elegant table settings, or beautiful decor are severely limited by the reproduction capabilities of newspapers. The best newspaper ads employ eye-catching but simple formats.

Even though selective placement in various newspaper sections or geographic editions allows for some target marketing, there is waste involved if you want to reach certain target markets. For example, an elegant gourmet restaurant may have a target market of businesspeople between the ages of 35 and 50 who earn over $75,000 a year. This restaurant's newspaper ads will reach thousands of residents who will not patronize the restaurant.

Magazines

There are many advantages to advertising in magazines. Unlike a newspaper ad that becomes obsolete daily, a magazine ad can last a week, a month, or even longer. Magazines may pass from one reader to another during their life spans. A magazine delivered to home subscribers will normally be saved until the next edition arrives. During this period, the magazine may be read by several family members as well as visitors. Magazines are seen in professional offices, airlines, and many other locations where people read to pass the time. As a result, an ad in a magazine may be read by five times the number of people in the magazine's circulation.

Unlike newspapers, most magazines reach a more select group of readers. There is a magazine designed for whatever target market you wish to reach. Whether the key factor is age, sex, income, vocation, geographic location, or interests, there is a magazine that is read by people possessing each key factor. For example, *Business Week* and *Fortune* appeal to high-income business executives.

Many readers are favorably impressed by the high quality of paper and the excellent reproduction magazines offer. You can use magazines to show off your operation's appetizing food items and beautiful food service facilities.

There are also disadvantages to magazine advertising. Magazine ads generally have much higher production costs than newspaper ads. Even though magazines offer less waste circulation than newspapers because of their targeted markets, there is still some waste. Many magazine readers are not conveniently located near the food service facility or do not fit into its target market for various reasons.

A full-color magazine ad may require many weeks or months to produce. Creating artwork, designing the layout, writing advertising copy, and producing color plates can take much time. Magazines have deadlines well in advance of their distribution, so an ad has to be finished and submitted weeks or months before it will appear. This means you will probably not have the opportunity to make last-minute changes or cancellations. This lack of flexibility can hurt if you are advertising a special discount on a particular item, and the cost of the item rises after the ad has been produced and submitted. Also, you cannot use magazine ads to react quickly to competitors because of these time constraints.

Radio

Each day over 83% of the U.S. population listen to the radio; radio ads can potentially saturate an entire local area. Another key advantage of radio advertising is its relatively low cost. Radio ads generally cost little to produce and the cost per person reached is also low in comparison to other media (see Exhibit 4.4). Radio ads can be produced very quickly and put on the air almost immediately.

Radio ads can be targeted to reach people within convenient driving distance of your property. In addition, you can reach specific target markets by matching the radio station's format and the time of day your ad is broadcast to the target market(s) of your property. For example, if your operation features jazz entertainment in its lounge, you might reach your target market by advertising on the local radio station featuring jazz. If businesspeople are a target, you could advertise on an "easy listening" or all-news station during early morning or late afternoon rush-hour time periods.

Exhibit 4.4 Sample Radio Ad Copy

GREY ADVERTISING INC.		RADIO
777 THIRD AVENUE, NEW YORK, N.Y. 10017		
CHICAGO • DETROIT • LOS ANGELES • MONTREAL • SAN FRANCISCO • TORONTO		

CLIENT: RED LOBSTER	COMML. NO.: /:30 (SECS)	F/C/A ☐
PRODUCT: local radio	TITLE:	FOR PROD. ☐
JOB NO.: 586-10-081	PROGRAM: / (NET)	AS REC. ☐
DATE:	AIR DATE:	WORD COUNT ____

ANNCR 1 If it's lobster you love, Red Lobster's got it.

COPY 2 If you savor shrimp, Red Lobster serves them tender and hot.

3 In fact, no other restaurant but Red Lobster can tempt you

4 with a world of seafood favorites. Every day.

5 Come in now for the finest fresh fish . . . the sweetest crab . . .

6 delicious seafood combination platters and so much more.

7 And with every meal, you'll enjoy Red Lobster's prompt

8 and friendly service. So bring your family, bring your

9 friends. And join the feast now at a Red Lobster near you.

10

11

12 (store locations)

Courtesy of Red Lobster and Grey Advertising, Inc.

Radio allows for high frequency of message distribution. You can have your ad repeated many times during the day on several different radio stations. Fast-food chains with new promotions often use radio stations to repeat their message continually.

Disadvantages of radio advertising include:

- *Short life span.* Radio ads have an extremely short life span. Unlike magazine ads that can be read several months later, once a radio ad is aired, it's gone forever unless repeated. Therefore, usually you can only use radio ads for messages about events in the near future, such as an upcoming Mother's Day brunch.

- *Audio only.* You cannot show delicious food or a pleasant atmosphere on the radio, so you are limited in the types of messages you can convey. No visual presentation means many listeners do not pay close attention.

Television

There are many advantages to television advertising. Its main advantage is combining sight with sound. No other medium makes such a highly appealing presentation. You can use television to highlight your food, beverages, atmosphere, decor, and other features. Television commercials can show chefs preparing food items and food servers giving friendly service and preparing specialty items tableside. Television maintains a high attention level so viewers may retain the advertising message (see Exhibit 4.5).

Television provides extensive coverage. Almost every household in the United States has at least one television set, and you can run a commercial several times a day on several stations to reinforce your message.

You can reach specific audiences by choosing television shows and time periods that appeal to an audience that matches one or several of your target markets. If you manage a fast-food or family restaurant, for example, you might want to run your television commercials on Saturday mornings during cartoon shows to reach the children's market. Sports bars may advertise during sporting events.

High cost is a major disadvantage of television advertising. Television commercials for network television can be very expensive to produce, and airtime can be extremely costly. A large commercial food service operation could spend as much as $100,000 to produce one television commercial. A one-minute commercial aired during prime time on national television can cost $250,000 or more. Even on local television, airtime can cost thousands of dollars per minute. Rates for cable television are typically lower, but would still be considered too expensive by many operations.

Producing and airing a television commercial can require many months of lead time. If you need to get your advertising message to the public quickly, television is not practical. Also, television commercials have a short life span, and there is a significant degree of waste coverage in television in spite of efforts to selectively target audiences.

Direct Mail

Direct mail advertising involves sending advertising messages (brochures, coupons, and other announcements) through the mail. Direct mail's main advantage is audience selectivity and specific target marketing. Private clubs are a good illustration of this point. The club's membership represents its total market since nonmembers cannot patronize the club. The club manager has perfect selectivity, because promotional information is mailed to members only.

Restaurant managers can develop a selective mailing list by collecting the business cards of guests. The names and addresses on these cards can then be compiled into a mailing list for announcing future special promotions. Another example of using direct mail advertising to target a specific market occurs when food service managers with banquet rooms send wedding package information to couples announcing their engagements in the local newspaper.

Direct mail advertising also offers great flexibility. You can personalize your advertising message to the recipients. Mailings can be started or stopped at your discretion without regard to lead time and cancellation deadlines.

Exhibit 4.5 Sample Television Commercial Copy

GREY ADVERTISING INC.   TELEVISION
777 THIRD AVENUE, NEW YORK, N.Y. 10017
CHICAGO • DETROIT • LOS ANGELES • MONTREAL • SAN FRANCISCO • TORONTO

CLIENT Red Lobster	PRODUCT National		DATE 11/16/89
TITLE Perfect Meal—Rev Party Platter Tag	SECS 25/5	JOB NO. 586-10-713	COMMERCIAL NO. GIRL-9843
PROGRAM			AIR DATE

☐ Live   ☐ F/C/A   ☐ FILM   ☐ FOR PROD.   ☐ TAPE   ☐ AS REC.   WORD COUNT

VIDEO		AUDIO
WATER WASHING OVER LOGO	1	It may be Red Lobster's
	2	most perfect meal.
FORKING DANISH LOBSTER	3	Petite Danish Lobster tails
DIPPING LOBSTER	4	Mmmm . . . the sweetest ever.
GRILLED SHRIMP IN FLAMES	5	Plus flame-broiled shrimp.
	6	Delicious!
SCAMPI DISH	7	Next: ahhh, sizzling scampi.
FULL PLATE	8	All this Lobster and Shrimp
	9	on one plate
	10	perfectly priced.
WATER WASHING OVER PRICE	11	Just $8.95
DISSOLVE TO LOGO	12	for a few weeks.
FULL PLATE SHOT WITH LEMON SQUEEZE	13	(SUNG) Red Lobster
	14	for the seafood lover in you.
PARTY PLATTER	15	And for the Holidays,
	16	call for Party Platters to go.
	17	Ready in just one hour.

Courtesy of Red Lobster and Grey Advertising, Inc.

With direct mail you have the advantage of being able to measure how well an ad or promotion has succeeded. If you send out 1,000 discount dinner coupons, for example, the number of coupons redeemed will indicate the success of the promotion.

Exhibit 4.6 Computing Direct Mail Costs

This formula is used to determine the costs *per response* of a direct mail effort. While the $8 figure calculated in this example may seem high, it is important to remember that this cost is a *front-end cost* only. "Front-end cost" refers to the cost per response from the initial mailing. Over a period of time, the respondents to the initial mailing will likely respond to additional offers. Therefore, the property will make money on the *back-end*—the subsequent responses.

Typical Costs Per Direct Mail Piece

LIST	$.065
COMPUTER	.005
LABEL	.005
LETTER	.025
BROCHURE	.040
RESPONSE DEVICE	.020
ENVELOPE	.020
LETTERSHOP	.020
POSTAGE	.120
TOTAL	**$.320**

$$\text{Cost per response} = \frac{\text{Cost per piece} \times \text{number of pieces mailed}}{\text{Number of responses}}$$

Assuming the cost per piece is $.32, and that 2,500 pieces were mailed and generated a response rate of 4%, the cost per response would be calculated as follows:

$$\frac{\$.32 \times 2,500 \text{ pieces}}{100 \text{ responses}} = \$8$$

Disadvantages to using direct mail include:

- *High cost.* Producing a high-quality, professional brochure or information packet is expensive. Other costs are for envelopes, postage, and the labor involved in compiling the mailing list (see Exhibit 4.6). The overall cost per potential guest reached is generally greater than for any other medium.

- *"Junk mail" image.* Another major disadvantage is the "junk mail" image that is associated with most direct mail. A direct mail piece may dispel this image if it's relevant and attractive.

Public Relations and Publicity

Public relations and publicity are marketing tools managers use to keep current guests and draw in new guests. Public relations and publicity efforts are much more indirect and subtle than sales and advertising efforts.

Public relations refers to the process of communicating favorable information about your operation to the public in order to create a positive impression. You should maintain good relations with guests; the media; your competitors; the chamber of commerce, the convention bureau, the trade and visitors' bureau, business groups, and other community organizations; trade associations; and government groups. The ultimate purpose of good public relations is to create goodwill and increase the number of guests who patronize your food service operation.

Satisfying your current guests and properly handling their problems and complaints is a major contribution to good public relations and to the success of your operation. Even handling emergency situations such as fires and accidents in the best possible way can create a favorable impression.

Charity work is a typical public relations activity. Food service operations help charities by collecting donations from employees, sponsoring fund raising activities, supporting telethons, and contributing company funds. Other examples of public relations activities are sponsoring bowling teams, Boy Scout and Girl Scout troops, and other community organizations.

Publicity is free coverage of an operation, its staff, or special property events by the media. The media can publicize your food service operation by discussing such items as food, beverages, service, atmosphere, table settings, prices, personnel, or physical surroundings. Unlike advertising, publicity usually appears in the editorial section of the medium because the medium, not the operation, controls the message and provides the space or airtime. You control the content and placement of advertising in the media, but you cannot control publicity about your food service operation.

Even though you cannot control publicity, you can try to generate as much positive publicity as possible. You can inform the media of upcoming events at your property in hopes of getting coverage. The media usually consider the grand opening of an operation or the celebration of a significant anniversary a newsworthy event.

The media can also be informed about significant accomplishments of food service employees. For example, the media might cover a story about an employee who saved a guest from choking. This story would focus favorable attention on the employee and the food service establishment.

You can also plan activities that the media may consider newsworthy. For example, you can plan parties at the operation to celebrate special events and invite the media to attend.

Some publicity is unplanned and unexpected. A typical example occurs when the media send a reviewer, unannounced, to evaluate the food service operation. Afterwards, the reviewer publishes or broadcasts his or her review. This type of unplanned publicity can be favorable or unfavorable.

Endnotes

1. More information about feasibility studies can be found in Rocco Angelo, *Understanding Feasibility Studies: A Practical Guide* (East Lansing, Mich.: Educational Institute of the American Hotel & Motel Association, 1985).

2. A more detailed discussion of marketing research and market plans can be found in Christopher W. L. Hart and David A. Troy, *Strategic Hotel/Motel Marketing*, rev. ed. (East Lansing, Mich.: Educational Institute of the American Hotel & Motel Association, 1986).

3. Much of the information in the marketing, sales, advertising, and public relations and publicity sections is adapted from James R. Abbey, *Hospitality Sales and Advertising*, 2d ed. (East Lansing, Mich.: Educational Institute of the American Hotel & Motel Association, 1993).

Key Terms

external selling
feasibility study
guest comment card
guest survey
internal merchandising

internal selling
marketing plan
publicity
public relations

Discussion Questions

1. What is a feasibility study?

2. If you were asked to invest in a new commercial food service operation, what would you expect a feasibility study to show in relation to: proposed location, demographic statistics, probable competitors, and projected financial success?

3. What three analyses typically are included in ongoing marketing research?

4. How can guest profile information be gathered?

5. What are the major tools used to reach marketing objectives?

6. What are three types of internal selling?

7. What are some advantages and disadvantages of advertising in newspapers? magazines?

8. What are the advantages and disadvantages of advertising on radio and television?

9. A food service operation should try to maintain good public relations with what groups?

10. How does publicity differ from advertising?

Part II

Menu Management

Chapter Outline

Nutrition: The Science of Food
    The Six Basic Nutrients
        Proteins
        Carbohydrates
        Fats
        Vitamins
        Minerals
        Water
    Nutrition Guidelines
        Recommended Dietary Allowances
        The Basic Four Food Groups Plan
        Nutrition Labeling
Nutrition and Food Service Managers
    Menu Planning
    Conserving Nutrients in Food
        How Nutrients Can Be Lost
Contemporary Dietary Concerns
    Calories
    Fats and Cholesterol
    Sodium
    Fiber

5

Nutrition

A GROWING NUMBER of Americans are concerned about nutrition. This can mean increased sales and repeat business for food service operations that include nutritious menu alternatives on their menus. While a commercial food service operation is not in business to educate guests about nutrition, managers should recognize that nutrition is becoming an increasingly important factor for many guests when they decide where to eat. This fact is changing the industry:

> Oat bran sales are booming. Cattle ranchers are breeding leaner animals. The race is on to bring calorie-free fat substitutes to market and quickservice restaurants are offering salads, low-fat milk and grilled chicken sandwiches. The food industry has realized that nutrition sells. In constant search of a higher quality lifestyle, many consumers are hungry for foods with improved nutritive value. Low-fat, high-fiber and cholesterol-free are attributive phrases that commonly appear in food promotions and on food labels. Twenty years ago a foodservice operator who catered to this market was considered odd or a health nut. But as the last decade of the twentieth century begins restaurateurs marketing to the nutritionally-aware patron are in the mainstream.[1]

Unfortunately, many food service professionals who have studied nutrition and use the information on the job do not take care of their own personal health. We hope you will! As you read this chapter, consider how the information can benefit you personally as well as professionally.[2]

Nutrition: The Science of Food

Let's begin our study of nutrition by defining two terms: food and nutrition. Food is material of either plant or animal origin that people eat. Once consumed, food nourishes and sustains the body and enables us to grow. Everyone needs food to live.

Nutrition is the science of food. When you study nutrition, you learn about the food you eat and how your body uses it to stay alive, to grow, to support good health, and, in general, to make you look and feel good.

Why is nutrition important? Good health is impossible without good nutrition. This is true not only when you are young and growing, but for every day of your life. Good nutrition allows you to function efficiently and resist infection and disease. Nutrition even influences how you look—it affects your hair, eyes, complexion, teeth, and gums.

Research indicates that children who do not receive proper nutrition before birth or as infants may suffer mental retardation.[3] It is obvious that the dietary intake of a mother is important to the health and well-being of her unborn child. If the mother nurses her child, the direct correlation between the mother's health and that of her child continues even after the baby is born.

Nutrition can affect your personality. Irritability often occurs when a nutritional deficiency develops. Your physical and mental efficiency is affected by nutrition. People who do not eat breakfast may not perform well late in the morning. Reaction time and work output can suffer. Overweight people may show changes in their personality because of self-consciousness.

It is important for you—as a person and a manager—to understand how food provides for energy, growth, maintenance, and repair. Your knowledge of food and nutrition will help you eat proper foods in the right amounts to keep yourself healthy. It will also help you on the job as you apply this knowledge to meeting the needs of your health-conscious guests.

The Six Basic Nutrients

Food contains nutrients (see Exhibit 5.1). There are six basic nutrients that supply energy, promote cell growth and repair, and regulate the body processes:

- Proteins
- Carbohydrates
- Fats
- Vitamins
- Minerals
- Water

Proteins. Proteins are essential elements in all living body cells. With the exception of water, they are the most plentiful substance in the body. Proteins are required to build, maintain, and repair all body tissues. They also assist with many other functions. Proteins help form chemicals that build resistance to disease. Enzymes, hormones, and hemoglobin contain protein.

Proteins are made of building blocks called amino acids. After digestion, proteins are broken down into separate amino acids that are then rearranged by the body to build required tissues.

Protein can be used as an energy source. This occurs when the diet does not provide enough energy from carbohydrates and fats or when more protein is consumed than is needed for other activities.

Which foods contain protein? Complete protein foods come from animal sources and include meat, poultry, fish, eggs, milk, and cheese. The term "complete protein" refers to foods which supply essential amino acids in amounts which closely approximate the body's requirements for proteins. (Essential amino acids are those that cannot be manufactured by the body and must be supplied in the diet.) Incomplete protein foods are those that lack enough of one or more essential amino acids to adequately meet body needs. Incomplete protein foods include nuts, dried peas and beans, soybeans, breads, and cereals. Fruits and most vegetables contain very little protein.

Exhibit 5.1 Sample Nutrient Chart

NUTRIENT	PURPOSE	PRINCIPAL SOURCES
Protein	• Builds and repairs body tissues. • Is a part of almost all body secretions (enzymes, fluids, and hormones). • Helps maintain the proper balance of body fluids. • Helps the body resist infection.	Protein of the best quality is present in eggs, lean meat, fish, poultry, cheese, and milk. Good quality protein is also found in soybeans and dried beans, peas, and nuts. Useful protein is present in cereals, breads, grains, and some vegetables; however, protein from these sources should be eaten with foods containing top-quality protein.
Carbohydrate	• Supplies energy for physical activity, bodily processes, and warmth. • Helps body use fat efficiently. • Saves protein for tissue-building and repair.	Starches: Cereals and cereal products such as bread, spaghetti, macaroni, noodles, and baked goods; rice, corn, dried beans, and potatoes; dried fruits and bananas. Sugars: Sugar, syrup, honey, jam, jellies, candy, confections, frostings, and other sweets.
Fat	• Supplies energy in concentrated form (over twice as much as an equal weight of carbohydrate). • Helps body use fat-soluble vitamins (A, D, E, and K). • Supplies elements of cell wall structure of all body tissues.	Cooking fats and oils, butter, margarine, mayonnaise, salad dressings, fatty meats, fried foods, most cheeses, whole milk, egg yolks, nuts, peanut butter, chocolate, and coconut.
Riboflavin (vitamin B_2)	• Helps body cells use oxygen to obtain energy from food. • Helps keep eyes healthy. • Helps keep skin around mouth and eyes healthy and smooth.	Milk and milk products, liver, heart, kidney, lean meats, eggs, dark green leafy vegetables, dried beans, almonds, and enriched breads and cereals. (Also present in a wide variety of foods in small amounts.)
Niacin (vitamin B_3)	• Helps body cells use oxygen to obtain energy from food. • Helps maintain healthy skin, digestion, and nervous system. • Helps maintain the life of all body tissues.	Tuna, liver, lean meat, fish, poultry, peanuts, whole grain enriched or fortified breads, cereals, and peas.
Vitamin D	• Helps the body use calcium and phosphorus to build and maintain strong bones and teeth. • Promotes normal growth.	Fish liver oils, vitamin D–fortified milk, irradiated evaporated milk, liver, egg yolk, salmon, tuna, sardines. (Direct sunlight also produces vitamin D.)
Vitamin B_6	• Helps body use protein to build body tissue. • Helps body use carbohydrates and fats for energy. • Helps keep skin, digestion, and nervous system healthy.	Pork, liver, heart, kidney, milk, whole grain and enriched cereals, wheat germ, beef, yellow corn, and bananas.
Folic Acid	• Helps body form red blood cells. • Aids metabolism within the cell.	Liver, lettuce, and orange juice.

(continued)

Exhibit 5.1 *(continued)*

NUTRIENT	PURPOSE	PRINCIPAL SOURCES
Vitamin A	• Helps keep eyes healthy and increases ability to see in dim light. • Helps keep skin healthy and smooth. • Helps keep lining of mouth, nose, throat, and digestive tract healthy and resistant to infection. • Aids normal bone growth and tooth formation.	Liver, deep yellow and dark green leafy vegetables, cantaloupe, apricots, and other deep yellow fruits, butter, fortified margarine, egg yolk, whole milk, and vitamin A–fortified milk.
Vitamin C	• Helps hold body cells together. • Strengthens walls of blood vessels. • Aids normal bone and tooth formation. • Aids in healing wounds and broken bones. • Helps utilize iron. • Helps resist infection.	Citrus fruits and juices, strawberries, cantaloupe, watermelon, tomatoes, broccoli, brussels sprouts, kale, and green peppers. Useful amounts also in cauliflower, sweet potatoes, white potatoes, and raw cabbage.
Thiamine (vitamin B_1)	• Promotes normal appetite and digestion. • Helps body change carbohydrates in food into energy. • Helps maintain a healthy nervous system.	Lean pork, heart, kidney, dry beans and peas, whole grain enriched breads and cereals, and some nuts.
Vitamin B_{12}	• Aids in normal function of body cells. • Helps body develop red blood cells.	Liver, kidney, milk, eggs, fish, cheese, and lean meat.
Calcium	• Helps build strong bones and teeth. • Aids in normal functioning of nerves, muscles, and heart. • Helps blood clot normally.	Milk, cheese, ice cream, sardines (including bones), and clams. Useful amounts in dark green leafy vegetables and oysters.
Iron	• Combines with protein to form hemoglobin, which carries oxygen to all parts of the body. • Helps cells use oxygen. • Prevents iron deficiency anemia.	Liver, heart, shellfish, lean meat, dark green leafy vegetables, egg yolk, dried peas and beans, dried fruits, whole grain and enriched breads and cereals, dark molasses.
Iodine	• Helps thyroid gland function properly. • Helps prevent some forms of goiter.	Iodized salt, saltwater fish, and seafoods.
Phosphorus	• Helps build strong bones and teeth. • Necessary part of all body cells. • Aids in normal functioning of muscles. • Helps body utilize sugar and fat.	Meat, poultry, fish, milk, eggs, milk products, nuts, and dried beans and peas.

Carbohydrates. Carbohydrates supply energy. They include starches, sugars, and cellulose. Carbohydrates come from such plant sources as fruits, vegetables, and grains. Some are also found in animal products; for example, milk contains lactose (milk sugar). Carbohydrates are the second most abundant type of nutrient in American diets; only water is consumed in greater quantities.

Carbohydrates provide a large amount of the total calories consumed by most Americans. A calorie is a measure of the energy contained in food. The body needs a certain amount of calories to work and perform effectively. However, when more calories are consumed than are needed, they are stored by the body in the form of fat. People who consume more carbohydrates than they need are often overweight.

What do carbohydrates do? They are the main source of fuel used for energy to conduct body processes such as digestion and respiration. They also help maintain proper body temperature and eliminate the need for the body to use protein as an energy source. This is important because, as noted earlier, protein is needed for other important uses such as tissue building and repair. Carbohydrates are necessary to form certain body compounds which regulate many body activities.

Fats. Fats are another type of nutrient that provides energy. Fats may be classified as saturated and unsaturated. Saturated fats are solid at room temperature; unsaturated fats, also called oils, are liquid at room temperature.

Fats that can be seen include butter, margarine, vegetable oil, and fat layers around and within meat. These visible fats provide approximately one-third of the fat in the American diet. Hidden fats in ice cream, cheese, whole milk products, meat, and egg yolks provide two-thirds of the fat in the American diet.

What are the functions of fats? First, they serve as concentrated sources of heat and energy for the body. They provide more energy (calories) per unit than any other nutrient. Second, fats are necessary to absorb certain vitamins. Third, fats contribute to the flavor, aroma, and palatability of food.

Many doctors feel that Americans eat too much fat. A rich diet is the main cause of people being overweight. Eating too much fat is especially troublesome if you do not exercise to burn up some of the excess calories.

Vitamins. There are many different vitamins which perform various functions. Before discussing specific vitamins, some general observations should be made:

- Vitamins are substances that are needed in very small amounts in order for the body to function properly.

- Vitamins cannot be made by the body; they must be provided by eating foods or taking supplements.

- Vitamins promote growth, aid reproduction, help digest food, help the body resist infection, prevent certain diseases, and help maintain mental alertness.

Some people are concerned that they do not consume enough vitamins. Vitamin deficiency diseases can occur. Most frequently, these diseases are caused by an inadequate intake of a vitamin, although in some cases a person's body may fail to properly absorb vitamins. Problems can also arise when too much of a specific vitamin is ingested.

Vitamins can easily be destroyed. Proper food handling techniques are important to preserve vitamins and other nutrients.

There are two basic categories of vitamins: fat-soluble and water-soluble.

Fat-soluble. Fat-soluble vitamins are absorbed into the body where they are stored and can be used as needed. Since they can be stored, fat-soluble vitamins need not be consumed with the same regularity as water-soluble vitamins. The fat-soluble vitamins are A, D, E, and K.

Vitamin A was the first vitamin discovered, and it has many important functions. Unfortunately, many American diets are deficient in vitamin A. Bones fail to grow their proper length without vitamin A. Vitamin A helps people see in dim light and keeps the skin soft and smooth. It helps the linings of the mouth, nose, throat, and digestive tract remain healthy. Vitamin A promotes fertility by assisting in sperm production in men and helping babies come to full term within the mother. Vitamin A also plays a role in tooth development and hormone production. Foods rich in vitamin A include liver, egg yolk, butter, whole milk, deep yellow and leafy dark-green vegetables, cantaloupes, apricots, and deep yellow fruits.

Vitamin D helps absorb calcium and phosphorus needed to form bones and teeth. Unfortunately, this vitamin is not found naturally in many foods. Fish, liver, and oils are the richest naturally occurring food sources. In the United States, milk fortified with vitamin D provides a very important source of the vitamin. The best source of vitamin D is the sun. When the sun strikes the skin, it changes compounds normally found in the skin into vitamin D.

Vitamin E is popularly called the fertility vitamin even though it has no influence on human reproduction. Functions of vitamin E include preventing the destruction of vitamins A and C and helping protect body fats and fatty substances from destruction. The best source of vitamin E is vegetable oils.

Vitamin K assists with blood coagulation. The best source of vitamin K is leafy dark-green vegetables. Some vitamin K is also found in fruits, potatoes, and cereals, with dairy products and meats supplying small amounts. Vitamin K is also formed in the intestine by microorganisms which live there.

Water-soluble. Water-soluble vitamins (those that can be dissolved by water) are absorbed into the bloodstream but are not generally stored in the body. Therefore, they must be consumed on a regular basis. The water-soluble vitamins are the B-complex vitamins and vitamin C.

B-complex vitamins help the body synthesize protein and use carbohydrates for energy. There are several vitamins in the B complex. While these vitamins perform specific functions, their activities are essentially interrelated. Three important B vitamins are thiamine, riboflavin, and niacin:

- Thiamine or vitamin B_1 helps body cells obtain energy from food, helps keep nerves in healthy condition, and promotes good appetite and digestion. Good sources of thiamine include lean pork, heart, kidneys, liver, dry beans and peas, whole grain enriched breads, cereals, and nuts.

- Riboflavin or vitamin B_2 helps body cells use oxygen to release energy from food. It helps keep the skin around the mouth and nose healthy and it also affects vision. Good sources of riboflavin include milk, liver, whole grain and enriched cereals, green vegetables, fish, and eggs.

- Niacin or vitamin B_3 helps body cells use oxygen necessary to produce energy. It promotes the health of the skin, tongue, digestive tract, and nervous system.

Good sources of niacin include liver, yeast, lean meat, poultry, fish, peanuts, and cereals.

Vitamin C is called ascorbic acid and is used to hold body cells together. It strengthens the walls of blood vessels and helps in healing wounds and resisting infections. Vitamin C produces healthy gums and helps increase the absorption of iron in the diet. Good sources of vitamin C include citrus fruits and juices, strawberries, cantaloupes, watermelons, tomatoes, green peppers, broccoli, cabbage, and spinach.

Minerals. Minerals serve as building materials and as body regulators. Only a small percentage of normal body weight is composed of minerals, but they are essential for building muscle, bones, teeth, and hair. They help maintain the correct amount of water in each cell and allow certain chemical reactions to occur within the body. Enzymes and hormones that help carry out many bodily functions contain minerals. Other minerals are needed to send nerve messages and contract muscles. The list of minerals used by the body is long and includes calcium, phosphorus, potassium, sulfur, sodium, chlorine, magnesium, iron, manganese, copper, iodine, bromine, cobalt, and zinc.

Some minerals perform only one known essential function; others are involved in various essential and often unrelated functions. Minerals are often found in food in a water-soluble form. Therefore, some of the same food preparation techniques discussed later in this chapter to conserve water-soluble vitamins are also recommended to conserve the mineral content of foods.

Some important minerals—calcium, iron, iodine, and phosphorus—are included in Exhibit 5.1. As you can see in this exhibit, many foods are sources of minerals. People need a balanced and varied diet to ensure that all minerals necessary for good health are consumed in the proper amounts.

Water. There is water in every body cell, outside every cell, in the blood, and in other body fluids. In fact, about 60% of an adult's and 70% of a baby's body is water. People can live longer without food than they can without water.

Water performs many important functions. It serves as a solvent so that other nutrients can be used by the body. Water transports waste from the body through the lungs, kidneys, and skin. It's also used as a building material for cells. Water regulates body temperature; it allows perspiration to occur and serves as a heat carrier as air is lost through breathing. Water is also essential as a body lubricant. Saliva helps us to swallow foods, and other liquids made up largely of water help move food through the gastrointestinal tract.

Almost all foods contain water (see Exhibit 5.2). Cucumbers and lettuce, which physically appear quite solid, actually contain a large amount of water. Whole milk and oranges are also mostly water (87%). By contrast, saltine crackers and English walnuts are less than 5% water.

An adult should drink six to eight glasses of water daily.[4] This approximates the amount of water lost each day from respiration through the lungs, skin perspiration, and the discharge of body wastes through the kidneys and gastrointestinal tract.

Exhibit 5.2 Percent of Water Content for Some Common Foods

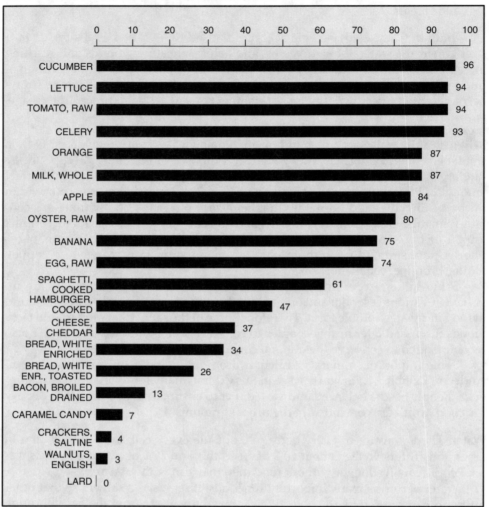

Source: U.S. Department of Agriculture.

Nutrition Guidelines

As you can see, there are many nutrients in a wide variety of foods that are important for health and well-being. It is important that the correct amount of each nutrient be provided in our diets. However, the amount of each nutrient necessary for proper health varies with each person's own unique needs. These needs are influenced by a person's sex, age, health, activity level, and other factors. Therefore, only general nutrition guidelines can be presented here.

Recommended Dietary Allowances. Recommended dietary allowances (RDAs) have been established by the Food and Nutrition Board of the National Academy of Sciences—National Research Council. These RDAs establish amounts of essential nutrients that experts believe to be adequate for the nutritional needs of most healthy people.

There are many misunderstandings about RDAs. RDAs represent average nutritional requirements only. RDAs are estimates of the nutrients that healthy people should consume. And RDAs provide estimates of nutritional requirements for selected nutrients, not all nutrients.

Knowledge about nutrition is constantly being updated, so the RDAs are periodically revised (the last revision was in 1980). The daily allowances recommended for each nutrient take into consideration the variation between healthy individuals. Except for calories, each allowance is set higher than the average need. For example, the average amount of protein intake needed by healthy people was determined, and then this amount was increased to provide a recommendation applicable to at least 95% of the population.

In addition to the RDAs established by the Food and Nutrition Board, the Federal Food and Drug Administration has established a set of allowances called the U.S. Recommended Daily Allowances, or U.S. RDAs (Exhibit 5.3). These are used as a basis for voluntary nutritional labeling of food products. U.S. RDAs are based on the RDAs established by the Food and Nutrition Board. Manufacturers can use this information to determine the percent of daily allowances a specific portion of their product provides.

The Basic Four Food Groups Plan. Many people have difficulty trying to translate a chart of recommended RDAs into a plan for nutritious eating. People see and deal with food, not nutrients, in their everyday lives. Fortunately, home economists, dieticians, nutritionists, and others have developed a simple way for us to focus on food rather than nutrients as we plan healthy diets. It's called the basic four food groups plan.[5] The four food groups are:

1. Milk (and other dairy products)
2. Meat (including poultry and seafood)
3. Fruits and vegetables
4. Grain

For a nutritious diet, you should eat something from each of the four groups each day (see Exhibit 5.4). How many servings to eat from each group depends on age and special conditions such as pregnancy (see Exhibit 5.5). The recommended servings pattern for adults is 2-2-4-4. In other words, each day a typical adult should consume two servings from the milk group, two servings from the meat group, four servings from the fruits and vegetables group, and four servings from the grain group. Other items should be consumed on an as-needed basis.

Although the recommended portion sizes and number of servings from each food group may have to be modified to meet the unique needs of some individuals, the basic four food groups plan is a simple way for most people to incorporate proper nutrition into their diets.

Exhibit 5.3   U.S. RDAs

	Adults and Children Over 4 Years		Children Under 4 Years		Infants Under 13 Months		Pregnant or Lactating Women	
Protein	65	g*	28	g*	25	g*	65	g*
Vitamin A	5,000	IU	2,500	IU	2,500	IU	8,000	IU
Vitamin C	60	mg	40	mg	40	mg	60	mg
Thiamine	1.5	mg	0.7	mg	0.7	mg	1.7	mg
Riboflavin	1.7	mg	0.8	mg	0.8	mg	2.0	mg
Niacin	20	mg	9.0	mg	9.0	mg	20	mg
Calcium	1.0	g	0.8	g	0.8	g	1.3	g
Iron	18	mg	10	mg	10	mg	18	mg
Vitamin D	400	IU	400	IU	400	IU	400	IU
Vitamin E	30	IU	10	IU	10	IU	30	IU
Vitamin B$_6$	2.0	mg	0.7	mg	0.7	mg	2.5	mg
Folacin	0.4	mg	0.2	mg	0.2	mg	0.8	mg
Vitamin B$_{12}$	6	mcg	3	mcg	3	mcg	8	mcg
Phosphorus	1.0	g	0.8	g	0.8	g	1.3	g
Iodine	150	mcg	70	mcg	70	mcg	150	mcg
Magnesium	400	mg	200	mg	200	mg	450	mg
Zinc	15	mg	8	mg	8	mg	15	mg
Copper	2	mg	1	mg	1	mg	2	mg
Biotin	0.3	mg	0.15	mg	0.15	mg	0.3	mg
Pantothenic acid	10	mg	5	mg	5	mg	10	mg

Key: g = grams; IU = international units; mg = milligrams; mcg = micrograms.
* If protein efficiency ratio of protein is equal to or better than that of casein, U.S. RDA is 45g for adults and pregnant or lactating women, 20g for children under 4 years of age, and 18g for infants.

Source: U.S. Food and Drug Administration.

Nutrition Labeling. To help consumers plan their diet, many packaged foods contain information on their labels about nutritional content. Nutrition labeling is voluntary for processed foods except when a nutrition claim is made or when a nutrient is added to the food—then nutrition labeling is mandatory. Manufacturers are providing nutrition information on more and more products. Food service managers in institutional operations, especially those dealing with various types of special diets, need this information. Nutrition information is currently of less importance to commercial operators, though this may change in the future.

Exhibit 5.6 shows a label from a can of sliced stewed tomatoes. Notice that the label provides basic information about: (1) serving size, (2) servings per container, (3) calories, protein, carbohydrates, and fats per serving, and (4) the percentage of U.S. RDAs.

Nutrition and Food Service Managers

The nutritional responsibilities of institutional food service managers and those of commercial food service managers differ.[6] An institutional food service operation must focus on nutrition. When such operations as hospitals and nursing homes are

Exhibit 5.4 Basic Four Food Groups and Recommended Portions

1. **Milk Group:** These foods supply significant amounts of calcium, riboflavin, and protein.

   1 cup milk, plain yogurt, or calcium equivalent.
      1 $1/2$ oz. cheddar cheese
      1 cup pudding
      1 $3/4$ cups ice cream
      2 cups cottage cheese

2. **Meat Group:** These foods supply significant amounts of protein, niacin, iron, and thiamine.

   2 oz. cooked lean meat, fish, poultry, or protein equivalent:
      2 eggs
      2 oz. cheddar cheese
      $1/2$ cup cottage cheese
      1 cup cooked, dried beans or peas
      4 tbsp. peanut butter

3. **Fruit-Vegetable Group:** Orange or dark green leafy vegetables and fruit are recommended 3 or 4 times weekly for vitamin A. Citrus fruit is recommended daily for vitamin C.

   Example of serving sizes:
   $1/2$ cup cooked vegetable or fruit, or juice
   1 cup raw
   Portion commonly served, such as medium-sized apple or banana

Some good sources of vitamin A:	Some good sources of vitamin C:
dark green leafy and deep yellow vegetables and a few fruits:	citrus fruits
apricots	grapefruits, an orange, or orange
broccoli	juice
cantaloupes	cantaloupes
carrots	strawberries
chard, collards, cress, kale, turnip	broccoli
greens	brussels sprouts
pumpkin	potatoes, baked in the jacket
spinach	apples
sweet potatoes	
tomatoes	
winter squash	

4. **Grain Group (whole grain, fortified, or enriched):** These foods supply significant amounts of carbohydrates, thiamine, iron, and niacin.

   Example of serving sizes:
   1 slice bread
   1 cup ready-to-eat cereal
   $1/2$ cup cooked cereal, pasta, or grits

5. **Others:** Foods and condiments such as oils and sugars complement, but do not replace, foods from the four food groups. Amounts consumed should be determined by individual caloric needs.

Source: *A Guide to Good Eating—a Recommended Daily Pattern.* Courtesy of the National Dairy Council.

Exhibit 5.5 Recommended Number of Servings from the Four Food Groups

Food Group	Child	Teenager	Adult	Pregnant Woman	Lactating Woman
Milk	3	4	2	4	4
Meat	2	2	2	3	2
Fruit-Vegetable	4	4	4	4	4
Grain	4	4	4	4	4
Other	Amounts should be determined by individual caloric needs				

Source: *A Guide to Food Eating—a Recommended Daily Pattern.* Courtesy of the National Dairy Council.

responsible for all or most of the meals served to their patrons, institutional managers must make sure that meals meet minimum nutritional requirements. Close attention to the nutritional content of meals is also important when a food service program is designed for such institutional facilities as college dormitories, military bases, and prisons.

The nutritional responsibilities of commercial food service managers are harder to define. Because guests of commercial operations can freely choose where to eat and what to eat, commercial food service managers clearly have less responsibility to meet the nutritional needs of guests than most institutional managers. But does that mean commercial managers have no responsibility at all? To complicate the issue further, there are many types of commercial food service operations: fast-food restaurants, snack shops, fine dining facilities, family restaurants, hot dog stands, and so on. Should a snack shop be expected to provide the same level of nutrition as a full-service restaurant?

Although in recent years the federal government has taken an interest in nutrition, no legislation has been proposed that would require commercial food service operations to meet minimum nutrition requirements. Ultimately, the nutritional responsibility of a commercial food service manager depends on the type of commercial operation and what that operation's guests expect. However, as noted in the chapter's introduction, a growing number of guests are becoming aware of the importance of nutrition. According to a recent study by the National Restaurant Association, the percentage of guests who choose nutritious menu items at restaurants went from 35% to 39% from 1986 to 1989. The study also revealed that the percentage of those guests who say they are unconcerned about eating healthful foods when dining out declined from 38% to 32% during the same period.[7] Because of these trends, an increasing number of commercial food service operations are offering menu alternatives that emphasize nutrition.

If commercial food service managers decide to offer menu items that emphasize nutrition, the managers should make sure these items are appealing. Most guests who want food that is good for them also want that food to look and taste good. Commercial managers can't serve nutritious food that is unappetizing if they want guests to keep returning to their properties.

Exhibit 5.6 Sample Label with Nutrition Information

```
                        NUTRITION INFORMATION
                            PER SERVING

            SERVING SIZE: 1 CUP ● SERVINGS PER CONTAINER: 2

    CALORIES .................... 70      CARBOHYDRATE ............... 18 g
    PROTEIN ..................... 2 g     FAT ........................... 0 g


        PERCENTAGE OF U.S. RECOMMENDED DAILY ALLOWANCES (U.S. RDA)

    PROTEIN ...................... 2      NIACIN ......................... 8
    VITAMIN A ................... 25      CALCIUM ...................... 8
    VITAMIN C ................... 50      IRON .......................... 6
    THIAMIN ...................... 8      PHOSPHORUS ................. 4
    RIBOFLAVIN .................. 4       MAGNESIUM ................... 8


    INGREDIENTS: CUT TOMATOES, TOMATO JUICE, SUGAR, SALT, DEHYDRATED ONIONS,
    DEHYDRATED  CELERY,  DEHYDRATED  PEPPERS,  FIRMING  AGENTS  (CALCIUM
    CHLORIDE AND/OR CALCIUM SULFATE), CITRIC ACID AND NATURAL FLAVORINGS.
```

Making nutritious foods appealing is also important to institutional managers, but for a different reason. While a commercial manager's goal is to maintain or increase sales, a goal for most institutional managers is to safeguard the health of patrons. Food that is served but not eaten will not contribute to a balanced meal or to a person's nutritional intake. Therefore, institutional managers also want to provide nutritious food that tastes good.

Menu Planning

Institutional food service operations must concern themselves with the nutritional content of their menu items. Using standard reference works, trained specialists can calculate the amount of each nutrient contained in each menu item offered. They can also regularly conduct nutrition audits. A nutrition audit is an assessment of a meal's nutrient value, assuming the entire meal is consumed.

There are many factors for managers of commercial food service operations to consider when planning menus. For those managers who have health-conscious guests, one factor is nutrition. The basic four food groups plan can be an excellent guide. For example, you can offer complete meals that have at least one serving from each food group. An à la carte menu can be planned so that the basic four food groups are represented and guests who want a nutritious meal can choose appropriate menu items. Or a buffet menu can include several items from each food group.

Food trends are another factor for commercial food service managers to consider when planning menus. Food trends are different from food fads. Food fads usually identify certain foods as cure-alls. Grapefruit, cranberry juice, and oat bran have taken their turns as the "hot" food item popularized in the media for having special qualities. Food fads surface quite frequently but are generally short-lived.

Food trends, on the other hand, are basic, long-term changes in the public's eating habits. Many recent food trends reflect the public's growing concern with nutrition and healthy eating. For example, there has been a trend in the United States away from red meats and toward seafood. Another trend is increased consumption of lower- and no-alcohol beverages. The "fresh is best" trend is also popular today. Wise food service managers keep up with food trends and try as much as possible to incorporate them into their menus.

Although the trend today is toward healthier eating, there will probably always be a number of guests who are relatively unconcerned about nutrition, who want traditional menu offerings like steaks, french fries, and rich desserts. Roughly one-third of today's guests are in this category.[8] Therefore, most commercial operations include items on the menu that appeal to this group of guests as well.

Conserving Nutrients in Food

Mishandling during storage or preparation can diminish the nutritional content of food. To protect food's nutritional value, food service managers must make sure employees practice basic principles of food preparation designed to retain nutrients.

How Nutrients Can Be Lost. Many food handling techniques discussed in detail in chapters 8 and 9 focus on nutritional concerns. However, several issues should be addressed here.

Cleaning and trimming. Food should not be cleaned or trimmed more than necessary. Vegetables should not be heavily pared since nutrients such as minerals are located just below the skin. If the skin and some of the underskin is removed, many nutrients are lost.

Oxidation. Some nutrients are destroyed on contact with oxygen. Cutting food into small pieces, grinding it, or exposing large surfaces to air can cause vitamin loss. Storage for an excessive amount of time can also cause oxidation.

Light. Sunlight destroys some color pigments and nutrients. Riboflavin (vitamin B_2) and pigments such as keratin (yellow) are especially susceptible to damage when exposed to sunlight.

Heat. Some nutrients such as vitamin C and thiamine are changed or destroyed by heat. Therefore, the longer that food is cooked, the greater the chance of destroying these nutrients. Proteins can also be damaged by heat. Toasting bread, for example, can destroy some of the bread's protein content.

Water. A large number of vitamins and minerals dissolve in water, so you should avoid soaking food if possible. To retain the maximum number of nutrients, foods that are soaked in water should be cooked in the same water. After the food is cooked, the water can be added to the stockpot or used to make soups, sauces, gravies, and related products.

Cooking food in the least amount of water in the least amount of time can also help preserve nutrients.

Misuse of ingredients. Some vitamins are destroyed in an alkaline medium. For this reason, baking soda should not be used in excess when baking nor should it be added to green vegetables during cooking.

Heavy paring of vegetables means waste and the loss of many nutrients.

Contemporary Dietary Concerns

Proper nutrition is only one factor in a healthy diet. As scientific evidence grows linking diet and disease, many Americans are making changes in their eating habits in an effort to live longer and be healthier (see Exhibit 5.7). Contemporary dietary concerns include those relating to:

- Calories
- Fats and cholesterol
- Sodium
- Fiber

Calories

Although some people want to gain weight, most people watching their calories want to lose weight. The number one issue for most diet- and health-conscious Americans is that food should be good but not fattening.[9] Few people want to be overweight. Overweight people tend to have more health problems and die younger. There is also strong social pressure to be thin.

As mentioned earlier, a calorie is a measure of energy contained in food. In general, people who consume more calories than they need gain weight; those who consume fewer than they need lose weight. If calorie intake equals the person's energy expenditure, the person's weight remains stable.

How many calories should a person consume? This varies with a person's age, sex, body type, and other variables. Calorie needs decline as people grow older. Women need fewer calories than men because women tend to have a higher

Exhibit 5.7 America's Changing Eating Habits

	Per Capita Consumption in Pounds		
	1972	1987	Percent Change 1972–1987
Dairy Products			
Whole Milk	207.5	109.9	−47%
Low-Fat Milks[1]	59.6	113.6	+91%
Yogurt	1.3	4.6	+254%
Butter	5.0	4.6	−8%
Cheese	13.0	24.0	+85%
Fresh Fruit, Total[2]	72.9	98.6	+35%
Citrus	26.5	27.2	+3%
Non-Citrus	46.3	71.5	+54%
Fresh Vegetables	64.9	78.6	+21%
Grains			
Wheat Flour	109.8	128.0	+17%
Corn Products[3]	9.7	11.5	+19%
Rice[4]	7.0	13.4	+91%
Pasta Products	8.6	17.1	+99%
Breakfast Cereals	10.8	15.2	+41%
Fats and Oils, Total[2]	53.4	62.7	+17%
Animal	13.3	11.1	−17%
Vegetable	40.1	51.5	+28%

[1]Includes low-fat, skim, buttermilk, and flavored drinks
[2]Total may not add due to rounding
[3]Includes corn flour and meal, hominy and grits, and starch
[4]Milled basis

Source: U.S. Department of Agriculture.

proportion of body fat and because they seem to be more efficient users of calories.[10] Activity is another important factor in deciding how many calories a person needs. Professional football players need far more calories than executives who work behind desks much of the time. Other factors include:

- *Body temperature.* A person running a fever uses more calories.

- *Environment.* People in a cold environment need more calories to stay warm.

- *Health.* People recovering from surgery, trauma, or illness need more calories.

One rule of thumb says that, if you are at your ideal weight, you can multiply that weight by 14 if you are not very active, by 15 if you are relatively active, or by 16 if you are very active. The number that results is the number of calories you need to eat each day to maintain your weight. For example, if you weigh 140 pounds and are relatively active, you should consume 2,100 calories to maintain your weight: 140 x 15 = 2,100.[11]

What if you are not at your ideal weight? There are many fad diets, pills, or even surgeries for reducing weight, and there are many people willing to try them.

For most people, however, the best way to lose weight is to consume fewer calories and increase their activity level.

Food service managers can meet the needs of people concerned about calories by offering such low-calorie menu alternatives as fresh fruit, diet beverages, sugar substitutes, low-fat milk, reduced-calorie salad dressings, and margarine. Menus should include information of interest to dieters, such as a menu item's total calories, important ingredients, and method of preparation.

Fats and Cholesterol

As mentioned earlier in the chapter, fats can be identified as saturated or unsaturated. Saturated fats are found primarily in animal foods—meats, lard, butter, whole milk, and eggs, for example. Two vegetable oils—palm and coconut—are also highly saturated. Unsaturated fats are found mostly in foods from plant sources—olives, nuts, corn, soybeans, etc.—and oils made from these and similar foods.

Fats should be avoided by people who wish to lose weight, since fat contains more calories (nine) per gram than any other nutrient. Experts generally recommend that only 30% to 35% of a person's daily calories should come from fats, and only a third of this percentage should be made up of saturated fats. Saturated fats should be avoided because they contribute to many types of cancer and to high levels of cholesterol. A high cholesterol level may lead to cardiovascular disease. Unsaturated fats are healthier and may even reduce cholesterol levels in some individuals.

Cholesterol is a fatty substance found in all animal foods. Humans need a certain amount of cholesterol to live. The human body uses cholesterol to make vitamin D, bile (a digestive substance), and various hormones. It is an important part of brain and nerve cells. In fact, the human body manufactures its own cholesterol in small amounts. However, when a large amount of animal foods—especially those high in saturated fats—are consumed, the body's cholesterol level can become too high. When this happens, cholesterol may collect in the walls of arteries and block the flow of blood to the heart and other vital organs. Cardiovascular disease and heart attacks may result.

Although the role of cholesterol in causing heart disease and other health problems such as high blood pressure and senility is not completely understood, experts generally agree that it is best to keep the dietary intake of cholesterol as low as possible.

Food service operations can help people control their intake of fats and cholesterol by using cooking methods that require no added fat, such as simmering, poaching, broiling, baking, grilling, and steaming. Even fast-food operations are banishing saturated fats from the kitchen. Burger King has advertised for years that its burgers are broiled, not fried. Other fast-food operations are moving from saturated fats to healthier vegetable fats.[12] Use of no-stick pans can eliminate or reduce the need for fat when sautéing or frying.

Food service managers can also provide alternatives to foods that are high in cholesterol—skim milk rather than whole milk, for example, or egg whites rather than whole eggs. Some egg yolks may be eliminated from some recipes. Salad dressings or gravy can be served on the side so guests on low-cholesterol diets can control how much goes onto their food. Some restaurants are exploring ways to make rich-tasting sauces without butter.[13]

Sodium

Sodium is a mineral component of table salt, which is used in seasoning or preserving food. Table salt is valued because it heightens the flavor of foods. Too much sodium in the diet, however, can cause hypertension or high blood pressure and may increase the risk of heart attacks, strokes, and kidney disease.[14]

Food service managers can meet the needs of people concerned with moderating their sodium intake by providing menu selections that are low in sodium and by providing menu information about ingredients and preparation methods. Table service restaurants can place a salt substitute next to the salt and pepper on the table.

Many people on a low-sodium diet prescribed by a doctor are on a no-added-salt diet. With this diet, salt may be used lightly in cooking, but no salt should be added at the table. Also, foods and condiments high in sodium such as pickles, olives, sauerkraut, ham, bacon, hot dogs, crackers, catsup, soy sauce, and garlic salt must be avoided. With a little planning, most food service managers can rather easily meet the needs of most people on no-added-salt diets.

Fiber

Fiber consists of the indigestible cell walls of plants. Fiber aids digestion by physically separating food particles in the digestive tract. It may prevent constipation, appears to help regulate cholesterol, and may even decrease the risk of colon cancer and heart disease.[15]

Some nutritionists recommend a daily intake of 15 to 18 grams of fiber; the National Cancer Institute recommends that healthy adults eat 20 to 30 grams of fiber each day.[16] The best way to make sure you're getting enough fiber in your diet is to eat a variety of high fiber foods: whole grain breads, bran cereals, brown rice, legumes, oatmeal, and fresh fruits and vegetables.

Food service managers can help guests meet their needs for fiber by including among their menu selections bran cereals (for breakfast), fresh fruits, raw or lightly steamed vegetables, brown rice, and whole grain breads.

Endnotes

1. National Restaurant Association Current Issues Report, "Nutrition Awareness and the Foodservice Industry," January 1990, p. i.

2. Parts of the following discussion are based on the U.S. Department of Agriculture, *Principles of Nutrition for Child Nutrition Programs* (Washington, D.C.: U.S. Government Printing Office, undated).

3. Lewis J. Minor, *Nutritional Standards* (Westport, Conn.: AVI, 1983), p. 150.

4. Henrietta Fleck, *Introduction to Nutrition*, 3d ed. (New York: Macmillan, 1976), p. 243.

5. This section is based in part on material adapted from Leslie E. Cummings and Lendal H. Kotschevar, *Nutrition Management for Foodservices* (Albany, New York: Delmar, 1989), pp. 54–59.

6. Some of the material in this section is based on Lendal H. Kotschevar, "Nutrition: Whose Responsibility?" *FIU Hospitality Review* 7 (Fall 1989): 10–18.

7. Paul Frumkin, "NRA Study: Consumers Leaning Toward Healthier Eating When Dining Out," *Nation's Restaurant News,* March 5, 1990, p. 38.

8. Frumkin, "NRA Study," p. 38.

9. Cummings and Kotschevar, *Nutrition Management,* p. 119.

10. Cummings and Kotschevar, *Nutrition Management,* p. 125.

11. From a 1989 U.S. Air Force pamphlet on nutrition. Used with permission.

12. Frumkin, "NRA Study," p. 38.

13. Carol Lally Metz, "F&B Faces a Challenge," *Lodging Hospitality,* January 1990, p. 98.

14. Cummings and Kotschevar, *Nutrition Management,* p. 173.

15. Cummings and Kotschevar, *Nutrition Management,* p. 67.

16. Cummings and Kotschevar, *Nutrition Management,* p. 67.

Key Terms

basic four food groups plan	minerals
calorie	nutrition
carbohydrates	proteins
cholesterol	recommended dietary allowances
fats	sodium
fiber	vitamins

Discussion Questions

1. Why should commercial food service operators be concerned with providing nutritious food for guests?

2. What are some important points that commercial food service managers should consider when assessing the nutritional content of food served in their operations?

3. How do each of the six basic nutrients contribute to a person's health and well-being?

4. What are some food sources of proteins? of carbohydrates? of fats?

5. Why is it important for a health-conscious individual to know the difference between fat-soluble and water-soluble vitamins?

6. Why is it important for food service managers to know about recommended dietary allowances established by the Food and Nutrition Board?

7. Why would a nutrition audit be more valuable to institutional food service operations than to commercial food service operations?

8. What are some of the ways nutrients can be lost through mishandling during storage or preparation?

9. How many calories should a person consume?

10. How can food service operations help people who need to control their intake of fats and cholesterol?

Chapter Outline

Menu Pricing Styles
     Table d'Hôte
     À la Carte
     Combination
Menu Schedules
     Fixed Menus
     Cycle Menus
Types of Menus
     Breakfast
     Lunch
     Dinner
     Specialty
Menu Planning
     Knowing Your Guests
     Knowing Your Operation
     Selecting Menu Items
     Menu Balance
Menu Design
     Copy
     Layout
     Cover
     Common Menu-Design Mistakes
Evaluating Menus

6

The Menu

EVERYTHING STARTS with the menu. The menu dictates much about how your operation will be organized and managed, the extent to which it will meet its goals, and even how the building itself—certainly the interior—should be designed and constructed.

For guests, the menu is much more than just a list of available foods. The menu also communicates the operation's image and contributes to the overall dining experience by helping to set a mood and build interest and excitement.

For production employees, the menu dictates what foods must be prepared. The tasks of service employees are also influenced by what items are offered on the menu.

For managers, the menu is the chief in-house marketing and sales tool. The menu also tells them what food and beverages must be purchased, the types of equipment they have to have, the number of workers they must hire, the skill level of those workers—in short, the menu has an impact on almost every aspect of a food service operation.

Because almost every guest will look at the menu, managers must be sure it conveys the right message. In an elegant restaurant with a romantic atmosphere, an elaborate menu tied with gold cord and printed on expensive paper can help set the tone for the guests' dining experience. Even the condition of the menu conveys a message. If the operation's managers allow torn, dirty menus to be handed out, what other areas of the operation are they uncaring about?

In this chapter we will take a look at menu pricing styles, how menus are scheduled for use, and the different types of menus. Menu planning and menu design principles will also be discussed. The chapter concludes with a section on evaluating menus. Most of the information and ideas discussed in the chapter can apply to institutional food service operations as well as commercial operations.

Menu Pricing Styles

There is a wide variety of menus, reflecting the wide variety of food service operations. Menus come in all shapes and sizes. Some are printed on parchment, others are written on a blackboard. But all menus can be categorized by how the menu items on them are listed and priced. Three basic categories of menus are:

- Table d'hôte
- À la carte
- Combination table d'hôte/à la carte

Table d'Hôte

A table d'hôte (pronounced "tobble dote") menu offers a complete meal for one price (see Exhibit 6.1). Sometimes two or more complete meals are offered on the menu, each meal having its own price. Some table d'hôte menus offer guests limited choices within the meal they select—for example, a guest may choose between a soup and a salad, or a choice of desserts may be offered. But for the most part, a meal on a table d'hôte menu is set by the menu planner and guests are given few, if any, choices. Table d'hôte menus are sometimes called prix fixe ("pree feeks") menus. Prix fixe is French for "fixed price."

À la Carte

With an à la carte menu, food and beverage items are listed and priced separately (see Exhibit 6.2). Guests need not choose a meal that has been planned for them; they can choose from the various appetizers, entrées, side dishes, and desserts listed to make up their own meal. The prices of the menu items they select are added together to determine the cost of the meal.

Combination

Many operations have menus that are a combination of the table d'hôte and à la carte pricing styles. Table d'hôte menus may offer a selection of individually priced desserts; many à la carte menus include a vegetable and potatoes or rice with the price of the entrée.

A few operations have combination menus that offer an extensive list of complete meal packages and an extensive à la carte section. Chinese and other ethnic-food restaurants are most likely to feature this type of combination menu.

Menu Schedules

Menus can also be categorized by how often they are used. Some operations have a fixed menu—a single menu that is used daily. Other operations use a cycle menu. A cycle menu is one that changes every day for a certain period of days, then the cycle is repeated.

Fixed Menus

Restaurants such as coffee shops and chain restaurants often use a single menu for several months (or longer) before replacing it with a new fixed menu. Daily specials may be offered to give guests some new menu selections, but there is still a set list of items that forms the basic menu. Fixed menus work best at restaurants and other food service establishments where guests are not likely to visit frequently, or where there are enough items listed on the menu to offer an acceptable level of variety.

Cycle Menus

Cycle menus are designed to provide variety for guests who eat at an operation frequently—or even daily. Institutional operations such as schools and hospitals

Exhibit 6.1 Sample Table d'Hôte Menu

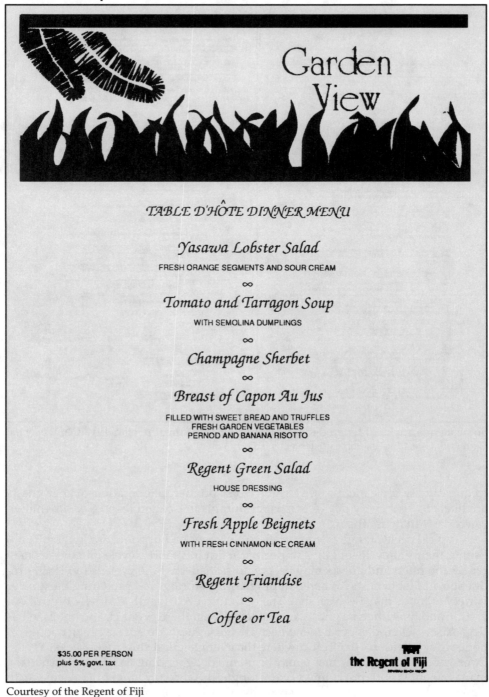

Garden View

TABLE D'HÔTE DINNER MENU

Yasawa Lobster Salad
FRESH ORANGE SEGMENTS AND SOUR CREAM

∞

Tomato and Tarragon Soup
WITH SEMOLINA DUMPLINGS

∞

Champagne Sherbet

∞

Breast of Capon Au Jus
FILLED WITH SWEET BREAD AND TRUFFLES
FRESH GARDEN VEGETABLES
PERNOD AND BANANA RISOTTO

∞

Regent Green Salad
HOUSE DRESSING

∞

Fresh Apple Beignets
WITH FRESH CINNAMON ICE CREAM

∞

Regent Friandise

∞

Coffee or Tea

$35.00 PER PERSON
plus 5% govt. tax

the Regent of Fiji

Courtesy of the Regent of Fiji

Exhibit 6.2 Sample à la Carte Menu

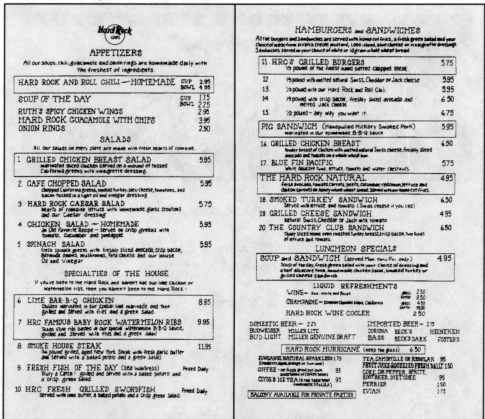

Some menus are hand-lettered to give them a more informal personality. (Courtesy of the Hard Rock Cafe, Chicago, Illinois; lettering by B. Perry White)

frequently use cycle menus (see Exhibit 6.3). Commercial operations whose guests are likely to visit every day—such as restaurants in isolated resorts, or downtown cafeterias—may use them.

Typical cycles range from a week to four weeks, but some are longer. Establishing the right cycle length is important. With too short a cycle, the menus may repeat too often and guests may become dissatisfied. If the cycle is too long, production and labor costs involved in purchasing, storing, and preparing the greater variety of foods may be excessive. The optimum cycle length varies by type of operation and how often its guests are expected to eat there. Some casino hotels in Las Vegas use a seven-day cycle menu because most guests do not stay long enough to notice the repetition.[1] In a resort where the average guest stays two weeks, a two-, three-, or four-week cycle menu may be planned, depending on how concerned the management is with providing variety for guests who stay longer than average. In a nursing home, a cycle menu of six weeks may be appropriate.[2]

Exhibit 6.3 Sample Cycle Menus

WEEK 1	MONDAY	TUESDAY	WEDNESDAY	THURSDAY	FRIDAY
ENTREES Choose 1	Hamburger with bun Chili	Submarine Sandwich Ground Beef and Gravy Bologna	Pizza Cheese Sandwich	Spaghetti w/ Meat Sauce Tunafish Sandwich	Tacos Sloppy Joes with Bun
FRUITS AND VEGETABLES Choose 2	French Fries Celery Sticks Applesauce	Mashed Potatoes Cabbage-Apple Salad Fruit Cocktail	Buttered Green Beans Carrot Sticks Fruit Gelatin	Tossed Salad Buttered Spinach Apple Crisp	"Round-about" Potatoes Orange Juice Banana
BREAD OR SUBSTITUTE	Sal (wi				
BONUS!					
MILK Whole or 2%	Mil				

WEEK 2	MONDAY	TUESDAY	WEDNESDAY	THURSDAY	FRIDAY
ENTREES Choose 1	Toasted Cheese Sandwich Meatloaf w/ Gravy	Pizza Turkey-Ham Sandwich	Fish in Bun Chicken or Turkey Supreme	Hamburger and bun Macaroni and Cheese	Lasagna Hot Dog and Bun
FRUITS AND VEGETABLES Choose 2	Mashed Potatoes Vegetable Soup Sliced Peaches	Buttered Corn Tossed Green Salad	French Fries Confetti Cole Slaw	Tater Tots Beets in Orange Sauce	Buttered Green Beans Finger Relishes
BREAD OR SUBSTITUTE	Hot rolls (with meatloaf)				
BONUS!					

WEEK 3	MONDAY	TUESDAY	WEDNESDAY	THURSDAY	FRIDAY
ENTREES Choose 1	Tacos Egg Salad Sandwich	Hot Dog and Bun Meat Turnover with Gravy	Spaghetti and Meat Sauce Turkey Sandwich	Pizza Tunafish Sandwich	Hamburger and Bun Ravioli
	sh Green d rots nge Smiles	Carrot Sticks Mexicorn Applesauce	Hashbrown Potatoes Cabbage-Apple Salad Pudding w/ Fruit		

WEEK 4	MONDAY	TUESDAY	WEDNESDAY	THURSDAY	FRIDAY
ENTREES Choose 1	Sloppy Joes with Bun Beef Stew	Baked Fish Beefaroni	Hamburger and Bun or Cheeseburger	Baked Chicken Toasted Cheese Sandwich	Pizza Submarine
FRUITS AND VEGETABLES Choose 2	Celery Sticks Buttered Corn Orange Slush				
BREAD OR SUBSTITUTE	Cheese Biscuit with Butter				
BONUS!	Peanut Butter Cup				
MILK Whole or 2%	Milk				

WEEK 1	MONDAY	TUESDAY	WEDNESDAY	THURSDAY	FRIDAY
ENTREES Choose 1	Hamburger with bun Chili	Submarine Sandwich Ground Beef and Gravy Bologna	Pizza Cheese Sandwich	Spaghetti w/ Meat Sauce Tunafish Sandwich	Tacos Sloppy Joes with Bun
FRUITS AND VEGETABLES Choose 2	French Fries Celery Sticks Applesauce	Mashed Potatoes Cabbage-Apple Salad Fruit Cocktail	Buttered Green Beans Carrot Sticks Fruit Gelatin	Tossed Salad Buttered Spinach Apple Crisp	"Round-about" Potatoes Orange Juice Banana
BREAD OR SUBSTITUTE	Saltines (with Chili)	Roll (with Ground Beef)		Italian Bread (with Spaghetti)	
BONUS!		Peanut Butter Cookie			Oatmeal Cookie
MILK Whole or 2%	Milk	Milk	Milk	Milk	Milk

These cycle menus are used at an intermediate school. Note that the menus are on a four-week cycle, and that the menus provide limited choices.

The daily menus used in a cycle can be à la carte or table d'hôte. Schools, hospitals, prisons, and other institutions may use table d'hôte menus in the cycle—that is, offer one set meal for each meal period (breakfast, lunch, and dinner) each day (although menus offering a choice are also used in many institutional operations). Restaurants that cycle menus may use à la carte menus—a hotel restaurant on a seven-day cycle could rotate seven different à la carte menus, for example.

Types of Menus

Menus can also be categorized by type. Three basic types of menus are breakfast, lunch, and dinner menus—menus designed around the three traditional meal periods. There are also a large number of specialty menus designed to appeal to a specific guest group or meet a specific marketing need. The types of menus a food service operation offers will depend on the number of meals it serves and the type of operation it is. Many operations have a separate breakfast menu because they have a cut-off time for serving breakfast. Combining lunch and dinner menus is a common practice. Whether or not to offer specialty menus depends on the operation and its clientele. An upscale restaurant may feel that a separate wine or dessert list adds to its image, for example.

Breakfast

Breakfast menus are fairly standard. Most restaurants offer fruits, juices, eggs, cereals, pancakes, waffles, and breakfast meats like bacon and sausage. Sometimes regional specialties, like grits in some southern states, are offered.

The watchwords for breakfast menu items are "simple," "fast," and "inexpensive." Guests are more price-conscious at breakfast than at other meals. Guests are also likely to be in a hurry to get to work or make some other appointment, so they want to be served right away. To keep prices down and make quick service possible, most breakfast menus are relatively limited, offering only the essential breakfast menu items.

Lunch

Like breakfast guests, lunch guests are usually in a hurry. Therefore, lunch menus must also feature menu items that are relatively easy and quick to make. Sandwiches, soups, and salads are important in many lunch menus.

Lunch menus must have variety; many guests eat lunch at the same restaurant several times a week because it is located close to where they work. To provide variety, most lunch menus offer specials every day. These specials can be printed on a separate piece of paper and clipped onto the lunch menu. Or a cycle menu can be used to provide variety, in which case the entire menu will change daily for a certain number of days.

Lunch menu items are usually lighter than dinner menu items, because most guests do not want to feel filled up and sleepy during the afternoon. Lunch menus are also less elaborate than dinner menus as a rule. If appetizers are offered at lunch, they are simpler to make and fewer in number. Lunch menus usually include desserts, and some include a list of alcoholic beverages.

Dinner

Dinner is the main meal of the day for most people, and menu items offered at dinner are heavier in character and more elaborate than those offered at breakfast or lunch. Dinner is more likely to be eaten in a leisurely fashion than breakfast or lunch because guests are often seeking a dining experience or celebrating a special occasion at dinner.

Guests are willing to pay more for dinner than for lunch, but they also expect a greater selection of menu items and place a greater premium on service, atmosphere, and decor. Therefore, dinner menus usually offer a wide variety of selections. Steaks, roasts, chicken, seafood, and pasta dishes like lasagna and linguine are typical dinner entrées. Wines, cocktails, and exotic desserts are more likely to be on a dinner menu than on a lunch menu.

Specialty

There is a wide range of specialty menus, from poolside menus to menus for afternoon teas. Some of the most common specialty menus are:

- Children's
- Senior citizens'
- Alcoholic beverage
- Dessert
- Room service
- Take-out
- Banquet
- California
- Ethnic

Children's. Children's menus do not necessarily have to blend in with the restaurant's theme or decor; the most important thing is to make sure the menu is entertaining (see Exhibit 6.4). The goal is to occupy the child long enough for the parents (and other guests) to eat in peace. Children's menus can be shaped like robots, animals, or rocket ships. Many children's menus feature bright colors, cartoons, pop-up designs, or black and white drawings that the child can color. Menus that fold into hats, masks, or other toys are good for small children; puzzles, word games, stories, and mazes can work for older children.

The food offered on children's menus should be simple and nutritious. Portions should be on the small side and prices should be modest.

Tassels, staples, or other potentially dangerous materials that can be removed and swallowed should never be part of a children's menu.

Senior Citizens'. The graying of America means that menus that appeal to the special wants and needs of senior citizens will become more important in the future. Such menus can be separate menus or separate sections of regular menus. More commonly, menu items that meet the needs of seniors are placed throughout the regular menu.

Exhibit 6.4 Sample Children's Menu

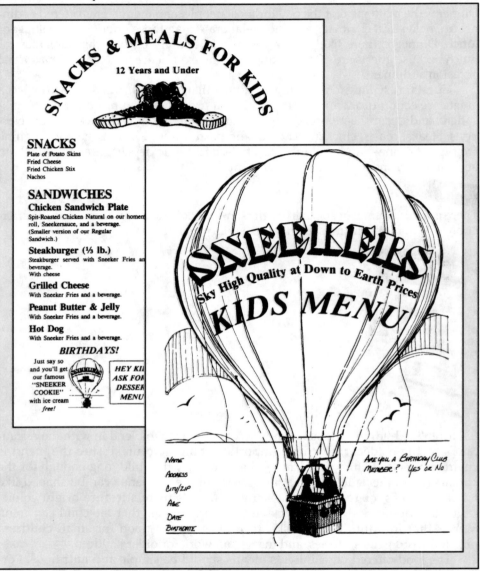

Children at Sneekers get a bucket of crayons along with their one-page take-home menus.
(Courtesy of Sneekers Restaurant, Lansing, Michigan)

Many seniors have dietary prescriptions or recommendations from their doctors. Most revolve around weight control, diabetes, cardiovascular problems or precautions, and gastrointestinal disorders. Other seniors are just more conscious of the need to eat properly.

Seniors watching their weight and diabetic seniors need simple, non-rich snacks, entrées, and desserts. A piece of fresh fruit served stylishly can allow a diabetic to enjoy dessert with others at the table.

Many seniors on sodium-restricted diets are on a "no added salt" diet. As mentioned in Chapter 5, with this diet it is okay to use salt lightly when cooking, but no salt should be added to the food when it reaches the table. Many good-tasting menu items can be prepared to meet this diet simply by omitting sodium-rich condiments and avoiding sodium-rich foods. Providing information on the sodium content of menu items can also help seniors on sodium-restricted diets.

Because of major advances in medicine, the diets of ulcer sufferers can be more "mainstream" than ever before. Many seniors with ulcers find that they have only minor limitations in choosing foods. Noting ingredients when items are described on the menu can help seniors make appropriate selections.

Alcoholic Beverage. Cocktails and wines can be listed on a separate menu or included on the regular menu. If included on the regular menu, the drink list should come before the food selections so guests desiring a drink before ordering their meal will have the necessary information. Operations that offer separate alcoholic beverage menus can have separate cocktail menus and wine lists, or can combine cocktails and wines on one menu. Separate beverage menus can be used in the lounge as well as in the dining room.

Food service operations should list alcoholic beverages in large, readable type, with brand names and prices included. Today many beverage menus include no- or low-alcohol drinks creatively named and described to help promote their sale.

Dessert. At the end of the meal, most guests cannot recall the dessert items they saw listed on the main menu. Food servers at some operations use dessert trays to remind guests of desserts. Some operations have a separate dessert menu so that food servers have something they can give to guests at the end of the meal to remind them of the desserts that are available.

There are many advantages to having a separate dessert menu:

- You can offer more desserts.

- There is more room for bold graphics and descriptive copy.

- You can devote a portion of the menu to dessert specials.

- If dessert prices change, you don't have to go to the trouble and expense of reprinting the main menu.

The types of desserts offered vary with the type of operation. Some elegant restaurants feature flaming desserts prepared tableside; many family restaurants offer cake and ice cream; even some fast-food restaurants now offer such simple dessert items as ice cream, pies, and cookies. Upscale restaurants often include after-dinner wines, cordials, brandies, and liqueurs on the dessert menu.

Room Service. Some hotels offer room service to guests. With a few exceptions, such as the room service menus found at luxurious hotels like The Ritz-Carlton, room service menus offer a limited number of menu items. They may offer items from the hotel's regular menu or feature items that are not on the regular menu.

Most room service menus are limited because it is difficult to offer high-quality food that does not deteriorate during transport from the production area to the guestroom, suite, or cabin. This is a problem in every lodging operation but especially in high-rise hotels where service staff must contend with elevators, and in resort-type properties where food servers must use a vehicle to transport the food to the guest.

One type of room service menu is the "doorknob" breakfast menu. A doorknob menu lists a limited number of breakfast items and times that the meal can be served. Guests select what they want to eat and the time they want the food delivered, then hang the menu outside the door on the doorknob. The menus are collected and the orders are prepared and sent to the rooms at the indicated times.

Take-Out. Some tableservice restaurants offer take-out menus in an effort to capture consumer dollars that otherwise might be spent at fast-food establishments or on convenience foods in supermarkets.

Like room service menus, take-out menus should be made up of items that can maintain an acceptable level of quality over a long period of time. Guests won't be satisfied unless the food they bought still looks and tastes good when they consume it.

Take-out menus should be inexpensive to produce since guests take them home. Some operations use their take-out menus as direct mail advertising pieces.

As noted in Chapter 1, some restaurants have installed fax machines in an effort to attract take-out business from busy executives. Home delivery services are another trend. Catering services are also becoming increasingly popular, according to some observers.

Banquet. Hotel food and beverage operations and restaurants that do extensive banquet business often develop pre-set banquet menus in varying price ranges from which guests may choose. They can also plan custom banquet menus when guests request them.

The pricing style for banquet menus is usually table d'hôte—a set meal with few if any choices offered at a set price. The meal tends to be elaborate, with appetizers, soups or salads, and fancy desserts served along with the entrée and its accompaniments.

Managers who plan banquet menus must be careful to select food that can be produced in quantity and still hold its quality.

California. Some restaurants offer breakfast, lunch, and dinner menu items on one menu, with all the items available at any time of the day: if a guest wants spaghetti for breakfast or pancakes for dinner, the guest can order it. This concept originated in California, so this type of menu has come to be called a California menu. Obviously, an operation that has no restrictions about when it will serve breakfast, lunch, or dinner items also gives up the production and scheduling convenience such restrictions provide.

Ethnic. Ethnic menus are offered by restaurants that seek to appeal to guests who like a particular cuisine. Restaurants that feature Italian, Chinese, or Mexican food are familiar ethnic restaurants. Ethnic restaurants that are not as familiar to most Americans include those offering Japanese, Polynesian, Scandinavian, Korean, Indian, and Thai cuisines.

An ethnic menu should feature a wide variety of dishes from the particular country or area. The names of the dishes should be in the original language and translated into English. The main ingredients of the dish should also be listed. How authentic should the menu items be? If most of the restaurant's guests are first-generation Americans of the ethnic background the menu seeks to appeal to, then the dishes should closely follow traditional recipes. However, if most of the clientele are second- and third-generation Americans and Americans from other ethnic backgrounds, the recipes can be "Americanized"—i.e., spices can be milder, some ingredients may be eliminated, etc.

Menu Planning

The success of a food service operation is to a large extent in the hands of its menu planner. Work will flow more smoothly, guests will be served more effectively, and profits will be greater when the menu has been properly planned. The opposite is also true: a poorly planned menu will cause significant operating problems that will affect guests, employees, and ultimately the financial objectives of the operation.

Not all food service managers will be called on to plan or help plan a menu. Managers at fast-food franchise restaurants, for example, may not do any menu planning; their menus will likely be planned at corporate headquarters after extensive market research. In hospitals and schools, menus are often planned by dietitians. At a large independent restaurant, a menu may be planned by a committee that includes the restaurant manager, the head chef, and perhaps the head of purchasing. Menu planning may be done by the owner or the head cook at a small restaurant.

Planning a menu is a very complex undertaking that requires a knowledge of the entire operation. Fortunately, it is rare that a menu planner has to start from scratch. Most menu planners revise an already existing menu. This means that the menu's pricing style—table d'hôte, à la carte, or a combination of the two—has already been chosen. The menu schedule has also been chosen—either fixed or cycle. And the type of menu has been determined—breakfast, lunch, dinner, or specialty.

For most menu planners, therefore, menu planning consists of selecting new menu items for an existing menu. How does a menu planner go about making these selections? The answers vary from operation to operation and from planner to planner, but two rules are basic: know your guests and know your operation.

Knowing Your Guests

The quality of all the decisions about the menu depends on knowing your guests well. What kinds of guests eat at your operation? What are they willing to pay for a meal? If your most important market is teenagers, your menu should look very different from a restaurant's whose main market is married couples with children.

What do your guests want to eat and drink? Some menu planners think their personal preferences are the same as their guests'. This is not necessarily true. When menu items are selected, the preferences of the guests—not the menu planner—must be considered. Guest preferences are learned by interviewing guests; reading surveys, comment cards, and trade journals; and studying production and sales records.

Knowing Your Operation

The type of operation helps determine what kinds of menu items are appropriate. At least five components of your operation have a direct impact on what kinds of menu items can be offered:

- Theme or cuisine
- Equipment
- Personnel
- Quality standards
- Budget

Theme or Cuisine. The theme or cuisine of the restaurant helps determine what types of menu items are appropriate. A Chinese restaurant has a very different menu than a family-oriented chain restaurant.

Equipment. A menu planner must know types and capacities of equipment in the kitchen. Menu planners can choose a wider variety of menu items if there is equipment on hand for baking, steaming, broiling, frying, etc. In contrast, an operation with limited equipment must have a limited menu.

When choosing menu items, planners should spread the workload evenly among the equipment. For example, if most of your entrées and a lot of your appetizers are fried, your fryers may be overloaded while the ovens and broilers are underutilized. For most restaurants, the entrées chosen should reflect a good distribution between frying, baking, broiling, roasting, and other methods of preparation.

Personnel. The number of employees and the skills of those employees will help determine what menu items can be placed on the menu. A menu planner should not put items on the menu that the kitchen staff does not have the skills to prepare.

Just as with equipment, a menu planner wants to avoid overwhelming some kitchen personnel while leaving others with little to do. Careful menu item selection can spread the workload evenly among kitchen personnel.

Quality Standards. Every item on the menu has to meet the operation's quality standards. A menu planner should not put items on the menu that can't be prepared and served while maintaining the proper quality.

Budget. Menu planners must recognize financial constraints when planning menus. Commercial properties cannot attain profit objectives and institutional operations cannot minimize expenses unless product costs fall within budgetary limits.

Selecting Menu Items

Hundreds of books have been written on the art and science of selecting menu items for menus. What follows is a simplified discussion of this complex subject.

The menu items listed on a menu can be categorized as appetizers, salads, entrées, starch items (potatoes, rice, pasta), vegetables, desserts, and beverages. How do menu planners create a "pool" of possible menu items in each of these categories from which to create or revise menus? There are many possible sources:

- *Old menus.* The operation's own previous menus may list menu items that were once popular but were dropped from the current menu for one reason or another. It may be time to consider them for the revised menu.

- *Books.* There are books for the food service industry devoted to recipes and new menu item ideas.

- *Trade magazines.* Trade magazines can be excellent sources of recipes for new menu items.

- *Cookbooks for the home market.* Cookbooks for home use can provide many new ideas for salads, soups, garnishes, entrées, and desserts. Of course, if they are chosen, the recipes have to be modified to yield larger quantities.

Only those menu items that marketing research has indicated that guests may like should be included in the pool. Once the pool has been narrowed down to "items our guests may like," some of these items must be eliminated because of:

- Cost
- Incompatibility with the operation's theme or cuisine
- Unavailable equipment
- Insufficient equipment capacity
- Insufficient kitchen space
- Insufficient number of employees
- Incompatibility with employee skills
- Unavailability of some ingredients
- Incompatibility with the operation's quality standards
- Sanitation problems

Once the pool has been narrowed down to menu items that guests will probably want and the operation can produce, the selection of items for the menu can begin.[3]

Entrées. Entrées are usually selected first. You must determine what kinds of entrées to offer: beef, pork, fish, entrée salads, etc. When planning, you may feel that you should have something for everyone and, therefore, be tempted to provide a wide range of entrées. This approach can create many operating problems. For example, a wider variety of food and ingredients must be ordered, received, stored, issued, and prepared. More equipment and more personnel with the necessary skills must be available. Production and service problems are more likely. The reverse—offering only a few entrées—reduces these problems. Many specialty or theme restaurants offer relatively few entrées. This minimizes many in-house production and serving problems.

As indicated earlier, menu planners must consider methods of preparation when selecting entrées. Production problems and service delays occur when all or most of the entrées are prepared the same way.

Some restaurants list sandwiches as entrée items on their menus. Sandwiches are the only entrées for some fast-food operations and delis. Sandwiches are usually not high-profit items, so restaurants that offer a lot of high-profit entrées usually try to downplay their sandwiches by listing them in smaller type separately from the entrées. Restaurants whose sandwiches are real money-makers and traffic-builders should give sandwiches a more prominent place on the menu.

Appetizers/Soups. Appetizers include fruit or tomato juice, cheese, fruit, and seafood items such as shrimp cocktail. Appetizers are supposed to enliven the appetite before dinner, so they are generally small in size and spicy or pleasantly biting or tart. The number and variety of appetizers on a menu is determined by the type of operation and its guests. Fast-food operations typically do not have appetizers; elegant restaurants may devote a whole page of their dinner menus to appetizers.

Many restaurants offer a limited selection of soups. Sometimes a "soup du jour" is listed (du jour means "of the day"). If more than two or three soups are offered, they are usually listed separately on the menu rather than lumped in with the appetizers. The kinds of soups offered are determined by the type of operation. Seafood restaurants usually offer soups like clam chowder and shrimp or lobster bisque, while Italian restaurants often have minestrone soup. Upscale restaurants may offer chilled soups such as vichyssoise.

Starch Items/Vegetables. The next items to be planned are usually the starch items and vegetables. Sometimes the starch item is a part of the entrée—sirloin tips in gravy served over rice, for example. At other times, the starch item is separate—a baked potato or a side dish of pasta. In many restaurants a vegetable is served with the entrée. Vegetables can also be offered as side dishes.

Again, the type of operation and its guests determine the variety of starch items and vegetables that are offered. The starch items at many seafood restaurants are limited to baked potatoes or french fries. A restaurant that features fine dining may offer a wide variety of rice, pasta, and potato items; potatoes, for example, may be baked, fried, creamed, mashed, prepared au gratin, etc. Chinese restaurants offer a great variety of vegetables; fast-food operations, few or none.

Salads. The first decision a planner must make about salads is whether they will be strictly side dishes, or whether some salads will be offered as entrées. If they are offered, salad entrées such as chicken salad, shrimp salad, or chef's salad are usually listed on the lunch menu. Tossed salad, coleslaw, potato salad, fruit salad, and cottage cheese salad are typical side-dish salads.

Desserts. The next menu items planned are the desserts. Desserts are typically high-profit items, so much so that even fast-food restaurants such as McDonald's have added a limited number of desserts to their menus. On the other end of the spectrum, many upscale restaurants offer a wide array of elaborate desserts. Low-calorie desserts can be offered for the health-conscious.

Beverages. Non-alcoholic beverages are often listed at the end of the menu. Coffee, tea, milk, and a selection of carbonated beverages are typical. Upscale restaurants may feature a wide variety of coffee—Colombian, Turkish, espresso, cappuccino, spiced coffee, and so on—and a number of teas such as Earl Grey and jasmine.

If an operation offers alcoholic beverages, a decision has to be made about how many beverages will be included. Should a few standard beers be offered, or should the operation carry a wide variety, including local and regional beers? How many different wines should be offered? Should dessert wines and cordials be included on the wine list? How many different brands of liquor should be offered? For chain restaurants and franchise operations, selection decisions are usually made at corporate headquarters. Managers in independent operations must make their own decisions, based on guest preferences, the restaurant's image, beverage inventory costs, space, and other factors.

Menu Balance

Once all the menu items have been selected for the menu, the menu should be reviewed for business, aesthetic, and nutritional balance.

Business balance refers to the balance between food costs, menu prices, the popularity of items, and other financial and marketing considerations. (Food costs and menu prices will be discussed in the next chapter.) In commercial operations, the menu must help the operation make a profit and the menu should be reviewed with that goal in mind.

Aesthetic balance refers to the degree to which meals have been constructed with an eye to the colors, textures, and flavors of foods. Obviously, balance is more important in a table d'hôte menu than in an à la carte menu, since guests are offered entire meals on a table d'hôte menu, and they have more freedom to choose their own food combinations with an à la carte menu. But even with an à la carte menu, some foods are commonly sold together—an entrée with an accompanying starch item and vegetable, for example.

Color is a very important component of a meal's attractiveness. A plate of baked whitefish, steamed cauliflower, and mashed potatoes makes for a boring and unappetizing presentation. Two or three colors on a plate are more interesting than one.

A meal should be composed of foods that vary in texture. Most guests would not like a meal of soup, stew, creamed corn, mashed potatoes, and chocolate pudding. In general, firm entrées should have tender or soft side dishes; soft entrées should have crisp or crunchy side dishes.

Putting compatible flavors together is a matter of experience as well as knowing traditional combinations. Ham and eggs, for example, go together better than shrimp and eggs. Imagine a meal of grape juice, sweet and sour pork, and cherry pie! Such a meal would have too many sweets and sours for most people.

Nutritional balance has historically been more important for institutional food service operations than for commercial properties. But, as noted in Chapter 5,

Exhibit 6.5 Sample Theme Restaurant Menu

Headings in this menu from the Beef Barron are reminiscent of the Old West. Line drawings and the lariats circling important dishes reinforce the Western theme. (Courtesy of
Hilton Hotels Corporation)

managers of commercial properties should make sure the components of a well-
balanced meal are available from among the menu items they offer. Nutritional
concerns are now important to many guests and must therefore be important to
restaurant managers.

Menu Design

After menu items have been selected, they must be organized into a menu that encourages guests to order. A well-designed menu complements a restaurant's overall theme, blends in with the interior decor, communicates with guests, and helps
sell the operation and its menu items (see Exhibit 6.5).

How a menu is designed depends on the type of operation. The menu in an
elegant hotel dining room is far different from the menu offered in a nursing home
cafeteria. In spite of these differences, there are many design and merchandising
techniques that are nearly the same for almost all food service operations.[4]

Many of you manage or will manage operations where the menu is designed by the fast-food franchisee, or by the corporate headquarters of a restaurant chain. There may be times in your career, however, when you will work at independent restaurants or other operations whose management will have a complete or partial say in what the menu looks like. A basic knowledge of menu design principles is helpful when you have menu planning responsibilities.

Menus are so crucial to an operation's success that the menu planners of many independent restaurants seek the help of advertising agencies or freelance artists and designers. The menu planner should tell the designer about the restaurant's guests, show the designer the restaurant's interior, explain the number and complexity of menu items, how often the menu will be changed, what the menu should achieve, and the budget for the project. The designer can provide many creative layout ideas and educate the planner as to production costs and options. The menu planner must be careful not to let the designer take over the project, however. The designer's natural inclination to make the menu a "work of art" should not outweigh the restaurateur's own judgment about what's best for the restaurant.

Copy

After the menu planner has selected the menu items that will appear on the menu, copy must be written. Many operations hire a professional copywriter to write menu copy.

Just as with all the other menu design elements, the appropriateness of menu copy depends on the operation, its guests, and the meal period. Copy on children's menus should be entertaining; copy on lunch menus, brief and to the point. Copy on dinner menus can be more descriptive because guests are more likely to have the time and inclination to read menu copy and take time in selecting menu items.

Menu copy can be divided into three elements: headings, descriptive copy for menu items, and supplemental merchandising copy.

Headings. Headings include major heads, subheads, and names of menu items. Major heads usually identify courses: "Appetizers," "Soups," "Entrées," etc. Subheads under the main heading "Entrée" could be "Steak," "Seafood," and "Today's Specials."

Menu item names must be chosen with care. Some operations choose simple descriptive names for their menu items. Others choose more elaborate names. For most operations it's best to keep menu item names simple so that guests are not confused.

If menu item names are in a foreign language, a simple description of the item in English will help guests who do not know the language and it may increase sales of the item. On the other hand, if many of your guests do not speak English, pictures of the menu items may be helpful.

Rules of grammar should be followed for the language that is used; if French is used, French grammar rules apply. A good language dictionary can help copywriters spell words correctly and use the correct accent marks. Menu copy in a foreign language works well only if the foreign language is used properly.

Descriptive Copy. Descriptive menu copy informs guests about menu items and helps increase sales. The menu item's main ingredient, important secondary ingredients, and method of preparation are often included in descriptive copy. The description should not be a recipe, though.

Flowery language, too many superlatives, and long sentences can turn guests off. Claims should be believable and made in short, easy-to-read sentences. A few well-chosen words are better than a long-winded paragraph.

Many variables determine when to use descriptive copy. Most entrées are high-profit items and they usually get the most copy. Specialties of the house deserve extra copy, since they help define an operation's character and appeal. Fancy appetizers and desserts, entrée-type salads, and wines are examples of other menu items that need descriptive copy. If an item's name is not very descriptive, more copy may be needed to explain the item. There should be no description when the item—"Low-Fat Milk," for example—is self-explanatory.

Truth-in-menu laws. One of the reasons that descriptive copy should not oversell a menu item is that it leads to disappointed guests. Another reason is that overselling can involve exaggerated claims that may be in violation of truth-in-menu laws. Some areas to be careful about include:

- *Grading.* If it is stated on the menu that a steak is USDA prime, then the steak served must be of that grade. Or if the copy says sirloin tips, then an inferior cut of meat cannot be substituted. Some foods are graded by size, and any size claims must be in line with official standards. If the menu says jumbo shrimp, for example, the item served must be jumbo shrimp, not extra large or large.

- *"Freshness" claims.* If the menu says an item is "fresh," then it cannot be canned, frozen, or "fresh-frozen."

- *Geographical origin.* You cannot make false claims about the geographical origin of a product. Cheese from Wisconsin cannot be sold as "imported Swiss cheese"; you cannot indicate "gulf shrimp" when the product is actually Pacific Ocean shrimp.

- *Preparation.* The copy must be accurate in regard to menu item preparation. Senior citizens, dieters, and other health-conscious guests are especially concerned about how menu items are prepared. If the menu says the item is baked, it cannot be fried instead.

- *Dietary or nutrition claims.* Do not make dietary or nutrition claims that are insupportable by scientific data.[5]

Supplemental Merchandising Copy. Supplemental merchandising copy is copy on the menu that is devoted to subjects other than the menu items. Supplemental merchandising copy includes basic information: address, telephone number, days and hours of operation, meals served, reservations and payment policies, etc. But supplemental merchandising copy can also be entertaining: a history of the restaurant, a statement about management's commitment to guest service, or even poetry. Many food service operations have a special feature, service, history, character, or locale that can make for interesting copy if handled well. Such copy can enhance an operation's image and help make it stand out from competitors.

How much supplemental merchandising copy is used depends on the menu space that's available and management's ideas about whether more copy or something else—more artwork, for example—is the way to encourage sales.

Layout

Once menu copy has been written, the menu must be organized into a layout—a rough sketch of how the finished menu will look. Coming up with a layout includes listing menu items in the right sequence, placing the menu items' names and descriptive copy (if any) on the page(s), determining the menu's format, choosing the right typeface and the right paper, and integrating artwork into the menu. Although these steps are presented separately in this section, in reality many layout decisions are made simultaneously because layout elements are so interrelated.

Sequence. A meal has a beginning, middle, and an end, and menu items should be placed on the menu to follow this order: appetizers and soups listed first, entrées next, and desserts last. How other menu items are placed—side orders, salads, sandwiches, beverages, and so on—will depend on the operation and the meal period. Salads may be listed with the entrées at lunch and with the appetizers at dinner. Alcoholic beverages are not listed at all on breakfast menus but may be listed first on dinner menus.

What order the various appetizers, entrées, etc., are placed in is usually determined by popularity and profitability. Those items that are most popular or are most profitable are typically listed first so guests can find them easily. The least popular or profitable items are usually listed last. Of course, this is not an unbreakable rule. There are many other ways to draw attention to a menu item besides putting it at the head of a list. Some designers may choose to draw a box around a high-profit item, place it in the center of a page, position eye-catching artwork next to it, or otherwise set it apart (see Exhibit 6.6).

Placement. Once menu items have been placed in a tentative order, designers can draw a rough sketch of the menu, with boxes or a series of horizontal lines to represent the approximate space the descriptive copy for each menu item will take up. Room must also be set aside for supplemental merchandising copy. Some designers may already know what kinds of artwork—drawings, borders, photos, etc.—they want to include on the menu. If so, space should be allowed for these elements as well.

Designers should be careful not to make the menu too crowded. Most designers favor a generous use of white space—blank areas not covered by words or artwork.

If an operation uses a clip-on regularly, then blank space should be provided for it on the regular menu because many guests won't lift up a clip-on to see what is printed underneath.

Format. Once a rough sketch of the menu is completed, planners can get an idea of what format will be most appropriate.

Exhibit 6.6 A House-Specialties Menu

TAKE OFF
WITH OUR HIGH FLYING FAVORITES
SNEEKER SPECIALTIES

SUPER PLATTERS!
A full meal served on a Monster Platter

BIG RIB PLATTER 9.99
Our signature special! A pound and a quarter of our famous
barbequed ribs.

FRIED ROUGHY PLATTER 8.59
Our sweet, delicate white fish lightly breaded and deep fried
to perfection.

HALF CHICKEN PLATTER   6.49
You'll love our chicken Spit-Roasted or BBQ'd in our famous
sauce. Crisp on the outside, moist on the inside.

RIBS AND CHICKEN KABOB PLATTER ... 9.99
Chicken breast marinated for flavor and tenderness then
charbroiled and served on a bed of rice next to our famous
BBQ ribs.

BARBEQUE PLATTER 9.79
The best of both worlds! One half pound of ribs next to a quarter
chicken charbroiled in our secret BBQ sauce.

All platters include fries, onion rings, apple sauce, roll, butter, and cole slaw

ENTREES

All entrees come complete with a garlic toast basket, a homebaked roll & butter, plus a choice of any two of the following.

- Tossed Salad
- Cabbage Salad
- Cottage Cheese

- Non-Alcoholic Beverage
- Baked Potato
- Sneeker Fries
- Mashed Potatoes

- Mixed Vegetables
- Rice Pilaf
- Soup of the Day

THE BIG MEATY RIBS
         Regular Large
.... 8.99 10.29
Falling-off-the-bone! Barbecued pork back ribs basted in our
"special sauce."

SPIT-ROASTED CHICKEN NATURAL
         Regular Large
.... 5.99 6.59
You'll love our chicken Spit-Roasted or BBQ'd in our famous
sauce. Crisp on the outside, moist on the inside.

CHICKEN GIZZARDS 6.49 6.99
Boiled in beer and seasoned, then lightly breaded and deep
fried. Served with natural gravy.

OFF THE HOOK

         Regular Large
ORANGE ROUGHY 7.29 8.69
A generous portion of the sweetest of white fish. Lightly
breaded and deep fried or broiled. Served with rice pilaf.

ORANGE ROUGHY (Cajun Style) 7.39 8.79
Cajun spice broiled into Roughy makes this fish a tangy treat.

CHICKEN PUFF PIE 5.99 6.99
Our version of Chicken a la King, but with more chicken and
fresh vegetables. Served with light, fluffy puff pastry rings.

CHICKEN KABOB 6.99 7.99
Marinated chicken breast, broiled and served with rice and
sauteed vegetables.

WHAT'S YOUR BEEF

SNEEKER SIRLOIN STEAK 8.99
A full one half pound of Choice Chunky Delight

CAJUN STYLE SIRLOIN 9.19

MIX AND MATCH (YOUR FAVORITES)

RIB & CHICKEN COMBINATION 9.89
Our favorite and most popular item. Two original greats!

RIBS & BUFFALO STYLE CHICKEN WINGS . 10.29
What could be better?? Enjoy two of our favorite items.

RIBS AND CHICKEN KABOB 10.29
Marinated chicken over rice with our famous BBQ ribs.

RIBS & BREAST OF CHICKEN STIX 10.29
Hand-breaded Breast of Chicken with our Ribs! Wonderful!

RIBS & STEAK 11.99
OUR Great Ribs along side our choice half pound chunky
sirloin.

SPECIAL NOTICE: Sneekers uses only real chicken in its products. Sometimes we miss 'em, so watch out for bones.

Boxes are used on this menu to draw attention to house specialties. (Courtesy of Sneekers Restaurant, Lansing, Michigan)

Exhibit 6.7 Menu Formats

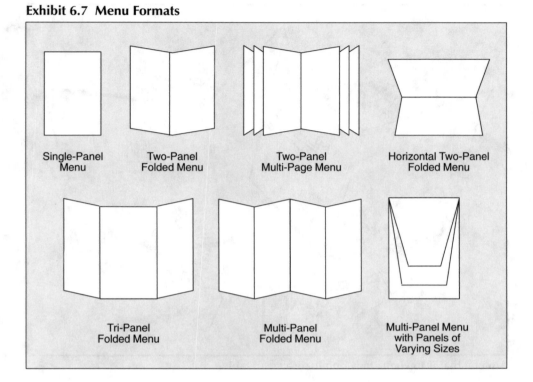

Single-Panel Menu	Two-Panel Folded Menu	Two-Panel Multi-Page Menu	Horizontal Two-Panel Folded Menu
Tri-Panel Folded Menu		Multi-Panel Folded Menu	Multi-Panel Menu with Panels of Varying Sizes

"Format" refers to a menu's size, shape, and general makeup. There are many menu formats to choose from (see Exhibit 6.7). There is no one "correct" format; decision-makers at each operation must decide what's right for them. There are a few general guidelines to keep in mind, however. A menu that is too large may dominate a small table or cause guests to knock over glasses when they pick it up—it may even catch fire if there is a candle centerpiece! Menus that are too small are hard to read and are often overcrowded. Menus with too many pages may confuse guests.[6]

Some adjustments may have to be made when working out the size and format of the menu. If there are too many menu items for the format chosen, the restaurateur has many options, including: (1) drop some menu items, (2) trim back some of the descriptive copy, (3) drop some of the supplemental merchandising copy, or (4) go to a format that provides more space. If there are not enough menu items to fill up the space, options include: (1) adding more menu items, (2) using the extra room for artwork or white space, or (3) going to a different format.

Typeface. At this point the typeface—the style of the menu's printed letters—should be chosen. Some operations that want to project an informal and relaxed image use hand-lettered menus. Most menus, however, are printed. How well guests can read the menu is determined to a large extent by the typeface used.

A menu that is too large may dominate a small table.

Type comes in various sizes, from small 6-point type to very large 72-point. The smaller the type, the harder it is to read. A good general rule is to never set menu copy in type that is smaller than 12-point.[7]

Lines of type should not be set too close together; that is, there should be a comfortable amount of space between lines. In general, type should be a dark color printed on light-colored paper for easy reading. Wise menu designers take into account the fact that lighting in restaurant dining rooms is usually much dimmer than in office work areas where menus are designed.

Uppercase letters are the capitals (A, B, C, etc.); lowercase letters are in lower case (a, b, c, etc.). Menu planners should remember that it is easier to read a combination of uppercase and lowercase letters rather than all capitals. Headings, menu item names, and copy that needs special emphasis should be the only copy in all uppercase letters.

Each typeface has its own personality. Some type has a dark and heavy appearance on the page; other typefaces have an open and light feeling. The typeface chosen should reflect the operation's personality, but the bottom line is that the typeface must communicate. If a strange, hard-to-read typeface is chosen, guests will react negatively and sales may suffer.

After the typeface is chosen and typeset, a page proof of the menu should be made to see how the type looks. A page proof is a copy of the page as it will look when printed. At this point more adjustments may have to be made. If the menu appears too crowded, for example, the designer may choose to enlarge the menu, use a different typeface, or stay with the same typeface but go to a smaller point size. After the designer decides what changes to make, a new page proof should be checked to make sure the changes solved the problems.

Artwork. As mentioned earlier, artwork includes drawings, photographs, decorative patterns, and borders that are used to attract interest, highlight menu copy, or reinforce the operation's image. If artwork will be included on the menu, the artwork should fit in with the interior design or overall decorative scheme of the restaurant. Artwork should not be so plentiful or complicated that the guest is overwhelmed or the menu is difficult to read. A cluttered, confusing menu is not inviting to guests and makes ordering difficult.

A freelance artist, or artists at the design house or advertising agency in charge of designing the menu, can create original art for the menu. An inexpensive alternative is to acquire books that include graphics and illustrations in the public domain that can be copied by printers. A restaurant with an Early American theme may find an inexpensive source of art for its menu in old prints, woodcuts, or engravings.

The more artwork involved, the harder (and costlier) it is to put the menu together. The cost of reproducing artwork goes up if you want the artwork to appear in a different color than other menu elements. One way to make artwork more cost-effective is to use it elsewhere—on postcards, newsletters, guest checks, napkins, posters, and matchbooks.

Paper. A menu is something that is touched and held. The kind of paper the menu is printed on communicates something about the operation to guests. An upscale operation's menu may be printed on expensive textured paper. A deli may use a single sheet of ordinary typing paper for its menu.

There are many different kinds of paper. The texture of paper can vary from coarse to silky smooth. Paper varies in how shiny or reflective it is. Too much reflection causes glare and makes reading the menu difficult. Paper also differs in strength, opacity (the amount of transparency), and ink receptivity. And, of course, paper comes in every color imaginable—menus do not have to be printed on white paper.

Many interesting things can be done with the paper the menu is printed on. A menu's pages can be foil-stamped. Foil stamping involves applying a thin foil film onto the paper. The foil can be artwork or copy—the name of the restaurant, for example. Paper can be embossed—that is, an image can be stamped in relief (either positive or negative) on the paper. Paper can be laminated (sealed in thin sheets of plastic). Many menu covers are laminated to protect them from stains and tears. Paper can be folded and die-cut for interesting designs. As mentioned earlier, children's menus often come in unusual shapes, and may even include pop-up art.

The right paper for the menu depends in part on how often the menu will be used. If the menu is only used for one day and thrown away, it can be printed on inexpensive paper. However, if, as in most cases, the menu must last for a while, a water-resistant paper should be chosen that can stand up to rough usage.

The entire menu doesn't have to be printed on the same kind of paper. The cover can be a heavier, coated paper stock while the inside pages can be lighter and more inexpensive.

Cover

A well-designed cover communicates the image, style, cuisine, even the price range of the operation. It helps set the mood and creates expectations of the dining experience to come.

The name of the restaurant is all the copy the cover needs. Some menus also include basic information on the cover, such as the operation's address, phone number, and hours of operation, but as a rule covers should not appear cluttered. Basic information may be better placed on the back cover. The back cover may be the place for other supplemental merchandising copy—the history of the restaurant, banquet information, take-out service information, and so on.

For most restaurants, cover stock should be heavy, durable, and grease-resistant (or laminated). The cover's design must be suitable to your operation. If the restaurant looks like an English pub, the cover should match this decor; a steakhouse's cover may have images of the Old West.

The colors on the cover should either blend in or contrast pleasantly with the color scheme of the restaurant. Colors must be chosen with care, because colors produce many conscious and subconscious effects. Colors can make people feel happy, sad, cold, hot, and so on. Pastel colors suggest a warm, soothing atmosphere; deep purples and reds suggest richness and opulence. Ethnic menus often have colors appropriate to the culture the food comes from. Bright reds, yellows, and oranges against a sand-colored paper suggest Mexico; black and red suggest Japanese or Chinese food; the colors of the Italian flag—red, white, and green—are often used on menus in Italian restaurants.[8]

Although most of a menu's colors are usually found on the cover, color may also be used on the interior pages, usually on a more limited basis. Color can be used in the background, as trim, or in artwork to create a mood or draw the guest's eye to specific items.

Color gives the menu variety, but cost increases as colors are added. The more colors you print on the cover (and in the interior), the more expensive the menu will be. Using one color—usually black—is the least expensive; four-color printing gives you all the colors in the spectrum and is the most expensive.

Common Menu-Design Mistakes

Common menu-design mistakes include the following:

- *Menu is too small.* Crowded menus are usually not very appealing and do not do as good a selling job because they're harder to read.

- *Type is too small.* Not every guest has 20/20 vision, and lighting in some dining rooms is quite dim. Guests can't order what they can't read.

- *No descriptive copy.* Sometimes the name of the menu item is not enough to go on, or does not do a good job of sparking guest interest. Good descriptive copy increases sales.

- *Every item treated the same.* A menu designer should use positioning, boxes, color, decorative borders, larger type, or some other device to call attention to the most profitable or best-selling items. If every menu item gets a low-key treatment, or if every item is in bold capital letters surrounded by exclamation points, the items you want to sell the most do not stand out from the rest.

- *Some of the operation's food and beverages are not listed.* Some operations do not list all of the wines or specialty drinks they offer, or they have a line like "Selected Desserts" rather than a complete listing of the desserts they sell. How can guests order items that are not on the menu?

- *Clip-on problems.* Operations that regularly use a clip-on should allow blank space for it on the menu so the clip-on does not hide important menu items. The clip-on itself should match the design and quality of the menu. A disorganized clip-on poorly printed on cheap paper can destroy the effect of a well-designed and expensive menu.

- *Basic information about the property and its policies are not included.* It's surprising how many restaurants do not include their address, phone number, hours of operation, payment policies, etc., on the menu.

- *Blank pages.* A blank menu page is a page that does nothing to sell the restaurant or its menu items. The back cover is the page that is left blank on many menus. Unless a blank back cover adds to the restaurant's image, there's nothing wrong with putting additional menu items or supplemental merchandising copy there. For example, a seafood restaurant can devote its back cover to listing the types of fish it serves and their unique flavor and texture characteristics.[9]

Evaluating Menus

No matter how well planned and designed, a menu should be evaluated periodically.

How can a menu be evaluated? First, management has to set standards that the menu is expected to help meet. For example, a standard for the lunch meal period might be, "The average guest check at lunch should be $6." A standard for dinner might be, "Each dinner guest should order a food item in addition to the entrée—an appetizer, a soup or salad, or a dessert." If these standards are not met, management must first determine if and to what extent other variables are contributing to the problem. Are food and beverage items meeting the operation's quality standards? Are menu prices correct? Are food servers doing their part to sell additional food items? If these and other variables check out, then managers must take a serious look at the menu because the menu may not be doing its part to meet management's goals.

There are many production and sales benchmarks managers can use to help them evaluate a menu. Production records and sales history records can be used to determine how well menu items are selling. If overall sales or the sales of particular menu items are not meeting management's projections or expectations, the menu is one of several areas that should be investigated.

Menus vary so greatly from operation to operation that each restaurant or other food and beverage outlet must establish its own methods of evaluation. General questions that most food and beverage managers can ask when evaluating a menu include:

- Have guests complained about the menu?

- Have guests said good things about the menu?

- How does the menu compare with the menus of competitors?

- Has the average guest check remained steady or increased?

- Is there enough variety in menu items?

- Are menu items priced correctly?

- Are you selling the right mix of high-profit and low-profit items?

- Is the menu attractive?

- Do the colors and other design elements match the operation's theme and decor?

- Are menu items laid out in an attractive and logical way?

- Is there too much descriptive copy? Not enough? Is the copy easy to understand?

- Is attention called to the items managers most want to sell, through placement, color, description, type size, etc.?

- Is the typeface easy to read and appropriate to the restaurant's theme and decor?

- Is the paper attractive and stain-resistant?

- Have the menus been easy to maintain so that guests always receive a clean, attractive menu?

Operations can create their own menu rating forms, with these and other questions listed on the form and grouped into categories such as "Design," "Layout," "Copy," "Merchandising," etc. When establishing evaluation criteria and creating evaluation forms, managers should keep in mind that an evaluation is worthless unless enough information comes out of it to help menu planners improve the menu.

Endnotes

1. Lendal H. Kotschevar, *Management by Menu,* 2d ed. (New York: Wiley, 1987), p. 51.

2. Eleanor F. Eckstein, *Menu Planning,* 3d ed. (Westport, Conn.: AVI, 1983), p. 81.

3. The menu planning sequence that follows—entrées, appetizers/soups, starch items/vegetables, salads, desserts, and beverages—is taken from Eckstein, *Menu Planning,* pp. 182–186.

4. John C. Birchfield, *Foodservice Operations Manual: A Guide for Hotels, Restaurants, and Institutions* (New York: VNR, 1979), Section 1, file code M–17.

5. Some of the information in this list was adapted from Nancy Loman Scanlon, *Marketing by Menu* (New York: VNR, 1985), pp. 134–136.

6. Scanlon, *Marketing by Menu*, p. 81.

7. Albin G. Seaberg, *Menu Design, Merchandising and Marketing* (New York: VNR, 1983), p. 36.

8. Scanlon, *Marketing by Menu*, p. 111.

9. Seaberg, *Menu Design*, pp. 53–54.

Key Terms

aesthetic balance
à la carte menu
business balance
California menu
cuisine
cycle menu
doorknob menu
fixed menu

nutritional balance
prix fixe menu
table d'hôte menu
take-out menu
truth-in-menu laws
typeface
white space

Discussion Questions

1. What are the three basic menu pricing styles?

2. What is a fixed menu? a cycle menu?

3. What are the differences between breakfast, lunch, and dinner menus?

4. What are specialty menus?

5. What are two basic rules in menu planning?

6. What five operational components have a direct impact on the kinds of menu items an operation offers?

7. In what three ways should a menu be balanced?

8. Menu copy can be divided into what three elements?

9. What are some common menu-design mistakes?

10. What are some of the questions food and beverage managers should ask when evaluating a menu?

Chapter Outline

Standard Recipes
    Developing Standard Recipes
    Recipe Sources
    Adjusting Standard Recipe Yields
Determining Standard Food Costs for Menu Items
    Calculating Portion Costs
    Calculating Dinner Costs
Determining an Overall Standard Food Cost
Determining Standard Beverage Costs
Pricing Menu Items
    Desired Food Cost Percent Markup
    Profit Pricing
    Competition and Pricing

Standard Product Costs and Pricing Strategies

W<small>HEN PLANNING MENUS,</small> managers must take into account not only the preferences of guests, but also the financial goals of the food service operation.

When standard product costs for food and beverage items are established, the manager knows how much it *should* cost to produce each menu item. This chapter explains how standard food and beverage costs can be determined for menu items that are prepared according to standard recipes. Standard cost information for menu items is used to establish an overall standard food cost. This overall standard cost information provides the manager with a benchmark by which to monitor actual food costs and evaluate how well the operation is meeting its financial objectives.

The final sections of the chapter address methods used to price menu items. Pricing strategies are important to commercial food service operations as well as to many institutional food service facilities. In order to ensure that the financial goals of the operation are met, managers must be able to determine the most effective selling price for each menu item.

Standard Recipes

A standard recipe is a formula for producing a food or beverage item. It specifies ingredients, the required quantity of each ingredient, preparation procedures, portion size and portioning equipment, garnish, and any other information necessary to prepare the item.

Exhibit 7.1 presents a sample standard food recipe. Note that this recipe yields 60 portions, each with a standard portion size of 6 ounces. The "Amount" column on the left margin can be used to adjust the yield to a larger or smaller quantity. To aid in portioning, the recipe's "Procedure" column specifies that a #60 scoop (which equals 60 level scoops, or servings, per quart) should be used. Note also that the recipe clearly indicates baking time, temperature, and the exact procedures for preparing the menu item.

The single most important advantage of using standard recipes is consistency. When standard recipes are followed correctly, items served to guests will be consistent in quality, flavor, and portion size. This consistency creates satisfied guests and enables a food service operation to build a solid base of repeat business. Also, when food service operations produce consistent products, managers can establish accurate standard costs. Managers need this information to ensure that economic goals will be met. If the cost of a menu item differs each time it is prepared because different types or quantities of ingredients are used or because of varying portion

Exhibit 7.1 Sample Standard Food Recipe

	Fish Fillet Amandine		**IX. MAIN DISHES—FISH 2** Baking Temperature: 450°F Baking Time: 14–15 min
Yield: _____ Size: _____		Yield: 60 Size: 6 oz	
Amount	**Ingredients**	**Amount**	**Procedure**
_____	Fish fillets, fresh or frozen 6 oz portion	22¹/₂ lb	1. Defrost fillets if frozen fish is used. 2. Arrange defrosted or fresh fillets in single layers on greased sheet pans.

_____	Almonds, toasted, chopped or slivered	1 lb	3. To toast almonds:
			  a. Spread on sheet pans.
			  b. Place in 350°F oven until lightly toasted.
			    Approximate time: 15 min.

_____	Margarine or butter, softened	2 lb 8 oz	4. Add almonds, lemon juice, lemon peel, salt, and pepper to softened margarine or butter.
_____ _____ _____	Lemon juice Lemon peel, grated Salt	¹/₂ cup 2³/₄ oz 4 tbsp	5. Mix thoroughly. 6. Spread margarine mixture on fillets as uniformly as possible. *Amount per fillet:* #60 scoop 7. Bake at 450°F for approx. 15 min or until fish flakes when tested with fork.
_____ _____	Pepper, white Weight: margarine-almond mixture	1 tbsp 4 lb	8. Sprinkle lightly with chopped parsley or sprigs of parsley when served.

Source: Adapted from G. Boyd, M. McKinley, and J. Dana, *Standardized Quantity Recipe File for Quality and Cost Control* (Ames, Iowa: Iowa State University Press, 1971).

sizes, there will be no consistent cost information available to help managers keep costs in line with budget constraints. The following are among other benefits derived from using standard recipes:

- More efficient purchasing practices result when managers know the exact amounts of ingredients needed to produce menu items.

- When managers know that the standard recipe will yield a specific number of standard-size portions, it is less likely that too many or too few items will be prepared.

- Since standard recipes indicate needed equipment and required production times, managers can more effectively schedule food production employees and necessary equipment.

- Less supervision is required since standard recipes tell the employees the quantity and preparation method for each item. Guesswork is eliminated; employees need only follow recipe procedures. Of course, managers should routinely evaluate the quality of items produced and ensure that standard recipes are followed correctly.

- If the chef is ill or the bartender doesn't show up, a product can be produced if a standard recipe is available. Granted, inexperienced employees will be slow and may make mistakes. However, if the recipe is in the head of an absent employee instead of on a standard recipe card, management will be in an even more awkward position.

Using a standard recipe does not require that the recipe be physically in the work area during production times. After a cook prepares a menu item several times, or a bartender mixes a drink several times, he or she will remember ingredients, quantities, and procedures. It would obviously be impractical if, before preparing a drink, a busy bartender had to refer to a standard recipe. A standard recipe must always be followed and must always be available, but it does not always need to be read.

Developing Standard Recipes

Developing standard recipes does not require throwing out existing recipes and starting over. Rather, it requires standardizing existing recipes according to a series of steps.

Select a time period for standard recipe development. For example, you may choose to standardize three recipes at each weekly cooks' meeting, or spend one hour each week with the head bartender to develop standard beverage recipes. At these meetings, ask the cook or head bartender to talk through the preparation of the item. What are the ingredients and how much of each ingredient is needed? What are the exact procedures? What are cooking/baking temperatures and times? What portion-control tools are, or can be, used? On what plate or in what glassware is the item served? What garnish is used? Double-check the recipe by closely observing the cook or bartender as the item is actually prepared.

Record the recipes in a standard format that will be helpful to those preparing the items. For example:

- Decide on the desirable yield. If 25 portions of a food item are prepared for slow periods and 60 portions are needed for busy times, recipes should be designed to yield these servings.

- List all ingredients in the order they are used.

- Decide whether to use weights or measures or both. Weighing is always more precise than measuring, and it is just as practical to weigh liquids, flour, etc., as it is to measure them. Exhibit 7.2 presents some equivalent weights and measures. Avoid confusion by using consistent abbreviations throughout all the standard recipes you are developing.

- Whenever possible, express all quantities in amounts that are practical for those preparing the item. For example, convert all measures into the largest possible units. Change $4/8$ cup to $1/2$ cup, four cups to one quart, or three teaspoons to one tablespoon. At this point you need to be sure that the proper equipment is

Exhibit 7.2 Equivalent Weights and Measures

1 pound	=	16 ounces	3/4 cup	=	12 tablespoons
1 tablespoon	=	3 teaspoons	1 cup	=	16 tablespoons
1/4 cup	=	4 tablespoons	1 quart	=	4 cups
1/2 cup	=	8 tablespoons	1 gallon	=	4 quarts
1/3 cup	=	5 1/3 tablespoons (or 16 teaspoons)	2 pints	=	1 quart
2/3 cup	=	10 2/3 tablespoons (or 32 teaspoons)	2 cups	=	1 pint

available. It does little good to specify a three-ounce quantity when an accurate measuring scale is not available. Also, when applicable, recipes should be developed that call for standard-size pans and other equipment.

- Record procedures in detailed, concise, and exact terms. Avoid ambiguous statements. For example, what does "one cup whipping cream" mean? Does it mean one cup of cream which has been whipped or does it mean one cup of cream which must be whipped? When mixing is called for, tell how to mix (by hand or by machine) and provide the exact time and speed if a machine is used. State the size and type of equipment needed and always list exact temperatures, cooking times, and other necessary controls.

- Provide directions for portioning. Indicate the type and size of the serving dish. Also, indicate portioning equipment, such as ladle or scoop, and specify the expected number and size of portions. If garnishes or sauces are needed, these should be listed.

After the standard recipes have been recorded, share them with other production staff. Solicit their ideas about accuracy and possible refinements.

Finally, test the recipes to be certain that they yield products of the desired quantity and quality. Many food service operations use a tasting committee or panel. This group may include management staff, cooks, other interested employees, and even guests. A rating scale similar to the one presented in Exhibit 7.3 can be used to evaluate a menu item on the basis of specific characteristics. For example, baked goods may be evaluated on the basis of external appearance and flavor; meats on the basis of aroma, tenderness, and juiciness; vegetables on the basis of color, moisture content, texture, and taste.

After successful testing, the recipe may be considered standardized. Production staff should now be given copies, trained in their use, and supervised to ensure compliance. In some instances, pictures can be used showing the finished product after portioning to give additional help to production and service staff.

Despite the advantages of using standard recipes, there may be some difficulties encountered in implementing them. Employees who have never used standard recipes may have negative attitudes about them. Cooks or bartenders, for example, may feel that they can no longer be creative in the kitchen or behind the bar. They may resent the need to put things down on paper. Other difficulties may be related

Exhibit 7.3 Sample Menu Item Rating Scale

Name of Menu Item: _____		Date: _____ Sample Number: _____			
Instructions: Check (✓) your feeling toward the characteristics specified for the menu item being evaluated.					
		Characteristics			
Your Rating:					
Like Very Much					
Like Moderately					
Like Slightly					
Neither Like/Dislike					
Dislike Slightly					
Dislike Moderately					
Dislike Very Much					
Comments					

to concerns about time. It takes time to standardize existing recipes, and it takes time to train production employees.

These concerns, however, are minor when compared to the points already noted in favor of using standard recipes. In addition, managers can minimize difficulties with implementing standard recipes by explaining to employees why standard recipes are necessary and by involving them in developing and implementing the recipes.

Recipe Sources

Trade magazines, quantity food cookbooks, and friendly competitors are examples of good recipe sources that can be useful to your operation. However, when standardizing the recipe of an item for your menu, always be sure that all ingredients required by the recipe will be available as long as the menu is used. Seafood, certain fruits, or fresh mushrooms may not be available or may become very expensive if a menu is used over several months. You may wish to exclude such items from the menu or, to avoid disappointing guests, simply qualify their listing on the menu with phrases such as "when available."

Regardless of the source, recipes must be tested. Even minor variations of equipment and temperature can make a big difference in the quality of the item produced. You should test the recipe at your operation and fine-tune it before adding the item to the menu.

When standardizing recipes from external sources it is especially important to address possible production concerns. Production and management staff must agree that the recipe is concise, accurate, and readable in regard to:

- Amounts
- Types of ingredients
- Production procedures
- Service procedures

Such agreement will ensure efficient use of time and energy and help eliminate human error as much as possible. Once the recipe has been adapted for use, the menu item's popularity with guests and the equipment, skills, and number of labor hours needed to produce the item should be routinely reviewed.

Adjusting Standard Recipe Yields

As noted earlier, a standard recipe yields a specific number of standard portion sizes. The yield from a standard recipe can be easily increased or decreased through the use of an adjustment factor. An adjustment factor is determined by dividing the desired yield by the original yield. For example, if a recipe yields 100 portions, and you want 225 portions of the same size, the adjustment factor would be calculated as follows:

$$\text{Adjustment Factor} \quad = \quad \frac{225 \text{ portions (desired yield)}}{100 \text{ portions (original yield)}} \quad = \quad 2.25$$

Each recipe ingredient is then multiplied by the adjustment factor to determine the amount needed for the desired yield. For example, if the original recipe required 8 ounces of sugar, the adjusted quantity would be:

$$\text{New Amount} \quad = \quad \underset{\text{(original amt.)}}{8 \text{ ounces}} \quad \times \quad \underset{\text{(adjustment factor)}}{2.25} \quad = \quad 18 \text{ ounces}$$

A similar procedure can be used to determine an adjustment factor if you alter the portion size. The adjustment factor in this case is determined by dividing the desired portion size by the original portion size. For example, if a recipe yields 40 three-quarter-pound servings, and you want 40 one-half-pound servings, the adjustment factor would be determined as follows:

$$\text{Adjustment Factor} \quad = \quad \frac{.5 \text{ (desired portion size)}}{.75 \text{ (original portion size)}} \quad = \quad .67 \text{ (rounded)}$$

Each recipe ingredient must then be multiplied by this adjustment factor to determine the amount of the ingredient required for the recipe. For example, if a recipe required 30 pounds of ground beef to yield 40 three-quarter-pound servings, to prepare 40 one-half-pound servings you would need 20.1 pounds of ground beef:

$$\text{New Amount} = \underset{\text{(original amt.)}}{30 \text{ pounds}} \times \underset{\text{(adjustment factor)}}{.67} = 20.1 \text{ pounds}$$

Some recipe ingredients, such as spices and yeast, should not be multiplied by the adjustment factor. Experience and taste-testing are necessary to make adjustments to these types of ingredients–especially when yields will be significantly altered.

Determining Standard Food Costs for Menu Items

After standard recipes and standard portion sizes have been established, standard food costs for individual portions or entire dinners can be calculated. The standard food cost for a menu item indicates the food cost that managers should expect when the item is prepared according to its standard recipe. This information must be known in order to stay within cost limitations imposed by the budget.

Portion costs are determined for items that are sold as a single menu selection. A portion cost is simply the cost of food incurred by preparing one portion of a menu item according to its standard recipe. *Dinner costs* are calculated for items that are combined to form dinners or other meals that are priced and sold as one menu selection. For example, a fish amandine dinner may include salad and dressing, potato, vegetable, and bread and butter in addition to the fish entrée. The portion cost of each of these individual menu items must be calculated and combined to determine the dinner cost for the complete dinner.

Calculating Portion Costs

A portion cost is determined by dividing the sum of the recipe's ingredient costs by the number of portions that the standard recipe yields. For example, if the cost to prepare a recipe is $75.00 and it yields 50 portions, then the portion cost for that item is $1.50 ($75.00 ÷ 50 portions). The prices for ingredients listed in standard recipes can be obtained from current invoices.

Exhibit 7.4 presents a sample worksheet that can be used to calculate the portion cost for a food item. Note that each recipe ingredient is listed in column 1 and the amount of each ingredient is recorded in column 2. It is impractical to cost some ingredients, especially a small amount of an inexpensive item. For example, no costs are included for salt and pepper. (The symbol "TT" means "to taste.") The cost per purchase unit is recorded in column 3.

To arrive at the total cost of each ingredient (column 4), the amount of the ingredient (column 2) is multiplied by the cost per unit (column 3). For example, the total cost of fish fillets is calculated as follows:

$$\text{Total Cost} = \underset{\text{(amount)}}{22.5} \times \underset{\text{(cost/unit)}}{\$2.85} = \$64.13 \text{ (rounded)}$$

The total ingredient cost for the recipe is indicated at the bottom of column 4. The total ingredient cost for preparing 60 portions of fish fillet amandine according to the recipe is $72.00. The portion cost for this menu item is calculated at the bottom of the worksheet:

Exhibit 7.4 Standard Portion Cost Worksheet: Menu Item

A. Name of Menu Item *Fish Fillet Amandine*

B. Portion Size *6 oz Fish/#60 Scoop Sauce*

C. Number of Portions *60*

Ingredient	Amount	Cost/Unit	Total Cost
1	2	3	4
Fish Fillets	22¹⁄₂ #	$2.85	$64.13
Almonds	1#	3.26	3.26
Butter/Margarine	2¹⁄₂ #	1.35	3.38
Lemon Juice	¹⁄₂ cup	1.90/16 oz (2 cups)	.48
Lemon Peel	3 lemons	.25/each	.75
Salt	TT	–	–
Pepper	TT	–	–
		Total	$72.00

$72.00	÷	60	=	$1.20
Total Cost (col. 4)		Number of Portions (C)		Standard Portion Cost

$$\text{Portion Cost} = \frac{\$72.00 \text{ (total cost)}}{60 \text{ (number of portions)}} = \$1.20$$

Therefore, the portion cost—the cost to prepare one portion of the recipe—is $1.20. Changes in the yield of a standard recipe that occur because of a change in the portion size will affect the portion cost. Anytime the portion size is altered, a new portion cost must be calculated.

Calculating Dinner Costs

The worksheet presented in Exhibit 7.5 provides a format for determining dinner costs. A dinner is a combination of menu items that is sold for one price. The cost of each item listed on the worksheet is obtained from completed portion cost worksheets. The costs of items offered as part of the dinner are totaled to arrive at the dinner cost of $2.45.

Because the vegetable varies from day to day, and because guests have choices in the potato, dressing, and juice categories, it would take an impractical amount of time to determine the dinner cost for all the different dinner combinations that are possible. Of the categories in which the guests have a choice, managers can choose the cost of the most popular item in the category to determine the dinner cost. For example, if baked potatoes are chosen most often by guests, then the portion cost of baked potatoes would be used to calculate the dinner cost. It is also possible to select the item with the highest portion cost in a category and use this when determining the dinner cost.

Exhibit 7.5 Standard Dinner Cost Worksheet

		Date of Last Cost
		8/1/00

Name of Dinner *Fish Fillet Amandine*

	Item	Portion Cost			
Entrée	*Fish Amandine*	$1.20			
Vegetable	*du Jour*	.12			
Potato	*Choice*	.12			
Salad	*Tossed Green*	.40			
Dressing	*Choice*	.15			
Juice	*Tomato/Pineapple*	.12			
Bread	*Loaf*	.15			
Butter	*Butter*	.06			
Other					
Garnish	*Orange/Lemon/Parsley*	.05			
Condiment	*Cocktail Sauce*	.08			
		$2.45			

The worksheet provides four more columns for calculating the dinner cost when the portion costs of items change (due to a change in an ingredient's price on the item's standard recipe). When this occurs, the new portion cost is added to the unchanged costs of the other dinner items to arrive at a revised dinner cost.

Determining an Overall Standard Food Cost

As pointed out in the previous section, the standard food cost for a menu item indicates the food cost that managers should expect when the item is prepared according to its standard recipe. However, these expected or potential costs cannot be compared with actual food costs because actual food costs are not computed on the basis of individual menu items. Actual food costs are the combined food costs associated with producing all the menu items sold over a given period of time. Therefore, an overall standard food cost that combines all the separate menu items' standard food costs must be established in order to evaluate actual food costs. The following sections demonstrate how to establish an overall standard food cost that is based on menu item sales during a given period of time.

First, a time period for a trial study must be selected. Over this trial period, accurate sales information for each menu item can be recorded on a worksheet similar to the one presented in Exhibit 7.6. By recording this information on a worksheet, total sales and overall food costs for the trial period can be easily calculated. Note that the worksheet in Exhibit 7.6 has space to record menu item sales for only sixteen days. Since accuracy increases with the length of the trial period, two or more worksheets should be used to tally item sales for at least one month.

Exhibit 7.6 Overall Standard Food Cost Worksheet

Item	Date 8/1	Date 8/2	Date 8/3	Date 8/4	Date 8/5	Date 8/6	Date 8/7	Date 8/8	Date 8/9	Date 8/10	Date 8/11	Date 8/12	Date 8/13	Date 8/14	Date 8/15	Date 8/16	Total Sold (A)	Sales Price (B)	Total Sales (A × B)	Food Cost (C)	Total Cost (A × C)	Food Cost % (C ÷ B)
								Number of Each Item Sold														
Soup	12	18	14	20	15	18	0	14	16	17	19	14	18	0	12	16	223	$ .90	$ 200.70	$ .32	$ 71.36	35.6
Eggplant	15	21	23	16	15	18	0	17	19	26	15	14	18	0	14	21	252	1.15	289.80	.35	88.20	30.4
Hamburger	35	41	38	42	30	37	0	37	39	41	41	29	37	0	33	40	520	2.35	1222.00	.95	494.00	40.4
Fish	20	18	16	24	26	18	0	22	16	19	23	26	18	0	20	15	281	2.95	828.95	.85	238.85	28.8
Steak	27	25	29	27	26	30	0	29	23	32	26	26	31	0	26	24	381	3.95	1504.95	1.15	438.15	29.1
Stew	30	35	40	37	39	30	0	32	33	43	36	38	31	0	30	35	489	3.85	1882.65	1.10	537.90	28.6
Diet Platter	11	15	17	12	15	14	0	13	13	20	11	13	14	0	10	15	193	2.95	569.35	.80	154.40	27.1
Sea Platter	30	31	35	29	34	30	0	32	29	38	28	32	31	0	30	30	439	4.25	1865.75	1.35	592.65	31.8
Plum Pie	12	10	18	12	11	15	0	14	8	19	11	11	16	0	12	9	178	1.95	347.10	.80	142.40	41.0
C. Eclair	15	11	21	13	14	11	0	17	9	24	12	13	12	0	14	10	196	2.15	421.40	.75	147.00	34.9
S. Remo	30	28	25	37	29	40	29	32	26	29	36	27	51	26	28	21	494	3.25	1605.50	.95	469.30	29.2
Oysters	29	30	31	27	26	48	31	31	28	34	26	27	49	28	27	30	502	2.90	1455.80	1.20	602.40	41.4
Gumbo	50	48	52	57	45	67	51	52	46	55	56	44	66	48	50	46	833	2.50	2082.50	.85	708.05	34.0
F. Amandine	70	65	63	67	70	78	40	72	63	66	66	68	77	37	65	66	1033	4.95	5113.35	2.45	2530.85	49.5
F. Shrimp	60	54	55	57	62	64	38	62	52	58	56	61	62	35	55	52	883	5.95	5253.85	2.01	1774.83	33.8
Sea Shrimp	45	45	35	38	41	47	25	47	43	38	37	39	45	22	40	43	630	6.25	3937.50	1.85	1165.50	29.6
N.Y. Strip	10	8	9	9	12	18	0	12	6	12	8	11	11	2	8	8	144	8.15	1173.60	3.45	496.80	42.3
Oyster Pie	19	17	18	18	20	23	10	21	15	21	17	21	22	8	19	17	286	5.95	1701.70	2.25	643.50	37.8
Pecan Pie	28	30	26	41	29	40	20	30	28	29	40	28	40	18	29	30	486	2.25	1093.50	.80	388.80	35.6
Brulot	15	14	15	16	10	25	5	17	12	18	15	11	25	3	14	16	231	3.55	820.05	.90	207.90	25.4
																		Totals:	$ 33,370.00		$ 11,892.84	

Recap:

$$\frac{\text{Total Standard Food Cost}}{\text{Total Sales}} \times 100 = \text{Overall Standard Food Cost Percent}$$

$$\frac{\$11,892.84}{\$33,370} \times 100 = 35.64\%$$

The number of menu items sold during the sixteen days are totaled in column A. The selling price of each menu item is listed in column B. The total sales figures represent the total income from sales of the individual menu items. These figures are calculated simply by multiplying the total items sold (column A) by the item's selling price (column B). For example, the worksheet indicates that 223 servings of soup were sold at 90 cents each, resulting in total sales of $200.70.

The food costs listed in column C are the standard food costs for individual menu items. If the item is sold individually, the food cost is the portion cost. If the item is a grouping of menu items, such as a fish fillet amandine dinner, the food cost is the dinner cost. As explained earlier in the chapter, portion costs and dinner costs are calculated from data provided by standard recipes.

The figures recorded in the "Total Cost" column represent the total standard food cost of the individual menu items sold during the trial period. These figures are determined by multiplying the total items sold (column A) by the item's standard food cost (column C). For example, the 223 servings of soup (column A) each had a standard food cost of 32 cents (column C). Therefore, the total food cost for soup sold during the trial period is recorded as $71.36 (223 servings multiplied by the 32-cent food cost).

The last column on the worksheet lists the standard food cost percent for each menu item. These figures are calculated by dividing the standard food cost of the menu item (column C) by its sales price (column B) and multiplying by 100. The standard food cost percent for the soup is 35.6%: $.32 ÷ $.90 = .356 (rounded); .356 × 100 = 35.6%.

The overall standard food cost percent is calculated at the bottom of the worksheet. The sum of the total standard food cost column ($11,892.84) is the overall standard food cost expressed in dollars. This sum is divided by the sum of the total sales column ($33,370.00) and multiplied by 100 to arrive at the overall standard food cost expressed as a percentage of sales. The overall standard food cost—the ideal cost managers can expect if everything goes exactly as it should—is the standard (expressed as dollars or as a percentage of sales) against which to compare actual food costs incurred during the trial period.

By comparing the overall standard food cost with the actual food cost, managers are able to assess the performance of the food service operation. If the actual food cost is greater than the overall standard food cost, managers need to investigate the cause(s) and, when necessary, take corrective action. This is very important because bottom-line profit is reduced by one dollar for each dollar that food costs are higher than needed. Every dollar that can be saved by reducing food costs will drop to the bottom line as profit.

Determining Standard Beverage Costs

Establishing a standard drink cost for beverages is relatively simple because usually there are few ingredients. A standard recipe form, such as the one shown in Exhibit 7.7 for a Manhattan, can provide space for listing ingredient costs and calculating the standard drink cost.

Ingredients are listed in column 1 of the standard recipe. The bottle size for each liquor ingredient is noted in column 2. (Most alcoholic beverages are sold by

Exhibit 7.7 Sample Standard Beverage Recipe

ITEM: Manhattan

	Date	Date	Date	Date
	6/19/—			
A) Drink Sales Price	$2.00	$ _____	$ _____	$ _____
B) Drink Cost	.375	$ _____	$ _____	$ _____
C) Drink Cost Percentage	18.8%	_____ %	_____ %	_____ %

Ingredients	Size	Bottle Data 6/19—				Drink Data				
		Cost	Cost	Cost	Cost	Size	6/19			
1	2	3	3	3	3	4	5	5	5	5
Whiskey, Rye	L (33.8 oz)	7.65				1.50 oz	.34			
Vermouth, Sweet	750 ML (25.4 oz)	.69				.75 oz	.02			
Angostura Bitters	16 oz	2.56				dash	.005			
Cherry						1 ea.	.010			
Water (Ice)						.75 oz	—			
TOTALS						3 oz	.375			

PREPARATION PROCEDURE:
Place ingredients into a mixing glass. Add ice and stir long enough to chill. Strain into cocktail glass. Garnish with a stem Maraschino cherry.

GLASS USED: 3$^{1}/_{2}$ oz Line Cocktail.

the liter rather than by the ounce. Therefore, because recipes and bar equipment use ounces as a unit of measure, it is usually necessary to convert liters to ounces before making recipe extensions or costing calculations.) The cost of the bottle of liquor is recorded in column 3. Since there are four columns in this section, three ingredient price changes can be noted before a new standard form must be used. The amount of each ingredient is listed in column 4. Column 5 shows the cost of each ingredient for one drink.

How are ingredient costs calculated? To determine the cost of the rye whiskey used in the Manhattan for example, first the price of the bottle of rye whiskey must be divided by the number of ounces in the bottle to obtain the cost per ounce:

$$\text{Cost per Ounce} \quad = \quad \frac{\$7.65 \text{ (price per bottle)}}{33.8 \text{ (ounces per bottle)}} \quad = \quad \$.226 \text{ (rounded)}$$

(When calculating a bottle's cost per ounce, some beverage managers deduct an ounce or two before dividing to allow for evaporation or spillage. This will increase the cost per ounce.)

Since 1.5 ounces of rye whiskey are used in a Manhattan, the ingredient cost for rye whiskey is $.34: $.226 × 1.5 ounces = $.339, or $.34 (rounded).

The costs of the rye whiskey and the other ingredients used to make the Manhattan are added together and the total drink cost ($.375) is recorded at the bottom of column 5. This figure is then transferred to Line B at the top of the recipe.

Line C at the top of the recipe indicates the drink cost percentage. The drink cost percentage expresses how much of the drink sales price (recorded on line A) the drink cost represents. The drink cost percentage is calculated by dividing the cost of the drink by the drink's selling price and multiplying by 100. The drink cost percent for the Manhattan in the sample recipe is calculated as follows:

$$\text{Drink Cost Percentage} \quad = \quad \frac{\$.375 \text{ (drink cost)}}{\$2.00 \text{ (selling price)}} \quad = \quad .188 \text{ (rounded)} \quad \times \quad 100 \quad = \quad 18.8\%$$

The standard drink cost is only one factor to consider when determining the selling price of a drink. The type of drink—highball, cocktail, or specialty—and the quality of liquor—house, call, or premium—are also taken into account when establishing a drink's selling price.

Pricing Menu Items

Commercial food service operations, as well as many institutional facilities, must establish selling prices for menu items. Although to a large extent prices determine whether financial goals of the operation are met, many managers use very subjective pricing methods. These pricing methods generally fail to relate selling prices to profit requirements or even costs. When the subject of menu pricing comes up, many managers speak about the "art" of pricing and suggest that intuition and special knowledge about the guest's ability to pay are the most important factors. Consider the following pricing methods, and notice that each is based simply upon the manager's assumptions or guesses about what prices should be:

- *The reasonable price method.* This method uses a price which the food service manager thinks will represent a value to the guest. The manager presumes to know—from the guest's perspective—what charge is fair and equitable. In other words, the manager asks, "If I were a guest, what price would I pay for the item being served?" The manager's best guess in answering this question becomes the product's selling price.

- *The highest price method.* Using this plan, a manager sets the highest price that he or she thinks guests are willing to pay. The concept of value is stretched to the maximum and is then "backed off" to provide a margin of error in the manager's estimate.

- *The loss leader price method.* With this plan, an unusually low price is set for an item (or items). The manager assumes that guests will be attracted to the property to purchase the low-priced item(s) and that they will then select other items while they are there. Beverage or food prices on some items are set low to bring guests into the property, but purchases of other items are necessary for the operation to meet profit requirements. This pricing method is sometimes used as an "early bird" or senior citizen discount to attract specific segments of the market.

- *The intuitive price method.* When prices are set by intuition alone, the manager takes little more than a wild guess about the selling price. Closely related to this approach is a trial-and-error pricing plan—if one price doesn't work, another is tested. The intuitive price method differs from the reasonable price method in that there is less effort to determine what represents value from the guests' perspective.

These methods may be common in the food service industry simply because they have been used in the past, because the manager setting prices has no information about costs or profit requirements to work with, and/or because the manager is not familiar with more objective methods. Objective pricing methods ensure that costs, the property's profit requirements, and the guest's perceived value of the dining experience are incorporated into the selling price. Two objective pricing methods are: (1) desired food cost percent markup, and (2) profit pricing.

Desired Food Cost Percent Markup

Some managers price menu items by using a desired food cost percent. For example, when a new food item is to be offered, the manager determines what would be a reasonable food cost percent for the item. Using intuition, a national average, or a previous food cost percent, perhaps the manager decides that a 33% food cost is desirable. The manager then refers to the item's standard recipe and calculates the standard food cost for the item at $1.50. The menu item's selling price is then determined by dividing the item's standard food cost by its desired food cost percent (as a decimal):

$$\text{Selling Price} = \frac{\$1.50 \text{ (item's standard food cost)}}{.33 \text{ (desired food cost percent)}} = \$4.55 \text{ (rounded)}$$

If the manager does not like this price, another price of $4.75, $4.95, or even $4.25 can be established; when such important decisions are guided by little more than intuition, there always seems to be a lot of room to play with the numbers.

While this method takes food cost into consideration, it is based on the assumption that the lower the percentage of income needed to pay for food, the larger the percentage of income available for all other expenses and profit. While this theory sounds good, it can be easily disproved. Consider the following example:

Menu Item	Food Cost	Menu Selling Price	Food Cost %	Contribution Margin
Chicken	$1.50	$4.50	33%	$3.00
Steak	$3.00	$7.00	43%	$4.00

In this example, chicken has the lower food cost percent (33% compared to 43% for steak). According to the traditional view, the sale of chicken should help the operation more than the sale of steak. However, as shown by the contribution margin (the menu item's selling price minus the item's standard food cost), only $3.00 is left from the sale of chicken to pay for all other costs and to make a contribution to the operation's profit requirements. In the case of steak, $4.00 remains. Which would you rather have left to pay for non-food expenses and to contribute to profit: $3.00 or $4.00? You want $4.00, of course.

With the food cost percent pricing method, the manager assumes that the markup will cover not only food costs, but also non-food expenses and profit requirements as well. It is, however, possible to use an even more objective pricing method—one which incorporates non-food expenses and profit requirements into the pricing decision from the very beginning.

Profit Pricing

The profit pricing method ensures that profit requirements and non-food expenses are factored into the pricing decision. This method first considers what an allowable food cost for the year would be if non-food expenses and profit requirements are subtracted from forecasted food sales.

For example, assume that an operation offers food service only and the budget prepared for the upcoming year forecasts food sales at $300,000, estimates non-food expenses at $189,000, and indicates that the owners require a profit of $15,000.[1] Given this information, allowable food costs for the year (food costs "allowed" by the annual operating budget) can be determined as follows:

$$\begin{array}{lll} \text{Allowable} \\ \text{Food Costs} \end{array} = \begin{array}{c} \$300,000 \\ \text{(forecasted} \\ \text{food sales)} \end{array} - \begin{array}{c} \$189,000 \\ \text{(non–food} \\ \text{expenses)} \end{array} - \begin{array}{c} \$15,000 \\ \text{(profit} \\ \text{requirements)} \end{array} = \$96,000$$

Once allowable food costs are determined, a budgeted food cost percent can be calculated simply by dividing allowable food costs by forecasted food sales:

$$\begin{array}{l} \text{Budgeted Food} \\ \text{Cost Percent} \end{array} = \frac{\$96,000 \text{ (allowable food costs)}}{\$300,000 \text{ (forecasted food sales)}} = .32, \text{ or } 32\%$$

The selling price of a menu item can then be determined by dividing the item's standard food cost by the budgeted food cost percent. If the menu item's standard food cost is $1.50, the selling price can be determined as follows:

$$\text{Selling Price} = \frac{\$1.50 \text{ (item's standard food cost)}}{.32 \text{ (budgeted food cost percent)}} = \$4.69 \text{ (rounded)}$$

In this example, the base selling price of the menu item would be $4.69. This base price would be adjusted by factors which include the value perceived by guests, competition, price rounding, and the prices currently or traditionally charged by the food service operation.

Competition and Pricing

One of the most important concerns in pricing decisions relates to your competition. Most operations have competitors that offer similar menu items and, perhaps, similar service and atmosphere. In order to price your menu items effectively, you must know your competitors: their menus, selling prices, and guest preferences.

One technique that can be used to attract guests from competitors is lowering your menu prices. This technique may succeed in bringing more people into your operation, but only if your lower-priced items are considered by guests as substitutes for what the competition offers. If there are no significant differences between what your operation offers and what the competition offers, then guests may see price as the determining factor in selecting your operation over the competition. However, if there are non-price-related differences that are important to guests (such as atmosphere, entertainment, etc.) this technique may not work.

Raising prices is also a way of responding to pressures from the competition. With higher prices, fewer menu items will need to be sold in order for the operation to maintain its required profit level. Does this technique work? The answer depends on the needs, desires, and preferences of guests. These factors determine whether or not people will continue to buy a menu item at a higher selling price.

Raising a menu item's price may be an effective strategy only if the increased revenue from the price increase makes up for the revenue lost as demand falls off and current guests begin to buy other menu items as substitutes. In some cases, a more effective strategy for increasing total sales revenue may be lowering a menu item's price. Lowering prices may increase the volume of sales and this increase may produce an increase in total sales revenue.

What we are really talking about here is the concept of elasticity of demand. Elasticity is a term economists use to describe how the quantity demanded responds to changes in price. If a certain percentage price change creates a larger percentage change in the quantity demanded, the demand is elastic and the item is considered to be price-sensitive. If, on the other hand, the percentage change in quantity demanded is less than the percentage change in price, the demand is inelastic. Before changing the established price of a menu item, it is important to know the elasticity of demand for that item—the extent to which demand changes as the price changes.

Endnotes

1. Profit pricing for an operation offering food and beverage service is more complicated. Interested readers are referred to Jack D. Ninemeier, *Planning and Control for Food and Beverage Operations,* 3d ed. (East Lansing, Mich.: Educational Institute of the American Hotel & Motel Association, 1991).

Key Terms

allowable food cost

budgeted food cost percent

contribution margin

dinner cost

elasticity of demand

portion cost

profit pricing

standard food cost

standard recipe

Discussion Questions

1. How does a food service operation benefit from using standard recipes?

2. What factors should a food service manager consider when standardizing existing recipes?

3. How can a food service manager convince a head cook or bartender of the need to develop standard recipes?

4. How is an adjustment factor used to increase or decrease the yield of a standard recipe?

5. What is the difference between portion costs and dinner costs?

6. What is the difference between the standard food cost of a menu item and an overall food cost?

7. What special factors must be taken into account when pricing beverage items?

8. Why is it incorrect to assume that the lower the percentage of income needed to pay for food, the larger the percentage of income available for all other expenses and profit?

9. Why is a markup from a budgeted food cost percent called a profit pricing method?

10. How can lowering menu prices produce an increase in total sales revenue?

Part III

Production and Service

Chapter Outline

Purchasing
    Why Is Purchasing Important?
    Goals of a Purchasing Program
        Buy the Right Product
        Obtain the Right Quantity
        Pay the Right Price
        Deal with the Right Supplier
    Security Concerns During Purchasing
    Ethical Concerns in Purchasing
Receiving
    Space and Equipment
    The Receiving Process
        Step One
        Step Two
        Step Three
        Step Four
        Step Five
        Step Six
    Other Receiving Tasks
        Marking and Tagging
        Rejecting Products
Storing
    Security
    Quality
    Recordkeeping
        Perpetual Inventory System
        Periodic Inventory System
        A Practical Approach
    Reducing Inventory Costs
Issuing
Special Beverage Management Concerns
    Purchasing
    Receiving
    Storing
    Issuing

8

Preparing for Production

WE HAVE COME to the point where we must focus on the flow of food and beverage products through the operation. In this chapter we'll first look at the basics of purchasing and then study guidelines for receiving, storing, and issuing food. The final sections of the chapter will review unique concerns in purchasing, receiving, storing, and issuing beverages.

Purchasing

Many activities make up the purchasing process. Food and beverage production employees need food, beverages, and other supplies to prepare menu items. They send requisitions (1)—written orders to withdraw items from storage—to storeroom personnel (see Exhibit 8.1), who then issue the requested products (2).

At some point, storeroom inventory—the amount of food, beverages, and other supplies on hand—will have to be replenished. To reorder supplies, storeroom personnel send purchase requisitions (3) to the purchasing department. Purchase requisitions are forms that specify the products that need to be reordered, how many are needed, and how soon they are needed. The purchasing department, through either a formal purchase order system or an informal purchase record system, orders these products from suppliers (4). Copies of the orders are given to receiving and accounting personnel (5).

Suppliers deliver the ordered products to the receiving area (6) and give receiving personnel a delivery invoice—the supplier's bill indicating the products that were delivered, their quantity and prices, and the total amount owed. Receiving personnel check the delivery against their copy of the purchase order or purchase record, and also check for such things as unauthorized substitutions and damage.

After the delivered products have been checked and accepted, they are transferred to the proper storage areas by property employees (7) and the delivery invoice is sent to the accounting department (8). This alerts accounting personnel that the supplier has delivered the products and they can process the necessary documents and pay the supplier (9).

While purchasing procedures vary from operation to operation, these basic steps are generally followed. As you can see, the purchasing process not only involves purchasing, but also receiving, storing, and issuing. Many people with various responsibilities are required to get food and beverages to the food and beverage department for production.

Exhibit 8.1 The Purchasing Cycle

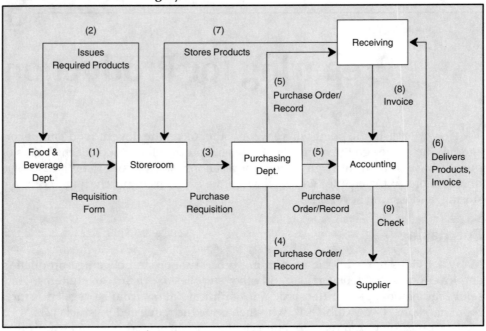

Why Is Purchasing Important?

On the most fundamental level, purchasing is important because a food and beverage operation has to purchase food, beverages, and other supplies in order to produce food and beverage items. But this is not the only reason that purchasing is important. Money can be made or lost based on how well the purchasing process works. For example, if too few items are purchased and stockouts occur, sales are lost and guests are disappointed. If too many items are purchased, money is tied up in unnecessary inventory and is unavailable to meet other obligations.

The importance of purchasing can be summed up in one simple phrase: purchasing directly affects the bottom line. Every dollar saved through effective purchasing increases a property's profit by one dollar. Only the best possible purchasing program can help food service managers achieve the best possible economic results.

Goals of a Purchasing Program

Whether purchasing is done by a specialist in the purchasing department of a large operation, or by a line manager at a small operation, the goals of a purchasing program are the same:

- Buy the right product
- Obtain the right quantity

- Pay the right price
- Deal with the right supplier

Buy the Right Product. The menu dictates what products must be purchased. If green beans are required for some menu items, for example, then green beans must be purchased. Questions about the type of green beans, the quantities to purchase, and the quality of the green beans then become important. What type of green beans is right for the operation?

To answer this question, managers must develop purchase specifications that reflect the operation's required standards. A purchase specification is a detailed description setting forth the quality, size, weight, and other factors desired for a particular item. Exhibit 8.2 illustrates one purchase specification format. Managers should develop a purchase specification for each of the expensive or otherwise important products purchased. Once developed, purchase specifications should be given to all suppliers. When you request price information, suppliers will know the product you want and the prices they quote will be more accurate.

The desired quality for each product is an important part of purchase specifications. While some operations are price-conscious and want the least expensive items available, others want only the highest-quality products because they know their guests will pay for them. Most operations fall between these two extremes. Therefore, for most operations, hard decisions must be made about what level of quality is acceptable for each product.

The quality level necessary for a product is determined in part by that product's intended use. If you want to use olives as garnishes, for example, colossal olives may have a quality level appropriate for this purpose. If you need olives to chop up for a salad bar topping, many operations would find colossal olives to have a higher-than-necessary quality. For these operations, lower-priced, smaller olives or even olive pieces would have an acceptable quality-level.

At independent restaurants, product quality decisions are likely to be made by the food service manager, the chef (for food products), and the beverage manager (for beverage products). At restaurant chains and fast-food franchises, most if not all product quality decisions are made at corporate headquarters.

Convenience foods. In some cases, convenience foods may meet the operation's quality standards and be the right products to buy. Convenience foods can be defined as foods that have been manufactured or processed to some extent so that less on-site labor is needed to prepare them. In addition to being less costly to make, convenience foods are usually easier to purchase, receive, store, issue, and prepare. For example, purchasing and preparing a frozen beef stew entrée takes less time, labor, and equipment than purchasing and preparing the beef, potatoes, carrots, broth, and other ingredients that make up a beef stew.

Many food service managers have negative attitudes about convenience foods, perhaps stemming from their experiences with the first frozen "TV dinners" introduced decades ago. But today there are many high-quality convenience foods available. If convenience foods can meet the operation's quality standards, food service managers should seriously investigate the possibility of purchasing and using them.

Exhibit 8.2 Sample Purchase Specification Format

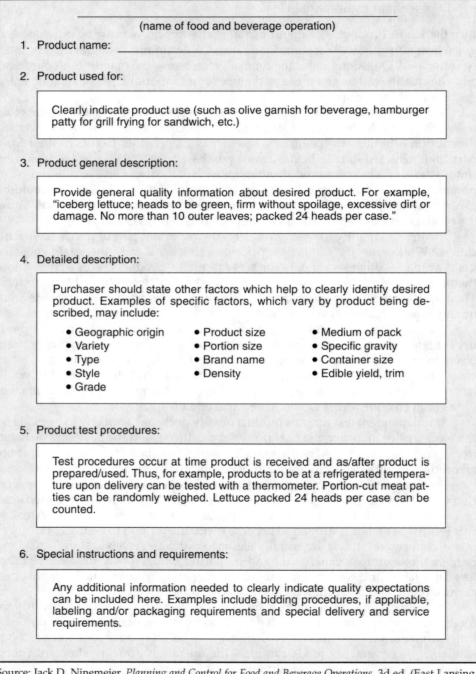

_____

(name of food and beverage operation)

1. Product name: _____

2. Product used for:

> Clearly indicate product use (such as olive garnish for beverage, hamburger patty for grill frying for sandwich, etc.)

3. Product general description:

> Provide general quality information about desired product. For example, "iceberg lettuce; heads to be green, firm without spoilage, excessive dirt or damage. No more than 10 outer leaves; packed 24 heads per case."

4. Detailed description:

> Purchaser should state other factors which help to clearly identify desired product. Examples of specific factors, which vary by product being described, may include:
>
> - Geographic origin
> - Variety
> - Type
> - Style
> - Grade
> - Product size
> - Portion size
> - Brand name
> - Density
> - Medium of pack
> - Specific gravity
> - Container size
> - Edible yield, trim

5. Product test procedures:

> Test procedures occur at time product is received and as/after product is prepared/used. Thus, for example, products to be at a refrigerated temperature upon delivery can be tested with a thermometer. Portion-cut meat patties can be randomly weighed. Lettuce packed 24 heads per case can be counted.

6. Special instructions and requirements:

> Any additional information needed to clearly indicate quality expectations can be included here. Examples include bidding procedures, if applicable, labeling and/or packaging requirements and special delivery and service requirements.

Source: Jack D. Ninemeier, *Planning and Control for Food and Beverage Operations*, 3d ed. (East Lansing, Mich.: Educational Institute of the American Hotel & Motel Association, 1991), p. 132.

Make-or-buy decisions. On the other hand, sometimes it is better for an operation to make a product on-site rather than to purchase it. Whether or not a product such as dinner rolls should be made by the operation rather than purchased should be investigated carefully, but there could be several possible advantages. Production of the product might be integrated with other ongoing work tasks, so the property might better utilize equipment and labor. Quality standards can be better maintained if the property produces the product. In addition, it is less likely that the property will run out of a product it makes on-site.

Perhaps the most important possible advantage is that products prepared on-site may be less expensive. One purpose of a make-or-buy analysis is to determine whether it is less expensive to make a product on-site than to purchase it. For example, managers at an operation that has always prepared its own Bloody Mary mix may discover a commercially prepared mix that meets their operation's quality standards. Should they purchase it?

The commercial mix costs $21 per case of 12 quart bottles. There is a 5% price reduction when the mix is purchased in five-case lots. The operation can purchase in this quantity and thus the cost per quart would be $1.66: $21 − 5% of $21 = $19.95; $19.95 ÷ 12 quart bottles = $1.66 (rounded).

The costs of making the Bloody Mary mix on-site are:

- Product cost: The current cost of ingredients used in the standard recipe, which yields two gallons (or eight quarts), is $10.45. The product cost per quart is, therefore, $1.31: $10.45 ÷ 8 quarts = $1.31 (rounded).

- Labor cost: The employee who prepares the mix is paid $5.89 per hour (including fringe benefits). It takes 15 minutes to prepare the mix. Therefore, the labor cost to prepare the eight quarts of mix is $1.47: $5.89 ÷ 4 = $1.47 (rounded). The labor cost per quart is $.18: $1.47 ÷ 8 quarts = $.18 (rounded).

The total estimated cost to prepare one quart of Bloody Mary mix on-site is $1.49: $1.31 (product cost) + $.18 (labor cost) = $1.49.

The final step in the make-or-buy analysis is to compare the cost of preparing the product on-site with the cost of the commercial mix:

Cost of commercial mix	$1.66 per quart
Cost of on-site production	$1.49 per quart
Savings per quart by preparing the mix on-site	$ .17 per quart

This make-or-buy analysis suggests that $.17 per quart can be saved if the operation continues to prepare its own Bloody Mary mix. While the per-quart savings may not seem significant, the operation saves $1.36 on mix each day, since the operation uses eight quarts per day. This is equal to a weekly savings of $9.52 ($1.36 × 7 days) or an annual savings of $495.04: $9.52 per week × 52 weeks = $495.04.

Obtain the Right Quantity. As mentioned previously, cash flow is adversely affected if inventory levels are too high; stockouts, lost sales, and guest dissatisfaction may result if inventory levels are too low. That is why purchasing food and beverage products in the right quantities is so important.

Some operations use a minimum/maximum system to make sure inventories are kept at optimal levels. Under this system, a par level—the minimum amount of a product that should always be in inventory—is established for most products in inventory. Par level equals the lead-time quantity plus the safety stock level of any given product. The lead-time quantity is the number of items of a particular product that will be withdrawn from inventory and used between the time the product is reordered and the time it is delivered. The safety stock level is the number of items of a product needed in case of emergencies, spoilage, or unexpected delays in delivery. When the inventory level of a product reaches the minimum quantity, additional supplies of that product must be ordered.

Maximum quantity is the greatest number or amount of a product that should be in stock at any given time. Every product in inventory with an established minimum level also has a maximum level. Maximum levels are established so that cash is not tied up in unnecessary inventory. The shelf-life of a product also affects the maximum quantity that can be stored.

Factors other than a property's minimum/maximum levels may affect the quantity of products purchased. Some of these factors are:

- *Changing prices.* Rising or falling prices may affect how much a property buys.

- *Available storage facilities.*

- *Storage and handling costs.*

- *Waste and spoilage concerns.*

- *Theft and pilferage concerns.*

- *Market conditions.* For example, some products may be in limited supply.

- *Quantity discounts, if any.*

- *Minimum order requirements imposed by suppliers.* If suppliers will not "break cases"—that is, sell partial cases—it may be necessary to purchase in "case lot" quantities only—which may be more than the optimal quantity desired.

- *Transportation and delivery problems.*

- *Order costs.* Costs to place and process an order can be high. If so, it may be better to place larger, less frequent orders.

Such perishable products as fresh produce, bakery goods, and dairy items must be purchased for immediate use and are often purchased several times a week. Since they are ordered so often, managers generally know the usage rates for these products, and so may not assign formal minimum/maximum levels to them. The quantity of perishable products to be purchased can be assessed by counting the number already on hand and subtracting this quantity from the amount managers know from experience will be needed.

Exhibit 8.3 is an example of a quotation/call sheet managers can use to prepare a perishable product order and select the supplier. This sheet has been filled out for a produce order. The top line shows that six cases of spinach are required for the period covered by the order. An inventory count reveals that two and a half cases are on hand. Ordering three and a half cases would bring the inventory level

Exhibit 8.3 Sample Quotation/Call Sheet

Item	Needed	On Hand	Order	A & B Co.	Green Produce	Local Supplier
		Amount			Supplier	
1	2	3	4	5	6	7
Spinach	6 cs	2 $1/2$ cs	4 cs	$22^{00}/cs = \$88.00$	$14^{85}/cs = \$59.40$	$21^{70}/cs = \$86.80$
Ice Lettuce	8 cs	1 cs	7 cs	$17^{00}/cs = \$119.00$	$16^{75}/cs = \$117.25$	$18^{10}/cs = \$126.70$
Carrots	3-20#	1-20#	2-20#	$14^{70}/bag = \$29.40$	$13^{90}/bag = \$27.80$	$13^{80}/bag = \$27.60$
Tomatoes	2 lugs	$1/2$ lug	2 lugs	$18^{60}/lug = \$37.20$	$18^{00}/lug = \$36.00$	$18^{10}/lug = \$36.20$
			Totals	$861.40	$799.25	$842.15

up to six cases; four cases, however, may need to be ordered if the supplier will not sell a partial case. After the perishable products on hand are counted and the quantities the purchaser needs to order are determined, three suppliers are called. Each is asked to quote a current price for the items needed. Each supplier has copies of the operation's purchase specifications for these products so that each supplier is quoting a price for the same quality of product.

After all suppliers are contacted, the manager has two choices. He or she can give the order to the supplier with the lowest total price for all products, or the order can be awarded on an item-by-item basis. Suppliers often place minimum poundage and/or dollar restrictions on orders. Therefore, it may not be possible to award only one item (such as 10 bags of radishes) to a supplier.

Pay the Right Price. Perhaps the most important purchasing objective is to obtain products and services at the right price. This is not necessarily the lowest price. Often, with "bargain" prices there is a gamble that the product may not be delivered or may not be of the proper quality.

There are many techniques that can be used to reduce purchasing costs. Professional purchasers know how and when to practice these techniques. Among them are the following:

- *Negotiate with the seller.* Bargaining over the price is a well-established practice. However, for each product there is a price below which a supplier will not go. This price is determined in part by prices charged by other suppliers, the supplier's operating costs, and the extent to which the supplier controls the market.

- *Consider purchasing lower-quality products.* If the required quality of products has not been researched and is not already known, this may be a reasonable alternative.

- *Evaluate the need for the product.* It may cost less to make the product on-site rather than to purchase it.

- *Discontinue some supplier services.* The price you pay for a product includes costs of delivering, extension of credit, technical assistance, etc. If some of these services are not needed, prices might be lowered.

- *Combine orders.* If fewer suppliers are used and each gets more of the purchaser's orders, prices may be decreased through volume purchases.

- *Re-evaluate the need for high-cost items.* For example, if prices for certain garnishes increase, these items might be replaced with less expensive garnishes.

- *Pay cash.* A supplier experiencing temporary cash flow problems may offer a lower price for cash transactions.

- *Speculate about price trends.* If you think prices will decrease, purchase lower quantities until the price stabilizes at a lower rate. If you think prices will rise, you may want to purchase more now.

- *Change the purchase unit size.* Product cost per unit may be less as larger purchase units are received. For example, one pound of flour may cost less when a 50-pound sack is purchased rather than a 10-pound sack.

- *Be innovative.* Cooperative purchasing or competitive bidding procedures may reduce prices. With reciprocal purchasing, food service managers may trade prepared meals and beverages for food supplies. A reciprocal purchasing arrangement should be entered into only after consulting legal counsel.[1]

- *Take advantage of suppliers' promotional discounts.*

- *Bypass the supplier.* Purchase directly from a distributor, manufacturer, or grower.

Product prices are also affected by the method of payment. If the supplier offers a discount for prompt payment, this option should be studied. Generally, payment terms should be negotiated after an agreement is reached on the price.

Deal with the Right Supplier. Experienced purchasers realize that factors other than price should be considered when a supplier is selected. These factors include:

- *Supplier's location.* A close location shortens delivery time. Also, many food service purchasers like to purchase from local businesses because they believe this fosters goodwill and improves community relations.

- *Supplier's facilities.* A visit can help the purchaser determine sanitation levels and processing procedures.

- *Financial stability.* Investigate the financial soundness of potential suppliers.

- *Technical ability of supplier's staff.* Good suppliers do more than just take orders. They know their products and are able to help customers understand how best to use them.

- *Honesty and fairness.* The supplier's reputation and business practices can reveal these qualities.

- *Dependability.* Many purchasers are willing to pay higher prices to suppliers who consistently meet the operation's quality standards and delivery schedules.

In short, food service buyers not only want reasonable prices, they also want prompt delivery, adequate quality, and good service. Each potential supplier should be evaluated on all these points before an order is placed.

Security Concerns During Purchasing

In small properties where the owner/manager is responsible for purchasing, there is less concern about theft. As operations grow, more people become involved in purchasing and the chances of theft increase.

There are many ways purchasers may choose to steal from an operation. They may purchase items for their own use or for other employees. They may take kickbacks or set up fictitious companies. Kickbacks occur when the property's purchaser works in collusion with an employee from the supplier's company: products purchased at higher-than-usual prices, with the difference in cost divided up and pocketed by the purchaser and supply company employee. Setting up a fictitious company enables a purchaser to steal by submitting invoices from the company and collecting money for products never received.

Ethical Concerns in Purchasing

Purchasers must meet high ethical standards in order to preserve one of their most valuable business assets: their personal integrity.[2] Purchasers are obligated to their operation, to colleagues, to suppliers, and to themselves to deal with suppliers in a fair and honest way. Ethical dealings encourage suppliers to compete for the operation's business, safeguard the operation's reputation, and help avoid legal problems.

Each operation should have purchasing policies and procedures reflecting ethical and professional standards. Should purchasers be allowed to accept gifts or meals from suppliers? How should travel and other expenses incurred in visiting a supplier be handled? Policies to answer these and other ethical questions vary from operation to operation. Exhibit 8.4 offers some guidelines for professional purchasers.

Receiving

In many operations, the receiving task is done by whoever is closest to the back door when products arrive. Proper receiving requires a knowledgeable person who follows specific receiving procedures.

Exhibit 8.4 Sample Code of Ethics for Purchasers

As a professional purchaser I accept the following obligations as I go about my work:

- To give primary concern to the best interests of my company
- To try to obtain maximum value for each dollar I spend
- To be active in professional groups that help improve my profession
- To desire and accept advice from colleagues, top management, and suppliers
- To be fair and honest in all my dealings with managers, employees, and supplier representatives
- To practice effective, ethical procedures that enhance relations with suppliers
- To learn as much as possible about all products and services that are needed and purchased
- To honor all my obligations and to be sure that all commitments are consistent with good business practice

Staff members who receive products must (1) check incoming products against purchase specifications, (2) know what to do when problems are uncovered, and (3) perform all other receiving tasks, including the completion of receiving reports.

In small operations, the same person—generally a manager, if not the owner—may be responsible for purchasing and receiving. When this person is the owner, there is little reason to worry about theft. If another person assumes both of these tasks, however, the possibility of theft increases. As operations grow, purchasing and receiving duties are split. Purchasing may be handled by a separate purchasing department while receiving and storage become the responsibilities of the accounting department.

Space and Equipment

In some operations, the receiving area is little more than a wide space in a hallway. Sufficient space should be set aside to permit a proper review of all incoming products. When possible, the receiving area should be located near the delivery door in order to restrict the access of delivery persons to other areas.

An accurate scale is needed to weigh incoming products. Every product should be weighed, counted, and/or measured. Other necessities include transport equipment to move products to storage, a desk and/or file cabinet to house receiving documents, a calculator to check order calculations, and small items such as a thermometer, a clipboard, and supplies for marking and tagging.

The Receiving Process

There are six steps to follow when receiving products.

Step One. Inspect incoming products against a purchase order (used at large properties) or a purchase record (used at small properties).

Purchase orders are orders for food or other supplies prepared by an operation's purchasing staff and submitted to suppliers (see Exhibit 8.5). Copies of the

Exhibit 8.5 Sample Purchase Order

Purchase Order Number: _____		Order Date: _____

Payment Terms: _____

To: _____
  (supplier)

_____

_____
  (address)

From/
Ship to: _____
  (name of food service operation)

_____

_____
  (address)

Delivery Date: _____

Please Ship:

Quantity Ordered	Description	✓	Units Shipped	Unit Cost	Total Cost

Total Cost _____

Important: This Purchase Order expressly limits acceptance to the terms and conditions stated above, noted on the reverse side hereof, and any additional terms and conditions affixed hereto or otherwise referenced. Any additional terms and conditions proposed by seller are objected to and rejected.

_____
Authorized Signature

Purchase orders are orders for food or other supplies prepared by an operation's purchasing staff and submitted to suppliers. In addition to identifying products, quantities, and prices, a purchase order may include other contractual information such as payment requirements and inspection rights.

orders are retained by the purchasing department. These documents identify the product, quantity, unit cost, and total cost of the order. In addition, a purchase order may include other contractual information such as guarantees, warranties, payment requirements, and inspection rights.

Purchase records are typically used by small operations that do not use purchase orders when placing some of their orders (see Exhibit 8.6). Rather than use written purchase orders, the purchaser for a small operation may telephone

Exhibit 8.6 Sample Purchase Record

(supplier)

Date Ordered	Item Description	Unit	Price	No. of Units	Total Cost	Invoice No.	Comments

A purchase record is a detailed record of all incoming shipments from suppliers. Purchase records are typically used by small food service operations.

suppliers and place orders. A purchase record is prepared so that the operation can keep track of what has been ordered. It is not submitted to the suppliers.

Receiving employees are provided with copies of the purchase order or purchase record so they know what products should be delivered, and so they can make sure they do not accept items that were not ordered.

Step Two. Inspect incoming products against the purchase specifications to confirm that the quality of the incoming products meets the operation's standards.

While this step is critical, it is often overlooked. How does the receiving clerk know if "fresh" fish actually is fresh or if it is frozen fish that was thawed before delivery? How can you tell that meat labeled "choice" really is choice? Although for some products certain tests can be run to verify quality, for many products the only way to know is to learn what the right product looks, smells, and/or feels like and carefully inspect delivered products with these subjective criteria in mind. As receiving personnel gain experience they learn what to look for.

Step Three. Inspect incoming products against the delivery invoice. If the invoice states that 75 pounds of ground beef were delivered, this should be confirmed by weighing the ground beef to be sure that 75 pounds were received. The price per unit and the arithmetic extensions may be verified by the receiving staff, or these tasks may be assumed by managers or employees from the accounting and purchasing departments.

If a product is not delivered for various reasons—the supplier is temporarily out of it, for example—or if a product is accepted but the quantity of the delivered product is different from the quantity stated on the invoice—for example, 70 pounds of ground beef were delivered instead of 75—a request-for-credit memo should be completed to adjust the amount of money due to the supplier (see Exhibit 8.7). This memo should be signed by the delivery person and a copy attached to the

Exhibit 8.7 Sample Request-for-Credit Memo

Request-for-Credit Memo

(prepare in duplicate) Number: _____

From: _____ To: _____
_____   (supplier)
_____   _____
_____   _____
                            _____

Credit should be given on the following:

Invoice Number: _____ Invoice Date: _____

Product	Unit	Number	Price/Unit	Total Price

Reason: Total: _____

_____   _____
(delivery person)   (authorizing signature)

A request-for-credit memo is a form filled out by the property's receiving clerk that lists products that were on the supplier's invoice but were not delivered, and/or lists products returned because of damage or other reasons. This memo should be signed by the delivery person and attached to the supplier's invoice.

delivery invoice. The accounting department should be sure to pay the adjusted—not the original—amount on the delivery invoice.

Step Four. Accept the products. The receiving clerk accepts the products for the operation by signing the delivery invoice. Beyond this point the responsibility for the products rests with the food and beverage operation, not the supplier.

Step Five. Move products to storage for quality and security reasons. It is a very poor practice to allow the supplier's delivery person to place items in storage. The delivery person should deliver products to the receiving area, where they are checked. After the delivery person leaves, the receiving clerk or another employee of the property can move items to storage areas.

Step Six. Complete the daily receiving report or other forms as required (see Exhibit 8.8). The daily receiving report helps an operation keep track of the suppliers who

Exhibit 8.8 Sample Daily Receiving Report

Date: 8/1/00													Page _1_ of _2_

							Distribution						
				No. of	Purchase		Food		Beverages				Transfer
	Invoice		Purchase	Purchase	Unit	Total							to
Supplier	No.	Item	Unit	Units	Price	Cost	Directs	Stores	Liquor	Beer	Wine	Soda	Storage
1	2	3	4	5	6	7	8	9	10	11	12	13	14
AJAX	10111	Gr. Beef	10#	6	$ 28.50	$171.00		$171.00					Bill
ABC Liquor	6281	B. Scotch	cs (750)	2	$ 71.80	$143.60			$143.60				Bill
		H. Chablis	gal	3	$ 8.50	$ 25.50					$ 25.50		Bill
B/E Produce	70666	Lettuce	cs	2	$ 21.00	$ 42.00	$ 42.00						
						Totals	$351.00	$475.00	$683.50	—	$102.00		

A daily receiving report helps managers keep track of the items that are received from suppliers each day.

made deliveries that day and what they delivered. The types of receiving records that have to be kept vary from operation to operation.

Other Receiving Tasks

Other receiving tasks include marking, tagging, and rejecting products.

Marking and Tagging. Marking and tagging facilitate proper stock rotation and inventory evaluation. Marking the date of delivery and price directly on the shipping or storage container before the product is placed in storage makes it easier to withdraw the oldest products from inventory first. When the value of the entire inventory must be calculated, having the cost of items noted on product containers makes this task easier.

Tagging involves attaching a tag to an item with the name of the item, its weight, cost, etc. written on the tag. The information on the tag is useful when employees fill out requisition forms, and the tags are used by some operations for control purposes.

Rejecting Products. Sometimes receiving personnel, using the property's general receiving guidelines as well as purchase specifications, may reject incoming products. Products may be rejected because they were not ordered or were not delivered on time. Or, their quality could be inadequate or their price incorrect. If the receiving clerk is aware of a potential problem, it is often the practice to contact the purchaser, chef, or other property official for a second opinion. If only a partial order is delivered or products are on back order, a manager may need to be contacted so that production plans can be re-evaluated if necessary.

Storing

After items are purchased and received, they must be stored. In far too many operations, storage means little more than putting items in storage areas and having an "open-door policy" that lets employees get products at any time. This is not a good strategy.

Storage policies must address three issues:

- Security
- Quality
- Recordkeeping

Security

Think of storerooms as bank vaults and food and beverage products within them as money. In many operations, products collectively worth thousands of dollars are kept in storage areas. Ask yourself, "If I had a roomful of money, how would I safeguard it?" Your answer will tell you how products in storage areas should be controlled.

Storage security measures include:

- *Lockable storage areas.* Walk-in refrigerators and freezers, dry storage areas, and liquor storage areas should be lockable.
- *Precious storage.* Keep very expensive items locked in special cabinets or compartments within storage areas.
- *Limited access.* Allow only authorized personnel to enter storage areas. Keep storage areas locked except when issuing products.
- *Effective inventory control procedures.* Control expensive and "theft-prone" items by using a perpetual inventory system (this system will be discussed later in the chapter).
- *Central inventory control.* At the end of a shift, items in work station storage areas should be put back in central storage areas for better inventory control.
- *Secure design.* Design storage areas with security in mind. Walls should extend to the ceiling and doors should be properly constructed and lockable. Make sure it is impossible to enter the storeroom through the ceiling. There should be no windows.
- *Lighting and monitoring.* Adequate lighting is necessary in storage areas. Some operations use closed-circuit television systems to monitor storage areas.[3]

It may not be practical to lock walk-in or reach-in refrigerators if employees need to get into them frequently. However, expensive items needing refrigerated storage—such as fresh meats, seafood, and wines being chilled—can be locked in special cages or compartments purchased or constructed for use in walk-in or reach-in refrigerators.

There usually is less need for production personnel to constantly enter walk-in freezers. Perhaps these can be kept locked at all times. If this is not practical, it may be wise to purchase or construct lockable storage units for use within walk-in freezers.

Quality

The effort you make to develop purchase specifications and to check incoming products against them will be wasted if you do not safeguard product quality during storage.

Safeguarding quality means more than just ensuring that food will not spoil. Spoiled items must be discarded, of course, but products that deteriorate even slightly in quality can cause problems. What happens when produce is just a little too ripe, for example? The use of such products might help reduce food costs but only at the risk of guest dissatisfaction.

Basic storage procedures that safeguard quality include the following:

- *Rotate food stocks.* Items which have been in storage the longest should be used first. This concept is referred to as first-in, first-out (FIFO). The FIFO rule is easier to follow when incoming products are placed in back of or underneath the products that are already there. As mentioned earlier, marking delivery dates on products before they are stored is also helpful.

- *Store foods at the proper temperatures.* Use accurate thermometers in storage areas to ensure that: (1) refrigerated storage temperatures are kept between 32°F and 40°F (0°C and 4°C), (2) dry storage areas are kept between 50°F and 70°F (10°C and 21°C), and (3) frozen items are kept in freezers with temperatures below 0°F (–18°C).

- *Clean storage areas.* Routine cleaning of all storage areas helps protect product quality.

- *Ensure proper ventilation and air circulation.* Keep items off the floor and away from walls to permit air circulation. Normally, items should be stored in their original packing containers. Items that absorb odors (such as flour) should be kept away from items which give off odors (such as onions). Store food in air-tight or covered containers.

Recordkeeping

An operation must keep track of the quantity and value of the products it has in storage. You have to know what is in inventory in order to know what should be ordered. The value of products in inventory is used to calculate the cost of goods sold when income statements are developed (income statements will be discussed in Chapter 13). When you want to determine food costs, the value of products withdrawn from storage must be assessed. This cannot be done accurately unless you keep inventory records.

Recordkeeping is also important in controlling theft. Detecting theft is difficult unless you can note differences between what should be and what actually is in storage.

Exhibit 8.9 Sample Perpetual Inventory Form

Perpetual Inventory								
Product Name: _P.D.Q. Shrimp_				**Purchase Unit Size:** _5 lb bag_				
Date	**In Carried Forward**	**Out**	**Balance** _15_	**Date**	**In Carried Forward**	**Out**	**Balance**	
Col. 1	Col. 2	Col. 3	Col. 4	Col. 1	Col. 2	Col. 3	Col. 4	
5/16		3	12					
5/17		3	9					
5/18	6		15					
5/19		2	13					

With forms such as this one, managers using a perpetual inventory system can keep inventory up to date by entering all additions to and subtractions from inventory.

There are two basic systems for keeping track of inventory: the perpetual inventory system and the periodic inventory system.

Perpetual Inventory System. A perpetual inventory system allows you to keep track of items in storage on an ongoing basis. The concept is identical to the way a checkbook record is maintained. As money (food) enters the checking account (storeroom), the running balance increases and is noted on an inventory form (see Exhibit 8.9). As checks are written (employees present requisitions and food is withdrawn), the running balance decreases and is subtracted from the running total on the inventory form. Therefore, at any time, you know what amount of money (food) is in the checking account (storeroom). This is useful for managers when they want to calculate food costs—the cost of food used to produce menu items over a given period of time.

Perpetual inventory records tell you the quantity of each product that *should* be in storage. This amount must be confirmed at regular intervals (usually monthly) by a physical count. Any discrepancy between what should be in inventory and what is actually in inventory can be investigated to determine whether theft, poor recordkeeping, or another problem exists.

For control purposes, the person who conducts the physical inventory should not be the same person who maintains the perpetual inventory records. Often, it's easier if two people take the physical inventory—one person can call out the count of inventory units while another person records the count on the form. For example, someone from management or the accounting department along with the chef (for food) or the head bartender (for beverages) may take the physical inventory.

Exhibit 8.10 Sample Periodic Inventory Form

		Physical Inventory					
Type of Product: _____		Month _____			Month _____		
Product	Unit	Amount in Storage	Purchase Price	Total Price	Amount in Storage	Purchase Price	Total Price
Col. 1	Col. 2	Col. 3	Col. 4	Col. 5	Col. 6	Col. 7	Col. 8
Applesauce	6 #10	4 ⅓	$15.85	$68.63			
Green Beans	6 #10	3 ⅚	18.95	72.58			
Flour	25# bag	3	4.85	14.55			
Rice	50# bag	1	12.50	12.50			
			Total	$486.55			

Managers using a periodic inventory system physically count what is in storage on a periodic basis—usually at the end of each month—and can use a form such as this one to record the quantity and value of inventory.

Periodic Inventory System. When a periodic inventory system is used, the operation does not keep track of what is added and subtracted from inventory on an ongoing basis. Rather, a periodic inventory system relies on physically counting what is in storage on a periodic basis—usually at the end of each month (see Exhibit 8.10).

An advantage of the periodic inventory system is that it avoids the trouble and cost of the paperwork involved with the perpetual inventory system. A disadvantage is that food cost information can only be figured out for each month. With a perpetual inventory system, food costs can be figured out for each day or any combination of days. Comparatively, then, the measurement of inventory and the accounting and operating information that can be calculated is much less accurate when a periodic inventory system is used.

A Practical Approach. Since there are advantages to each inventory system, managers at many operations use both to keep track of inventory. They use the perpetual inventory system to keep track of expensive or otherwise important products in inventory, because keeping close track of them is worth the trouble and cost of the paperwork and labor involved. Inexpensive inventory items, on the other hand, are kept track of quickly and easily by physically counting them on a regular basis, typically at the end of each month.

Reducing Inventory Costs

As previously mentioned, cash flow problems and quality problems can occur when inventory levels are too high. The following procedures are among those you can use to effectively manage your inventory:

- *Carry a smaller amount of inventory.* This may be possible if you can obtain more frequent deliveries and purchase smaller quantities of products.

- *Be sure that required levels of inventory are correct.* Periodically examine minimum/maximum inventory levels to make sure they are set properly.

- *Decrease the number of product types that you carry.* For example, perhaps you need only two or three—rather than four or five—different sizes of shrimp.

- *Refuse to accept early deliveries.* You will have to pay for these products sooner than you would have to if they were delivered as originally scheduled.

Issuing

Issuing involves distributing food and beverages from storerooms to authorized individuals who requisition these products. Large food and beverage operations may have one or more full-time storeroom employees who issue products. These employees may also receive goods. Small properties usually do not have full-time storeroom employees.

Issuing procedures will depend in part on what kind of recordkeeping system the operation is using to keep track of inventory. If an operation is using the perpetual inventory system for every item in storage, a requisition must always be used to withdraw products from inventory. As mentioned earlier in the chapter, a requisition is a written order identifying the type, amount, and value of items needed from storage (see Exhibit 8.11). Requisitions should be signed or initialed by an authorized official such as the chef.

At the end of each day (or on some other regular basis), the storeroom clerk or another employee may use the requisition forms that have been collected to update perpetual inventory records. These requisition forms can then be forwarded to a manager or to the secretary/bookkeeper for review and calculation of daily food cost information.

As you can imagine, issuing every product using the perpetual inventory system would require a great deal of time and trouble. That is why many operations simplify inventory recordkeeping, and therefore issuing procedures, by using the perpetual inventory system for selected products only.

Another way to simplify issuing is to have employees obtain all the products needed for production at one time. Not only does this help control, it also increases employee productivity—time is not lost by employees constantly leaving production areas to retrieve items from storage.

Special Beverage Management Concerns

Let's look at special concerns in purchasing, receiving, storing, and issuing beverages.

Exhibit 8.11 Sample Requisition Form

Food Requisition

Storage Type (check one):

☐ Refrigerated

☐ Frozen

☑ Dry

Date: _____

Work Unit: _____

Approved for Withdrawal: _____

Item	Purchase Unit	No. of Units	Unit Price	Total Cost	Employee Initials Received By	Employee Initials Withdrawn By
Col. 1	Col. 2	Col. 3	Col. 4	Col. 5	Col. 6	Col. 7
Tomato Paste	CS-6 #10	2 ½	$28.50	$ 71.25	JC	Ken
Green Beans	CS-6 #10	1 ½	22.75	34.13	JC	Ken
			Total	$596.17		

Requisition forms such as this one are filled out by production personnel to identify the type, amount, and value of items needed from storage.

Purchasing

Whereas purchase specifications are an important part of purchasing food, there is less need for an operation to develop purchase specifications for alcoholic beverages, since many alcoholic beverages are purchased by brand name.

In many states, laws and other restrictions regulate the purchase of alcoholic beverages. Some states operate "state stores" from which all alcoholic beverages must be purchased, and prices for many beverages may be set by law, making negotiating and shopping for better values pointless. Even in less regulated states, calling suppliers in search of the best deal may not work as well with alcoholic beverages as with food. If a particular brand of alcohol is desired, there may be only one wholesaler in the area who carries the brand.

A house brand is a beverage brand served when no special brand is requested by the guest. How do you determine which house brands to purchase? Attitudes of beverage managers can range from: "Don't use anything you wouldn't be proud to display on the back bar" to "Use the least expensive—let the guest pay extra for a premium brand." In practice, middle-range brands—neither the least nor the most expensive—are generally used for house brands.

Sometimes beverage managers make the mistake of trying to please everyone.

Call brands are specific beverage brands that guests request by name when they place an order. Deciding what kinds of call brands to carry is a marketing decision. Sometimes beverage managers make the mistake of trying to please everyone. They offer many brands, each of which must be ordered, stored, issued, and controlled. Beverage operations would be more efficient if they had a selection of brands available to meet the needs of most regular guests instead of trying to satisfy everyone's tastes. If one call brand is not available, usually a reasonable substitute can be offered.

From time to time beverage suppliers in some states may offer special deals. An example is a per-bottle or case discount when a specified volume is purchased. However, before making a large-volume purchase to take advantage of a discount, consider these questions:

- How much cash will be tied up in inventory?

- Will cash flow be affected negatively?

- Will the greater risk of theft warrant the purchase?

- If deals are for brands not normally carried by the property, will guests accept the change?

- In areas where property taxes must be paid on items in storage, will increased inventory taxes eliminate much of the savings?

Another factor to consider before making a large-volume beverage purchase is that inventory turnover rates are generally lower for beverages than for foods. This is because foods are more perishable than beverages. For example, a property's food inventory may turn over (on average) 26 times per year—the value of goods on hand equals the approximate amount of foods used during a two-week period. By contrast, a property's beverage inventory may turn over only 12 times per year—the amount of beverage inventory on hand approximately equals the cost of beverages purchased for one month's use. Therefore, any extra beverages purchased to take advantage of a volume discount may be in storage for a long time.

Receiving

Because beverages are more prone to theft than food, some of the receiving principles for food noted earlier in the chapter should be re-emphasized here:

- Cases should be opened and bottles checked to make sure all incoming beverages noted on the delivery invoice were, in fact, delivered.

- After beverages are received, they should be moved immediately to secure storage areas. The longer beverages remain in receiving areas, the greater the chance of theft.

- Purchasing and receiving tasks should be separated for beverages unless both tasks are assumed by the owner/manager in a small operation. Even when these tasks are separate, the possibility of collusion between purchasing and receiving staff must be guarded against.

Storing

Prevention of unauthorized physical access, the need to keep effective records, and sanitary storage are as important for beverages as for food.

In addition to a central beverage storage area, many operations have behind-the-bar storage. This storage area should be locked when the facility is closed for business. Generally, quantities of beverages in a behind-the-bar or other non-central storage area should be minimal, since security controls are less effective in these areas. The main concern is to establish correct bar "pars"—the number of bottles that should be on hand behind the bar.

When possible, wines, beer, and other refrigerated beverages should be stored away from refrigerated food items. If this is not possible, a locked storage area for beverages should be provided.

Closely monitoring the beverage inventory is critical. Normally, all alcoholic beverages can be kept under a perpetual inventory system; quantities should be verified by physical count at least monthly.

Issuing

Beverages should be issued on a bottle-for-bottle basis to replenish bar pars. If, for example, the bar par for house Scotch is five bottles and at the end of the shift two bottles are empty, two bottles must be issued to maintain the bar par. The empty bottles should be presented to whoever is in charge of issuing beverages from inventory—usually a manager—before he or she issues full replacement bottles. The empty bottles must then be broken or disposed of in compliance with local or state ordinances.

Normally, beverages should be issued once each shift—preferably at the end. If bartenders frequently run out of a certain beverage before a shift ends, this suggests the need to re-examine its par level.

As beverages are issued, bottles should be marked in order to:

- Identify a bottle as coming from the property's central storage.

- Indicate the date of issue. Managers might question why a bottle of fast-selling liquor is at the bar for a long time.

- Identify to which bar, when a property has several, a bottle has been issued.

Managers also may wish to write the purchase price directly on the bottle label. When done inconspicuously, this can help employees complete requisitions for beverages. When bottles of liquor are used for tableside flaming of food or when bottles of wine are served at the table, this labeling practice may be impractical.

Some managers believe that the key to the locked beverage storage area should be kept at the bar, since there may be times when a manager with a key is not on duty. This practice, however, lessens management's control over issuing. It is usually better to set bar par levels high enough so that keeping a key behind the bar does not become necessary.

Even when bar par levels have been carefully set, some managers may still feel that a key should be on hand just in case something extraordinary occurs and there is a need to replenish bar pars in the middle of a shift when a manager with a key is not on duty. In this case, a storeroom key can be left behind the bar, but the key should be placed in an envelope and lines drawn in ink across the envelope flap before the flap is taped shut. The bartender can still get into the storeroom by tearing open the envelope and using the key, but management staff will be able to tell that this occurred. The amount of liquor behind the bar and in the storage area can then be checked to make sure all is properly accounted for.

Endnotes

1. William B. Virts, *Purchasing for Hospitality Operations* (East Lansing, Mich.: Educational Institute of the American Hotel & Motel Association, 1987), p. 34.

2. Some of the following material was adapted from Virts, *Purchasing,* pp. 37–39.

3. Jack D. Ninemeier, *Food and Beverage Security: A Systems Manual for Restaurants, Hotels and Clubs* (Boston, Mass.: CBI, 1982), pp. 97–99.

Key Terms

call brands
credit memo
delivery invoice
first-in, first-out (FIFO)
house brands
inventory

issuing
purchase order
purchase record
purchase requisition
purchase specifications
requisition

Discussion Questions

1. What one phrase summarizes the importance of purchasing?

2. How can quality requirements be incorporated into the purchasing process?

3. What is meant by the term "make-or-buy decision"?

4. What factors affect purchase quantities?

5. How can buyers attempt to get reduced prices while maintaining quality?

6. When selecting a supplier, what factors should be considered?

7. What steps make up the receiving process?

8. What is the meaning of FIFO?

9. How does a perpetual inventory system differ from a periodic inventory system?

10. How can the issuing process be simplified?

Chapter Outline

Production Planning
Food Production
    Food Production Principles
Preparing Fresh Fruits and Vegetables
    Fresh Fruits
    Fresh Vegetables
    Fruit and Vegetable Salads
        Salad Dressings and Marinades
    Fruit and Vegetable Garnishes
    Fruit and Vegetable Cookery
        Cooking Methods
        Vacuum Processing
Preparing Meat and Poultry
    Tenderness
    Cooking Considerations
        Cooking Methods
        Other Cooking Procedures
Preparing Fish
    Cooking Considerations
Preparing Eggs and Dairy Products
    Eggs
        Cooking Considerations
        Cooking Uses
    Dairy Products
        Cooking with Milk
        Cooking with Cheese
Preparing Baked Products
    Common Baking Ingredients
        Flour
        Leavening Agents
        Fat
        Liquids
        Eggs
        Sugar
    Mixing Batter and Dough
Preparing Coffee and Tea
    Coffee
    Tea
Control During Food and Beverage Production

9

Production

IT IS CRUCIAL to produce food and beverage products that conform to quality standards. Excellent service, an inviting ambience, and clean surroundings cannot overcome the negative effects of improper or ineffective production procedures. Quality is a constant concern. Managers must define quality standards for each product. Then, they must supervise and evaluate to ensure that standards are met. Personnel must be trained to follow standard procedures. Quality standards must be incorporated into production activities through standard recipes, purchase specifications, and proper tools and equipment.

Countless books and articles have been written about food and beverage production. Since this text is an introduction to food and beverage operations, it does not attempt to provide extensive details about preparation.[1] Instead, it presents basic information for new or prospective food and beverage managers and other personnel who must understand fundamental principles and procedures of food preparation.

Production Planning

Production planning is the first step toward providing dining experiences that meet or exceed guest expectations. Operations of all sizes need to plan for production in order to have food and beverages, personnel, and equipment available when needed.

Production planning should always be tailored to the needs of the specific operation. In small operations, the manager alone may plan for production. In larger operations, production planning is a formal task undertaken at regularly scheduled production meetings attended by various personnel.

The primary task of planning is to determine the quantity of menu items to be prepared. Many operations use sales history records to estimate production needs for the upcoming week. These records indicate for each date the total meals served, the number of portions of some or all menu items served, the weather, and special events or activities. Exhibit 9.1 shows one type of sales history record. By noting the total meals served on similar dates with similar weather and other conditions, restaurateurs can estimate the total number of guests for days of the week being planned. Lodging operators often use occupancy levels to estimate the number of guests that hotel dining rooms might expect.

Many large food service operations take information generated from sales history records and expand it into master food production planning worksheets, such as the one shown in Exhibit 9.2, which show production personnel the exact

Exhibit 9.1   Sample Sales History Record

Date	1	2	3	4	5	6	7	8	9	10	11	12	13	14	15	16	17	18	19	20	21	22	23	24	25	26	27	28	29	30	31	Total Sold
Day	SU	M	TU	W																												
Weather	Rain	Clear	Clear	Clear																												
Meals Served	386	391	379	397																												
Special Events	—	—	Sale	Sale																												

Number of Portions Served

Item	1	2	3	4	5	6	7	8	9	10	11	12	13	14	15	16	17	18	19	20	21	22	23	24	25	26	27	28	29	30	31	Total Sold
Soup	12	18	14	20																												
Eggplant	15	21	23	16																												
Hamburger	35	41	38	42																												
Fish	20	18	16	24																												
Steak	27	25	29	27																												
Stew	30	35	40	37																												
Diet Platter	11	15	17	12																												
Sea Platter	30	31	35	29																												
Plum Pie	12	10	18	12																												
C. Eclair	15	11	21	13																												
S. Remo	30	28	25	37																												
Oysters	29	30	31	27																												
Gumbo	50	48	52	57																												
F. Amandine	70	65	63	67																												
F. Shrimp	60	54	55	57																												
Sea Shrimp	45	45	35	38																												
N.Y. Strip	10	8	9	9																												
Oyster Pie	19	17	18	18																												
Pecan Pie	28	30	26	41																												
Brulot	15	14	15	16																												

Exhibit 9.2 Sample Master Food Production Planning Worksheet

Day __Tuesday__
Date __8/1/00__

Master Food Production Planning Worksheet

Local Weather Forecast __Cloudy & mild__
Special Plans: Party of 15 — steaks

Items	Standard Portion Size	Forecasted Portions			Adjusted Forecast	Requisitioning Guide Data		Remarks	Number of Portions Left Over	Actual Number Served
		Guests	Officers*	Total Forecast		Raw Materials Requested	State of Preparation			
Appetizers										
Shrimp Cocktail	5 ea	48	—	48	51	12 lbs of 21–25 count	RTC		—	53
Fruit Cup	5 oz	18	1	19	20	See Recipe for 20 Portions			—	19
Marinated Herring	2 1/2 oz	15	1	16	16	2 1/2 lbs	RTE		—	14
Half Grapefruit	1/2 ea	8	—	8	8	4 Grapefruit			—	9
Soup	6 oz	30	3	33	36	Prepare 2 Gallons			5	32
Entrées										
Sirloin Steak	14 oz	28	—	28	29	29 Sirloin Steaks (Btchr.)	RTC		—	28
Prime Ribs	9 oz	61	1	62	64	3 Ribs of Beef	RTC	Use Re-heat if necessary	out at 10:45 P.M.	62
Lobster	1 1/2 lb	26	—	26	28	28 Lobsters (check stock)			—	26
Ragout of Lamb	4 oz	24	2	26	26	12 lbs lamb fore (3/4" pcs)		Recipe No. E.402	1+	25
Half Chicken	1/2 ea	34	2	36	38	38 halves (check stock)			—	39
Vegetables & Salads										
Whipped Potatoes	3 oz	55	1	56	58	13 lbs	AP		2–3	56
Baked Potatoes	1 ea	112	3	115	120	120 Idahos			out at 11:10 P.M.	120
Asparagus Spears	3 ea	108	—	108	113	8 No. 2 cans			2	110
Half Tomato	1/2 ea	48	4	52	54	27 Tomatoes			2	52
Tossed Salad	2 1/2 oz	105	3	108	112	See Recipe No. S.302			—	114
Hearts of Lettuce	1/4 hd	63	2	65	67	18 heads			—	69
Desserts										
Brownie w/ice cream	1 sq./1 1/2 oz	21	2	23	26	1 pan brownies			—	24
Fresh Fruits	3 oz	10	—	10	11	See Recipe No. D.113			—	10
Ice Cream	2 1/2 oz	35	3	38	40	Check stock			—	43
Apple Pie	1/7 cut	21	—	21	21	3 Pies			out at 10:50 P.M.	21
Devils Food Cake	1/8 cut	8	—	8	8	1 cake			1	7
Total No. of Persons		173	5	178	185					180

Abbreviations: AP—as purchased; RTC—ready-to-cook; RTE—ready-to-eat

number of portions needed each day. Some operations have computerized forecasting capabilities.

Production planning meetings serve other purposes as well. For example, having an estimate of the number of meals to prepare makes it possible to schedule labor and equipment.[2] If there are special events such as banquets or other catered functions scheduled for the upcoming week, you will need to plan, communicate, and coordinate to ensure that no problems result.

As a result of planning, there is a greater likelihood that resources are not over- or under-utilized as activities are undertaken by different departments. Effective planning minimizes potential problems.

Beverage operations usually require very little production planning if adequate bar par inventory levels have been established and if an effective minimum/maximum inventory system is used in central storage areas. What planning there is typically focuses on scheduling employees and maintaining a constant supply of required brands of liquors and wines.

Food Production

Food production comprises a number of functions that may be performed in one or more types of kitchens. The number of functions and the type of kitchen or kitchens depend on the characteristics of the specific operation—large or small, cafeteria or table service, limited menu or extensive menu, and so forth.

Typical major functions include preparing cold foods, cooking, baking, and preparing beverages. Each of these major functions encompasses other functions and has many applications. For example, there are many types of cooking methods for many types of foods. Cooking methods can be broadly categorized as moist-heat and dry-heat, as shown in Exhibit 9.3. Moist-heat methods require water or another liquid. Dry-heat methods require hot air or hot fat.

In this chapter, we will address the major preparation functions under the categories of fresh fruits and vegetables, meat and poultry, fish, eggs and dairy products, baked goods, and coffee and tea. But first, some important food production principles to keep in mind.

Food Production Principles

We cook or otherwise prepare food for several reasons: (1) to develop, enhance, or alter flavor; (2) to improve digestibility; and (3) to destroy harmful organisms. Too much cooking or other improper preparation destroys vitamins, affects the potency of proteins, and can unfavorably change the color, texture, and flavor of food. Therefore, foods should be prepared according to basic principles. These include, but are not restricted to, the following:

- Begin with quality food, which is not necessarily the most expensive.
- Make sure food is clean.
- Make sure food is properly handled.
- Use proper seasonings.

Exhibit 9.3 Examples of Moist-Heat and Dry-Heat Cooking Methods

---

Moist-Heat Methods

Boiling—cooking food in 212°F (100°C) water. Blanching and parboiling are types of boiling in which foods are partially cooked for a short time.

Poaching—cooking food in liquid below the boiling point of water. The food may or may not be covered with liquid.

Simmering—cooking food in a liquid which is below water's boiling point.

Steaming—using water converted to an invisible vapor or gas by heating it to the boiling point. Cooking with steam helps retain nutrients.

Stewing—a process in which small cuts of poultry or meat are simmered in a thickened liquid.

Dry-Heat Methods

Baking—cooking with dry heat in an oven.

Roasting—essentially the same as baking but applicable to meat and poultry as opposed to other foods.

Broiling—cooking food at a high temperature on a rack that is located above, below, or between hear sources.

Barbecuing—broiling, grilling, or roasting while basting with a sauce.

Grilling—cooking on an open grid over gas, charcoal, or electric heat.

Griddling—cooling on a solid heated surface, usually with a small amount of fat.

Ovenizing—cooking foods on greased pans in ovens at high temperatures.

Frying—cooking quickly in fat. Frying includes pan-frying, stir-frying, sautéing, deep-frying, and pressure-frying. All but deep-frying and pressure-frying use a small amount of fat.

- Use the right preparation techniques and equipment.
- Follow standard recipes.
- Don't cook in quantities that are larger than necessary.
- Serve food as soon as possible after preparation.
- Serve hot food hot and cold food cold.
- Make every presentation something special.
- Never be satisfied with a mediocre product. Always try to make it perfect.

Preparing Fresh Fruits and Vegetables

Increased nutritional awareness is leading Americans to consume a larger quantity and variety of fresh fruits and vegetables. The quality of these products is constantly improving. Excellent choices of fresh fruits and vegetables are often available year-round because of the diverse climates in the United States and because technology has improved storage and transportation systems.

Fresh Fruits

The term "fruit" refers to the matured ovary of a plant, including the seeds and adjacent parts. It is the reproductive body of the seed plant. Fruits are high in carbohydrates and water and are excellent sources of minerals and vitamins.

Normally, only ripe fruit is used for food production. When fruit is ripe, it is at full size, the tissue is soft and tender, the color is good, the taste is better because the starch in fruit has turned to sugar, and aroma has developed.

Fruit costs are affected by:

- Perishability
- Pesticides
- Weather conditions
- Consumer preferences
- Packaging
- Processing

There are many precautions to take and procedures to follow when working with fresh fruit. Careful washing is a must. Fresh fruit should be handled as little as possible to avoid bruising. Citrus fruit is easier to peel after it has been steamed, which can be done efficiently in a compartment steamer. To prevent darkening of low-acid fruits after cutting, the cut fruit should be placed in orange or lemon juice to slow the browning process, or the cut fruit should be covered with a sugar solution to prevent contact with oxygen, which causes the color change.

Remember that fresh fruits are often more palatable and nutritious than cooked fruit. Try to find innovative ways to serve fresh fruits.

Usually, fresh fruits are best stored in the refrigerator. Bananas are an exception and should be purchased for immediate use because they are highly perishable. Several weekly deliveries of bananas are much better than infrequent deliveries.

Fresh Vegetables

The term "vegetable" refers to any plant grown for an edible part other than the ovary, which is classified as fruit. (The term "vegetable fruits" is used in the list below to describe those vegetables which technically are classified as fruits because they contain the ovary of the plant.) Generally, vegetables have less sugar and more starch than fruits. The structure of a vegetable is formed by cellulose and can be maintained only when water remains in the cell. Vegetables shrink and wilt as they dry.

Vegetables are classified by the part of the plant from which they come; for example:

- Roots—sweet potatoes, beets, carrots, parsnips, and turnips
- Tubers or underground stems—potatoes
- Bulbs—onions, garlic, and leeks
- Stems—celery, rhubarb, and asparagus

- Leaves—lettuce, spinach, and cabbage
- Flowers—cauliflower, broccoli, and artichoke
- Pods and seeds—green beans, peas, and lima beans
- Sprouts—soybeans and alfalfa
- Vegetable fruits—tomato, eggplant, squash, pumpkin, okra, pepper, and cucumber

Vegetables are rich in minerals and vitamins. They generally cost less when they are in season and when there is an abundant supply.

Careful washing is important when preparing fresh vegetables. Wilted vegetables can be soaked in cold water or covered with ice to help regain crispness; however, this doesn't restore lost nutrients. To avoid unnecessary waste, do not throw away usable leaves of lettuce and outer stalks of celery. When paring potatoes and other vegetables, pare them thinly so that nutrients and product are not lost.

Fresh vegetables should be purchased only for immediate consumption and should be stored in a cool, well-ventilated space. Most vegetables—except those classified as roots or tubers—require refrigeration.

Fruit and Vegetable Salads

Fruits and vegetables for salads should be fresh and have fine flavor and color. Salads may be served as accompaniments to entrées or as meals by themselves. The following guidelines are helpful in salad-making:

- Use fresh, ripe products.
- Use a variety of colors.
- Use varied textures—crisp, soft, and smooth combinations work well. Mushiness is unacceptable.
- Use good tools such as a clean vegetable brush, sharp knives, and a special cutting board.
- Freshen vegetables (after they have been washed) in very cold water, but only until they are crisp. Drain well before using.
- Chop or cut salad ingredients in pieces of uniform size; avoid crushing.
- Handle prepared salad ingredients gently. Toss mixed salads together lightly.
- If salad dressings are added to salads rather than served on the side, add them just before serving to avoid wilting the salad.
- Keep salad ingredients, finished salads, and salad dressings refrigerated until serving time.

There appear to be no limits to the types of salads that can be made today—hot or cold. Some of the more common types include tossed salads, cabbage slaws, pasta salads, molded salads, fruit salads, hot vegetable salads, and protein salads. Note that many of these types overlap; that is, fruit salads can be tossed, layered, frozen with whipped cream, molded in gelatin, have a cream or cottage cheese base, or be arranged in any number of ways. Fruits can be diced and served with other complementary foods or served as halves or sections.

Tossed salads are made with one or more kinds of salad greens. Salad greens include iceberg, romaine, Boston, and Bibb lettuce; escarole; endive; and chicory. Parsley and spinach also are frequently used in tossed salads. Slaws are made with chopped or shredded green and/or red cabbage mixed with other shredded vegetables or, perhaps, mixed fruit, marshmallows, nuts, cheese, or onions.

Molded salads generally have a plain gelatin or dessert gelatin base. They can be layered with fruit, vegetables (cooked or raw), meat, fish, cheese, or cream. Salads made with meats, poultry, fish, or dairy products (especially cheeses) are common entrees.

Salad Dressings and Marinades. Salad dressings and marinades are special enhancements that are typically coupled with vegetables and fruits. Marinades are also used in preparing meat, poultry, and fish.

There are almost as many types of salad dressings as there are types of salads, but many have certain characteristics and ingredients in common. Most salad dressings are either stable or unstable emulsions. An emulsion is a mixture of two ordinarily unmixable liquids. Stable emulsions are those that do not separate, such as mayonnaise. Unstable emulsions are those that separate when left standing, such as oil and vinegar. Unstable emulsions must be shaken to be evenly mixed. Other types of dressing include cooked or boiled dressings and yogurt or sour cream-based dressings.

Marinades are seasoned liquids. Usually they contain vegetable or olive oil and an acid such as wine, vinegar, or fruit juice. Herbs, spices, or vegetables are often added for flavoring. Foods are marinated when they are soaked in a marinade. The marinade may be used to tenderize as well as enhance the flavor of the food item. Marinades can also be used as a cooking medium and as a sauce for the cooked food.

Fruit and Vegetable Garnishes

Fruits and vegetables are frequently used as garnishes to decorate plates and platters of food. Garnishes should contribute form, color, and texture to the foods with which they are served. There is an endless variety of fruit and vegetable garnishes, ranging from lemon slices to exotic truffles.

Actually, the range of garnishes is limited only by one's imagination and the requirement that the garnishes be edible. Fruits and vegetables are not the only foods used as garnishes. Other examples are sieved egg whites, chocolate curls, stuffed anchovies, croutons and toast points, and edible flowers.

Fruit and Vegetable Cookery

Preparation for cooking fresh vegetables and fruits is the same as preparation for cold vegetables and fruits: the produce must be washed and sometimes trimmed, cut, torn, or soaked. Most fresh produce should be cleaned and stored as soon as possible after delivery, especially if it will be held several days or more. Vegetables such as potatoes and carrots require scrubbing while others such as greens require soaking. Water used to clean vegetables should not be reused.

General principles for cooking fruits and vegetables are based on common sense and are simple to learn and practice. Goals are to retain nutrients, to yield a high level of flavor, and to produce a product that is tender, firm, and colorful. Normally, only a small amount of water should be used and products should be cooked until tender and firm but not soft.

As noted earlier, overcooking destroys many valuable nutrients and distorts color, flavor, texture, and shape. Preparation should be scheduled as close to serving time as possible. Most vegetables should be cooked in covered cooking vessels. Green vegetables, however, should be cooked without a cover. Baking soda (or any other alkaline chemical) deepens the green color of vegetables, but it also can cause a loss of vitamin C, and therefore should not be used.

When heating canned vegetables, remember that these vegetables already have been fully cooked. Only a very short heating time is needed, and heating time should be scheduled as close to serving time as possible. Canned vegetables lend themselves to batch cooking methods. Batch cooking is a method in which small quantities of products are prepared immediately before serving. For example, if 75 portions of cooked carrots are needed over a two-hour period, the chef might prepare 25 portions at a time. While more effort is required to prepare three batches instead of one, the advantage of higher quality at the time of service often makes this effort worthwhile.

Cooking Methods. Fruit and vegetable cooking methods include, but are not limited to steaming, baking, frying, boiling, and microwaving.

Steaming. Steaming is one of the best cooking methods for fruits and vegetables. Steaming uses water that has been converted to an invisible vapor or gas. Compartment steamers have low-, high-, or room-pressure compartments into which steam is injected. The direct application of steam quickly cooks the food while maintaining high quality and nutritional levels. The instructions from the steam equipment manufacturer should be followed closely. Steamed vegetables should normally be salted and seasoned *after* they are cooked.

Baking. Baking is a dry-heat cooking method using hot air. It is appropriate for some fruits and vegetables—such as potatoes, squash, eggplant, apples, and tomatoes—that contain enough water to form steam.

Frying. One frying method particularly suitable for fruits and vegetables is stir-frying. Stir-frying is a popular cooking method using high heat, a small amount of oil in an open skillet or wok, and a short amount of cooking time. Stir-fry vegetables should be diced or cut into small uniform-size pieces and crisp-cooked. Sautéing—cooking quickly in a small amount of hot fat—is similar to stir-frying.

Deep-frying is appropriate for such vegetables as potatoes, eggplants, and onions. Deep-frying uses a large amount of fat and requires vegetables to be rinsed and dried before frying. Tempura is a method of deep-frying in which products are parboiled, dried, and breaded—usually in a flour and water batter—before they are deep-fried in fat.

Microwaving. Vegetables to be cooked in a microwave oven should be placed in a covered microwavable dish with a very small amount of liquid. Since vegetables cook quickly, timing is critical to prevent overcooking.

Boiling. Boiling entails cooking food in water or other liquid at a temperature of 212°F (100°C). When boiling, bring water to a full boil, add vegetables, cover the cooking container (if applicable), lower the temperature, and continue cooking at a gentle boil. Cooking in water can destroy water-soluble vitamins. The problem worsens when the water used in cooking is thrown out rather than being used in preparing the product.

Blanching is another form of boiling. When foods are blanched, they are submerged in boiling water for a short time. Peaches and tomatoes may be blanched so their skins are easier to remove. Blanching is also used in preparing fruits and vegetables for freezing. Vegetables are often blanched as a preliminary process in cooking, then, just before serving, blanched vegetables may be cooked by another process. Vegetables can also be parboiled, which is similar to blanching. This process involves immersing products in boiling water until they are partly cooked in preparation for roasting.

Vacuum Processing. Vacuum processing produces partially cooked or prepared food. Fruits and vegetables can be partially cooked and vacuum-packed in plastic pouches. The pouches are then refrigerated (not frozen). To reheat, pouches may be dropped in boiling water or steamed in a special oven. If they have been processed by the *sous vide* method, they may require steaming in a special oven. Vacuum-packed commercially processed foods can be purchased or operations can use vacuum-processing techniques on-site. Advantages include potential labor savings, increased shelf life of food, and higher quality products. A potential disadvantage involves sanitation problems if packaging is done improperly.

Preparing Meat and Poultry

Meats and poultry are often the most expensive and important items on a menu. Great care should be taken in purchasing, preparing, and serving these entrees. Popular meats include beef, pork, veal, and lamb; chicken and turkey are probably the most popular types of poultry. While meat and poultry are separate entities, they have many common characteristics, including their four primary components:

- *Muscle fiber.* Muscle is made of fibers held together by connective tissue. The thickness of the fibers, the size of fiber bundles, and the amount of connective tissue will determine the grain of the meat.

- *Connective tissue.* Connective tissue holds muscles together and determines the tenderness of the meat. This tissue covers the walls of muscle fibers, binds fibers into bundles, and surrounds the muscles. Tendons and ligaments that attach the muscle to the bone are composed of connective tissue. Less tender meat cuts have more connective tissue.

  There are two types of connective tissue: (1) collagen (white) which breaks down into gelatin when heat is applied, and (2) elastin (yellow) which does not break down when heated. Tenderer meat contains collagen instead of elastin. The type of connective tissue within the meat determines the cooking method.

- *Fat.* Fat is distributed inside meat in small layers called marbling. Fat contributes to tenderness and flavor. Exterior layers of fat cover the muscle.

- *Bone.* Bone is not edible. A high proportion of meat to bone is favorable because there is a lower cost per edible unit. The shape of bone helps identify the meat cut. Bones are used in soup stocks to add flavor.

Tenderness

Tenderness is important in selecting, preparing, and serving meat and poultry. As noted above, tenderness is influenced by the connective tissue which is present. Fat and age also affect tenderness. Tender meat contains more fat, and young animals yield tender meat. The location of the muscle also affects tenderness. The least-used muscles (loin and rib cuts in meat) are more tender than fully developed muscles such as chuck and round.

Temperature influences tenderness. The higher the cooking temperature, the tougher the meat, especially if the meat is overcooked. Grinding, pounding, and other techniques can be used to tenderize meat. Aged meat (hung in a refrigerator during the time of after-death changes) will be more tender. Enzymes injected into meat before or after the slaughtering process are also tenderizers.

Cooking Considerations

Goals of meat cooking include improving flavor, changing color, tenderizing the product, and destroying harmful organisms. Cooking at a low temperature for longer periods of time is better than using a hot temperature for shorter cooking times, because there will be less weight and nutrient loss.

Some meats (portion-cut items) can be cooked from their frozen state. If done properly, there is little difference in tenderness, juiciness, and flavor of frozen or thawed meats. Frozen meats should be processed at a lower temperature for a longer period of time.

Microwave cooking has not proven to be a generally useful technique for cooking meats. While cooking time is faster, the product often is drier and there is more shrinkage. Unless special heating elements are used in microwave cooking, no surface browning occurs on the meat.

Cooking Methods. Cooking methods for meat and poultry include but are not limited to:

Roasting. Roasting in an oven is a common dry-heat method of cooking meat. Meat to be roasted should be placed on a rack in a roasting pan with the fat side up so the meat can baste itself. A meat thermometer should always be used, inserted in the thickest part of the muscle away from the bone. Do not rely on charts that list minutes per pound or other roasting factors. While these can be used as a guide, careful use of the meat thermometer is always best.

Guests will have different preferences about how their meat is prepared. Some people prefer meat that is well-done (no pink color; gray throughout). Others like rare meat (browned surface with a red interior). Still others like their meat between these stages (a thicker layer of gray surface with a pink interior). Popular cooking references vary in the recommended interior temperatures necessary to attain different stages of doneness. Experienced cooks have their own standards. Food service

Overcooking destroys a steak's tenderness—not to mention its flavor.

managers should work with chefs to develop cooking procedures that will meet the operation's food quality standards.

Meat continues to cook after it is removed from the oven. Therefore, it should be removed when the product is a few degrees cooler than the desired temperature.

Pork should always be cooked until it is well-done—with an internal temperature of at least 150°F (66°C). This prevents trichinosis, a disease caused by a tapeworm which may be present in the meat because of improper care of the animal before slaughter or poor sanitary practices after slaughter.

Broiling. Broiling uses direct radiant heat. Meats should be approximately half-cooked when turned with tongs or a spatula. Normally, high temperatures should be used when broiling meat, poultry, and other food.

Pan broiling. With this technique, meat is broiled in a heavy fry pan and cooked slowly. The pan should not be covered and water or fat is seldom added. Fat from cooking should be poured off as it accumulates.

Frying. There are many types of frying, as we have already noted. All except deep-frying use a small amount of fat. Deep-frying uses a large amount of fat.

Braising. Braising is a process in which meat is first browned in a small amount of fat, then cooked slowly in a small amount of liquid in a covered cooking vessel.

Simmering. When simmered, meat is cooked in a small amount of water or broth in a covered pan until tender. The temperature of the water should be below the boiling point.

Pressure cooking and steaming. Meat can be cooked under pressure in a compartment steamer or steamed in an oven. When steaming meat in an oven, cover the meat with aluminum foil to prevent moisture loss. Trapped moisture becomes steam which helps cook the meat.

Other Cooking Procedures. Meat stocks are used in preparing many meats and other products. Stocks are made from cracked bones, cut meat pieces, and other ingredients. These ingredients are covered with water, simmered for several hours, and then vegetables and spices are added. After cooking, the stock is strained, chilled, and degreased. Further processing can then be done. If a brown stock is desired, bones are roasted before simmering. If a white stock is needed, bones are not roasted. Bouillon is a brown stock that has been clarified by adding egg whites.

Preparing Fish

There are two types of edible fish: (1) finfish that have bony skeletons and come from saltwater or freshwater, and (2) shellfish that don't have bony skeletons and come mainly from saltwater. There are two types of shellfish. Mollusks have hard-hinged shells (oysters, clams, scallops, mussels) and crustaceans have segmented shells (lobsters, shrimp, crabs).

The fat content of fish ranges from less than 1% (cod and haddock) to more than 25% (such as in salmon, mackerel, and lake trout). The fat content is an important factor in determining the cooking method. The nutrient value of fish is generally quite high. Fish is a good source of minerals and protein and presents a good alternative to meat protein. Fish with a high fat content is a good source of vitamins.

Cooking Considerations

Fish has relatively little connective tissue compared to meat and poultry, and therefore requires shorter cooking times. Fish should be cooked at a moderate temperature long enough for flavor to develop, connective tissue to break down, and protein to coagulate.

Fish should not be overcooked because it becomes tough. The flesh is cooked sufficiently when it falls into clumps or flakes when tested with a fork. If the cooking is not stopped at this point, the product will become tough, dry, and flavorless. Fish that is properly cooked breaks up easily, so careful handling is necessary during cooking and serving.

Fish can be prepared without heat, using a marinade with an acid such as lemon or lime juice. The acid in the marinade speeds the coagulation of the fish protein, causing it to turn white. Marinated products such as pickled herring are favorites with many guests. Fish is also served raw with sushi (rice with vinegar) in some establishments featuring Japanese cuisine.

Popular cooking methods include such dry-heat techniques as broiling, baking, and frying. Moist-heat methods such as poaching and steaming also can be used. Low-fat fish may require some fat in the cooking process. However, fat normally will not be needed when a high-fat fish product is prepared.

Shellfish can be cooked by placing the product in simmering water. Shrimp is usually steamed, baked, charbroiled, or deep-fried.

Preparing Eggs and Dairy Products

Eggs

Eggs are a good source of vitamins and minerals. They can be served alone in various styles or used as an ingredient in other menu items. There is no relationship between the color of the eggshell (brown or white) and the quality or taste of egg products.

Cooking Considerations. Eggs prepared in various ways are popular breakfast entrées. The following guidelines should be kept in mind:

- Use eggs as soon as possible after purchasing. Flavor and appearance deteriorate with age.

- Boiling causes eggs to become rubbery. When cooking eggs in the shell, place the eggs in boiling water, then turn down the heat to a simmering temperature or remove the eggs from the heat.

- Eggs to be cooked soft in the shell should be cooked for no longer than one to three minutes.

- Hard-cooked eggs should be cooked no more than 15 minutes.

- After removing eggs cooked in the shell from the water, immerse them in cold water and peel them immediately to prevent yolks from turning green.

- To poach eggs, bring water to a simmer before adding the eggs. Eggs should be broken into a separate dish before they are added to the poaching vessel.

- Cook eggs at the lowest possible temperature.

Cooking Uses. There are many different ways to use eggs in cooking. When eggs are heated, the protein in the yolk coagulates. This makes eggs useful as thickening agents and for coating other foods. When heat is applied to the egg white, it changes from a transparent to a soft white color. When sugar is added to any egg mixture, higher heat is necessary for coagulation; when salt is added, a lower temperature is needed. When an acid such as lemon juice is added, the temperature for coagulation is also lowered and a fine gel is produced.

    Binding and coating. Eggs help make the ingredients stick together in products such as meat loaf and in batters for deep-fried products.

    Leavening agent. Leavening involves incorporating gases into a product to increase the product's volume and make it lighter. Beaten egg whites create a foam made up of air bubbles surrounded by thin layers of egg-white film. When this foam is incorporated into a mixture and heated, the air bubbles expand and the film hardens. This process occurs in making omelets, souffles, and sponge cakes. Egg whites should be beaten only until the peaks stand straight. If they are overbeaten, the volume of the foam will be reduced. If sugar is added to egg whites while being beaten, the resulting foam will be more stable.

    Egg yolks can also be used as a leavening agent: when heated, they increase in size. However, because of the presence of fat, yolks are less effective leavening agents than egg whites.

Emulsifying agent. Oil and vinegar separate unless the oil droplets are coated with egg or some other emulsifier to prevent the separation. Egg yolks are used as an emulsifier in mayonnaise, ice cream, and cake.

Interfering substance. Eggs prevent ice crystals from combining to create a larger mass. They are used in this way when sherbets are made.

Clarifying agent. When egg protein coagulates, it traps particles in the substance so they can be removed. This makes liquids clear and free from impurities. Broths, for example, are clarified with egg whites.

Dairy Products

Milk is the single most naturally nutritious product. It is usually pasteurized and homogenized. Pasteurization is a process of controlled heating which destroys bacteria to make milk safe to use. Homogenization is a process that breaks up fat particles so they will remain suspended. This prevents milk from separating into fat and liquid parts.

Milk has many cooking uses, but it is delicate. Milk curdles and scorches easily, and it is highly perishable. While there are many types of milk available, basic cooking procedures are the same regardless of which milk product is used.

Cooking with Milk. Acids such as lemon juice, tomato juice, and vinegar can cause milk to curdle. This is a frequent problem. To prevent curdling, heat should be kept as low as possible during cooking, and salt should be withheld until the product is served. Warming the milk first, or blending a small amount of the acid mixture at a time with the milk, helps prevent curdling.

To prevent scorching, milk should be heated in a double boiler, a steam-jacketed kettle, or a steamer. When milk is heated, its flavor and odor can be affected by prolonged cooking, or a surface skin can form. The latter can be prevented by covering the milk, stirring it, or by placing a bit of fat such as butter on the surface of the milk. Low heat and frequent stirring are two of the most important preparation principles to follow when cooking with milk.

Cooking with Cheese. The basic cooking procedures for milk are also important when cooking with cheese. There are many cheese varieties and, like milk, cheese is a very nutritious food. Expensive cheeses are not necessarily higher in food value. The extra expense is due to the cost of popular flavoring techniques and the "supply and demand" characteristics of the marketplace.

Remember that protein coagulates with heat. Cheese can become tough and rubbery when it is overheated. This can occur when it is heated for too long or at too high a temperature. Fat in cheese is solid at room temperature. As it warms, it softens. When cheese is heated its fat melts.

Cream cheese is frequently used in cooking since it is so easy to blend. Cheddar is the most popular cheese used in cooking and should be chopped or grated before being added to a sauce or cooked dish. This increases the cheese's surface area and hastens the melting process.

A bakery chef adds his final touch—a frosted floral sculpture—to a cake he has created.

Preparing Baked Products

Some food service operations bake all, or at least part, of their bread and dessert products. Bakeshop production is both an art and a science. Sometimes it is difficult—even with the best recipes—to develop quality bakery products. Altitude, humidity, and the moisture content of the specific flour being used affect baking times and temperatures and the amount of ingredients that must be added to some baked products.

Common Baking Ingredients

Flour. Flour is made by grinding and sifting wheat, rye, barley, or corn. It also can be made from rice, potato, or soy products. Wheat is the most popular flour and is

Exhibit 9.4 Types of Wheat Flour

Whole wheat graham flour—this wheat flour contains the entire wheat kernel.

Bread flour—high in protein content, this flour is used for yeast breads. The protein ingredients develop into gluten which gives the bread structure, elasticity, and strength.

All-purpose flour—made of blended wheats with a lower protein content than bread flour. All-purpose flour has less strength and elasticity and is used for pastry, cookies, and homemade bread.

Pastry flour—this type of flour has a lower protein content than all-purpose flour and is used in the commercial baking industry for pastries and cookies.

Cake flour—cake flour has very low protein content and is very finely ground. It is bleached white and, as the name suggests, is used in cake production.

Instant flour (quick mixing)—this type of flour does not need to be sifted and creates no flour "dust."

Self-rising flour—a leavening agent such as baking soda is added to self-rising flour.

Gluten flour—this flour is very high in protein content (approximately 41%) and is used for special bakery purposes.

Enriched flour—enriched flour has B vitamins and iron added. Other ingredients are added as well.

classified by "hardness." "Hard" wheat flour has a higher protein content and produces a larger volume and finer texture of bread product. "Soft" wheat flour has a lower protein content and is used to make cakes, pastries, and cookies. The highest protein content is in durum wheat, used to make macaroni and similar products. There are many types of wheat flour; some of the most popular are noted in Exhibit 9.4.

Leavening Agents. Leavening agents are used to make dough light and porous. Dough products can be leavened by incorporating air or by forming gas.

Air can be incorporated into dough by beating eggs or by creaming fat and sugar. Gas can be formed in dough by turning water in the dough into steam (a gas) which then expands the dough. Examples of products leavened entirely by steam include popovers and cream puffs.

Carbon dioxide (CO_2) is a gas created by the action of yeast on sugar. The types of yeast most commonly used for baking purposes are pressed yeast and dry yeast. Pressed yeast (in which live yeast cells are pressed into a cake) and dry yeast (where yeast is dried in granular form) are packaged in metal foil to avoid contact with the air. Carbon dioxide can also be produced by using baking soda with water. Baking powder (which is made of dry acid, baking soda, and starch or flour) is another popular leavening chemical. Whenever baking powder or baking soda is used, it should always be added with the dry ingredients so that the gas-forming reaction can be delayed until the water is added as one of the final steps in the preparation process.

Fat. Fat creates a tenderizing effect by coating flour particles and preventing them from coming together. The term "plasticity" refers to a fat's ability to be molded. More "plastic" fats—those that have a waxy texture—tend to hold their shape in a batter or dough, have a high melting temperature, and have greater shortening power. Shortening power refers to the ability of shortenings to surround flour particles and other ingredients, lubricating them so that they cannot stick together.

Liquids. Liquids are used for several purposes in baking. For example, they can be used to hydrate (add water to) starch and gluten. Liquids are also used to dissolve salt, sugar, and baking powders. In addition, liquids can be used to moisturize baking powders and sodas to start carbon dioxide production.

Eggs. Eggs are used to incorporate air into batter and add flavor and color. Since egg proteins coagulate, eggs add rigidity to the structure of baked products.

Sugar. Sugar adds sweetness, creates a browning effect, and serves as a yeast food. Sugar also tenderizes by interfering with development of the gluten in the flour and helps contribute to the fine texture of bakery products.

Mixing Batter and Dough

Flour mixtures can be classified as either dough or batter. Doughs for pie or bread are thick enough to be rolled or kneaded on a board. By contrast, batter can be poured, as in cake-making, or dropped, as in cookie preparation.

There are several methods of mixing batter and dough. When the muffin method is used, dry ingredients are sifted together first. Then eggs are beaten, and liquid and fat are added to the eggs. This liquid is then blended with dry ingredients. When the pastry method is used, dry ingredients are sifted together and fat is blended with the dry ingredients. The liquid is added last. When the conventional cake method is used, fat and sugar are first creamed together and then eggs are added. Dry and liquid ingredients are alternatively blended with the fat/sugar/egg mixture.

Preparing Coffee and Tea

Coffee and tea are two of America's most popular beverages. Guests often judge their entire meal by the quality of these beverages. Food service professionals must take great care to make sure the flavor and consistency of the coffee and tea they serve meets or exceeds their guests' expectations.

Coffee

Blends of coffee used in food service operations are specially designed to maintain quality for relatively long periods of time. Coffee normally is made in an urn or in an automatic coffee-maker.

When an urn is used, ground coffee is carefully measured and placed in a container that is lined with a filter. Fresh cold water is poured into the container and the coffee is brewed at the proper temperature. Temperatures, times, and recipes vary depending on the type of coffee-maker, the manufacturer, the type of coffee, and the operation's recipe. It is important to follow manufacturers' directions. One rule of thumb calls for one pound of ground coffee for each two and one-half gallons of water.[3] When the coffee is brewed, grounds should be removed immediately. Then, half of the coffee should be drawn and poured back into the urn to mix the stronger, bottom-of-the-urn liquid with the rest of the coffee.

Procedures for using an automatic coffee-maker are similar. Coffee should be held at approximately 185°F (85°C); it should *never* be allowed to boil. And it should not be held longer than one hour. Coffee-makers should be rinsed after each use and cleaned regularly according to manufacturers' instructions.

Coffee to be used as iced coffee is often made double strength to allow for dilution from ice.

Tea

Tea can be made with loose tea or tea bags. When making tea, the water should be at the boiling point when it is poured over the loose tea or the tea bag. The teapot/cup should be kept hot and the tea should be allowed to steep for no more than five minutes. It should be served immediately.

Iced tea is often prepared with one-ounce tea bags immersed in water that has reached the boiling point. The normal proportion is two ounces of tea to one gallon of water. Like hot tea, iced tea should steep for no more than five minutes and then be poured into a glass with ice. When this is impractical, tea should be pre-cooled and ice should be added to the glass when the tea is served. Since ice will dilute the tea, it should be made stronger than hot tea.

Control During Food and Beverage Production

The primary concerns of managers during food and beverage production are (1) to make quality ingredients available for food and beverage production, and (2) to ensure that quality requirements are met.[4]

Some control activities to preserve quality and maximize food production efficiency include the following:

- Require that all standard cost control tools (standard recipes, standard portion sizes, etc.) be used.

- Make sure that weighing and measuring tools are available and always used.

- Ensure that only the amount of food actually needed for production is issued.

- Train personnel to constantly comply with required food production procedures.

- Minimize wasted food.

- Monitor and control employee eating/drinking practices.

- Make sure that items taken out of storage but not used are put back in secure storage areas.

- Inspect and approve items to be discarded because they spoiled in storage or weren't properly prepared.

- Maintain production records; use them for revising quantities of items to be produced in the future.

- Analyze sales and production records to determine how much income each menu item is generating.

- Study and resolve production bottlenecks.

- Study systems for managing equipment, layout and design, and energy usage. Implement procedures to reduce costs without lowering quality standards.

- Make sure that labor-saving convenience foods or equipment items reduce labor costs.

- Recruit, train, and schedule personnel who are genuinely concerned about preparing and offering high-quality products that meet the property's standards.

Endnotes

1. An in-depth treatment of food production is offered by the Educational Institute in its *Food Production Principles* course. For information, contact the Institute at Box 1240, East Lansing, MI 48826.

2. Details about scheduling are found in Jack D. Ninemeier, *Planning and Control for Food and Beverage Operations,* 3d ed. (East Lansing, Mich.: Educational Institute of the American Hotel & Motel Association, 1991), Chapter 14.

3. John W. Stokes, *How to Manage a Restaurant or Institutional Foodservice,* 3d ed. (Dubuque, Iowa: Brown, 1977), p. 238.

4. This section is adapted from Jack D. Ninemeier, *Planning and Control for Food and Beverage Operations,* 3d ed. (East Lansing, Mich.: Educational Institute of the American Hotel & Motel Association, 1991), Chapter 8.

Key Terms

dry-heat cooking
emulsion
fruit
garnish
homogenization
leavening agent

marinade
moist-heat cooking
pasteurization
vegetable
vegetable fruit

Discussion Questions

1. What is the main purpose of production planning?

2. What are the two basic classifications of cooking methods?

3. Why should fruits and vegetables be pared as thinly as possible?

4. What guidelines should be followed in making salads?

5. What are the effects of overcooking?

6. What factors influence the tenderness of meat and poultry?

7. Why does fish generally require shorter cooking times than meat and poultry?

8. What causes eggs to become rubbery?

9. When cooking with milk, what precautions should be taken?

10. What steps can be taken to control foods and beverages during production?

Chapter Outline

Types of Service
    Table Service
        American
        English
        French
        Russian
    Buffet Service
    Cafeteria Service
    Other Types of Service
Providing an Enjoyable Experience for Guests
    Standard Operating Procedures
    Guest Service Training
    Teamwork
Pre-Opening Concerns and Activities
    Inspecting Facilities
    Following Reservation Procedures
    Assigning Food Server Stations
    Performing Sidework
    Holding Food Server Meetings
Providing Guest Service
    A Service Sequence
    Special Situations
        Serving Alcoholic Beverages
Food and Beverage Income Control Procedures
    Income Control and Servers
        With Guest Check Systems
        With Precheck Registers
        Income Collection Systems
    Income Control and Beverage Personnel
        Shopper Services for Bartender Control
Enhancing Food and Beverage Sales
    Suggestive Selling
    Selling Beverages

Food and Beverage Service

FOOD AND BEVERAGE SERVICE is the culmination of the planning and production processes. It centers on the guest—more specifically, on providing an enjoyable experience for the guest. Food and beverage service is a complex subject, comprising a wide range of characteristics, activities, and procedures. Characteristics include such things as the type and size of the operation, the type of service it offers, and its ambience or atmosphere. Activities include transferring food and beverage products from production personnel to serving personnel, serving the guests, clearing the table, and so on. Procedures to carry out each activity should be standardized so that guests' expectations can be met or exceeded time after time.

Food and beverage servers are key personnel. Servers represent the operation to the guests. Servers interact more frequently with guests than do other employees, so the responsibility of providing an enjoyable experience for the guest rests in large part with them. In many ways, an operation's reputation and financial success depend on its service staff.

Because service differs so much from one type of operation to another, and because there are so many types of operations, this chapter first addresses different approaches to service. It then explains why standard operating procedures are important in providing an enjoyable experience for guests. It goes on to describe principles and procedures that are typical of many table service dining rooms. The focus is on table service because it is more service-oriented and more guest-centered than other approaches to service.

Types of Service

There are many different approaches to serving food. An operation should use a service style—or a combination of service styles—that best satisfies its guests' wants and needs.

Table Service

Traditional table service provides service for guests who are seated at tables. Servers bring food and beverages to the guests. The servers or other service personnel are also responsible for clearing and resetting the tables. There are four common styles of table service: American, English, French, and Russian.

American. American service is the most frequently used service style in the United States. It has many variations, but the variations usually have these steps in common: (1) servers take guests' orders after the guests are seated; (2) orders are given to the kitchen where food is prepared and portioned onto plates; and (3) plates are brought to the table by the server and presented to the guests.

A variation of American service is often used for banquets—group events at which everyone eats a pre-planned meal at the same time. There are many ways of handling banquet service, depending on the occasion, the type of menu planned, the type of service desired, and so on.[1]

English. English or family service is, for many guests, much like service at home. That is, quantities of foods are placed in bowls or on platters to be passed around the table. The food is brought to the table by servers who present the food to the guests. The guests then pass the food around the table, helping themselves to the amounts they desire. Some operations use family service when featuring family-oriented themes. Other operations use family service only on holidays.

French. French service is used in some dining rooms featuring gourmet foods and an elegant atmosphere. A characteristic of French service is that many food items are partly or completely prepared at tableside. Food for preparation may be brought to tableside on a cart with some type of heating unit. Steak Diane, flaming desserts and drinks, and Caesar salads are some popular items that are prepared in this manner. French service requires experienced employees. Some operations use French service in combination with American service; that is, they feature some specialties served in the French tradition along with their regular fare.

Russian. With Russian service, food production employees portion and arrange foods attractively on platters. Servers then carry the platters directly to the table and, after presenting the food to guests, serve portions onto the guests' plates. Russian service can be as elegant as French service, but it's faster and more practical than French service. It's sometimes used for banquets.

Buffet Service

For buffet service, foods are attractively arranged on platters that are placed on large serving tables so that guests may serve themselves. Sometimes, a separate table is used for each course. Plates, flatware, and other necessary items are conveniently located.

Some restaurants offer only buffet service. Some offer buffets part of the time; table service operations may have special buffets on weekends and holidays, for example. Others offer a combination of table and buffet service all the time; soup, salad, and dessert bars are examples of buffet service combined with table service.

Buffet service is sometimes used for banquets in combination with limited table service—usually for beverages.

Cafeteria Service

In most cafeterias, guests advance through serving lines, selecting their food items as they go. The most expensive or hardest-to-serve food items are usually portioned by service staff. In some operations, however, cafeteria service is similar to buffet service; guests help themselves to items on display. Traditionally, cafeterias have required guests to enter the serving area, move along a straight-line serving counter, and pay for their meals at the end of the counter or as they exit the dining room. Today there are alternatives such as "scramble" layouts in which guests enter a cafeteria line and can bypass one another, going to separate serving stations that feature various types of foods. For example, there may be a salad bar, soup station, hot and cold sandwich area, entrée center, beverage center, and dessert bar. There is less of a waiting-in-line feeling when a scramble system is used.

Other Types of Service

Table service, buffet service, and cafeteria service are just a few of the most common approaches to food service today. Fast-food service, deli service, counter service, and tray service are among the others.

Fast-food operations generally offer seating as well as drive-through and take-out services. Service is limited to taking the guests' orders and giving the food to the guests on trays or in carry-out sacks or cartons.

Delis feature take-out service and also may offer limited seating at tables or at counters. Some restaurants have limited deli service. For example, fresh-baked breads and desserts may be available for guests to purchase when leaving the restaurant.

Counter service is often found in bars, lounges, snack shops, and coffee shops.

Tray service has been traditionally associated with institutional food service. Meals are plated, put on trays, kept hot or cold in special transport carts, and moved from preparation/plating areas to service areas as needed. A variation of tray service is used in the airline industry. All items except the hot entrée are placed on individual trays and kept chilled. After the entrée is heated, it's added to the tray and served.

Providing an Enjoyable Experience for Guests ──────────

Standard Operating Procedures

The primary goal of most table service operations is to provide an enjoyable experience for guests by meeting or exceeding guest expectations. This goal requires effective standard operating procedures that are consistently performed by all employees. Each operation should set its own policies and standard operating procedures.

Producing and serving quality products consistently is a prerequisite for success in the food and beverage business. Standard operating procedures are essential tools in this battle for consistency because they detail exactly what must be done and how it should be done. Managers cannot rely on employees' common sense to do the right thing at the right time. Tasks must be identified in job breakdowns, and procedures to perform the tasks must be spelled out clearly in step-by-step fashion. Exhibit 10.1 is a sample job breakdown incorporating standard operating procedures.

Performance standards that are measurable and observable should be tied to each operating procedure. Performance standards help managers and employees determine whether procedures are being performed correctly. Exhibit 10.2 is an example of performance standards developed for a food server.

Exhibit 10.1 Sample Job Breakdown

Job Breakdown

Job Breakdown #36: The ability to assist guests in making food and beverage selections.
Equipment needed: Guest check, pen. (Guests will already have menus and wine list.)

What to Do	How to Do It	Additional Information
1. Approach the table.	1. Stand erect. Look at the guests, smile, and greet them pleasantly. Introduce yourself. If you know their names, use them when you greet them. Be courteous.	1. You win the table with your first contact when you are pleasant and personable.
2. Take cocktail order.	2. Ask if guests would like a cocktail or appetizer wine. Be sure to get the complete details of the order, such as on-the-rocks, straight up, or extra olives. Remember which guest ordered each cocktail.	2. Most guests know which drinks they prefer. Be prepared to make suggestions, if appropriate. Do not push your personal preferences. Do not act surprised when a guest orders some non-standard drink.
3. Serve cocktails.	3. Place a cocktail napkin in front of each guest. Serve all beverages from the right with the right hand, when possible. Place cocktail glasses on napkins. Do not ask who ordered each drink. (You must remember.) As each drink is served, state what it is, such as Scotch and water, double martini, or Scotch-on-the-rocks.	3. Knowing who ordered what shows that you care about the order. Guests feel special when you repeat their order as you serve their drinks.
4. Check back for a second cocktail order.	4. Be courteous and bring the second round, if ordered, following the same procedure as the first round. Remove all first-round empty glasses and napkins. Put down new napkins and serve the drinks.	4. Check back when drinks are approximately two-thirds consumed.
5. Take the food order.	5. Ask the guests if they are ready to order. Explain the chef's specialty and answer any questions about the food. Take orders beginning with the women, when possible. Suggest appetizers, soup, or salads, as appropriate, to help them plan a complete meal. Proceed to the male guests. Be sure to inform the guests of the approximate cooking times of their selections. Communicate with the guest during this very important step. It is more than taking orders. It should be menu planning.	5. Guests expect you to know about the food. When you are asked a question and do not know the answer, do not bluff. Go to the kitchen or manager and find out the answer. Then go back and tell the guest. Suggesting menu items helps a hesitant guest make a decision he/she really wanted, especially if they may require some wait.

Exhibit 10.1 *(continued)*

What to Do	How to Do It	Additional Information
6. Take the wine order.	6. Ask, "Have you chosen a wine?" When you are asked to help, ask whether the guest prefers red or white, dry or semi-sweet, and other questions to get some idea of his/her preferences. Then point out two or three choices that fall within the characteristics described. The guest can choose according to price or other factors. Excuse yourself from the table and assure the guests that you will be right back with the first course.	6. Know the wine list. Always be careful to recognize the timid guest who is a novice at selecting wines. Be prepared to coach the guest through a selection process that will meet his/her needs. Experienced wine drinkers will usually know what they want to order and will not expect much assistance. This is not the time to feed your ego by demonstrating your technical wine knowledge and intimidating the guest. Be confident, but be courteous.

Source: Lewis C. Forrest, Jr., *Training for the Hospitality Industry*, 2d ed. (East Lansing, Mich.: Educational Institute of the American Hotel & Motel Association, 1989), pp. 32–33.

Guest Service Training

Every reasonable concern that a guest might have should be addressed in the standard operating procedures for guest service that are taught to all service personnel in training sessions. The old saying "the guest is always right" still applies, and that is the attitude that servers should convey. What is needed to improve service in many operations is not expensive equipment or an elaborate atmosphere, but a genuine concern for guests and the use of consistent service procedures.

Training service staff to properly welcome and serve guests is one of the chief responsibilities of dining room or food and beverage managers. Each component of the meal, beginning with before-meal drinks and appetizers and ending with after-dinner beverages or desserts, should be served according to standard operating procedures. Service staff must be polite, properly groomed, and have a genuine interest in helping guests enjoy the dining experience.

Servers must be able to identify properly plated entrées and other menu items; they need to know what these items should look like and what garnishes should be used. If an item doesn't look right—if a salad is made with brown-tinged lettuce, for example—servers need to know what procedures to follow to correct the fault.

Training should include sanitation and safety, topics which are covered in the next chapter. Serving, sanitation, and safety go hand in hand. Proper service cannot be provided if unsafe or unsanitary conditions exist.

Supervision throughout the service shift is necessary to prevent or solve problems, to ensure timely service, and to evaluate the training effort.

Teamwork

Cooperation and good communication between kitchen, bar, and dining room personnel are essential to the success of any restaurant. Making the guest's experience

Exhibit 10.2 Sample Performance Standards

Job Performance Standards: Food Server, Lunch Shift

A food server's performance in taking care of assigned tables for the lunch shift is considered good when the server performs the following duties according to the procedures documented in job breakdowns that were covered during training:

1. Arrives in the dining room by 10:30 A.M., rested and ready for work in a complete, clean uniform.
2. Has all assigned tables fully set up with tablecloths, napkins, glass and silverware, condiment sets, ashtrays, and matches by 11:15 A.M.
3. Greets guests cordially. Approaches the table as soon as guests are seated to provide necessary service.
4. Suggests a cocktail order while guests are deciding on food selections.
5. Engages in positive communications with the guests concerning daily specials and other menu selections; attempts suggestive selling of food and beverage offerings.
6. Attempts to sell a bottle, carafe, or glass of wine with lunch.
7. Writes orders on guest checks legibly, correctly using approved abbreviations.
8. Places orders in kitchen as soon as they are taken, following the kitchen call system for orders.
9. Picks up and delivers orders promptly; serves orders to all guests at a table at one time.
10. Serves food plates from guest's left side with left hand whenever possible.
11. Serves beverages from guest's right side with right hand whenever possible.
12. Serves wine and cocktails according to approved procedures.
13. Serves standard condiments with food orders without guest having to ask; serves special condiment requests quickly and pleasantly.
14. Checks back on each guest often for refills of beverages and to be sure that all guest requests are quickly filled.
15. Clears china, glassware, and silver from tables as guests complete courses; clears quietly from guest's right with right hand, removing serviceware to a tray on a sidestand nearby.
16. Attempts to sell desserts to all guests.
17. Offers coffee service at the end of the meal for all guests.
18. Presents the guest check promptly as soon as final course has been served.
19. Thanks guests for coming.
20. Immediately clears and resets table as soon as guests leave the dining room.

Source: Lewis C. Forrest, Jr., *Training for the Hospitality Industry*, 2d ed. (East Lansing, Mich.: Educational Institute of the American Hotel & Motel Association, 1989), p. 43.

an enjoyable one is not the responsibility of just one person. It requires the combined efforts of the chef, the chef's assistants, salad preparation personnel, food and beverage servers, buspersons, and others.

Teamwork between service and production employees is a must. Servers should turn in guests' orders to the kitchen in proper form and at the right time. Orders should be readied in the kitchen in reasonable time for all servers. Everyone must work together to obtain the best results.

Teamwork builds morale and esprit de corps—a spirit of cooperation that guests recognize and appreciate, and one that makes everyone's job easier and more enjoyable. Developing this spirit and maintaining it from pre-opening to end-of-shift activities is every food service manager's challenge.

Pre-Opening Concerns and Activities

While every dining room is unique, there are basic concerns that are common to all and certain tasks that are typically performed before any dining room is opened to guests. These include:

- Inspecting facilities
- Following reservation procedures
- Assigning food server stations
- Performing sidework
- Holding food server meetings

The person or persons responsible for carrying out these tasks will vary from one dining room to another. A dining room manager might be responsible for making inspections, assigning food server stations, and holding food server meetings. A host or receptionist may be responsible for taking reservations. Servers and buspersons generally perform sidework.

Inspecting Facilities

Facilities need to be inspected before the dining room is opened to ensure that any problems with room temperature, lighting, and so on are identified and resolved. Such safety hazards as rips in carpeting, loose banisters, wobbly tables, and wall decorations not securely fastened should be promptly corrected. A safety checklist can be used to remind you to check these and other potential problems. Additional inspection is necessary for sanitation purposes. Have the dining and public areas been properly cleaned? Are the tables set correctly? Are the chairs clean?

Some dining areas can be viewed from the street. You should go outside, look at the dining room from that perspective, and ask yourself, "If I were a potential guest, would the dining room and adjacent areas be attractive to me?"

Following Reservation Procedures

Some operations do not take guest reservations. Others have systems that allow guests to reserve seating at a specified time. Reservations are important to some guests, and the operation can benefit as well because staffing needs and production volumes can be more accurately estimated.

One type of reservation system offers reserved seating only at certain times—for example, 7:00 P.M. and 9:00 P.M. A more typical system offers reservations at staggered intervals during the entire meal period.

Many properties take telephone reservations. When this is done, it's critical that all required information be received. To avoid confusion, only a few employees should be permitted to accept reservations.

Since a reservation is a commitment that a table will be ready when required, managers must plan carefully. No-shows and diners who stay longer than usual make planning difficult. What should the dining room manager do when guests don't show up, come early or late, change the number in the party, or request a table other than the one reserved? Managers must anticipate these issues so that equitable and consistent procedures can be developed before problems arise.

Assigning Food Server Stations

Food server stations are generally assigned before the dining room opens. A food server station is a certain section of tables for which a server is responsible. In some operations, servers do not have assigned stations; instead, they are assigned tables by turns, as guests are seated. This means that food servers may wait on tables scattered throughout the dining room. Normally, this procedure is not recommended.

The number of tables assigned to a food server should depend on the:

• Number of seats

• Frequency that seats turn over

• Experience of the server

• Distance to the kitchen and bar

• Number of food servers scheduled for a specific meal period[2]

Needs of the specific operation are very important. A food server in a busy coffee shop, where tables turn over several times in a short interval, may not be able to serve the same number of guests as a server in a dining room featuring leisurely dining and having low seat turnover.

Performing Sidework

Setup and cleanup work must be done before dining rooms are opened. These activities are referred to as "sidework." Examples of sidework include filling salt-and-pepper shakers, filling bun warmers with rolls, watering dining room plants, polishing tabletops, and replenishing server supply stations. Food service employees know this work must be done, but they may object to doing it. Sidework tasks can be rotated among service personnel so that no employee consistently gets the "easy" or "hard" assignments.

Emphasize to all employees the importance of doing sidework to prepare the dining room for service. If the work is not done, supplies will likely be needed at the busiest times when service staff are not available to do the work, and safety and sanitation problems will eventually arise. Teach new employees that sidework is an important part of their job. With proper supervision, you can reduce or eliminate problems that many operations have in keeping up with sidework.

Holding Food Server Meetings

A brief food server meeting before the dining room opens can be helpful. At this time, server stations should be reviewed, daily specials explained, questions answered, and menu prices reviewed. This time can also be used to taste new dishes and provide training on how menu items are made. Food server supply stations should be checked to ensure they are properly stocked. A final discussion with the chef and opening service staff will confirm that everything is ready and that the dining room can be opened.

Providing Guest Service

Guests should be welcomed cordially as they enter the dining room—by a host, maître d', receptionist, or someone in a similar position. If the dining room accepts reservations, the guests should be asked whether they have made one.

Seating may be handled by the same person who welcomes the guests. When seating guests, satisfy requests for special tables if possible. Provide assistance to handicappers if they ask for it. A no-smoking section should be set aside for guests who wish to dine in a smoke-free area. This is required by law in many localities.

Always provide the best available table. Tables in traffic aisles, next to kitchen doors, or near server supply stations are less desirable and should be held until no better tables are left. The employee responsible for seating should work closely with food servers to ensure that the workload is evenly distributed. There is a fine balance between rotating tables so that all food servers get a fair chance at tips and providing quality service to guests.

There is no one step-by-step serving process.[3] Each operation has its own way of serving guests. To simplify discussion, this section looks at one example of a dinner service sequence in a table service restaurant using American service and offering alcoholic beverages. More details about serving alcoholic beverages will follow in the next section.

A Service Sequence

In the service sequence that follows, all serving activities are performed by servers. In many operations, some of the activities would be carried out by buspersons or other personnel. The sequence begins after guests have been seated:

- *Welcome the guests.* Extend a personal welcome to guests; be friendly, and make the guests feel comfortable.

- *Serve or pour water.* Use tongs or a scoop for ice.

- *Present the menu and the wine list.* The menu and wine list, whether open or closed, should be right side up.

- *Take the beverage order.* Carefully note how the guests wish their beverages to be served.

- *Serve the beverages.* Generally, beverages are served from the guest's right with the right hand.

- *Ask the guests if they wish to order appetizers.* They also may wish to order another drink.

- *Serve the appetizers.* Food is generally served from the guest's left with the left hand.

- *Take the food order.* Suggest any specials of the day. Answer any questions. Make sure you know who ordered what.

- *Take the wine order.* Make suggestions if appropriate.

Taking the guests' orders.

- *Remove the appetizer dishes.* Clearing is usually performed from the guest's right with the right hand.

- *Follow order-placing procedures for food items.* Write your orders carefully; use the correct abbreviations.

- *Serve the wine.* See the section on wine service which follows.

- *Serve salad and bread.* Soft bread is usually served warm; hard rolls usually at room temperature. Salads should be chilled.

- *Remove salad dishes.* But first, make sure the guests are finished. Some guests continue eating their salads when their entrées arrive.

- *Serve the entrée and its accompaniments.* Place the entrée plate so that the main item is closest to the guest. Place side dishes to the left.

- *Ask if everything is prepared satisfactorily.* Know what to do if something is not satisfactory.

- *Clear the table.* But make sure the guests are finished before clearing.

- *Take the dessert order.* After-dinner drinks might be included in any suggestions.

- *Serve dessert and/or after-dinner drinks.* Guests may want water and/or coffee with their desserts.

- *Present the guest check.* This is a critical point. Do not make the guests wait for their check. Present it as soon as possible after determining that they do not wish to order anything else.

The list just presented is purposely sketchy. It's meant only to suggest what must be done to meet guests' basic expectations in some dining rooms. What it takes to exceed guests' expectations is often unique to each operation and its servers. Servers can go a long way toward making the experience a pleasant and memorable one by putting themselves in the guests' position and thinking of how they would like to be treated if they were guests. Exhibit 10.3 is an example of advice that dining room managers can give to servers to educate and motivate them.

Special Situations

There are a multitude of concerns in serving: what to do when a guest is in a hurry, when a guest complains, when a guest is difficult, and so on. Exhibit 10.4 identifies some of the ways in which guest complaints can be addressed. While it's impossible to detail what might be done in any number of operations, it's important to point out that policies and procedures dealing with special situations should be established.

Some special situations and concerns relate to the serving of alcoholic beverages.

Serving Alcoholic Beverages. Bartenders often serve as well as prepare drinks. Bartenders and beverage servers must be trained so they will know exactly what their job involves and how to perform it properly. On-the-job training programs and using bar backs (assistant bartenders who perform backup tasks while learning bartending procedures) are two training methods. After bartenders and beverage servers are trained, they must be well-supervised to ensure that service procedures are followed.

Effective procedures for serving beverages should fit the needs of the specific operation. The following are among important practices in taking beverage orders:

- The guest's exact order must be noted and followed; that is, "on the rocks" (with ice), "up" (no ice), a specific brand, a particular garnish, and so on.

- Drinks should be carried on a cocktail tray.

- The cocktail tray should rest in one hand while drinks are served from the other; it should never rest on the table.

- Drinks are typically served from the guest's right with the right hand.

- Glasses should be cleared from the table as soon as they are empty (from the guest's right with the right hand), and guests may be asked if they wish to order another drink.

Exhibit 10.3 Advice for Servers

Serving is a very old and honorable occupation dating back many centuries. As in any job, fully knowing your craft (and the standards your restaurant expects of you) is the most important starting point. Here are a few other helpful hints:

1. Always have a positive attitude. Never give off "negative vibes" to a guest.

2. Make sure your personal appearance—from you hair, to your nails, to your shoes—is the best it can be. Always look neat and clean. Don't use overpowering colognes or perfumes.

3. Always be aware of what your guests may need. Psychics would make perfect servers because they would always know ahead of time what their guests needed. But, if you pay attention and use common sense, often you'll be able to predict what your guests need before they need it (condiments, more beverages, and so on).

4. Use the "Golden Rule." If you treat your guests the way you wish you were treated when you dine out, you should have some very happy people at your tables.

5. Remember that you are in charge of your tables. *Everything* that goes on at your tables reflects on you. Make sure your "assistants" (buspeople, chefs, bartenders, and managers) know that you will serve only the best. You *must* have high standards and keep them up.

6. Two of the most important service skills are timing and organization. Without these skills, just waiting on one table can be a problem. You must work on your timing and organization skills—they don't come overnight.

7. Always make time for your guests. When you are at a table, make sure you're there mentally as well as physically—don't be thinking about what you need to get for the next table. No matter how busy you are, always slow down when you are at tableside serving guests. Most guests don't mind waiting a few minutes for you if you give them time when you are with them.

8. Always check the condition of your tables at the beginning of your shift, and as much as possible during the shift. Remember, this may be the first time your guests have dined with you; you want them to remember you for the perfectionist you are.

9. Be *very* knowledgeable about the food you serve. Know how *everything* is prepared. Be aware of what you are able to do for guests on special diets.

10. Be knowledgeable about where you work. This is especially important here at Opryland Hotel. You'll always be asked questions, and it's important to know the correct answers.

11. Stay with your tables. Don't talk with another employee or do unnecessary sidework while your guests need you. Always be there for them.

12. Don't be afraid to make suggestions on food and wine. You work here, you should know about these things! Always have some suggestions ready that you feel very comfortable with. The importance of knowledge about what you serve can't be overstated.

13. Take a real interest in what your guest says to you—most people really appreciate a good listener. Manners are also very important. Make sure you always behave in a proper way.

14. Realize when your guests need to be left alone. You'll see many romantic couples and many businesspeople who don't want you to hover over them. "Read" your guests—you must be able to know when they need or want you around and when you are in the way.

15. Don't let unfortunate incidents get to you. You can't let dropping a tray of food or not receiving a tip from a guest interfere with your work. These things happen to every server on occasion—the best thing to do is to recover and keep going.

16. Last but not least, always be professional. Treating your work seriously and learning all you can about the craft of serving can make you feel better about yourself and your job, and may lead to higher tips from more satisfied guests.

Courtesy of Opryland Hotel, Food & Beverage Training Department, Nashville, Tennessee

Exhibit 10.4 Handling Guest Complaints

In spite of all efforts that food service managers and employees undertake to please guests, some complaints are still likely to occur. Suggestions for handling guest complaints include the following:

- Remember that you are dealing with a person and his or her feelings, not just with a problem.
- Look at the situation from the guest's perspective; consider how you would feel and how you would want to be treated.
- Listen with concern and give the guest your undivided attention.
- Maintain eye contact and avoid interruptions.
- Stay calm and in control of the situation.
- Apologize for the problem. Even when you disagree with guests, apologies may make them feel better.
- Empathize. Showing empathy tells guests you know how they feel. Be sensitive to the problem and communicate this understanding to them.
- Ask questions and be prepared to take notes. Learn as many details as you can about the problem so that you can determine the best solution.
- Offer solutions. Tell the guests what you can do and if possible offer several options. However, don't make promises you can't fulfill.
- Act on the problem. Follow your property's standard procedures and do exactly what you promised the guest. Tell the guest how long it will take to resolve the problem.
- Monitor progress. If another employee or department is involved, stay in touch to help assure the problem gets corrected.
- Follow up. If you feel it won't disturb the guest, check back to make sure he or she is satisfied once the problem has been corrected.

Source: *Front Office: Handling Guest Complaints* (East Lansing, Mich.: Educational Institute of the American Hotel & Motel Association, 1986). Videotape.

Serving wine. Wine is increasingly popular in the United States, and many guests are knowledgeable about wines. Therefore, it's important that servers know at least some basics about wine and wine service.

The quality of a wine is determined by the grape that is used in its making and the skill of the wine-maker, among other factors. The color of a wine depends partly on how the grapes are handled and partly on their color. Color is extracted from the skin, not the juice, so red grape skins are carefully removed from red grapes being fermented for white wine. Red wine can only be made from grapes with red skins and fermentation is done "in the skins." The alcoholic content of most wines ranges from 11% to 13%.

Many operations offer "house" or "jug" wines for sale by the glass or carafe. For these wines, service is quite simple; servers merely ask the bartender for a glass or carafe of the wine the guest ordered, and serve it properly.

Service becomes more complicated in operations that offer bottled wines and wine lists. Here are some guidelines that can be followed when guests order wine by the bottle:

- Bring the bottle to the table before opening it. The bottle should rest on a white napkin or towel as the label is shown to the guest who ordered the wine.

- When the guest approves the wine, open the wine following the correct procedures: hold the bottle, cut the foil top and peel it away, wipe the cork and the bottle rim with the napkin or towel, insert the corkscrew and twist until it holds, then pull the cork out and place it at the right side of the guest who ordered the wine. (The guest may wish to examine the cork.)

- After the cork is removed, wipe the rim again.

- Allow the host to sample a small amount of the wine.

- After the host approves, fill the wine glasses of all the guests at the table. The proper amount per glass differs from operation to operation; usually a "full" glass is no more than two-thirds or one-half full.

- Know what to do if the host does not approve of the wine.

- The wine bottle should be placed at the right of the host's wine glass. If the wine is red, no ice bucket is necessary; red wine is normally served at room temperature. If the wine is white, it should be placed in an ice bucket draped with a clean napkin.

Serving alcohol with care. Managers have a personal, professional, and social responsibility to serve alcohol with care. Drunk drivers are responsible for approximately half the driving fatalities in the United States each year. Alcohol is also a factor in up to 70% of all drowning deaths and in about 30% of suicides.[4]

Many states have passed legislation establishing third-party liability for accidents involving intoxicated drivers. Such laws, called Dram Shop Acts, often state that bartenders, servers, and owners can be jointly held liable if they unlawfully sell alcoholic beverages to a minor or an intoxicated person who then causes injury to others.

In some states without a specific Dram Shop Act, operations and servers have been held liable for damages under common law. The factor behind this liability is server negligence. Negligence is "failure to exercise the care that a reasonably prudent person would exercise under like or similar circumstances."

Today's legislation regarding third-party liability can change rapidly. Regardless of the specific third-party liability in your location, good sense dictates responsibility in your service of alcoholic beverages. No one should sell beverages to minors or to those who are intoxicated. Service staff should be taught to identify minors by recognizing false identification and observing characteristics and actions frequently exhibited by minors, such as nervousness, sticking closely to a group, and pooling money and giving it to another person to buy drinks.

Employees should understand that a 12-ounce glass of beer, a 4-ounce glass of wine, and a 1-ounce serving of 100-proof liquor all have approximately the same $1/2$-ounce of pure alcohol. They should know the legal definition of intoxication. While this varies, in many states someone is legally intoxicated when the blood-alcohol concentration (BAC) in his or her blood reaches .10 gram of alcohol or higher per 100 milliliters of blood.

How many drinks can someone consume before becoming intoxicated? There is no precise answer to this question because so many factors influence the effects of alcohol. However, one approach relates the weight of an individual to the number

Exhibit 10.5 A BAC Chart Based on Weight

KNOW YOUR LIMITS

**CHART FOR RESPONSIBLE PEOPLE WHO MAY SOMETIMES
DRIVE AFTER DRINKING!**

Approximate Blood Alcohol Percentage

DRINKS	1	2	3	4	5	6	7	8
100	.04	.09	.13	.18	.22	.26	.31	.35
120	.04	.07	.11	.15	.18	.22	.26	.29
140	.03	.06	.09	.13	.16	.19	.22	.25
160	.03	.06	.08	.11	.14	.17	.19	.22
180	.02	.05	.07	.10	.12	.15	.17	.20
200	.02	.04	.07	.09	.11	.13	.15	.18
220	.02	.04	.06	.08	.10	.12	.14	.16
240	.02	.04	.06	.07	.09	.11	.13	.15

Body Weight in Pounds

| Influenced Rarely | Possibly | Definitely |

Subtract .01% for each 40 minutes or .03% for each 2 hours of drinking.
One drink is 1 1/4 oz. of 80-proof liquor, 12 oz. of beer, or 4 oz. of table wine.

**SUREST POLICY IS…
DON'T DRIVE AFTER DRINKING!**

Source: Distilled Spirits Council of the United States, Inc.

*This chart is provided for information only. Nothing contained in this chart shall constitute an endorsement by the Educational Institute of the American Hotel & Motel Association (the Institute) or the American Hotel & Motel Association (AH&MA) of any information, opinion, procedure, or product mentioned, and the Institute and AH&MA disclaim any liability with respect to the use of such information, procedure, or product, or reliance thereon.

Source: *Serving Alcohol with Care,* 2d ed., an industry-taught seminar (East Lansing, Mich.: Educational Institute of the American Hotel & Motel Association, 1988), p. 38.

of drinks that may be consumed before reaching a BAC of .10 (see Exhibit 10.5). A large, heavy person experiences fewer effects with the same amount of alcohol than does a smaller, lighter person. However, care must be taken in relying on this chart since it only considers weight and number of drinks consumed. An active, fit individual has a high percentage of muscle in relation to fat and is typically less influenced by alcohol. Since women tend to have a higher percentage of body fat than men, women may absorb more alcohol into their bloodstreams than men of the

Exhibit 10.6 Traffic Light Rating System

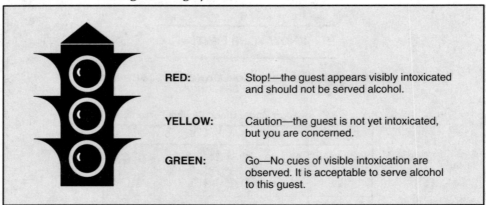

RED:		Stop!—the guest appears visibly intoxicated and should not be served alcohol.
YELLOW:		Caution—the guest is not yet intoxicated, but you are concerned.
GREEN:		Go—No cues of visible intoxication are observed. It is acceptable to serve alcohol to this guest.

Source: *Serving Alcohol with Care,* 2d ed., an industry-taught seminar (East Lansing, Mich.: Educational Institute of the American Hotel & Motel Association, 1988), p. 41.

same weight consuming a like number of drinks. Fatigue and many common illnesses also affect how the body responds to alcohol. When alcohol is consumed by someone in a weakened condition, the result is quicker intoxication.

There are several behavioral warning signs that can help service employees recognize that a guest is becoming intoxicated. These include:

- Relaxed inhibitions

- Impaired judgment

- Slow reactions

- Decreased coordination

The traffic light rating system (see Exhibit 10.6) can be used to help determine if guests should continue to be served alcoholic beverages. Monitoring alcohol consumption begins in the green zone when servers first observe guests and look for behavioral warning signs of intoxication. Each time a guest orders another drink it's important to re-evaluate the guest's rating. As guests rated green become more relaxed and less inhibited, the rating may change to yellow. A person in the yellow zone will exhibit relaxed inhibitions and impaired judgment. Slow reaction time and loss of coordination will be exhibited by a drinker in the red zone. No person in the red zone should ever be allowed to drive.

It's important for service employees to communicate their observations about guests to other servers, bartenders, and managers. The server or manager should intervene when necessary to "cut off" intoxicated guests. The following suggestions can help reduce the possibility of a troublesome confrontation:

- Alert a backup.
- Remove alcohol from the guest's sight and reach.
- Be non-judgmental.

- Be firm.

- Minimize the confrontation.

- Remind the intoxicated guest that driving while intoxicated is dangerous and against the law, and suggest an alternate form of transportation.

- Consider calling the police if a person insists on driving while intoxicated.

- Keep a personal record of the incident.

Food and Beverage Income Control Procedures

As a manager, you must be concerned about controlling sales income during food and beverage service. Procedures must be implemented to help ensure that income is received for all items served.[5]

There are many ways that dishonest employees try to "beat the house." As a manager, you should ask: "If I were an employee who wanted to steal, how would I do it?" To the extent that you can answer this question, possible problems are identified. You must resolve them. Do not assume your employees are honest and will never steal. While the majority of employees may be honest, there are likely to be others who are not.

Income Control and Servers

With Guest Check Systems. With a guest check system, no order for a food or beverage product should be taken from the guest without listing each item on a guest check, and no food or beverage order should be prepared if it's not on a guest check. When a guest check control system is used, numbered guest checks are issued to food servers and these guest checks become their responsibility. The amount of sales income that a food server should have collected is determined by adding the totals on all the guest checks they wrote.

Many properties use duplicate guest checks. The copy is given to production employees and can, at a later time, be compared with the original given to the guest and retained by the cashier.

With Precheck Registers. A precheck register is like a cash register except that no cash drawer is used. When precheck registers are used, a server takes the guest's order, writes it on a guest check, and goes to the precheck register. The check is inserted into the machine, a clerk key (identifying which server is using the machine) is pressed, and the guest's order is entered into the machine. Use of the precheck register authorizes the order on the guest check to be prepared. The order is taken to the kitchen (or it can be sent by a remote printer) and prepared. Before the server leaves at the end of the shift, the orders he or she entered into the precheck register are totaled to assess the amount of sales income due from the guest checks the server wrote. The actual guest checks are totaled and this amount is compared with the server's total from the precheck register.

Income Collection Systems. There are two basic income collection systems. With the server banking system, the server keeps all income collected from guests until the end of the shift. With the cashier banking system, the cashier (or bartender)

Exhibit 10.7 Receipt of Cash Bank

By signing on the last unsigned line below, I acknowledge receipt of cash in the amount of $ to be used as a cash register bank. The total amount is due and payable before checking out at the end of the shift.		
Name	Date of Shift	Returned (Signature of Manager on Duty)

operates a cash register, collects guest checks or drink tickets and cash from food servers, and retains the funds until the end of the shift.

The amount of sales income due from servers is determined by totaling and comparing precheck register totals with guest check totals. This amount of money is collected from the server (if a server banking system is used) or from the cashier (if a cashier banking system is used).

Income Control and Beverage Personnel

The bartender is unique within a food and beverage operation. What other position is responsible for taking and preparing guest orders, determining the amount of money that should be collected, collecting sales income, and ringing up sales into the cash register? Bartenders serve guests at the bar, and at tables when service personnel are absent. Bartenders may also be responsible for serving food. Frequently, there is no practical way to separate all of these tasks.

Bartenders must be given a cash bank at the beginning of their shifts. In many properties, a bartender must complete a form similar to the one shown in Exhibit 10.7. In this way the bartender certifies that the cash bank has been received and that he or she is responsible for the amount of cash in the bank until the bank is returned at the end of the shift.

Certain income control procedures should be performed at the end of each bartender's shift.[6] The bartender must account for all beverage guest checks. The amount of money in the cash register must be verified with tallies of guest checks, precheck register totals, and a review/verification of sales rung for each server. Use of precheck registers and guest checks along with sales journal tapes located in the cash register provide information to verify the amount of sales income for which the bartender is responsible. Issuing procedures are also an important part of the bartender's closing procedures. Management should ensure that the amount of liquor at the bar at the beginning of the bartender's shift is accounted for at the end of the shift (this includes keeping track of empty bottles).

Supervising a bartender is difficult, especially when the operation is busy. Nevertheless, managers should take some time to observe what the bartender is doing. Common theft methods include working from the tip jar instead of the register and not ringing up drinks that are served. A dishonest bartender can use the "no sale" key to deposit money collected from guests into the cash drawer. Because it was entered into the register as a "no sale," this money is not recorded or accounted for on the register tapes. Swizzle sticks, maraschino cherries, bent matches, a slip of paper with several tears, etc., are common methods dishonest bartenders use to track unrecorded drinks representing cash they are "owed" from the cash drawer. Managers should occasionally go behind the bar, read the amount of sales rung on the register, and replace the first cash drawer with a new one. The amount of money in the first drawer should equal the original cash balance plus the amount of sales rung up on the register since the beginning of the shift. More money than this may represent income deposited as "no sales" that the bartender intends to steal.

Other methods of theft and precautions that can be taken to protect against them are listed in Exhibit 10.8.

Shopper Services for Bartender Control. Sometimes a shopper service is used to check bartenders. A shopper service provides a "shopper" to pose as a guest to observe the beverage operation. Shopper services may be used primarily for detecting bartender theft, but the service can also be used to look at the entire operation with the aim of making improvements.

All bartenders should be checked routinely. (Bartenders should be told when hired that shoppers may be used.) New bartenders or persons that the managers have reason to suspect may be shopped more frequently. Obviously, the bartenders must not know or recognize the shopper.

Shoppers should meet with management staff before visiting the bar to get acquainted with all pertinent procedures and systems. If there are special problems, the shopper can be told about them during the meeting.

When the shopper visits the bar, he or she should order a drink and carefully observe the bartender as he or she takes the order, prepares the drink, serves it, and collects cash for the drink. How the bartender rings it up on the cash register should also be noted. The shopper can remain at the bar and casually observe various transactions and interactions. However, it's important for him or her to visit the restroom, look at other public areas, and react as a guest to the total experience.

At the conclusion of the visit, the shopper reports all findings to the manager. The shopper may have observed signs of dishonesty, such as misuse of the cash register; pouring free drinks; or suspicious conversations between the bartender and employees or guests. With this information, the manager can take steps to deal with the problem.

Beverage servers also can manipulate beverage products and/or money in order to steal from the property. Common types of beverage server theft are listed in Exhibit 10.9.

Enhancing Food and Beverage Sales

Maximizing economic objectives while meeting the needs of guests is a goal common to all food and beverage managers in commercial operations. To meet this goal, they need the help of their guest-contact employees: the servers.

Exhibit 10.8 Bartender Control Techniques

Common Types of Bartender Theft	Precautions
Violating procedures for cash register operation, incuding bunching sales, no rings, and working out of the tip jar.	• Specific register operating procedures should be developed. • The tip jar should not be near the register. • Supervision is necessary to ensure that all required procedures are followed consistently.
Under-pouring or diluting drinks and pocketing cash from the sale of the "extra drink."	• Require that a shot glass or jigger be used when preparing all drinks.
Bringing in personal bottles of liquor, preparing drinks from these bottles, and keeping the money.	• Mark bottles and check them often enough to eliminate this practice.
Accumulating drink sales from liquor served from the entire bottle, recording a "bottle sale" (usually at a lower sales price than the drinks) and pocketing the difference.	• Implement effective cash register operating controls. • Supervise employees closely. • Establish a rule that all drinks served must be tallied on guest checks.
Selling drinks for cash and recording drinks as spilled, returned, or complimentary.	• No drinks should be served without charge unless approved by the manager. • Returned drinks should not be discarded without the manager's approval.
Serving and ringing up a low quality brand but charging the higher call-brand price when a call brand is requested. The bartender pockets the extra cash resulting from the substitution.	• All drink orders should be written on a guest check. • The amount rung up and printed on the guest check should equal the total charge on the check.
Bartender working in collusion with beverage server(s) so drinks are served but income is not received.	• Use a rotating schedule for employees. • Be aware of gossip about employee relationships. • Monitor beverage cost percentages.
Lowering sales income value written on the guest check and rung into the register (undercharging).	• Routine audits of guest checks should be made to audit pricing errors.
Trading liquor with the cook for food products.	• All employee eating and drinking policies should be enforced. • Be aware of signs of against-policy eating and drinking by employees, such as plates and glasses hidden in work stations or restrooms.
Using stolen checks to replace cash.	• No checks should be accepted without the manager's approval.
Using counterfeit guest checks to collect sales income.	• Use unique, hard-to-duplicate guest checks.
Taking cash from the cash drawer.	• A basic sales income control system can determine how much money should be in the cash drawer. • Consider making the bartender liable for all cash shortages (if legal in your locality).
Giving away drinks to promote a bigger tip, or giving drinks to friends.	• No complimentary drinks should be given without the manager's approval. • Guest checks must be in front of each guest at all times.

Exhibit 10.9 Beverage Server Control Techniques

Common Types of Beverage Server Theft	Precautions
Receiving beverages from the bar without recording them on a guest check.	• No beverages should be given to personnel without a copy of the guest check unless cash is paid for drinks when they are picked up.
Collecting cash from the guest without a guest check and pocketing the cash.	• Same as above.
Reusing paid checks or collecting cash from one guest with a guest check that has already been presented to another.	• All guest checks given to the beverage server should be recorded by number and matched with duplicates. • Servers must not remove a beverage from the preparation area without a check
Collecting cash and destroying the guest check.	• Same as above.
Under-adding checks or omitting items for friends in order to influence the amount of the tip.	• Guest checks should be audited to check arithmetic. • Original and duplicate copies should be matched.
Providing high-priced items to friends and recording them at a lower price.	• Match original and duplicate checks to ensure that items picked up from the bar were, in fact, the items for which payment was received.
Collecting sales income from guests and alleging that they left without paying.	• Close supervision of all guest service areas will minimize walk-outs. • Any server with more than an infrequent rate of walk-outs should be retrained and closely supervised.
Collecting income, destroying the check, and stating that the check was lost while turning in the allegedly correct amount.	• Where legal, servers should be assessed and charged for lost checks. • Servers with more than an infrequent rate of lost checks should be retrained and closely supervised.
Collecting sales income for a check, deleting items because of alleged returns, and pocketing the cash.	• All returns should be reported to the manager as they occur.
Serving guests, collecting sales income, deleting items (for example, a guest allegedly didn't have a drink) and pocketing the cash.	• Original and duplicate copies of the check can be matched.
Eating food and drinking beverages.	• All policies regarding employee eating and drinking should be enforced.

Suggestive Selling

Suggestive selling embraces a variety of techniques that servers can use to encourage guests to buy certain menu items.[7] Suggestive selling calls for tact on the part of servers. When guests know what they want, absolutely no effort should be made to change their minds. However, some guests may not know what they want and might appreciate some assistance.

Two objectives of suggestive selling are to (1) increase sales of the most profitable items, and (2) increase the check average (check average refers to the total dollars of food and beverage sales divided by the total number of guests consuming a meal).

Let's look first at suggestive selling aimed at increasing sales of the most profitable menu items. The food server can draw the guest's attention to these items and make recommendations when the menu is presented. This technique works especially well when the operation has planned its menu around the items it wants to sell. For example, items that head a list, are boxed, or have written descriptions may sell with greater frequency than other items.

To increase the check average, food servers should ask questions that cannot be answered with a "No": "Our strawberry shortcake is fantastic and the chef's own special cherry pie just came out of the oven—which would you like?" Or, "Would you like a white or a red wine with dinner?"

"You've probably noticed all of the desserts we've prepared tableside this evening. Everyone raves about our cherries jubilee and flaming crepes—which would you prefer?" is an example that illustrates another important concept of suggestive selling: people are influenced by what they see being consumed around them. If guests see a Caesar salad being prepared tableside, this may strongly influence them to order the salad.

Suggestive selling can be applied to cafeteria service as well as table service operations. A server can make suggestions to guests as they pass through the cafeteria's serving line. Suggestive selling also has implications for buffet service. The way that items are placed on the buffet line and the use of garnishes can affect the guests' desire to take portions of the menu items.

Selling Beverages

The sale of alcoholic beverages can be of great economic value to food and beverage operations. Contribution margins are high from beverage sales; after product cost is subtracted from income, there is a significant amount left over to contribute to profits. That's why in the "old days" many food service managers made special efforts to "push the alcoholic beverages."

Today, however, the emphasis is on serving alcohol with care. While many observers feared significant losses in profitability as the new social concerns about alcohol emerged, these fears have proven unfounded. Operators have been able to enhance dining experiences for their guests and increase profits while still being socially responsible.

To effectively sell beverages, employees should know:

- Exactly what drinks are available
- Something about the drinks
- How to make suggestions
- Which wines to suggest with menu items
- How to present, open, and serve wine

To increase beverage sales most effectively, service staff must be trained.

A well-rounded wine list is very important. Entire books have been written on the topic.[8] A good list should include dry and sweet wines, white and red wines, and champagne (sparkling wine) at low, medium, and high prices.

The wine list is an important marketing tool. Descriptions of the wine—even if it's only two or three words—can be of great help. Recommended wines can be listed next to appropriate items on the food menu. Wine displays set up around the dining room, wine tasting stations where guests can sample various wines at no cost, table tent cards, and menu inserts may also help sell wine. Some properties employ a wine steward (sometimes called a sommelier) who is very knowledgeable about wines to suggest wines to discriminating guests.

Some operations specialize in exotic tropical or flaming drinks. These operations should be sure that proper in-house merchandising is done. The manager should provide drink menus, table tent cards, and other merchandising items to make guests aware of the special drinks. The service staff must reinforce these messages. The manager can help motivate the staff by noting that as more beverages are sold, check averages increase and so should tips.

Seasonal drinks are relatively easy to sell. Tom and Jerry drinks during the Christmas season, green beer on St. Patrick's Day, and special fruit punch drinks during summer months are examples.

Many of the techniques used for alcoholic beverages can be used for in-house merchandising of non-alcoholic beverages. Part of the secret of selling non-alcoholic beverages is for them to be expertly prepared and attractively presented. Standard recipes are an important first step. Selection of distinctive glassware and appropriate garnishes also helps in suggestive selling.

Contests among employees can help boost beverage sales. A free bottle of wine or free meals for a service employee and guest are examples of incentives for service staff to sell beverages.

The bottom line is that you must always try to meet the guests' wants in the type of products, service, and atmosphere you provide. If you can find some way to distinguish your beverage products from those of the competition—or from the products the guest can make at home—you are more likely to increase beverage sales.

Endnotes

1. See Anthony M. Rey and Ferdinand Wieland, *Managing Service in Food and Beverage Operations* (East Lansing, Mich.: Educational Institute of the American Hotel & Motel Association, 1985), pp. 243–275.

2. Carol A. King, *Professional Dining Room Management* (Rochelle Park, N.J.: Hayden, 1980), p. 32.

3. A detailed account of professional guest service is beyond the scope of this book. Interested readers are referred to Rey and Wieland, *Managing Service*, Chapters 9–12. Also, two videotapes—*Professional Dining Room Service, Parts I and II*—are available from the Educational Institute.

4. This discussion is based largely on *Serving Alcohol with Care*, 2d ed., an industry-taught seminar (East Lansing, Mich.: Educational Institute of the American Hotel & Motel Association, 1988). *Serving Alcohol with Care* is also available on videotape.

5. For more information, see Jack D. Ninemeier, *Planning and Control for Food and Beverage Operations,* 3d ed. (East Lansing, Mich.: Educational Institute of the American Hotel & Motel Association, 1991).

6. Details of bartender closing procedures are beyond the scope of this chapter. For more information, see Ninemeier, *Planning and Control,* 3d ed.

7. Suggestive selling by food and beverage servers is the topic of *Food & Beverage Suggestive Selling* (East Lansing, Mich.: Educational Institute of the American Hotel & Motel Association, 1988). Videotape.

8. An excellent reference on beverages is Harold J. Grossman, *Grossman's Guide to Wines, Beers, and Spirits,* 6th rev. ed., revised by Harriet Lembeck (New York: Scribner, 1977).

Key Terms

buffet service	negligence
cafeteria service	sidework
Dram Shop Acts	suggestive selling
food server station	table service
intoxication (legal definition)	

Discussion Questions

1. How does the French style of table service differ from the Russian style?

2. How does English table service differ from American table service?

3. What is the primary goal of most table service operations?

4. Why are standard operating procedures important?

5. What factors should be considered when determining the number of tables to assign to food servers?

6. What are some important points that servers should know in order to serve alcoholic beverages with care?

7. What are some guidelines that food service managers and servers can follow to help reduce the possibility of a troublesome confrontation with an intoxicated guest?

8. How does a server banking system differ from a cashier banking system?

9. What precautions can managers take to protect against theft by bartenders?

10. From the food service operator's perspective, what are the two primary objectives of suggestive selling?

Chapter Outline

Sanitation
- What Causes Unsafe Food?
    - Chemical Poisoning
    - Harmful Germs
- Foodborne Illnesses
    - Food Poisoning
    - Food Infection
- Personal Cleanliness and Health
- Sanitary Procedures for Safe Food Handling
    - Purchasing
    - Receiving
    - Storing
    - Preparing
    - Serving
- Cleaning Up
    - Ware Washing
    - Cleaning Kitchen and Dining Areas
    - Procedures for Handling Garbage and Refuse

Safety
- OSHA
- Food Service Accidents
    - Burns
    - Muscle Strains and Falls
    - Cuts
    - Equipment Accidents
    - Fire
- First Aid
- Accident Reports

Management's Role in Sanitation and Safety Programs
- Inspections

11

Sanitation and Safety

SANITATION AND SAFETY are two topics some food and beverage managers ignore at their peril. If an outbreak of food poisoning can be traced to your operation, the costs in human suffering, salaries and productivity (if employees become ill), medical and hospital expenses, bad publicity, and lost business can be devastating. The costs in human suffering, and the monetary costs to the operation, can also be great if a worker or guest is injured on your property because of unsafe conditions.

Sanitation must be addressed at every stage of the food handling process. Serious illness and even death can be caused by the failure to follow simple, basic food sanitation procedures. Safety concerns are just as vital. Food service managers have a personal, professional, and legal responsibility to provide safe conditions for employees and guests.

Sanitation

Food products must be purchased, received, stored, prepared, and served under sanitary conditions. Clean equipment must be used and sanitary work habits must be practiced. One of your most important duties as a food service manager is to make sure that the food being served to guests is safe and wholesome.[1]

Guests are concerned about sanitation. A nationwide survey conducted for the National Restaurant Association asked people to rank factors they consider important in choosing or returning to a restaurant. Cleanliness ranked number one when people wanted a fast-food or moderate-service restaurant. When people considered full-service restaurants, cleanliness ranked second only to food quality and preparation.[2]

The Food and Drug Administration's 1993 Food Code, upon which some of the recommendations in this chapter are based, contains sanitation guidelines designed to safeguard the public health. It is important to note that food service operations must comply with their own state and local recommendations, even though the state and local regulations may differ from the federal recommendations contained in the Food Code.

What Causes Unsafe Food?

In order to serve safe food, you must know what causes food to become unsafe. There are two causes of unsafe food: chemical poisoning and harmful germs.

Chemical Poisoning. Chemical poisoning occurs when toxic substances contaminate foods or beverages. Chemicals may be added before the food reaches the restaurant (apples may have pesticide residues on their skins, for example) or while the food is at the restaurant. An employee who is untrained, has reading problems, or to whom English is a second language may mistakenly substitute harmful cleaning chemicals for cooking ingredients, for example. Or improperly manufactured cooking containers or utensils may react with foods (especially those containing acids) to cause a relatively common type of chemical poisoning.

You can take many common-sense precautions to minimize the possibility of chemical poisoning. One obvious precaution is to buy food only from dependable sources. This may mean not purchasing food from "backdoor salespersons" who offer special buys on food that was grown or slaughtered locally. Another simple precaution is to wash fruits and vegetables to remove any pesticide residues or other chemicals.

Use caution when spraying for flies, cockroaches, and other insects; and when spreading chemicals for mice and rodents. Pesticides should be handled by someone trained in their use. Be careful with chemicals used to clean kitchen equipment. These cleaners must be approved for use around food and should be applied according to the manufacturer's instructions. Store all chemicals in appropriate containers away from areas where food is kept.

Harmful Germs. Germs are small living organisms all around us that are too small to be seen without a microscope. They vary in length, but it takes 2,500 to 13,000 of them, placed end to end, to make one inch.

Not all germs are harmful. Some are required to produce such foods as cheese, sauerkraut, and bread. Others help manufacture drugs and useful chemicals. Still others are in our bodies and help us digest and absorb vitamin K.

Some germs are dangerous. They cause illness and disease if they are allowed to multiply and spread to humans through food or some other means.

There are several types of harmful germs that can make food unsafe. Examples include bacteria, molds, parasites, and viruses. Unfortunately, the germs most harmful to people like many of the same foods we do: non-acidic, high-protein foods such as meat, fish, poultry, eggs, and milk; and baked goods with cream fillings. High-protein foods are most susceptible to germ growth and are classified as potentially hazardous. While all foods must be handled with care, potentially hazardous foods should be given special attention.

Germs need certain conditions in order to multiply. First, germs need moisture. Freezing or drying foods will not necessarily kill germs. Rather, since moisture is removed (in drying) or changed into another form (ice crystals in freezing), germs may become dormant but begin multiplying when moisture is again available—for example, when moisture is added to dry products or when frozen products are thawed.

Germs also need comfortable temperatures to thrive. A food temperature danger zone exists between 41°F (5°C) and 140°F (60°C). Germs will multiply rapidly if they are in foods that are within this temperature range. Food production and service personnel should do everything possible to keep foods out of this danger zone.

Acidity also affects the ability of germs to grow. Some germs can live in very acidic foods such as citrus fruits, but most germs grow best in "neutral" foods—foods that do not contain large amounts of acids. Unfortunately, many foods high

Germs need comfortable temperatures to thrive.

in protein (meats, seafood, eggs, milk, etc.) are in the neutral acid range. This reinforces the need to give special attention to protein foods.

Many other factors affect the optimal growth of germs. If you understand these factors and know how to make the environment "uncomfortable" for germs, you will be on your way to a safe, sanitary food service operation. Later in the chapter we will discuss germ-fighting strategies when purchasing, receiving, storing, preparing, and serving food.

Foodborne Illnesses

Harmful germs can cause foodborne illnesses (see Exhibit 11.1). There are two basic types of foodborne illnesses:

1. Food poisoning—illness caused by germ-produced poisons
2. Food infection—illness caused by germs in food

Food Poisoning. Food poisoning occurs when germs get into food and produce wastes that are poisonous. With food poisoning, it is the poison—not the germs themselves—that produces the illness.

Once a food is poisoned by germs, there is nothing you can do to make it safe for consumption. For example, if heat is applied to the food it will kill the germs, but it will not eliminate the poison. Another problem with the poison is that it often has no taste, odor, or color, so the common practice of smelling or tasting the food to see if it is all right is ineffective. At best, you will not be able to tell whether the food is safe. At worst, you may get sick yourself from tasting foods that contain poison.

Exhibit 11.1 Overview of Foodborne Illnesses

Type of Illness	How People Become Infected	Foods Commonly Associated With This Illness	How This Illness Can Be Prevented
Staph poisoning	Eating food infected by careless food handlers: Germs from cuts Coughing or sneezing around food	Potentially hazardous food that is high in protein content: Custard and cream dishes Meat dishes (especially ham, poultry, and meat salads)	Careful food handling habits School food service employees free from infections Thorough cooking of food followed by immediate serving or refrigeration
Botulism	Eating food containing poison from the bacteria	Canned goods which are not processed properly such as beans, corn, meat, and fish	Careful processing of canned foods School food service personnel not using home- or school-processed canned goods
Sam poisoning	Eating improperly cooked foods contaminated by: The organism Contact with fecal material (often from rodents)	Foods high in protein content, especially: Meats Poultry Eggs and egg products Baked products with cream fillings	Good personal habits of food handlers Thorough cooking and immediate serving or refrigeration of foods Good food storage practices
Clostridium perfringens	Eating food contaminated by: Food handlers Insects	Foods high in protein content, especially: Meats Poultry Sauces, soups, and gravies made with meat and poultry	Thorough cooking and immediate serving or refrigeration of foods Good food storage practices Good personal habits of food handlers
Strep	Eating foods contaminated by: Coughing or sneezing Dust, dirt from clothing, facility air	Foods high in protein content, especially: Milk, milk products Egg products Meats and poultry	Good personal habits of food handlers Pasteurization of milk Thorough cooking and immediate refrigeration of foods
Trichinosis	Eating pork products which are contaminated	Pork and pork products	Cooking pork and pork products thoroughly (155°F or 68°C minimum in center) Local, state, federal pork inspection
Tuberculosis	Eating food infected by food handlers who carry the disease	Foods high in milk or milk products	Milk pasteurization Proper sanitation of all eating, drinking, and cooking utensils Careful food handling Routine health exams for school food service employees

Remember: 1. Handle foods properly:
   a. Follow good personal hygiene habits.
   b. Be careful with all foods high in protein content.

2. Keep foods at proper temperature:
   a. Minimize the time that foods are in the temperature range of 41°F (5°C)–140°F (60°C).
   b. Keep foods hot and keep foods cold or don't keep the food at all.

Source: U.S. Department of Agriculture, Food and Nutrition Services, *Principles and Practices of Sanitation and Safety in Child Nutrition Programs*, Washington, D.C., undated.

Types of food poisoning. Staphylococcal poisoning—staph—is a common type of food poisoning. Staph germs are found on the skin and in the nose and throat of people with colds and sinus infections. Foods most often involved in staph poisoning are meats—especially ham, poultry, and meat salads—and cream foods such as cream puffs and cream-filled cakes. Illness usually occurs within four hours of eating the food. Symptoms are nausea, vomiting, abdominal pains, and diarrhea.

Another illness caused by poison in food is botulism. Fortunately, botulism is rare. It can be fatal, however. Botulism often results from eating improperly

Exhibit 11.2 Sample Procedures for Investigation of Alleged Food Poisoning

Here are some steps a food service manager may take if a guest calls the operation complaining of food poisoning. Managers should follow their own operation's policies, which may involve contacting upper management and the operation's attorney before any other action is taken.

1. Obtain the name, address, and phone number (at home and at work) of the guest.

2. Ask for specific signs and symptoms of the illness.

3. Get details about the menu items the guest consumed and when they were consumed; when the guest became ill; the duration of the illness; any medication taken for the illness; known allergies; and any medication or inoculation taken before the illness.

4. Obtain the name of the physician consulted and/or the hospital visited by the guest. If the guest has not seen a physician, encourage him or her to do so for a proper diagnosis of the illness.

5. If the property has a doctor on retainer, alert him or her to the problem. Do not call the doctor at night unless the guest wants to speak with the doctor.

6. *Notify the Board of Health authorities if food poisoning is diagnosed by a physician.*

7. A committee comprising the food and beverage manager, executive chef, and key kitchen personnel should be notified *immediately* in order to analyze the entire production process and determine where and how the menu items could have been contaminated.

8. Find out how many portions of the menu item(s) responsible for the food poisoning were served. If possible, collect samples and specimens and send to a lab for analysis.

9. Determine which employee(s) prepared the suspected menu item(s). Send these employees to a physician for a medical examination to determine if they are ill or are germ carriers.

10. Re-examine cleaning standards in the areas where the suspected menu items were prepared and served. Take swabs from the equipment and send them to a lab for analysis.

11. Review sanitation inspection forms/checklists covering the production areas involved in the incident. Evaluate the need for stricter sanitation measures in these areas.

processed canned foods. With new methods of canning and processing, cases of botulism from commercial sources are rare. However, botulism can occur when improperly processed homegrown canned goods are used.

The presence of botulin (the toxin that causes botulism) cannot be detected by tasting, smelling, or looking at the food. Illness generally occurs within 12 to 36 hours after the contaminated food is eaten. Symptoms include dizziness; double vision; difficulty in swallowing, speaking, and breathing; weakness in the muscles; and paralysis.

Exhibit 11.2 outlines basic procedures that an operation may follow when a guest complains of food poisoning. Procedures will vary from operation to operation.

Food Infection. Food infections are caused by bacteria and viruses in food that are consumed with the food and later reproduce inside the body. With food infection, it is the germs themselves—not the poison they produce—that cause the illness.

Types of food infection. Salmonellosis—sam—is a common form of food infection. Sam germs live in the intestinal tract of people and such animals as hogs and chickens. Foods especially susceptible to salmonellosis include ground beef, pork, and poultry; fish; eggs and egg products; and baked goods containing cream fillings. Illness usually occurs within 12 to 48 hours. Symptoms include abdominal pains, diarrhea, fever, vomiting, and chills.

Clostridium perfringens is a germ found almost everywhere: in the soil, in the intestinal tract of people and animals, and in dust. Food sources are soups, gravies, and stews kept lukewarm in deep containers for long periods of time. Illness usually occurs within 8 to 12 hours after eating the contaminated food; symptoms are abdominal pains and diarrhea.

Personal Cleanliness and Health

Many foodborne illnesses are traced to the employees who handle foods. Food service employees should not cough or sneeze into their hands, smoke cigarettes, scratch their heads, touch their faces, or otherwise practice habits that will contaminate their hands and the food they work with (see Exhibit 11.3).[3]

All food service employees should have regular physical examinations by a medical doctor. Many local laws require blood tests, chest X-rays, and examinations when a food service worker is hired and on a regular basis thereafter.

Food service employees who are sick should not report to work. An employee with a cold, cough, open sore, or boil could easily contaminate food. An employee who has been exposed to an infectious disease should consult a doctor before returning to work.

Employee eating habits have an impact on sanitation. Establish and enforce rules about where and when employees can eat. Designate specific areas for employee use and permit eating only in those areas. Employees should be required to wash their hands after they finish eating.

Sanitary Procedures for Safe Food Handling

Proper food handling is more a matter of developing a proper attitude than memorizing an extensive list of do's and don'ts. If you and your employees understand the need to be careful with food and know basic sanitation principles, many of the specific rules become a matter of common sense. The first step in proper food handling is simply making it clear to everyone that sanitation is a priority when purchasing, receiving, storing, preparing, and serving foods.

Purchasing. Restaurant personnel should only purchase food that is wholesome and suitable to eat. Food should be obtained from commercial sources that comply with all applicable local, state, and federal sanitation laws.[4]

Generally, meat and poultry products shipped to other states or shipped within a state must be inspected by agents from the United States Department of Agriculture (USDA) to make sure these products are suitable for human consumption. Inspection is done at the processing plants to make sure that (1) meat and poultry products have the proper quality, (2) the plant is clean, and (3) proper procedures are used by the plant's employees.

Exhibit 11.3 Sample Personal Cleanliness Guidelines for Food Service Employees

1. Bathe daily and use deodorant and anti-perspirant.

2. Shampoo your hair as often as necessary to keep it healthy and clean. Wear it in a simple, easy-to-manage style.

3. Wear clean clothes or uniforms.

4. Keep your fingernails clean, well-trimmed, and free of nail polish.

5. Do not wear excessive makeup and perfume.

6. Do not wear jewelry other than unadorned wedding bands. This guideline is primarily for sanitary reasons, but it also helps protect both you and your jewelry.

7. Wear clean, low-heeled, properly fitting shoes with non-skid soles. The heel and toe should be completely enclosed for sanitation and safety reasons. Do not wear tennis shoes, slippers, or sandals.

8. Always wash your hands with soap and warm water before beginning work and before beginning a new food-handling operation. Your hands should also be washed before returning from the restroom, after touching your face or hair, and after handling soiled articles, including money.

9. Wash hands in handwashing basins, not preparation or dishwashing sinks.

10. Use disposable towels to dry your hands, not dish towels, aprons, or your clothes or uniform.

11. Employees should wear hair restraints; they should not use hairspray as a substitute. Avoid hairpins and barrettes because they can slip out.

12. Do not comb your hair, use hair spray, file your nails, or apply makeup in food service areas.

13. Do not smoke or chew gum in any food production areas.

14. Do not cough or sneeze near food. It is unsanitary to carry used handkerchiefs in your pocket. If needed, disposable tissues should be used and then discarded.

Government agencies other than the USDA are also involved in food inspection. For example, the Public Health Service helps ensure the wholesomeness of milk; the Department of the Interior—Bureau of Commercial Fisheries administers an inspection program for all types of processed fish products—fresh, frozen, cured, and canned.

A wise purchaser buys only federally inspected meat and poultry products or makes sure that state or local inspection programs are acceptable substitutes for federal inspection before buying local products. Eggs and such egg products as frozen egg whites and yolks, pressed egg yolks, etc., are also generally inspected for wholesomeness by the USDA. Inspection of cheese and fresh and processed fruits and vegetables is not required by law and is done for producers and growers who request (and pay for) this service.

Purchasers should be aware of the difference between inspection and grading. Inspection refers to an official examination of food to determine whether it is wholesome. Grading refers to the process of analyzing foods relative to specific, defined standards in order to assess its quality (see Exhibit 11.4). Inspection is often required by law, but grading is optional. Many purchasers prefer to buy graded products because they know those products have met specific quality standards—that's one reason producers are willing to pay to have their fruits, vegetables, cheese, and other products graded. Purchasers should be aware, however, that products are graded at the processing plants; improper handling by delivery or restaurant personnel can adversely affect quality.

Receiving. All incoming foods should be checked to make sure they meet quality standards stated in the operation's purchase specifications. Employees who receive meats and poultry for the operation should look for the USDA "Inspected and Passed" labels. The following are examples of sanitation guidelines for receiving:

- Look at the condition of the delivery vehicle. Does the interior look clean? Is it an open-bed truck or an enclosed truck? The chance that products may be contaminated is greater with an open-bed truck.

- Carefully inspect every case that appears damaged; there is a possibility that the food within may be contaminated.

- Check all deliveries for evidence of insect or rodent contamination.

- Check incoming products for unusual or foul odors. Such odors generally mean a problem exists.

- Don't accept frozen foods that feel partially or completely thawed, or appear to be spoiled.

Storing. Food should be stored as soon as possible after receiving. Keep stored foods covered. Uncovered food may dry out or absorb odors. It is also possible for debris or other objects to fall into uncovered food from storage shelves above. Store frozen foods in their original containers because these containers are usually moisture- and vapor-proof. Store staples such as flour, cornmeal, and rice in rust-proof and corrosion-resistant containers with tight-fitting lids. Do not use metal containers; they are hard to clean, sanitize, and maintain.

Keep stored food away from walls and dripping pipes. Place food on slotted shelves that are at least two inches away from the wall and six inches off the floor to facilitate air circulation and floor cleaning. Don't line shelves with paper or other materials because this will block airflow. All shelves must be clean.

Food that cannot be stored on shelves because of size or bulk should be stored on easily movable dollies or skids, not on the floor. Even if it is in containers, food should never be stored on the floor because containers may be placed on kitchen counters to be opened and emptied. That would allow soil on the bottom of the containers to contaminate the counter.

Recommended temperatures in refrigerated storage areas vary with the type of food being stored (see Exhibit 11.5). Freezer temperatures should be 0°F (−18°C) or below. Food products not requiring refrigeration or freezing should be stored in clean, cool, and moisture-free areas that are well-ventilated and free from rodents and insects. Temperatures for dry food products should be between 50°F (10°C) and 70°F (21°C); relative humidity should range from 50% to 60%.

Exhibit 11.4 Inspection and Grading Stamps

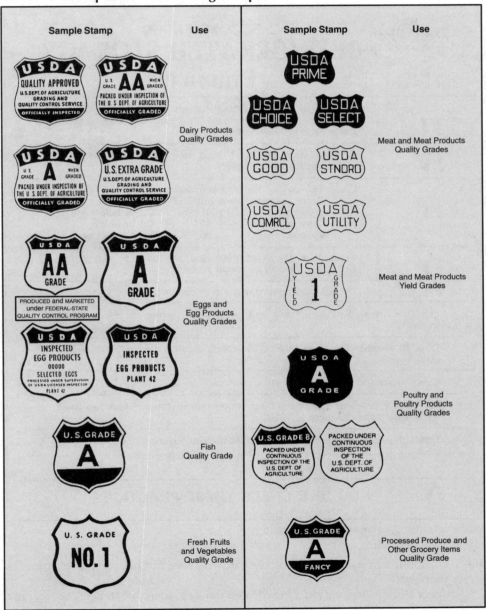

Sample Stamp	Use	Sample Stamp	Use

Issue food to preparation or service areas on a first-in, first-out (FIFO) basis. In other words, products that are in storage the longest should be used first. Before storing a product, mark the date it was received on the package or container it came in. As mentioned in Chapter 8, this will help with stock rotation. Products

Exhibit 11.5 Recommended Refrigerated Storage Practices

RECOMMENDED
REFRIGERATED STORAGE
Practices

NATIONAL RESTAURANT ASSOCIATION

| ✓✓ | All cooked food or other products removed from original container must be enclosed in clean, sanitized, covered container and identified. |

| ✓✓ | Do not store packaged food in contact with water or undrained ice. |

| ✓✓ | Check refrigerator thermometer regularly. |

Recommended temperatures

produce	45° F. (7° C.) or below
dairy and meat	40° F. (4° C.) or below
seafood	30° F. (−1° C.) or below

| ✓✓ | Store large pieces of meat and all foods to permit free circulation of cool air on all surfaces. |

| ✓✓ | Do not store food directly on floor or base. |

Schedule cleaning of equipment and refrigerated storage rooms at regular intervals.

Date all merchandise upon receipt and rotate inventory on a "first-in—first out" basis.

Check fruits and vegetables daily for spoilage.

Store dairy products separately from strong odored foods. Store fish apart from other food products.

Establish preventive maintenance program for equipment.

✓✓ DOUBLE CHECK THESE PRACTICES

Source: *Sanitation Operations Manual*, p. A21.

that seem spoiled or unusable should be thrown away, but be sure that employees notify you first!

Inspect storage areas often. Do not keep poisons, toxic substances, or cleaning materials in food storage areas.

Preparing. Basic sanitation procedures should always be followed when working with and around food (see Exhibit 11.6). Keeping hands clean during food preparation is a must. The use of disposable gloves is often practical.

Clean food preparation tools and other equipment properly. Sanitize contact surfaces between every food processing task.

Exhibit 11.6 Food Service Sanitation Procedures

Employee Activity to be Avoided	Reason for Avoidance	Suggestion
1. Don't leave inventory on the loading dock.	Spoilage of perishable goods through bacterial growth.	Count inventory immediately and store in proper area, refrigerators, freezers, and dry storage.
2. Don't store food on the floor.	Food is easily contaminated by dirt on floor.	
3. Don't store food against the wall.	Prevents air circulation.	Food should be two inches away from the wall to ensure circulation.
4. Don't leave leftover food out.	To avoid contamination.	Refrigerate food as soon as possible.
5. Don't hold food in temperatures between 45–140°F.	To avoid contamination.	
6. Don't refreeze food.	Quality decreases, bacterial count increases.	Use completely or store after product is cooked.
7. Don't cook food incompletely.	To avoid contamination.	Heat food without interruption.
8. Don't taste suspicious-looking food.	Preservation of employee's health.	If it looks suspicious, throw it out.
9. Don't serve unwashed fruits or vegetables or open cans with unwashed tops.	To avoid contamination.	
10. Don't leave food particles on equipment, glasses, flatware, or dishware.	To avoid contamination.	Clean all equipment after use and inspect glasses, flatware, and dishware before service.
11. Don't use cracked or chipped glasses or dishware.	Bacteria can grow in the cracks.	
12. Never handle glasses by the rim, utensils by the eating portion, or tops of plates.	Transfer of bacteria from hands to dishware.	Touch dishes only by the edge, cups by handles, glasses near the base, and utensils by the handles.
13. Never place soiled dishes on the same tray with food that is to be served.	Possible contamination.	Use buspersons or clear the table with a separate tray.
14. Don't allow food to stand on the service counter.	Cooling food increases chances of bacterial growth.	Serve it at once.
15. Never sit on counters or tables; don't lean on tables.	Contaminants on clothing are transferred to tables.	
16. Don't have hair loose.	Hair falls in food and causes contamination. It is also not appetizing.	Wear hairnets or hats.
17. Keep your hands away from your face and hair and out of your pockets; do not touch money unless necessary.	Possible contamination.	If you must do any of these things, wash hands thoroughly afterward.
18. Never chew gum or anything of a similar nature.	It can spread infection.	
19. Never carry the check or pencil in your mouth. Don't put a pencil in your hair.	Bacteria can be spread.	Check should be carried in your hand; pencil in your pocket.
20. Avoid sneezing, yawning, or coughing.	Spreads infection.	If unavoidable, be sure to turn away from food or guests and cover your mouth.
21. Do not spit.	Spreads infection.	
22. Don't eat or nibble on the job; never eat from bus trays or soiled dishes.	Disease can spread.	Eat at designated break times and wash hands thoroughly when finished.

(continued)

Exhibit 11.6 *(continued)*

Employee Activity to be Avoided	Reason for Avoidance	Suggestion
23. Never smoke on duty.	The nicotine virus can be transferred as well as disease.	Smoke in designated areas during breaks; wash hands thoroughly afterward.
24. Never use your apron as a towel.	Clean hands are contaminated on a dirty apron.	Use disposable towels.
25. Never work with dirty hands.	Possible contamination.	Wash hands using warm, soapy water. Lather well and rinse with clear water. Dry hands with disposable towels.
26. Never handle clean dishes if hands have not been cleaned after touching soiled dishes.	Possible contamination from soiled dishes.	Wash hands thoroughly between these two stages. This is for all personnel—dishwashers, servers, and buspersons.
27. Never touch or pick up food with hands.	Spread of infection from the skin.	Use the proper serving tool or gloves.
28. Don't report to work in soiled clothes.	Soil can harbor infection.	Always wear a clean uniform and apron.
29. Avoid excessive jewelry.	Food particles can collect and cause contamination.	Wear a minimum of jewelry.
30. Don't arrive at work needing a bath.	To avoid bacterial contamination.	Bathe and use deodorant daily.
31. Never use the same knife and cutting board for meats and vegetables without washing.	Salmonella and other very small organisms can spread.	Use a different knife and board, or wash board and use a sanitizer.
32. Don't report to work if sick.	Increases the chances of spreading the illness.	Call in so a replacement can be located.
33. Don't work with exposed wounds.	Increases risk of wound infection and of spreading it.	Always keep wounds covered with the proper type of bandage.
34. Don't report to work if your health card has expired.	Prevents the spread of communicable disease, tuberculosis, and venereal disease.	Keep track of the expiration date and renew it immediately.
35. Never wash hands in sinks used to prepare food.	Contamination of food.	Use designated handwashing sink.
36. Never taste food with your finger.	Contamination of food by saliva.	Use a tasting spoon and only once.
37. Never re-serve food.	Handling of the food by guests can spread disease.	Throw food away; avoid giving an excess of rolls, etc., when serving.
38. Never serve pork rare.	To prevent trichinosis.	Cook pork until done to kill trichina organisms.
39. Never leave racks of glasses bowl-side up.	Airborne illness can collect.	Store glassware inverted.
40. Never store food in an open container.	Airborne particles can contaminate foods.	Always store food in sealed containers.
41. Don't leave prepped food out.	Possible contamination.	Prepare just prior to cooking or serving.
42. Never dry dishware, glasses, utensils, or cooking equipment with a towel.	Possible bacterial contamination.	Let air dry or dry in dishwashing machine's cycle.
43. Don't store garbage with food.	Increases chances of infection.	Have the proper places for each.

Source: Adapted from material originally developed by Jeanne Picard, School of Hotel, Restaurant and Tourism Administration, University of New Orleans, 1980.

Wash the tops of cans before opening them. Do not use cans that have swelling at the tops or bottoms, or those with dents along the side seams. Swelling could mean that germs have contaminated the product; dents along the side seam may indicate the can's seal is broken. If canned products have unusual or unfamiliar odors, or if the contents seem foamy or milky, don't use them.

Wash all raw fruits and vegetables thoroughly before preparation or serving. Be especially careful when handling and preparing meat, eggs, fish, shellfish, and other foods high in protein. Do not use meats that smell strange or have slimy surfaces. Generally, any type of food that appears moldy, cloudy, or that has a strange smell should be discarded. Do not taste foods, since this test proves nothing and can make you ill.

Never leave food out overnight to thaw. Potentially hazardous foods should be thawed in one of the following ways:

- In refrigerated units

- Under running water at a temperature of 70°F (21°C) or below

- In a microwave oven if the product will be immediately transferred to other cooking equipment

- As part of the cooking process—for example, when steaks are charbroiled from their frozen state

Do not refreeze thawed products. Freezing, thawing, and refreezing can create sanitation problems and destroy food quality.

Prepare perishable foods as close to serving time as possible. To kill any germs that may be present, all foods should normally be heated to at least 145°F (63°C) in the center of the food mass. Some foods require a higher temperature. The center of poultry, poultry stuffings, stuffed meats, and stuffings containing meat should be heated to 165°F (74°C), pork to 155°F (68°C). On the other hand, rare roast beef and rare beefsteak need to be heated only to 130°F (54°C). Meat and poultry temperatures should be checked with a cooking thermometer.

Keep cold foods refrigerated until serving begins (or during service, in the case of a cafeteria or buffet operation). Many kitchens have refrigerators where prepared foods can be kept until service.

A common problem in many food service operations involves holding hot foods that are prepared in advance of service. Casseroles, stews, gravies, and other products high in protein are often kept in a hot water bath at lukewarm temperatures for long periods of time. If germs get into these products, conditions are ideal for food poisoning or infection. Protein foods must be kept above 140°F (60°C) or below 41°F (5°C) or they should not be kept at all.

Rapid cooling is important for potentially hazardous foods that are left over after service or are cooked for use during later work shifts. Preparation staff must minimize the time that these foods are within the food temperature danger zone. Be concerned about the temperature in the center of the food mass, not the temperature on the food's surface. Frequent stirring, refrigerating hot foods as soon as possible after cooking, and ensuring effective air circulation are examples of good sanitation procedures to hasten cooling.

Leftovers must be handled carefully. After removing them from the production or service area, put leftovers in proper containers and quickly refrigerate or freeze them for use as soon as possible.

Serving. The need for sanitary work procedures does not end after food is prepared. Food must be safely handled when it is being portioned and served to guests.

For food quality and sanitation reasons, employees in table service operations should "plate" food when it is needed for pickup for service—not before. Employees should not touch food with their hands when portioning it. Tongs, scoops, spatulas, or other tools should be used instead. These tools must be cleaned properly between uses. All too often a ladle used to portion a protein-rich casserole is placed in a container of lukewarm (and quickly soiled) water, then rinsed and used to portion some other dish.

Employees serving beverages should use a scoop to dispense ice. They should never use their hands or a drinking glass as a scoop. Using their hands could spread germs; if a glass is used and it breaks, glass will be scattered throughout the ice and the entire ice bin will have to be cleaned.

Most operations that serve food in salad bars or buffet or cafeteria lines are required by law to use sneeze-guards or breath protectors. These are various types of panels, often made of transparent plastic, that minimize the possibility of guests or servers coughing, sneezing, or breathing on displayed food items.

Food servers or buspersons must be especially careful with dishes and flatware when serving guests. They should pick up flatware by the handles and dishes by the edges, never touching the eating surfaces. Following the operation's procedures for wiping down tables is also a responsibility of servers or buspersons. Many guests place flatware and food such as rolls on the table's surface. If the table is not clean, it can easily contaminate flatware and food.

Servers should discard rolls, butter, or cream in pitchers if they are not consumed by the guest. No food items should be reused unless they are individually wrapped items such as small packages of cream, crackers, or bread sticks.

Last but not least, servers and buspersons should not eat food that has been served to guests but not eaten, and kitchen employees should never reuse food that has been served to guests but returned to the kitchen uneaten.

Cleaning Up

The effective cleaning and sanitizing of dishes, flatware, pots, pans, and the facility itself is one of the most important jobs in food service. Topics that will be discussed include ware washing, cleaning kitchen and dining areas, scheduling cleaning tasks, and handling garbage and refuse properly.

Ware Washing. In this section we will discuss cleaning dishes and other small wares manually or with a dishwashing machine.

Manual cleaning. Often, local ordinances specify equipment and procedures that should be used for manual cleaning of dishes, flatware, pots, and pans. Some general guidelines are included in Exhibit 11.7.

There are two ways to properly sanitize dishware washed manually:

- *Hot water.* Water must be at least 180°F (82°C) to sanitize dishware. To raise water to that temperature you need a booster heater or an electrical heating element that can be immersed directly in the water. Since employees cannot

Exhibit 11.7 General Guidelines for Manually Cleaning Small Wares

1. Remove large quantities of soiled food from dishware with a spatula, brush, or other utensil before washing. Inspect dishware during washing and discard cracked, chipped, or unusable items. Often, a presoaking process is required to properly wash heavily soiled dishware.

2. Wash dishware in a sink with at least three or four compartments. If a three-compartment sink is used, procedures will involve washing, rinsing, and sanitizing. If a four-compartment sink is used, the normal process will involve prewashing, washing, rinsing, and sanitizing. Always follow local and other health codes.

3. Use the proper type and quantity of dishwashing soap, based on information from the soap's manufacturer or supplier. Provide employees with the proper measuring equipment.

4. Use plastic brushes with firm bristles to wash dishware. Don't use dishcloths, dish mops, or soft sponges—they are very difficult to keep clean. Don't use metal cleaning brushes because they can leave metal slivers in or on items being washed. Wash glasses with a glassware brush.

5. The normal order of washing is: glassware, flatware, dishes, trays, and pots and pans.

6. Frequently drain wash water and refill with clean, fresh, hot water.

7. After they are washed, glasses, cups, and bowls should be placed upside down in rinse racks. They should be placed loosely in the racks so that rinse water will reach all surfaces. For the same reason, dishes, trays, and pots and pans should not be crowded on the rinsing racks.

8. Place flatware in the rinse baskets with handles up.

9. Remove all detergent from dishes before placing them in the rinse sink.

10. Fill rinsing sink with clean water at approximately 180°F (82°C) if sanitizing with hot water. If sanitizing with chemicals, it's possible to sanitize with water at a much lower temperature. (Different chemicals may call for different temperatures—always check the manufacturer's instructions.)

11. Change rinse water frequently.

remove items from 180-degree water with their hands, they must use tongs or other devices.

- *Chemicals.* It's frequently more practical to use a chemical sanitizing agent to sanitize dishes. If chemicals are used the water does not need to be excessively hot. Use proper chemical sanitizing agents in the correct amount. Determine the quantities to use and provide appropriate training and measuring utensils to employees.

Cleaning with dishwashing machines. The following are guidelines for using a dishwashing machine:

- The dishwashing machine should be operated according to the manufacturer's instructions. Carefully follow procedures for using automatic detergent dispensers, wetting agents, etc.

- Inspect the machine before using. Remove bits of food, broken glass, or other foreign objects. Ensure that spray arms are clean and working properly.

- Make sure temperature gauges for wash and rinse water are functioning.

- Rinse dishes and flatware before running them through the machine. Rack them properly so all surfaces are exposed to wash and rinse water.

- Air-dry dishware and other items after washing; never use towels. Towel-drying can recontaminate sanitized dishes.

- Handle clean dishes and flatware with plastic gloves or clean hands.

Wash water temperature for dishwashing machines must normally be between 150°F (66°C) and 160°F (71°C). If you are sanitizing with hot water during the rinse cycle, the water's temperature must be above 180°F (82°C) for the time specified by local sanitation codes. You will need a booster heater to raise the water temperature to the proper level. If you are sanitizing with chemicals, it's important to follow the manufacturer's recommendations and applicable local regulations.

Cleaning Kitchen and Dining Areas. All floors, walls, ceilings, and equipment within kitchen and dining areas must be kept clean and in good repair. Generally, cleaning should be done when the least amount of food is exposed. Dustless methods such as wet mopping or vacuuming are recommended for floor cleaning.

Properly constructed facilities and equipment are more easily cleaned than those that fail to incorporate recommended guidelines for construction and maintenance. Wall coverings should be smooth and non-absorbent. Smooth, durable floor materials such as sealed concrete, terrazzo, or ceramic tile are best in most food service areas.

A cleaning schedule for all kitchen and dining areas is important to help ensure that the property's sanitation goals are met. Typical cleaning schedules list the equipment or area to be cleaned, the employee responsible, when the cleaning should be done, and the appropriate cleaning manuals and written cleaning procedures that should be consulted. It's very important to have written cleaning procedures. For each equipment item and area to be cleaned, there should be a written description of the cleaning task, steps needed to complete the job, and the correct materials and tools to be used. Every piece of equipment can have its cleaning procedures posted next to it. These same cleaning procedures should be used for on-the-job training sessions. Managers must follow up to make sure all areas and equipment are cleaned effectively.

Procedures for Handling Garbage and Refuse. Each independent operation, restaurant chain, or institution will have its own unique garbage and refuse handling procedures, but some guidelines are universal. Cover all garbage containers in food preparation areas. Use easily cleanable containers and thoroughly scour and disinfect them on a routine basis to prevent odors and protect against rodents, insects, and germs. Provide a suitable area to undertake the cleaning process.

Take inside garbage containers outside and empty them as soon as they are full or on a regular basis throughout the day. Outside garbage areas and containers can attract rodents and insects that may enter and infest the operation's building(s), so outside garbage-storing areas and containers must be clean. Keep all garbage stored outside in closed containers and have it collected regularly. Normally, pick-ups should be scheduled several times weekly; more frequent service will be required for high-volume properties and/or during warm weather when spoilage and odors are more likely.

Safety

Safety relates to the prevention of accidents, especially those that can harm guests and employees. Most accidents are caused by someone's carelessness; most can be prevented. The most important issue is: what can a food service manager do to help protect others from danger or injury while at the property? Of secondary importance, but still of concern to food service managers, is preventing damage to or loss of equipment and other physical assets.[5]

All employees should be trained in what to do in case of an accident. If an accident occurs at the property, managers should learn from it to help ensure that a similar accident does not happen in the future.

In this section we will talk about the Occupational Safety and Health Administration (OSHA) and its impact on safety in the workplace. We will review types of food service accidents and list safety principles that, when followed, can help prevent accidents. This will be followed by a discussion of first aid procedures and accident reports.

OSHA

OSHA is an agency of the United States Department of Labor that was created to help make working conditions safer for employees. OSHA has:

- Required employers to furnish employees with jobs and places of employment that are free from recognized safety hazards

- Established mandatory job safety and health standards

- Developed an enforcement program

- Constructed reporting procedures that deal with job injuries, illnesses, and fatalities

- Created and implemented many procedures to help improve working conditions

- Implemented programs to encourage employers and employees to reduce hazards in the workplace

OSHA regulations usually apply to every employer with one or more employees, so restaurants and food service operations in hotels and institutions of all types are generally covered.

OSHA permits states to develop their own programs for occupational safety and health. State programs must be at least as effective as federal programs. In effect, federal standards indicated by OSHA become standards that state plans must meet or exceed.

There are three major components of OSHA laws that affect food service operations:

- *Recordkeeping requirements.* OSHA requires employers to maintain certain records. These range from a daily inspection report on any vehicle used by an employer to transport guests, to reports dealing with employee injuries and illnesses.

- *Inspections.* OSHA inspectors may visit an operation to look for potential safety hazards. After an inspection, OSHA officials may hold a meeting with representatives from the operation to discuss and review any violations. Plans for remedial action are covered at these meetings. A follow-up inspection may be scheduled.

- *Fines.* If a food service operation does not comply with OSHA requirements and fails to take remedial actions suggested by OSHA officials, fines are possible. Failure to correct a violation within the allotted time can result in a fine of $1,000 a day until the violation is corrected. Falsifying records is punishable by fines of up to $10,000 and/or six months' imprisonment.[6]

OSHA has developed training information to help educate food service managers and employees about safety concerns. Also, its representatives are trained to provide creative suggestions to resolve safety-related problems. OSHA representatives are more than just inspectors; they are consultants who work with food service establishments to identify and resolve problems which, left undetected and uncorrected, could cause injury or death to the property's employees or guests.

Food Service Accidents

Let's look at the most common types of food service accidents and ways to protect employees and others.

Burns. Many accidents in food service operations result in burns. The following are among actions that can be taken to prevent burns:

- Follow recommended procedures when using any cooking equipment or when lighting gas equipment.

- Plan ahead. Always have a place prepared for hot pans before removing them from a range or oven.

- Use dry potholders; a wet or damp potholder can cause a steam burn. Never use an apron, towel, or dishcloth.

- Don't use pans with loose handles (they can break off) or rounded bottoms (the pans may tip).

- Don't fill pots, pans, or kettles too full. Open pots carefully by raising the back of their lids so steam will escape away from you.

- Stir food carefully with long-handled spoons or paddles; avoid spattering and splashing.

- Don't reach into hot ovens; use a puller or other proper tool.

- Allow equipment to cool before cleaning it.

- Know how to put out fires. If food catches on fire, spread salt or baking soda on the flame; do not use water. Know how to use fire extinguishers and other safety equipment.

- Prohibit horseplay.

- Be careful when pouring coffee and other hot liquids.

- Use caution around heat lamps.[7]

Muscle Strains and Falls. To avoid muscle strains, always have a firm footing before attempting to lift a heavy object. Keep your back straight; do not bend forward or sideways. Bend your knees to pick up low objects and lift with your legs, not your back. Employees should not try to carry too many items at one time or items that are too heavy for them. When carrying a heavy load, ask for help or use a cart.

Next to traffic accidents, falls kill more people than any other kind of accident. Most falls are not from high places but are slips or trips at floor level.[8] Precautions to prevent falls include the following:

- Keep floors clean and dry at all times. Wipe up spills immediately. Use "slip-resistant" floor waxes and use "Caution" or "Wet Floor" signs when appropriate.

- Keep hazardous objects such as boxes, mops, and brooms off floors. Replace loose or upturned floor tiles as soon as they are noticed.

- Repair cracked or worn stair treads.

- Wear properly fitting shoes with low heels and non-skid soles. Never wear worn-out shoes, thin-soled shoes, slippers, high heels, tennis shoes, or sandals. The heel and toe of the shoe should be completely enclosed. Keep shoestrings tied to prevent tripping.

- Walk, don't run, and use caution when going through swinging doors.

- Use a sturdy stepladder if it is necessary to reach high places.

- Make sure that entrances and exits are clean and safe. This includes removing snow and ice if the property is located in an area where this is a potential problem in winter. Keep floor mats or other protective devices clean and in good condition.

- Keep any areas in which employees must work or walk well-lighted; pay special attention to exterior areas and steps where accidents are more likely to occur.

Cuts. Cuts are constant hazards for food preparation employees. Employees must be alert when using knives, slicers, or similar equipment.

There are many common guidelines for using knives. Always place food to be cut on a table or a cutting board. Cut away from your body; the food item should be firmly grasped and sliced by cutting downward. When chopping food with a knife, hold the food with your free hand and keep the point of the chopping knife on the block. Dull knives cause more problems than sharp knives because dull knives require employees to exert more pressure, and slippage problems are more likely to occur.

Discard or repair knives with loose handles. Don't leave knives on the edge of a counter—push them back so they cannot fall on the floor or on someone's foot. Don't try to catch a falling knife. Never play with knives or use them as substitutes for screwdrivers or can openers. Don't use knives to open cardboard cartons; use the proper container-opening tool.

Cuts can also occur when knives or other sharp tools are washed. For this reason, all sharp tools should be washed separately. Never place knives or other sharp tools in sinks filled with soapy water. Clean all sharp tools with caution. Use a folded heavy cloth and work slowly and carefully from the center of the blade to the outside cutting edge. When cleaning a slicer, make sure the blade of the slicer is in the position recommended for cleaning. Unplug the unit and refer to the manufacturer's operating and maintenance manual for specific cleaning instructions.

Minimizing the use of glass in the kitchen can help prevent cuts. Any broken glass should be cleaned up immediately with a broom and dustpan, not your fingers. If glass is broken in a dishwasher, drain the dishwasher and pick up the glass with a damp cloth. Always place broken glass or china in a separate refuse container.

Here are some additional precautions for preventing cuts:

- Keep knives, cleavers, saws, and other sharp tools in racks or special drawers when not in use.

- Use the correct-size cutting tools and make sure they have the proper blade.

- Use safety guards and any other safety items provided on equipment.

- Be careful with grinders. Use the feeder/tamper.

- Use caution when operating slicers and other electric cutting tools.

- When using sharpening steels, be sure there is a finger guard between the handles and the steel.

Equipment Accidents. Safety precautions should be used whenever employees work with equipment. Don't take shortcuts when operating potentially hazardous food service equipment; always follow the manufacturer's instructions carefully. Place the instructions on or near equipment so that employees can refer to them.

Train employees in how to use, maintain, and clean equipment. New employees should be carefully supervised to ensure that proper procedures are followed. Whenever possible, disconnect equipment from power sources before cleaning.

Properly maintain equipment. Improper maintenance can lead to unsafe working conditions. Conduct regular and detailed equipment inspections with maintenance personnel or representatives from the equipment supply company. Make sure all gas connections conform with applicable regulations. Gas equipment should bear the seal of approval of the American Gas Association.

Here are some special precautions for working with electrical equipment:

- Ensure that all electrical equipment and connections conform to national, state, and local electrical code requirements. Electrical equipment should, where applicable, bear the Underwriters Laboratories seal of approval.

- Carefully follow the manufacturer's instructions whenever operating electrical equipment.

- Always unplug electrical equipment before cleaning it. Never touch metal sockets and electrical equipment when your hands are wet or you are standing on a wet floor.

- Practice preventive maintenance. A qualified electrician should inspect all electrical equipment, wiring, switches, etc., on a regular basis.

Fire. Another potential accident in food service operations is fire. The following precautions can help lessen the danger of fire:

- Properly clean and maintain cooking equipment and exhaust hoods/filters.

- For sanitation as well as safety reasons, limit smoking to restricted areas.

- Be sure there is adequate fire extinguishing equipment on hand. Personnel should know where it's located and how to use it. Consult local fire authorities about the purchase, use, and inspection of fire extinguishing equipment.

- Consider using fire detection devices. These may be specialized equipment items that can detect smoke, flames, and/or heat.

- Consider using automatic sprinkler systems. They are a very effective way to control fires.

Sprinkler systems may be required by local fire ordinances, but even if they are not, they may be a wise investment. Special fire extinguishing equipment under ventilation filters is frequently required by local ordinances. Regardless of the type (dry chemical, carbon dioxide, or chemicals in special solutions), this equipment can only be effective if it is professionally designed, installed, and maintained.

Employees should know where all emergency exits are located, and fire drills should be conducted. Contact the local fire department for specific help in designing emergency procedures. Make sure all doors to the property open out and that fire exits are kept clear at all times. Fire department telephone numbers should be located near telephones.

First Aid

Immediately after an accident occurs, first aid is the primary concern. It is very important that someone trained in first aid apply treatment. People without first aid training normally should only undertake common-sense procedures. In case of a serious injury, you should make the person as comfortable as possible (without risking further injury) and call for medical help; in case of a minor injury, give the person whatever aid is necessary from the property's first aid kit, fill out an accident report, and urge the victim to see a physician if that seems appropriate.

Encourage employees to receive first aid training. The American Red Cross provides excellent training throughout the United States. If possible, training should be given to several employees so that it's more likely that someone with first aid training will always be on the premises.

Exhibit 11.8 Sample First Aid Poster

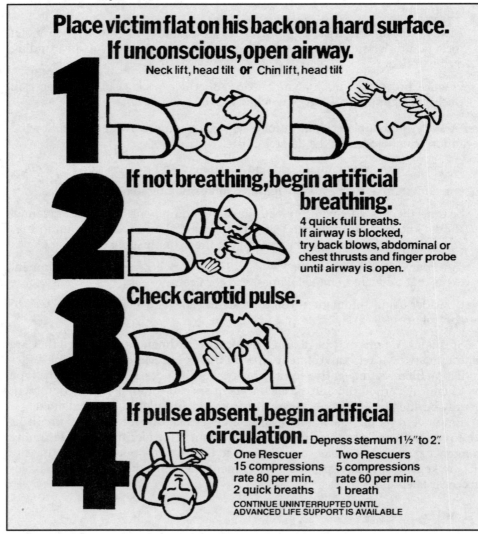

Courtesy of the American Heart Association

An operation should have first aid equipment and supplies on-site in a convenient area. OSHA and some state labor departments, municipal regulatory agencies, and insurance companies have first aid equipment requirements. In large operations, particularly those with more than one floor, several first aid kits may be needed.

Display first aid information. Post various types of medical and first aid posters in appropriate places throughout your food service operation (see Exhibit 11.8).

Accident Reports

OSHA regulations and state workers' compensation laws require that accidents that occur in the workplace be reported. Exhibit 11.9 illustrates required information for workers' compensation purposes in one state. As a result of this report and, perhaps, investigations by state labor officers or insurance company investigators, a settlement consistent with the applicable state compensation laws will normally be made. You can also use accident reports created by the National Restaurant Association or other industry sources, or develop your own in order to gather more information and develop procedures to prevent an accident's recurrence.

The steps in any accident investigation should be to (1) assess exactly what happened, (2) determine why the accident occurred, (3) suggest what should be done to prevent recurrences, and (4) follow up. It's important that managers see all the reports on an accident and follow up to ensure that preventive action has been taken.

Management's Role in Sanitation and Safety Programs

Although all members of the food service staff are members of the operation's sanitation and safety team, the development of sanitation and safety programs really begins with a commitment from management. Managers have the ultimate responsibility for developing, implementing, and monitoring the property's sanitation and safety efforts. The role of managers includes:

- Incorporating sanitation and safety practices into operating procedures

- Ensuring that sanitation and safety concerns take priority over convenience

- Training employees in sanitary and safe work procedures

- Conducting sanitation and safety inspections

- Completing accident reports, assisting in investigations, and doing whatever is necessary to ensure that problems are quickly corrected

- When necessary, assisting in treatment and seeking medical assistance for injured employees or guests

- Reporting needed repairs or maintenance, changes in work procedures, or other conditions that are potential problems

- Conducting sanitation and safety meetings

- Urging the active participation of all staff members in solving sanitation and safety problems

Inspections

Inspections are usually at the heart of management's effort to ensure that sanitation and safety procedures are consistently followed. You can develop inspection forms or checklists that focus attention on equipment, facilities, food handling practices, and/or food service employees. Persons with special knowledge (insurance representatives, state or local fire inspectors, and so on) can help you create these checklists. A sample safety checklist is shown in the appendix to this chapter.

Exhibit 11.9 Sample Accident Report Form

Form 100
Rev. 1-82

OSHA`
Case or File No. _____

DEPARTMENT OF LABOR

Bureau of Workers' Disability Compensation

EMPLOYER'S BASIC REPORT OF INJURY

COPIES TO BE DISTRIBUTED
Yellow and Green — Bureau of Workers'
  Disability Compensation, Lansing, Mich.
Blue — Insurance Company
Pink — Employer File
White — Employee

Employers must report to the Bureau on Form 100 all injuries, including diseases, which arise out of and in the course of the employment and cause: 1. Seven (7) or more days of disability not including Sundays or the day of injury. 2. Death. 3. Specific Losses. In case of DEATH also file immediately an additional report on Form 106.

1. **INJURED EMPLOYEE** _____ Soc. Sec. No. _____/____/____
2. Address _____ Telephone No. _____
3. Birthdate - Month _____ Day _____ Year _____ If under 18, date working permit issued _____
4. Sex: ☐ Male ☐ Female   Number of injured employee's children under age 16 living with injured _____
5. Marital Status: ☐ Married ☐ Single   If married male, is wife living with him? ☐ Yes ☐ No
6. Number of other family members or relatives at least 50% supported by injured _____
7. **DATE OF INJURY** _____ Last day worked _____ Did employee die? ☐ Yes ☐ No If yes, date _____
8. Location of Injury City _____ State _____ County _____
9. Was place of accident or exposure on employer's premises?   ☐ Yes   ☐ No
10. Name and address of physician _____
11. If hospitalized, name and address of hospital _____

12. DESCRIPTION OF ALLEGED INJURY (Complete and specific information needed for each category)

A. Describe the injury or illness
   Examples: Amputation, Burn, Cut, Fracture, Sprain, etc.

B. Part of body - The part of body directly affected by the injury or illness.
   Examples: Head, Arm, Leg, Circulatory system, etc.

C. Describe the events that caused the injury. Examples: Fell, Operating machinery, Exposure to chemicals, etc.

D. Name the object or substance which directly injured the employee.
   Examples: Knife, Band Saw, Acid, Floor, Oil, Punch Press, etc.

13. Occupation of injured employee (be specific) _____
14. Department _____ Foreman or supervisor _____
15. Total Gross Wages - Highest 39 of 52 weeks preceding date of injury
    Total Gross Weekly Wages $ _____ No. of weeks used in calculation _____
                              Average weekly wage $ _____
16. Complete the following only if the injured employee received wages from a second employer.
    Name of second employer _____
    Mailing address _____
17. Date returned to work _____ or estimated lost time from work _____

18. IS EMPLOYEE CERTIFIED AS VOCATIONALLY HANDICAPPED?   ☐ Yes   ☐ No
19. IS EMPLOYEE RECEIVING UNEMPLOYMENT INSURANCE BENEFITS?   ☐ Yes   ☐ No

20. **EMPLOYER**   MESC. No. _____
    A. _____ Federal ID No. _____
    B. _____
21. Location (if different from mail address) _____
22. **TYPE OF BUSINESS** _____
23. **NSURANCE COMPANY (Not agent)** _____ Carrier ID No. _____
24. **HAS WHITE COPY OF THIS REPORT BEEN GIVEN TO EMPLOYEE?**   ☐ Yes   ☐ No
              Questions or errors should be immediately reported to the employer representative indicated below

Date of Report _____ Prepared by _____
                              Signature (in ink) **Employer** or Representative   Tele. #

Source: Michigan Department of Labor.

How often you make sanitation and safety inspections depends, in part, on how well your property measures up during the first inspection. A complete inspection should be made at least monthly. However, if necessary you should also conduct daily inspections of specific work station areas or equipment.

A primary reason to conduct sanitation and safety inspections is to correct potentially dangerous conditions. Corrective measures should be taken promptly! If time must lapse before a problem is corrected, inform employees of any possible hazards and alert upper management that a problem has been found and steps are being taken to correct it.

After an inspection is completed, inspection forms and checklists should be filed for later reference. Looking back at earlier forms and checklists can give you an indication of the long-range effectiveness of your sanitation and safety programs. Also, should any inquiries be made by OSHA, insurance companies, or other agencies, the forms are evidence of your efforts to maintain a sanitary and safe food and beverage operation.

Endnotes

1. This chapter provides only a basic overview of sanitation. Readers desiring more detailed information about sanitation are referred to Ronald F. Cichy, *Quality Sanitation Management* (East Lansing, Mich.: Educational Institute of the American Hotel & Motel Association, 1994).

2. *Sanitation Operations Manual* (Chicago: National Restaurant Association, 1979), p. iii.

3. Personal hygiene is one of the subjects covered in *Sanitation: Conquering Kitchen Germs* (East Lansing, Mich.: Educational Institute of the American Hotel & Motel Association). Videotape.

4. Details about purchasing procedures are found in William B. Virts, *Purchasing for Hospitality Operations* (East Lansing, Mich.: Educational Institute of the American Hotel & Motel Association, 1987).

5. Safety issues are covered in more detail in Raymond C. Ellis, Jr., and the Security Committee of AH&MA, *Security and Loss Prevention Management* (East Lansing, Mich.: Educational Institute of the American Hotel & Motel Association, 1986).

6. David Wheelhouse, *Managing Human Resources in the Hospitality Industry* (East Lansing, Mich.: Educational Institute of the American Hotel & Motel Association, 1989), p. 333.

7. Information about accident prevention in this chapter is based on U.S. Department of Agriculture, *Sanitation and Safety Practices for Child Nutrition Programs* (Washington, D.C.), pp. 85–96, and *Safety Operations Manual* (Chicago: National Restaurant Association, 1981), pp. A24–A29.

8. *Safety Operations Manual*, p. A27.

Key Terms

chemical poisoning	food poisoning
food grading	food temperature danger zone
food infection	Occupational Safety and Health Administration (OSHA)
food inspection	potentially hazardous foods

Discussion Questions

1. What basic precautions can be taken to prevent the chemical poisoning of food?

2. What conditions must be present for germs to multiply?

3. How is food poisoning different from food infection?

4. How can food service managers help ensure that incoming products are wholesome?

5. What are some guidelines for preparing food in a sanitary way?

6. What procedures can service personnel follow to help ensure that guests are served wholesome food?

7. What major components of OSHA laws affect food service operations?

8. What are common types of accidents that occur in food service operations?

9. What are some precautions that can be taken to prevent falls?

10. What is management's role in sanitation and safety programs?

Appendix

Sample Safety Checklist

The following checkilst covers both physical factors in the property and work practices of your personnel. During your inspection be as aware of unsafe acts as you are of unsafe conditions.

Area	Yes	No	Comments
Receiving Area:			
Are floors in safe condition? (Are they free from broken and defective floor boards? Are they covered with non-skid material?)			
Are employees instructed in correct handling methods for various containers, etc., that are received?			
Are garbage cans washed daily in hot water?			
Are garbage cans always covered?			
If garbage disposal area is adjacent to a part of the general receiving area, is there a program that keeps floors and/or dock areas clear of refuse?			
Is there a proper rack for holding garbage containers? Are garbage containers on dollies or other wheel units to eliminate lifting by employees?			
Are adequate tools available for opening crates, barrels, cartons, etc. (hammer, cutter, cardboard carton opener, and pliers)?			
Is crate, carton, and barrel opening done away from open containers of food?			
Storage Area:			
Are shelves adequate to bear weight of items stored?			
Are employees instructed to store heavy items on lower shelves and lighter materials above?			
Is a safe ladder provided for reaching high storage?			
Are cartons or other flammable materials stored at least two feet away from light bulbs?			
Are light bulbs provided with a screen guard?			
Is a fire extinguisher located at the door?			
Are employees carefully instructed in the use of detergents to prevent agitation of dermatitis, etc.?			
Do you have a program for disposition of broken glass or china?			
Where controls are in a passageway, are they recessed or guarded to prevent breakage or accidental starting?			
Are dish racks in safe condition (if wooden, free from broken slats and smoothly finished to eliminate splintering; if metal, free of sharp corners that could cause cuts)? Are these racks kept off the floor to prevent tripping?			

Source: Adapted with permission from the National Safety Council, Chicago, no date.

Area	Yes	No	Comments
Serving Area:			
Are steam tables cleaned daily and maintained regularly (are gas or electric units checked regularly by a competent serviceperson)?			
Is safety valve equipment operative?			
Are serving counters and tables free of broken parts and wooden or metal slivers and burrs?			
Do you have regular inspections of: Glassware? China? Silverware? Plastic equipment?			
If anything breaks near the food service area, do you remove all food from service adjacent to breakage?			
Are tray rails adequate to prevent trays from slipping or falling off at the end or corners?			
Are floors and/or ramps in good condition (covered with nonskid material, free from broken tile and defective floorboards)?			
Are these areas mopped at least daily and waxed with nonskid wax when necessary?			
Is there effective traffic flow so that customers do not collide while carrying trays or obtaining foods?			
Dining Area:			
Are floors free from broken tile and defective floor boards? Are they covered with nonskid wax?			
Are pictures securely fastened to walls?			
Are drapes, blinds, or curtains securely fastened?			
Are chairs free from splinters, metal burrs, broken or loose parts?			
Are floors "policed" for cleaning up spillage and other materials?			
Is special attention given to the floor adjacent to water, ice cream, or milk stations?			
Are vending machines properly grounded?			
If customers clear their own trays prior to return to dishwashing area, are the floors kept clean of garbage, dropped silver, and/or broken glass and china?			
If dishes are removed from dining area on portable racks or bus trucks, are these units in safe operating condition (for example, are all casters working, all shelves firm)?			
Soiled Dish Processing Area:			
Are floors reasonably free of excessive water and spillage?			
Are floor boards properly maintained and in safe condition (free from broken slats and worn areas that cause tripping)?			
Are all electrical units properly grounded?			

Area	Yes	No	Comments
Are switches located to permit rapid shutdown in the event of emergency?			
Can employees easily reach switches?			
Pots and Pans Room or Area:			
Are duckboards or floor boards in safe condition (free from broken slats and worn areas which could cause tripping)?			
Are employees properly instructed in use of correct amounts of detergent and/or other cleaning agents?			
Are adequate rubber gloves provided?			
Is there an adequate drainboard or other drying area so that employees do not have to pile pots and pans on the floor before and after washing them?			
Do drain plugs permit draining without the employee placing hands in hot water?			
Walk-in Coolers and Freezers— (Refrigerators):			
Are floors in the units in good condition and covered with slip-proof material? Are they mopped at least once a week (and whenever spills occur)?			
If floor boards are used, are they in safe condition (free of broken slats and worn boards which could cause tripping)?			
Are portable and stationary storage racks in safe condition (free from broken or bent shelves and set on solid legs)?			
Are blower fans properly guarded?			
Is there a by-pass device on the door to permit exit if an employee is locked in (or, is there an alarm bell)?			
Is adequate aisle space provided?			
Are employees properly instructed in placement of hands for movement of portable items to avoid hand injuries?			
Are heavy items stored on lower shelves and lighter items on higher shelves?			
Is the refrigerant in the refrigerator nontoxic? (Check with your refrigerator service manual.)			
Food Preparation Area:			
Is electrical equipment properly grounded?			
Is electrical equipment inspected regularly by an electrician?			
Are electrical switches located so that they can be reached readily in the event of an emergency?			
Are the switches located so that employees do not have to lean on or against metal equipment when reaching for them?			
Are floors regularly and adequately maintained (mopped at least daily and waxed with nonskid wax when necessary; are defective floor boards and tiles replaced when necessary)?			

Area	Yes	No	Comments
Are employees instructed to immediately pick up or clean up all dropped items and spillage?			
Are employees properly instructed in the operation of all machines?			
Are employees forbidden to use equipment unless specifically trained in its use?			
Are machines properly grounded?			
Don't Overlook:			

Lighting—is it adequate in the:
    Receiving Area?
    Storage Area?
    Pots and Pans Area?
    Walk-in Coolers and Freezers?
    Food Preparation Area?
    Cooking Area?
    Serving Area?
    Dining Area?
    Soiled Dish Processing Area?			

Doors—do they open into passageways where they could cause an accident? (List any such locations.)			
Are fire exits clearly marked and passages kept clear of equipment and materials? (List any violations.)			
Stairways and Ramps:			
Are they adequately lighted?			
Are the angles of ramps set to provide maximum safety?			
If stairs are metal, wood, or marble, have abrasive materials been used to provide protection against slips and falls?			
Are pieces broken out of the casing or front edge off the steps?			
Are clean and securely fastened handrails available?			
If the stairs are wide, has a center rail been provided?			

Ventilation—is it adequate in the:
    Receiving Area?
    Storage Area?
    Pots and Pans Area?
    Walk-in Coolers and Freezers?
    Food Preparation Area?
    Cooking Area?
    Serving Area?
    Dining Area?
    Soiled Dish Processing Area?			

Other Safety Concerns:			
Do employees wear good shoes to protect their feet against injury from articles that are dropped or pushed against their feet?			
Is employee clothing free of parts that could get caught in mixers, cutters, grinders, or other equipment?			

Area	Yes	No	Comments
Are fire extinguishers guarded so they will not be knocked from the wall?			
If doors are provided with a lock, is there an emergency bell or a by-pass device that will permit exit from the room should the door be accidentally locked while an employee is in the room?			
Is there a pusher or tamper provided for use with the grinders?			
Are mixers in safe operating condition?			
Are the mixer beaters properly maintained to avoid injury from broken metal parts and foreign particles in food?			

Part IV

Design, Finances, and Automation

Chapter Outline

The Planning Process
    Preliminary Considerations
        The Planning Team
        Equipment and Space Needs
        Redesign Goals
        Blueprints and Specifications
Redesigning the Kitchen
    Design Factors
        Cost
        The Menu
        Food Quantity
        Food Quality
        Equipment
        Utilities
        Space
        Sanitation and Safety
        Type of Service
    Layouts
        L-Shaped Layout
        Straight-Line Layout
        U-Shaped Layout
        Parallel Layout
Redesigning Other Areas
    Receiving and Storage Areas
    Dining Room Areas
        Server Supply Stations
        Cashier Work Station
    Lounge Areas
        Bars
Food and Beverage Equipment
    Factors in Equipment Selection
        Cost
        Sanitation and Safety
        Design and Performance
        Maintenance
        Capacity
        Construction
        Other Factors
    Types of Food Service Equipment
        Refrigerated Storage Equipment
        Ranges
        Ovens
        Tilting Braising Pans
        Steam Cooking Equipment
        Broilers
        Deep Fryers
        Other Equipment
Types of Beverage Equipment

Facility Design, Layout, and Equipment

A FOOD SERVICE FACILITY'S design and layout have a great impact on its appeal to guests and employees. If facilities are poorly designed, guests will be inconvenienced and may receive slow service. Production employees will lose time in extra walking and extra motions when preparing food; service employees may have to walk farther between food pickup areas and guest tables. Like good design and layout, the right equipment improves employee productivity and food quality; the wrong equipment can lead to many problems.

Because an operation's design, layout, and equipment influence how profitable it will be, owners are also concerned with these factors. Design and layout affect capital costs. If more space is designed into the facility than is needed, capital and labor costs will be greater than necessary. Unnecessary operating costs for servicing the extra space (heating, ventilating, air-conditioning, cleaning and maintenance, etc.) will be incurred.

Government agencies have a role to play, too, through regulatory laws for design, layout, and equipment that managers must adhere to.

You obviously would like the food service facility to be used for a long time. What if a menu change requires new and different types of equipment? Are there ways to design flexibility into the facility? The best designs and layouts are flexible.

You probably did not help design the facility in which you now work. However, you may be involved in remodeling projects. Even simple re-arrangements of the production equipment or dining room tables should be based on some very basic principles. Therefore, regardless of your management role, some knowledge about design and layout is helpful.

The Planning Process

Planning a facility's construction or remodeling should focus on the following goals:

- Management negotiates the best price possible for contracted labor, building materials, furniture, fixtures, and equipment.

- The remodeled facility appeals to guests and employees.

- There is a maximum return on investment.

- There is an efficient flow of people and products within the facility, and equipment is well-placed.

If more space is designed into the facility than is needed, capital costs will be greater than necessary.

- The facility provides safe working space for employees and public access space to guests.

- Design and layout take sanitation issues into account.

- The facility lends itself to employee work efficiency so that fewer employees are needed to meet quality standards and labor costs are lower.

- Facility maintenance costs are low. Since energy costs are a concern, buildings and equipment should be energy-efficient.

- Facility design makes employee supervision and other management activities easy.

Effective planning takes time and generally requires the specialized knowledge of such people as contractors, food service suppliers, and interior designers.[1]

Preliminary Considerations

There are many steps and people involved in the planning process. The commitment of capital funds is likely to be substantial; the amount of planning to help ensure that project goals are met without surprises also involves a substantial time commitment.

The Planning Team. The first step is to form a planning team. Of course, the general manager and the owner must be members of the team. In most cases, an architect will be needed. Unless you are thoroughly familiar with the complex task of interior space design, a food service facility consultant may also be a member of the team.

After the planning team is in place, the team must develop concepts and ideas for the facility. Does the remodeling project involve the exterior and/or the interior of the facility? Does it include the entire kitchen or just one area? Factors such as the type of facility (commercial or institutional); its size and hours of operation; the menu; and quality requirements of production, service, and atmosphere should be reviewed. By developing a thorough idea of the project, you will help ensure its successful completion.

It's important to think through exactly what activities are performed in an area before redesigning it. While it's not possible to look ahead many years, it's still important to think about general work activities and provide some flexibility in the design.

Equipment and Space Needs. The menu is a primary factor in dictating equipment and space needs. Other factors include employee skills and the variety and volume of food and beverages the operation produces.

A food service operation is usually designed or redesigned by first considering individual work stations. A work station is a place where one employee works or where one menu item is made. Work stations are put together to form work sections that are then organized into the larger work area. For example, the work station for one bartender may be designed first. It can then be matched with similar bartender work stations to form a work section—the bar. This work section must be appropriately placed in the work area—the lounge.

Preliminary layout and equipment plans help with space allocation; floor plans can show the general arrangement of equipment, work aisles, and the relationship of one work area to another. Cost estimates can be based on these plans. If estimated costs are greater than the amount budgeted for redesign and renovation, adjusting the plans may be necessary.

Redesign Goals. Managers must determine what they want the redesign to accomplish. For example, managers of an elegant facility may want the dining room to project an atmosphere of luxury; a fast-food establishment that depends on a high guest turnover may use bright, hot colors in its dining room as a subtle means of persuading guests not to linger over their meals.

Managers must also keep government safety regulations in mind when redesigning food service areas. These laws may restrict equipment placement in the kitchen, the number of guests that can be seated in the dining room, emergency lighting, the placement and number of exits, and so on.

Blueprints and Specifications. When preliminary information has been reviewed and approved, final blueprints can be drawn and equipment specifications prepared. These are used to solicit price quotations and make decisions about hiring contractors and suppliers. Construction and installation tasks follow. Contractors, equipment suppliers, and the operation's planning or management team should agree on a schedule and stick to it.

Redesigning the Kitchen

Plans to redesign the kitchen should address several concerns, including the following:

- *Physical fatigue.* A great deal of physical work takes place in the kitchen. Everything possible to reduce physical fatigue should be built into the kitchen's design. Examples are reducing distances that employees must walk, adjusting heights of work areas to best suit employees, and providing comfortable locker room, restroom, and employee dining facilities.

- *Noise.* Excessive noise makes employees uncomfortable and can distract employees and guests. Noise can be minimized with soundproofing materials and quiet equipment.

- *Lighting.* Much detail work is done in kitchen preparation areas. Adequate lighting helps employees work safely without eyestrain.

- *Temperature.* Kitchen areas can be hot. Cooking and cleaning equipment that generates heat and steam can make working conditions uncomfortable. Heating, ventilating, and air conditioning plans must deal with these problems.

- *Government safety codes.* Government safety codes designed to safeguard workers typically regulate the design, size, and placement of kitchen ventilation systems. Construction materials, exits, plumbing and electrical systems, and locations of fire extinguishers also may be regulated by local, state, and/or federal laws.

Design Factors

Kitchen design factors include:

- Cost
- The menu
- Food quantity
- Food quality
- Equipment
- Utilities
- Space
- Sanitation and safety
- Type of service

Cost. Scarce funds often limit kitchen remodeling. If preliminary planning reveals the project can't be completed with the funds available, the planning team has at least three options: (1) it can defer the project until funds are available, (2) it can adjust the plans to match the money budgeted for the project, or (3) it can cancel the project. Experienced managers, contractors, and others on the planning team will know which option is best.

The Menu. The menu is one of the most important determinants of kitchen needs. The menu items that an operation's employees must prepare help determine what kind of kitchen space and equipment are necessary. One example of how the menu affects kitchen design is the amount and type of convenience foods included on the menu. If a facility uses many convenience foods, the operation needs less space, less equipment, and fewer employees.

Food Quantity. The quantity of food the operation handles must be considered when redesigning. If a large volume of food is purchased, received, stored, issued, produced, and served, more kitchen equipment and space will be needed.

Food Quality. Food quality is often enhanced when food is prepared as close as possible to the time of service. However, "batch cooking"—dividing food into small batches and cooking batches as needed during the meal period—has space, cost, and equipment implications. For example, batch cooking requires less production equipment; capital costs may be decreased. On the other hand, batch cooking may result in higher labor costs. The restaurant's managers must decide what level of quality is acceptable for various food items and purchase the type and amount of equipment that will deliver that quality.

Equipment. There is a wide variety of equipment available to perform almost any storage, production, or service requirement. Today, many food service equipment items are mobile and can be moved easily for quick installation in new work stations or areas. It's often wiser to purchase multi-purpose equipment such as tilting braising pans and vertical cutter/mixers than one-purpose specialty equipment.

Utilities. Utility concerns are closely aligned with equipment needs. It's time-consuming and expensive to install equipment in areas without convenient access to utilities (plumbing, electricity, gas, etc.). The availability and cost of utilities during the life of the equipment must also be estimated.

Space. When facilities are remodeled, kitchen space has already been allocated. Unfortunately, often the original designers minimized kitchen space in order to provide more room to seat guests. Making room for more guests may not necessarily lead to more guests, however. When kitchen space is limited, so is the quantity of food that can be produced, which may lead to dissatisfied guests because of service delays. If your kitchen is cramped, part of the redesign might be to enlarge the kitchen.

Sanitation and Safety. As mentioned in Chapter 11, sanitation and safety concerns should be incorporated into kitchen design. As a food service manager, you are responsible for providing a sanitary and safe operation for guests and employees. As already noted, some sanitation and safety precautions are required by law. Operations must include areas for washing and sanitizing dishware and flatware (if disposable items are not used). Sanitary storing and holding facilities are also important. For safety reasons, kitchen lighting should be good and work aisles in front of production equipment should be wide.

Type of Service. The type of service an operation provides to guests is another factor to consider when redesigning the kitchen. For example, banquet service may require large quantities of food to be prepared and portioned quickly. This calls for a different type of kitchen than one in a coffee shop offering counter service.

Layouts

The process of redesigning a kitchen is complex. Work flow—the traffic patterns employees form as they go about their work—is another factor that must be considered.

Exhibit 12.1 L-Shaped Layout for Bakeshop Area

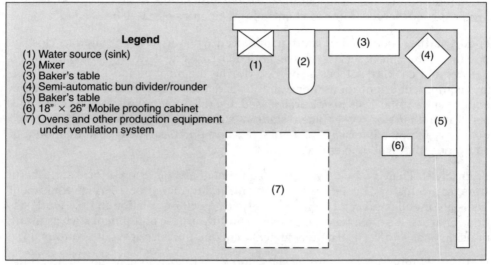

Legend
(1) Water source (sink)
(2) Mixer
(3) Baker's table
(4) Semi-automatic bun divider/rounder
(5) Baker's table
(6) 18" × 26" Mobile proofing cabinet
(7) Ovens and other production equipment under ventilation system

Note that the sample layouts shown in this section are designed to minimize employee backtracking.

L-Shaped Layout. The L-shaped layout presented in Exhibit 12.1 shows a work area found in many institutional food service kitchens—a bakeshop. This layout is a good one for the types of tasks performed in a bakeshop. Consider the task of making dinner rolls; an L-shaped layout makes this easy for the worker. Dinner rolls, like many other baking recipes, call for water. Therefore, time can be saved if a sink (see number 1 on the exhibit) is located next to the mixer (2). Because bread products such as dinner rolls must be kneaded, portioned, and shaped, a bakery table (3) is close to the mixer. Dinner rolls can be quickly shaped with a bun divider/rounder (4); this item is located close to the table. When proportioned and shaped rolls come out of the divider, they must be put onto pans; a table (5) makes this easier. After the rolls are panned, they must be proofed and transported to ovens. A mobile proofing cabinet (6) helps with this task. Since bakeshops use ovens frequently, ovens should be located close to the bakery area (7).

Straight-Line Layout. The straight-line layout in Exhibit 12.2 shows how pots and pans may be washed. First, soiled pots and pans are brought to the soiled pot counter (1). Leftover food can be scraped and sprayed into a garbage disposer trough (2 and 3) before washing. Depending on local sanitation codes, sinks for washing, rinsing, and sanitizing (4, 5, 6) are needed. After sanitizing, space is necessary for clean pots and pans to air dry; a clean pot counter (7) serves this purpose. Items must be stored after drying; a mobile pot rack (8) can be used for storing and transporting pots and pans to work areas for their next use.

Exhibit 12.2 Straight-Line Layout in Pot/Pan Wash Area

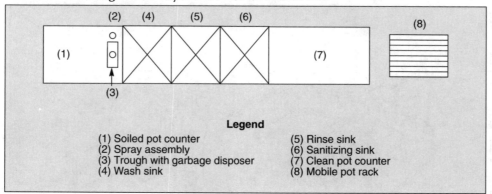

Legend

(1) Soiled pot counter
(2) Spray assembly
(3) Trough with garbage disposer
(4) Wash sink

(5) Rinse sink
(6) Sanitizing sink
(7) Clean pot counter
(8) Mobile pot rack

Exhibit 12.3 U-Shaped Layout in a Dishwashing Area

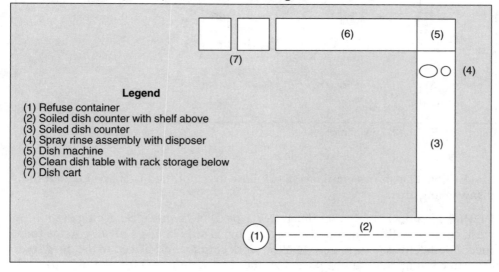

Legend

(1) Refuse container
(2) Soiled dish counter with shelf above
(3) Soiled dish counter
(4) Spray rinse assembly with disposer
(5) Dish machine
(6) Clean dish table with rack storage below
(7) Dish cart

U-Shaped Layout. Exhibit 12.3 illustrates a U-shaped layout for a dishwashing work area. The process begins at the refuse container (1) where service staff transport tubs and trays of soiled dishes. Shelves above the soiled dish counter (2) can be used for racks of glasses and cups. The shelf below the soiled dish counter can be used to stack soiled dishes until they are washed. The next counter (3) is used to rack soiled dishes before pre-rinsing (4) and running through the dishwashing machine (5). As with pots and pans, clean dishes must be air dried, so a clean dish table (6) is necessary. After dishes are dry, they must be stacked and transported to the serving counter or food service stand; mobile dish carts (7) may be needed.

Exhibit 12.4 Modified U-Shaped Layout in Dishwashing Area

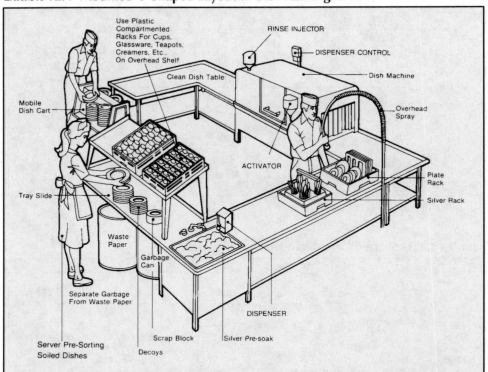

Courtesy of Ecolab, St. Paul, Minnesota

Exhibit 12.4 shows employee work flow in a modified U-shaped layout for a dishwashing area.

Parallel Layout. Exhibit 12.5 illustrates a parallel layout for a frying station. A work counter with refrigerated storage below (1) can be used to store items to be fried. Food items can be battered on the work counter and placed in the deep fryer (2). After frying, they can be placed on the work counter (3) for plating. The cook can then turn to the work counter/pickup station (5) and give the items to food servers or place them on dishes prepared by other cooks. In some operations, the fryer cook also works the grill; in this case, the range oven with grill (4) should be located close to or in the work station.

Redesigning Other Areas

Other areas that food service managers may be involved in redesigning include:

- Receiving and storage areas
- Dining room areas
- Lounge areas

Exhibit 12.5 Parallel Layout in a Frying Station

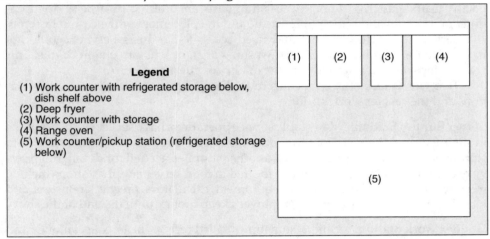

Legend
(1) Work counter with refrigerated storage below, dish shelf above
(2) Deep fryer
(3) Work counter with storage
(4) Range oven
(5) Work counter/pickup station (refrigerated storage below)

When redesigning dining room and lounge areas, managers should include conveniences for handicapped guests if these conveniences are not already present. Examples of conveniences include widened doorways, lowered or full-length mirrors in restrooms and grab bars near toilets, and no raised thresholds. These and other conveniences are required by law in many localities.

Receiving and Storage Areas

As mentioned in Chapter 8, receiving should take place in non-public areas. The receiving area should be as close as possible to the receiving door, and it should be large enough to handle all items ordinarily received. There should be room for a scale, dolly or cart, and other receiving equipment.

Storage areas include spaces for dry, refrigerated, and frozen products. Some large properties have separate storage spaces for produce, meats, seafood, and dairy products. For security reasons, dry storage areas should be designed with floor-to-ceiling walls and with ceilings that cannot be entered from an adjoining area. Some facilities have a lockable "precious storage" area for expensive items. It's common to have centralized walk-in refrigerators and freezers for all items needing cold storage.

Dining Room Areas

The planning team must pay special attention to the redesign of dining room areas. Guest reactions to food and its service often depend on the atmosphere of the dining room. Many things contribute to atmosphere: cleanliness; dining room furniture; dining room lighting; the amount of natural light (if any); the type of fabric and color(s) of tablecloths (if used); the types and color(s) of glass- and dish-ware; the type of flatware used; paintings, photographs, wall hangings, or other decorations; artificial, natural, or no plants; style of table settings; and many other factors.[2]

The size of the dining area must be matched with the kitchen's production capacity. Traffic patterns of employees and guests are affected by aisle width, location of restrooms and other public areas, and the placement of the cash register(s).

Servers in the dining room may need access to bar areas. Servers should not have to go through the kitchen, dishwashing area, or lobby to obtain drinks. This wastes steps and time, and lowers the quality of guest service.

Two work areas of special concern in the dining room are server supply stations and the cashier work station.

Server Supply Stations. Many table service operations have server supply stations in dining areas. These stations are often screened from guests and can be used to store soiled and clean dishes, as well as other supplies needed for dining room service. Equipment items that might be located in food server supply stations include microwave ovens, beverage service equipment, calculators, precheck registers, and lockable cash drawers (if service employees keep money until the end of the shift).

Cashier Work Station. Cashiers, sometimes called receptionists, collect money and visit with guests as guests enter and leave the facility. This work station's design and placement should be chosen carefully. If the station is placed in any available corner, guests who pay for their meals at the cash register may be inconvenienced; servers who take guest checks to the register may have to take many unnecessary steps.

Guests should be required to pass the cashier work station(s) as they leave the dining area. This reduces the possibility of "walk-outs" (guests who leave without paying). A convenient location is better for guests as well; they will not have to go out of their way as they leave.

The cash register is the primary equipment item located in this area. It should be placed so the cashier and the guest can see the transaction rung up in the display window. Other items that should be located in this area include the following:

- *Telephone.* A telephone enables the cashier to take reservations. Many credit card and check acceptance companies require pre-authorizations by telephone.

- *Miscellaneous items for sale.* Some food service operations have a variety of items for sale at the cashier's work station, including cigars, cigarettes, and recipe books. A place to store and protect these items against theft is necessary.

- *Menus.* Guests may wish to examine the menu while waiting to be seated. Offering take-home menus is another option.

- *Protected storage.* This is needed for guest checks when the cashier is responsible for them until they are processed by the manager or accounting personnel.

- *Dining room sketch and server station assignments.* Space for a dining room sketch and a list of server station assignments may need to be available.

Lounge Areas

The atmosphere in the lounge should be exactly what your property wishes to project. Many of the same factors discussed for dining room atmosphere—cleanliness, furniture, lighting, decorations, etc.—apply to lounges as well.

When designing the lounge, keep in mind that beverage personnel may have to interact with the restaurant cashier/receptionist (for example, when processing beverage transfers). Therefore, the location of the lounge relative to the dining room's cashier work station may be important. If food is served in the lounge, the lounge's location relative to kitchen or food pickup areas is a concern. Guests who only want food service should not have to pass through the lounge to get to the dining room, because non-drinking guests may not wish to enter the lounge. A foyer, a coatroom, or public restroom may be used to separate the lounge from the dining room. Server traffic flow is also important.

Bars. The design of a bar is just as important as the design of the kitchen, dining, and lounge areas.[3] The bar is an integral part of the food and beverage operation and generates sizable profits. It's unwise to allocate space to the bar based only on what's left after food service needs are met.

There are three basic types of bars: service bars, public bars, and combination public/service bars. Exhibit 12.6 shows the layout for a public/service bar. Two bartenders are required in this layout. One bartender works the service bar to provide drinks to employees who then serve guests in the restaurant or lounge. A second bartender serves guests at the public bar. The primary work stations are around the two speedrails, which hold bottles of the most frequently ordered liquor. Other often-used items (soda gun, ice, and glassware) are also located in these areas. The refrigerator and sinks can be shared by each bartender because they are installed in a convenient location for both. The overall design of the bar must be compatible with the lounge as a whole.

Beverage preparation areas are designed by first developing individual work stations. Usually, the length of a public bar is determined by the need for equipment space behind the bar, rather than the need for a specific number of seats (or amount of standing room) for guests.

Work simplification should be built into a bar's design. The task of preparing a variety of drinks in a short time requires carefully placed equipment. The bar's layout can greatly influence a bartender's work speed. Here are some bar layout guidelines:

- The bartender should be able to perform related activities in one place. For example, fruit garnishes can be cleaned, prepared, and stored in one specific area.

- Sufficient lighting and work counters at proper heights should be provided. Countertops should be approximately 34 inches from floor level.

- Doorways or pass-throughs should be wide enough to accommodate products and supplies that must be placed behind the bar. Too often, half-barrels or other sizes of draft beer kegs are difficult to bring into bar areas.

- Work space should accommodate employees. Bartenders should have ample space to produce drinks; beverage servers need room to place and pick up orders. Space is also required to store items that the servers may need, such as napkins, bar picks, and ashtrays.

Exhibit 12.6 Sample Layout of Public/Service Bar

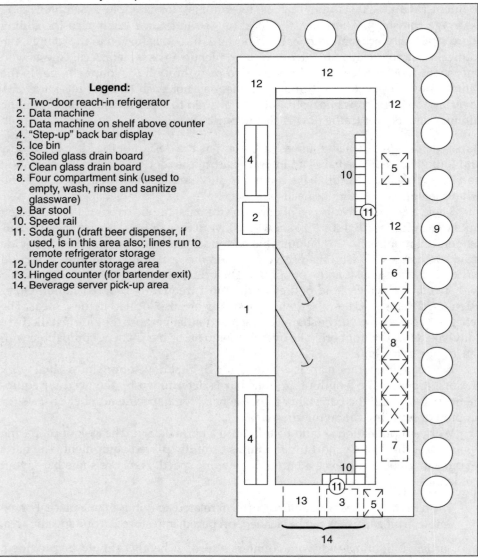

Legend:
1. Two-door reach-in refrigerator
2. Data machine
3. Data machine on shelf above counter
4. "Step-up" back bar display
5. Ice bin
6. Soiled glass drain board
7. Clean glass drain board
8. Four compartment sink (used to empty, wash, rinse and sanitize glassware)
9. Bar stool
10. Speed rail
11. Soda gun (draft beer dispenser, if used, is in this area also; lines run to remote refrigerator storage
12. Under counter storage area
13. Hinged counter (for bartender exit)
14. Beverage server pick-up area

Source: Jack D. Ninemeier, *Beverage Management: Business Systems for Restaurants, Hotels, and Clubs* (New York: Lebhar-Friedman, 1982), p. 74.

Food and Beverage Equipment

Food and beverage employees cannot effectively store, prepare, or serve products without the right equipment. Today there is a wide range of food and beverage equipment available. Equipment is often expensive, and equipment decisions will affect the property for a long time—the useful life span of many items is more than

15 years. How can you decide which item is best? Part of the answer is to involve supervisors and employees in the decision-making process. They are the ones who use the equipment and know how it works, so you should solicit their ideas about equipment selection.

Factors in Equipment Selection

There are many factors to consider when purchasing equipment. Many of them are similar to those considered when redesigning kitchens. While some factors address broad concerns important to every equipment purchase, other factors are specific to the property and the item in question. The following factors are important for most equipment purchases:

- Cost
- Safety
- Sanitation
- Design and performance
- Maintenance
- Capacity
- Construction
- Other factors

Cost. The purchase price is not the only cost to assess. Financing charges (interest) often dramatically increase equipment costs. Operating costs, including utility charges, can be substantial. If energy costs are expected to increase in the near future, this factor will have an even greater impact on purchase decisions. As mentioned earlier, installation expenses can be high. For example, some equipment may need a new ventilation, plumbing, or electrical system. If utility hook-ups are not available where needed, expenses to provide them can be significant. You should consider repair, depreciation, and insurance expenses as well. All relevant costs must be identified and considered in the purchase decision.

Sanitation and Safety. Equipment should be easy to clean. The National Sanitation Foundation (NSF) periodically develops and issues guidelines on sanitary aspects of equipment design and construction.[4] These guidelines can help with the equipment selection process.

Buy equipment made of materials that can withstand normal wear, including the corrosive action of food and beverages and cleaning compounds. Equipment must not impart odor, color, or taste to food. All food contact surfaces should be smooth, easily cleanable, corrosion-resistant, non-toxic, stable (no wobbly tables, for example), and non-absorbent. Use non-toxic solder in all food contact areas. Some materials used for food service equipment include:

- *Wood*. While lightweight and economical, wood is difficult to keep clean because it's porous. Wood can easily absorb food odors and stains, so its use should be restricted. It's frequently used for shelving in production and storage areas.

Exhibit 12.7 Government/Industry Groups Concerned with Equipment Safety and Sanitation

Name of Group	Type	Special Concerns
1. Occupational Safety and Health Administration (OSHA)	Government	Equipment safety and related concerns
2. National Sanitation Foundation (NSF)	Private	Equipment sanitation
3. Underwriters Laboratories (UL)	Private	Electrical equipment safety
4. American Gas Association (AGA)	Private	Safety for gas-fueled equipment
5. Municipal and State Agencies	Government	Safety and sanitation
6. National Electric Manufacturers' Association (NEMA)	Industry	Electrical equipment safety
7. Food and Drug Administration (FDA)	Government	Sanitation
8. American Society of Sanitary Engineers	Industry	Facility design

- *Metal.* Metal, especially stainless steel, is commonly used for food preparation equipment and food contact work surfaces. Steel, copper, or brass can be plated with chromium, tin, or nickel. These treatments are frequently used on food service equipment items to produce a shiny finish. Copper utensils are usually plated to make them corrosion-resistant, and steel plating is often used to line equipment. Steel sheets can be treated, covered with zinc, and used to make galvanized metal for sinks, tables, and related service equipment. Over time, however, this metal is subject to wear and the steel can be exposed, resulting in rust and corrosion.

- *Glass.* Glass is sometimes used in equipment doors.

- *Plastic or rubber-based products.* Plastic or rubber-based equipment items are gaining popularity. These materials resist cuts and odors and are lightweight, non-porous, and easy to clean. Plastic or rubber-based equipment items are often much less expensive than metal-based products.

Equipment must also be safe to use. The Occupational Safety and Health Act (OSHA) has established laws to help ensure that equipment is free of hazards. These laws can provide meaningful safety information to guide purchase decisions.

Check for Underwriters Laboratories (UL) approval on electrical equipment and American Gas Association (AGA) approval on gas equipment. Look for such features as safety catches on steamer doors, safety pilot lights on gas equipment, and overload protection on electrical equipment.

Exhibit 12.7 lists some government and industry groups that are concerned about equipment safety and sanitation.

Design and Performance. Equipment should be simple to use, provide value (price relative to quality), incorporate sanitation and safety standards, and help employees provide high-quality products in the volume and with the speed that are necessary.

Multi-purpose equipment with optional features can often be purchased at little additional cost. For example, a mixer with the proper attachments can be used to slice, grind, or shred food products. On the other hand, some equipment may have built-in features that increase the purchase price but will never be used. Performance features might best be assessed by talking with industry professionals using similar equipment.

Since some equipment is easier to operate than others, the skills and abilities of employees must be considered. Buy equipment that's easy to operate whenever possible.

Maintenance. Most equipment requires careful periodic maintenance to operate effectively. Can maintenance be done by on-site staff or must skilled technicians be contracted? How often and at what cost must these activities be performed? How long does maintenance take? Will there be a need to make menu or other adjustments during this time? If the equipment being considered is a newer model of the equipment currently being used, managers should review the old equipment's maintenance and repair record (see Exhibit 12.8). Excessive repairs suggest that either the equipment is unsuitable or that it's being used improperly. Equipment that is frequently "down" is of little value.

Capacity. Obviously, managers should choose equipment with the right capacity for the operation. Inadequate equipment will impair efficiency; production staff may need to prepare several batches of food instead of one, for example.

Construction. The National Sanitation Foundation has developed detailed construction specifications for many types of food service equipment.[5] Consult this source when considering equipment construction standards. Reputable manufacturers and suppliers are more likely to provide high-quality equipment.

Properly constructed equipment is more expensive than lower-quality equipment. However, because of its extended life and other advantages, expensive equipment is generally worth the additional investment. When you consider that a dishwashing machine can easily cost as much as a high-priced luxury car, the importance of proper design and construction is clear.

Other Factors. Normally, equipment should be made for commercial—not home—use. Food service employees are not always careful with equipment, so equipment items must be durable. Appearance is important for serving and production equipment visible to guests.

New equipment should be compatible with existing space and other equipment items already in use. For example, a dishwashing machine that fits into the old dishwashing machine's space is convenient. In some operations, the quietness of equipment and/or its mobility will be an important concern.

Generally, "stock" is a better choice than "custom" equipment. Stock equipment is available in catalogs and can be ordered through dealers without modification to basic designs. Custom equipment tailored to the operation is much more expensive and managers must allow a considerable lead-time when ordering it.

Exhibit 12.8 Preventive Maintenance and Repair Record

Service	Type Machine	Equipment Number
Location	Serial Number	Model Number
Make	Date Purchased	Purchase Cost

Preventive Maintenance Procedure	
Function	Interval

Special Instructions

Specifications	
Voltage	Drive
Amperage	Belts
Phase	Fuse
Pressure	Lubrication
Horsepower	Filter
RPM	Fluids

Spare Parts Required			
Part	Mfr. Part Number	Hotel Stock Number	Quantity

Types of Food Service Equipment

Food service equipment items include:

- Refrigerated storage equipment
- Ranges
- Ovens
- Tilting braising pans
- Steam cooking equipment
- Broilers
- Deep fryers
- Other equipment

Refrigerated Storage Equipment. There are two basic types of refrigerated equipment: walk-in units and reach-in or roll-in units.

Walk-in units. Refrigerated walk-in units are used for central storage purposes. They can also be used to hold items awaiting production or service. Walk-in freezers are used to store items awaiting production and, sometimes, frozen leftovers.

For safety reasons, it should be possible to open the doors of walk-in refrigerators and freezers from the inside even if the door is locked. A thermostat, perhaps with an accompanying high-temperature-alert device, can be used to monitor the internal temperature of the unit.

Walk-ins can be sectional (installed in sections after the building is constructed) or built-in. Separate refrigeration systems should generally be used for walk-in refrigerator and freezer compartments. Refrigeration systems feature water- or air-cooled compressors. The compressor, condenser, and evaporator must be fitted to the size of the refrigeration unit.

Walk-in refrigeration units should be built with locking panels to ensure an airtight, durable seal. Normally the manufacturer will warrant refrigerated units for several years under normal usage. Insulation is usually foamed-in-place or made of a froth-type urethane. If prefabricated units are installed on concrete floors, a floor made of insulated panels may also be necessary. To prevent floor distortion, a flooring load of at least 300 pounds per square foot is generally recommended. Metal plates or floor coverings should be used when there is continual use of heavily loaded transport equipment.

Reach-in or roll-in units. Smaller refrigerated units are referred to as reach-ins or roll-ins. They are used to store food products at point-of-use in production areas. These units are often used in server or guest areas as well. They may also be used as central storage units at small operations.

Reach-ins have doors that swing open like a home refrigerator's or swing up like a chest-type freezer's. Reach-ins or roll-ins may open on one side only or be a pass-through type with doors on each side. They may have from one to three or more sections of full-length doors or two to six or more sections of half-size doors. Reach-ins may have fixed shelves or slides for modular pans. Some reach-ins are designed to accommodate roll-in carts. Under-the-counter units used to store small quantities of food items in preparation/service areas are also available.

A line of heavy-duty ranges: (1) Range with two 12-inch solid tops and one 12-inch open top, standard oven below; (2) range with three 12-inch open tops, standard oven; (3) range with two 18-inch solid tops and 36-inch cheese-melter mounted above, standard oven below; (4) single broiler with warming oven mounted over it, convection oven below. (Courtesy of The Montague Company, Hayward, California)

A pass-through reach-in is generally located between a preparation area and a service area. In a cafeteria operation, salads, sandwiches, and refrigerated desserts can be prepared in the kitchen, placed in the pass-through, and retrieved through the other side by servers or guests.

As with walk-in refrigerators and freezers, the proper size of the compressor, condenser, and evaporator for a reach-in or roll-in unit is essential. Foamed-in-place or froth-type urethane insulation is necessary. Reach-ins or roll-ins should have a seamless interior construction with self-closing doors. Adjustable legs that make the equipment level with the floor, an automatic defroster-timer for the freezer, an exterior-mounted thermometer, and locking doors are useful options.

Ranges. A range can be used to do almost any type of cooking. Ranges may be operated by either gas or electricity.

Ranges have been very popular and widely used in commercial and institutional food service operations for years. However, specialized equipment has reduced dependence on ranges. Several ranges installed in a straight-line work station are being replaced in some operations by a work station consisting of one range, a high-speed pressure steamer, a pressure fryer, and other specialized equipment items.

There are two basic types of ranges: solid-top and open-top. Solid-top ranges apply heat uniformly over the entire top section of the range. Open-top ranges have individually heated units which can be adjusted separately. Combination solid-top/open-top ranges are also available. While most ranges come equipped with ovens underneath, some countertop models have shelves or storage cabinets below.

A separate specialty grill that allows cooks to grill food with wood and charcoal. (Courtesy of Hickory Specialties, Inc., Brentwood, Tennessee)

Specialized ranges include chop suey ranges and range griddles. A griddle or a grill can be purchased as a separate piece of equipment, but it's usually placed close to the range. Griddle-top units are usually equipped with a grease collection pan underneath and a splashback to prevent spillage.

Carbon dioxide or non-toxic chemical fire extinguishers that meet applicable regulations should be placed near ranges. Generally, ventilation systems above ranges have fire extinguishing systems built into them. The danger of a grease fire is always present when cooking with range equipment. Managers should stress safety to employees and provide them with safety training.

Ovens. There are many types of ovens. *Range ovens* have been a traditional and versatile piece of production equipment in most food service operations. Many ranges have ovens beneath them.

Deck ovens are decked (stacked) on top of each other to increase capacity without requiring additional floor space. These units are available with single or multiple decks and in combination with roasting or baking ovens.

A *roasting oven* typically has an interior cavity 12 to 15 inches high, while the interior cavity of a *baking oven* is usually about 8 inches high. However, both types of ovens are available in a wide range of interior lengths and widths.

Gas-powered deck ovens in a pizzeria. (Courtesy of Bakers Pride Oven Co., Inc., New Rochelle, New York)

Convection ovens have fans or blowers to circulate heat and air in the closed oven chamber. This allows heat to penetrate food products more quickly and shortens cooking time. It also permits the use of lower oven temperatures. There are several types of convection ovens: single-deck, double-deck, and roll-in (roll-in convection ovens allow a mobile rack to be wheeled directly into the oven).

Many items that can be prepared with a conventional range or deck oven can also be prepared in a convection oven. Since items can be cooked in a shorter time and at a lower temperatures in convection ovens, food quality is often enhanced. This also increases output, and, because the convection oven itself is smaller than a conventional deck oven, more efficient use is made of available floor space.

Rotary or *revolving tray ovens* use flat shelves suspended between two reels. Food items to be roasted or baked are loaded onto the trays as they appear at the door opening. These ovens are designed to prevent the escape of hot air when the door is opened. Rotary ovens are frequently used in large food service operations.

Microwave ovens use radiation (electromagnetic waves) to heat food. As the waves penetrate food, they cause molecules in the food to move, producing friction and heat. The advantages of microwaves include fast cooking, easy cleaning, and fewer fire hazards.

Microwaves have many uses. They can be used for many products that do not need browning. Some microwave ovens are even equipped with browning units which give characteristic color to bakery and other products.

Typical applications for microwave ovens in quantity food operations include thawing, heating, and reheating small portions of food; and cooking short-order products.

Infrared (quartz) ovens may be used to heat, roast, and brown products. They are especially useful for reconstituting frozen foods packaged in bulk. A quartz oven is very good for broiling and for browning to finish dishes that have been heated in a microwave.

Recon ovens are used to reconstitute frozen, prepared entrées. They can also be used as high-speed conventional ovens. Recon ovens have many uses and come in various sizes to accommodate most needs.

Tilting Braising Pans. A tilting braising pan is a flat-bottomed cooking item that can be used as a kettle, griddle, fry pan, steamer, oven, or warmer/server. The bottom of an electric tilting braising pan is a heavy stainless steel plate which is heated by an electric heating element.

A tilting braising pan can reduce the total cooking time of many food products by as much as 25%. It's very flexible and can be used for a wide variety of food products. Since it tilts, both pouring and cleaning are easy.

Steam Cooking Equipment. Steam cooking equipment is used in many food service operations. There may be a self-contained boiler that produces steam for the equipment. It's a common practice to purchase steam equipment with a larger than necessary boiler so that more steam equipment can be added. Steam equipment can also be purchased without a boiler and connected to a centralized steam source. With some steam equipment—a steam-jacketed kettle, for example—steam does not come in contact with the food being cooked. With other steam equipment—a compartment steamer, for example—steam comes into direct contact with the food.

Steam-jacketed kettles. Steam-jacketed kettles are large cooking pots which range in capacity from several quarts to 100 or more gallons. They are generally used to steam, boil, or simmer. Steam-jacketed kettles have a double wall: food is heated by steam that is in a jacket surrounding the interior wall of the kettle. In some kettles, the double wall extends only approximately three-fourths of the way up the side. In other kettles the double wall extends up the entire side. As with any steam equipment, proper safety features are a must. These include pressure-reducing and safety valves.

Steam-jacketed kettles can be used to prepare meats, poultry, casseroles, eggs, soups, fresh or frozen vegetables, sauces, and pie fillings. These kettles reduce the amount of range space and number of top-of-range cooking utensils necessary. Large kettles allow cooking in one vessel rather than many. Because steam-jacketed kettles tend to heat evenly, scorching problems are reduced.

Some steam-jacketed kettles can be tilted to remove food products and draw off water used to clean the kettle. Tilting kettles may also have draw-off valves. In non-tilting kettles, food or water must be removed by ladling or by a draw-off valve.

It's a good idea to have a water source close to the kettle because water is a common ingredient in many of the items usually prepared in this equipment. A nearby drain makes it easier to clean kettles.

Compartment steamers. A compartment steamer is a heating vessel that cooks food directly with steam. A compartment steamer works much like a pressure cooker. It can be used to cook almost any food except items that need to be deep-fat fried, sautéed, or cooked with dry heat.

A conventional low-pressure compartment steamer usually operates at approximately five pounds per square inch (psi) of steam pressure. Low-pressure compartment steamers are found in the kitchens of many large volume food service operations. They can be used to prepare large quantities of food, so they are excellent for cooking vegetables, macaroni, and eggs. Low-pressure compartment steamers also thaw frozen products and perform many of the tasks done by steam-jacketed kettles.

High-pressure compartment steamers are often placed on cooking lines in commercial properties. These equipment items operate at approximately 15 psi. They are designed to cook small quantities of food quickly. High-pressure compartment steamers are used to prepare convenience foods such as frozen or refrigerated pre-portioned items in pouches, fresh shellfish, and a variety of other items that can be reconstituted on an as-needed basis.

Convection steamers. Room-pressure convection steamers are very useful for cooking seafood, vegetables, and other items for which nutrient retention is especially important.

Broilers. Broilers use radiant heat to cook foods rapidly and are fueled by either gas or electricity. There are two common types of broilers: overhead broilers and underfired charbroilers.

Overhead broilers. Overhead broilers have heating units that radiate heat down to foods placed on a shelf below. The shelf is usually adjustable so that food can be placed closer to or farther away from the heat source. This will affect the broiling time. For example, a thick piece of meat placed close to the heat source may burn on the outside before it's done on the inside, so the shelf should be placed farther away. A thinner cut of meat might be placed closer to the heat source.

A small overhead broiler, also called a shelf broiler or salamander, can be mounted on top of a range. While the capacity of shelf broilers is small, they are adequate in operations with low broiling loads. They are usually used as finish broilers (for example, to melt cheese or brown bread crumb toppings) and as auxiliary broilers during slow periods.

Charbroilers. Underfired charbroilers use a heat source under the food rather than above it. Food items to be charbroiled are placed on a grate above a radiant-hot surface. During cooking, the food juices drip directly onto the hot surface and burn, creating the typical charcoal flavor and appearance. Since this process produces smoke and odors, charbroilers—like most other pieces of cooking equipment—must be placed under an efficient ventilation system.

Charbroilers with small cooking surfaces are available for light use. Some larger units have an expandable grate area.

Deep Fryers. Deep fryers can be fueled by electricity or gas. Conventional fryers (tabletop models) may hold 15 pounds or less of frying fat. Large freestanding fryers may hold 130 pounds or more of frying fat.

Pressure fryers have sealed lids. When the unit is in operation, pressure builds up within the fryer. This reduces frying time and is ideal for items such as deep-fried chicken.

Large volume operations may use a continuous-type deep fryer. These units have a conveyor to move products through the fat. The food's position on the conveyor determines the cooking time. Items that require more cooking time are placed at the end of the conveyor so that they remain in the fat longer.

High-quality fat enhances food flavor and lasts longer. A fat's quality and smoke point (the temperature at which the fat disintegrates and smokes) are important concerns in selecting frying fat.

Deep fryers must have a rapid recovery rate. A recovery rate is the amount of time it takes a deep fryer to reheat the fat to proper cooking temperatures after cold food is added. Without rapid recovery, food products will absorb grease and food quality will suffer.

Conventional and pressure deep fryers are often equipped with two frying baskets. This is useful for frying large quantities at one time or for alternating baskets. Newer models are equipped with automatic filtering systems and computerized controls to automatically lower frying baskets into the fat, time the food while it's frying, and then raise the basket(s).

Many of the kitchen fires that occur originate at the deep fryer. For this reason, the area must be well ventilated and have fire extinguishing equipment nearby. Personnel should be carefully trained in proper fryer use. Since breading or other preparation activities are frequently necessary for products being deep fried, sufficient work space close to the fryer is important. Work space must also be provided to set down products removed from the unit. In too many operations, this work space is across the aisle from the fryer and the aisle quickly becomes unsanitary and unsafe because breading, batter, and frying fat drips on the floor as products are removed.

Other Equipment. Most of the equipment discussed thus far in this section cooks food. Other food service equipment includes:

- Mixers

- Cutters, choppers, and slicers

- Coffee-making equipment

- Dishwashing machines

- Inexpensive equipment

Mixers. A mixer is a mechanical device used to combine or blend foods. An electric motor drives a mixing arm. Mixers are commonly used in preparation areas for making salad dressings, whipping potatoes, and blending casserole mixtures. In the baking area, a mixer is necessary to produce dough and batter.

Mixers are of two general types: table models with a capacity of 5 to 20 quarts and floor models with a capacity of 20 to 80 quarts or more.

Special attachments can be used with a mixer to cut, shred, grind, or chop food products for casserole dishes, salads, and other items. A floor-model mixer has three standard attachments: (1) a paddle beater for general mixing which can be used to mash, cream, mix, or blend food products; (2) a whip that incorporates air into light mixtures and can be used to blend dry mixes, whip cream or egg whites, or mix light icings; and (3) a dough hook that can be used to mix heavy dough with a folding and stretching action.

The drive shaft of a mixer can also be used to operate a wide array of food processing attachments such as knife sharpeners, juice extractors, and food slicers. Three other popular mixer attachments are cutters, choppers, and grinders. Cutters and choppers cut vegetables and other food as the food passes against or between rotating blades. Grinders push food items through grinding plates or blades. If properly used, these attachments can significantly increase kitchen staff productivity.

Cutters, choppers, and slicers. Cutters, choppers, and slicers can also be purchased as stand-alone pieces of equipment. Food cutters/mixers are available in table as well as floor models.

A table-model food chopper is another popular item. Items to be chopped are placed in a bowl that revolves and pushes the products through revolving knives. The chopped food is removed when the bowl has turned once. For finer chopping, the bowl is allowed to turn additional times.

Some stand-alone food slicers automatically move food across a blade. Manual slicers are more common, however. Slicers can be very dangerous if used improperly. The manufacturer's instructions should always be followed. Managers must train employees in safe operation and cleaning.

Coffee-making equipment. There is a wide variety of coffee-making equipment available to meet the needs of almost any food service operation. Manual, semi-automatic, or automatic equipment is available to produce one cup or many gallons at one time. Some equipment is stationary, mounted on a counter or directly on the floor; some can be mounted on a cart for mobile use.

Small coffee-making units for hotels and restaurants use manual, pump, or siphon systems to pour water over and through coffee grounds into glass carafes. Urns ranging in size from 3 to 150 gallons are also available for use in banquet and institutional operations.

Proper maintenance of coffee-brewing equipment is a must. So are procedures for correctly making and handling coffee. Coffee distributors usually offer a wide variety of information for use in employee training programs.

Dishwashing machines. A dishwashing machine is a valuable and expensive appliance that comes in many types. The most basic is a rack-type machine in which dishes are racked and inserted into the machine for washing. Most machines have an automatic washing and sanitizing cycle which eliminates the need for operator control of these cycles. Large rack-type machines are also available. With these machines, dishes are racked and placed on a conveyor that pulls the racks through the machine. They are then removed from the conveyor belt at the other end by a dishwashing machine operator.

Dishwashing machines may have automatic dispensers for detergent and other chemicals such as drying agents. Most machines require a booster heater to bring the water temperature up to the required 180°F (82°C) minimum temperature necessary for sanitization. Some units use lower temperatures and sanitize dishes chemically.

Table-model cutter/mixer capable of chopping 7 pounds of meat in 25 seconds; mixing 10 pounds of potato salad in 60 seconds. (Courtesy of Stephan Machinery Corporation, Columbus, Ohio)

The dishwashing machine is the single most expensive equipment item in many facilities. Associated costs include the costs of counters, disposers, racks, dish carts, and the dishwashing area itself. Proper layout and design is important to ensure that employees can work efficiently. You must also train employees to properly operate and maintain equipment to protect the owner's investment.

Inexpensive food service equipment. The list of inexpensive food service equipment is long and includes toasters, warmers, ladles, peelers, scales, knives, pots and pans, egg beaters, measuring spoons, pastry brushes, rolling pins, muffin and pie tins, funnels, strainers, thermometers, can openers, mixing and chopping bowls, graters, poultry shears, cutting boards, butter spreaders, and much more. There are no universal guidelines for the types and quantities of inexpensive equipment items an operation should have; each operation must assess its own unique needs.

Types of Beverage Equipment

Most operations need far less beverage equipment than food service equipment.[6] In recent years, a wide variety of automated beverage equipment has become available. Examples include equipment that measures the liquor used in drinks and equipment that actually mixes drinks. Whether an operation uses automated beverage equipment is a decision that must be made by its management team, based on issues like maintenance costs and the marketing implications of using such equipment. (Some guests do not like automated beverage equipment, for example.) If managers opt to install automated equipment, they should also develop plans for what to do if the equipment breaks down. (Chapter 14 will discuss automated beverage equipment in more detail.)

Other beverage equipment includes refrigerators, frozen drink machines, glass storage areas, sinks, blenders, and hand tools such as bar strainers, shakers, and corkscrews.

Beverage equipment visible to guests should be attractive and compatible with the operation's atmosphere. Dirty, noisy, rusty, or dented equipment is never acceptable.

Endnotes

1. For additional information about the planning process, see Edward A. Kazarian, *Food Service Facilities Planning*, 2d ed. (Westport, Conn.: AVI, 1983).

2. Anthony M. Rey and Ferdinand Wieland, *Managing Service in Food and Beverage Operations* (East Lansing, Mich.: Educational Institute of the American Hotel & Motel Association, 1985), pp. 353–364.

3. This discussion is loosely based on Jack D. Ninemeier, *Beverage Management: Business Systems for Hotels, Restaurants, and Clubs* (New York: Lebhar-Friedman, 1982), pp. 65–78.

4. *Food Service Equipment Standards* (Ann Arbor, Mich.: National Sanitation Foundation, 1976).

5. *Equipment Standards.*

6. Rey and Wieland, *Managing Service*, pp. 320–321.

Key Terms

broiler	steam-cooking equipment
deep fryer	tilting braising pan
oven	traffic pattern
range	walk-in unit
reach-in unit	work flow
roll-in unit	work station

Discussion Questions

1. What concerns should be addressed when redesigning a kitchen?

2. What are four types of work-area layouts?

3. When redesigning receiving and storage areas, what are some things a food service manager should keep in mind?

4. What are some factors that contribute to a dining room's atmosphere?

5. What items are typically found at a cashier work station?

6. What are three basic types of bars?

7. What are some bar layout guidelines?

8. When selecting food service equipment, what are some factors managers must consider?

9. What are some common types of food service equipment? beverage service equipment?

10. What are some common types of ovens?

Chapter Outline

Uniform System of Accounts
The Operations Budget
    As a Profit Plan
        Projecting Revenue
        Determining Profit Requirements
        Estimating Expense Levels
    As a Control Tool
The Income Statement
    Restaurant Income Statement
    Hotel F&B Department Income Statement
The Balance Sheet
    Assets
    Liabilities
Ratio Analysis
    Liquidity Ratios
    Solvency Ratios
    Activity Ratios
    Profitability Ratios
    Operating Ratios
        Food Cost Percentage
        Beverage Cost Percentage
        Labor Cost Percentage
        Average Food Service Check
        Seat Turnover
Food Service Payroll Accounting
    The Fair Labor Standards Act
    Payroll Accounting for Tipped Employees
    Minimum Wage Tip Credit
        Using the FLSA Formula to Compute the Tip Credit
        Using Actual Tips Received to Compute the Tip Credit

13

Financial Management

Financial management deals with the economic aspects of food service operations. In today's fast-paced world of business, food service managers need to know as much as they can about the financial aspects of their operations. Today, few managers can operate out of a cigar box or keep bills in a desk drawer and magically come out all right at the end of the month. Fortunately, effective accounting systems have been developed to ease the food service manager's task in areas of accounting and financial management.

Groups such as the American Accounting Association and the American Institute of Certified Public Accountants establish the rules and standards used by all businesses. In the hospitality industry, food service operations can use accounting systems developed for their specific type of operations. The major purpose of accounting systems is to generate accurate and timely information to help managers make decisions. These uniform accounting systems are discussed early in this chapter.

The existence of uniform accounting systems does not mean that accounting should be left completely to the accountants. As mentioned in Chapter 2, controllers and other accountants are most often in a staff or advisory relationship to the restaurant manager and other line managers. Knowledge about accounting principles and the basic financial statements helps line managers gauge the soundness of their accountants' analysis and advice.

This chapter focuses on the financial aspects of a food service operation that managers need to know in order to perform their jobs effectively. The operations budget—management's profit plan and control tool—is examined in some detail. Basic financial statements, particularly the income statement and the balance sheet, are discussed from a management perspective. Also, a section on selected financial and operations ratios centers on how these ratios help a manager evaluate the success of the food service operation. The final sections of the chapter address aspects of payroll accounting that are unique to food service businesses.

Uniform System of Accounts

Several major trade associations related to the food service industry have published manuals defining accounts for various types and sizes of operations. A food service business using the uniform system of accounts manual designed for its segment of the hospitality industry may select from the manual those accounts that apply to its operations and ignore those that do not. These manuals may also provide standardized financial statement formats, explanations of individual accounts, and sample bookkeeping documents. A uniform system of accounts serves as a turnkey accounting system because it can be quickly adapted to the needs and requirements of new businesses entering the food service industry.

The idea of a uniform system of accounts is not new and is not unique to the hospitality industry. The *Uniform System of Accounts for Hotels* was first published in 1926 by a number of outstanding hoteliers who had the foresight to recognize the value of such a system to the hotel industry. Although there have been several revised editions since the 1926 publication, the fundamental format of the original uniform system has survived. This is a testament to the success of the system in meeting the basic needs of the industry.[1]

Following the lead of the lodging industry, the National Restaurant Association published the *Uniform System of Accounts for Restaurants* in 1930. Its objective was to give restaurant operators a common accounting language and to provide a basis upon which to compare the results of their operations. This uniform accounting system has been revised five times and today many restaurant operators find it a valuable accounting handbook.[2]

There are many uniform accounting systems serving the needs of the various food service segments of the hospitality industry. The *Uniform System of Accounts and Expense Dictionary for Small Hotels, Motels, and Motor Hotels* provides a standardized accounting system for full-service properties (those with extensive food and beverage facilities) and limited-service properties (those that have limited food and beverage facilities or that lease out food and beverage operations).[3] There are also uniform accounting systems for conference centers, clubs, and hospitals.

The uniform accounting systems are continually revised to reflect changes in acceptable accounting procedures and changes in the business environment that may affect hospitality accounting. They now enjoy widespread adoption by the industry and recognition by banks and other financial institutions as well as the courts.

Food service managers gain many benefits from adopting the uniform system of accounts appropriate for their operations. Perhaps the greatest benefit is that the uniformity of account definitions provides a common language with which managers from different food service businesses may discuss their operations. This common language permits useful comparisons among properties of the same size and service level. When managers and executives from businesses using the same uniform system of accounts gather to discuss the industry, they know that they are all speaking the same language.

Another benefit of a uniform accounting system is that regional and national statistics can be gathered and the industry can be alerted to possible threats and/or opportunities posed by developing trends. Industry statistical reports also serve as general standards by which to compare the results of individual operations. For example, the percentages listed in Exhibit 13.1 provide national averages for the sources and uses of income for several different types of restaurants. Exhibit 13.2 presents similar statistics for the food and beverage departments of various sizes of hotels. These industry statistics are meant to be used only as guidelines for general comparison purposes. A significant variance between the results of a particular food service operation and the industry average may be due to circumstances that are unique to that operation or locality. If that is the case, there may not be cause for alarm or any need for action.

Exhibit 13.1 The Restaurant and Resort Industry Dollar

	Full-Menu Table Service	Limited-Menu Table Service	Limited-Menu No Table Service	Cafeteria
Where It Came From*				
Food Sales	81.3	83.5	98.1	97.1
Beverage Sales	16.8	14.6	1.6	1.2
Other Income	1.9	1.9	0.3	1.7
Where It Went*				
Cost of Food Sold	29.5	28.3	31.1	36.9
Cost of Beverage Sold	4.6	3.9	0.4	0.4
Payroll	26.9	28.9	23.5	25.4
Employee Benefits	2.6	4.5	3.1	4.1
Direct Operating Expenses	6.9	6.4	5.7	4.2
Music and Entertainment	1.0	0.5	0.3	0.1
Advertising and Promotion	2.6	2.6	4.8	1.3
Utilities	2.8	3.0	2.9	2.7
Administrative and General	3.8	4.3	4.4	3.7
Repairs and Maintenance	1.9	1.7	2.1	1.3
Rent	4.7	3.7	6.8	6.4
Property Taxes	0.6	0.7	0.7	0.5
Other Taxes	1.3	0.5	0.4	0.6
Property Insurance	1.3	1.2	0.9	0.8
Interest	1.1	1.1	0.6	0.8
Depreciation	2.9	2.9	3.0	3.6
Other Deductions	0.5	0.5	0.4	0.6
Net Income Before Income Taxes	5.0	5.3	8.9	6.6

*All Figures are weighted averages. Based on 1988 data.

Source: *Restaurant Industry Operations Report '89* (National Restaurant Association and Laventhol & Horwath, 1989), p. 9.

The best standard against which to measure the financial performance of a food service operation is the financial plan developed by management in the form of an operations budget.

The Operations Budget

The operations budget is a profit plan and a control tool for a food service business that addresses all revenue and expense items appearing on the business's income statement (discussed later in the chapter). Annual operations budgets are commonly divided into monthly plans. These monthly plans become standards against which management can evaluate the actual results of operations each month. Thus, the operations budget enables management to accomplish two of its most important functions: planning and control.[4]

In small food service operations, the manager/owner generally develops the budget. In larger operations, other staff members provide important help. Supervisors might budget expense levels for their areas of responsibility in consultation with senior management personnel, or a budget committee may review each department's income and expense plans before a property-wide budget is approved. When staff members are allowed to provide real input into the budget process, they

Exhibit 13.2 Hotel Statistics

	Size Classifications				Hotels Built During Past 15 Years	
	Under 250 Rooms	250 to 500 Rooms	501 to 1,000 Rooms	Over 1,000 Rooms	500 Rooms and Under	Over 500 Rooms
Rooms Department:						
Rooms Net Revenue	100.0%	100.0%	100.0%	100.0%	100.0%	100.0%
Departmental Expenses:						
Salaries and Wages Including Vacation	14.8%	13.6%	12.7%	13.9%	13.4%	11.9%
Payroll Taxes and Employee Benefits	4.2	4.5	4.9	5.8	4.5	4.7
Subtotal	19.0%	18.1%	17.6%	19.7%	17.9%	16.6%
Laundry, Linen, and Guest Supplies	3.7	3.9	3.9	4.6	3.9	4.2
Commissions and Reservation Expenses	2.7	2.7	2.9	3.1	2.7	2.8
All Other Expenses	3.0	3.1	2.6	2.7	3.2	3.2
Total Rooms Expense	28.4%	27.8%	27.0%	30.1%	27.7%	26.8%
Rooms Departmental Income	71.6%	72.2%	73.0%	69.9%	72.3%	73.2%
Food and Beverage Department:						
Food Net Revenue	100.0%	100.0%	100.0%	100.0%	100.0%	100.0%
Cost of Food Consumed	36.1%	34.8%	32.5%	30.4%	35.0%	32.9%
Less: Cost of Employees' Meals	2.0	2.1	2.2	2.9	2.2	2.2
Net Cost of Food Sales	34.1%	32.7%	30.3%	27.5%	32.8%	30.7%
Food Gross Profit	65.9%	67.3%	69.7%	72.5%	67.2%	69.3%
Beverage Net Revenue	100.0%	100.0%	100.0%	100.0%	100.0%	100.0%
Cost of Beverage Sales	24.4	22.2	20.7	17.5	22.6	20.5
Beverage Gross Profit	75.6%	77.8%	79.3%	82.5%	77.4%	79.5%
Total Food and Beverage Revenue	100.0%	100.0%	100.0%	100.0%	100.0%	100.0%
Net Cost of Food and Beverage Sales	31.1	29.9	28.0	24.8	29.9	28.1
Gross Profit on Combined Sales	68.9%	70.1%	72.0%	75.2%	70.1%	71.9%
Public Room Rentals	3.0	3.1	3.1	1.9	3.1	2.4
Other Income	2.6	2.1	2.5	2.8	2.3	2.6
Gross Profit and Other Income	74.5%	75.3%	77.6%	79.9%	75.5%	76.9%
Departmental Expenses:						
Salaries and Wages Including Vacation	31.1%	31.8%	32.4%	30.2%	31.7%	30.6%
Payroll Taxes and Employee Benefits	8.8	10.7	12.4	12.5	10.2	12.0
Subtotal	39.9%	42.5%	44.8%	42.7%	41.9%	42.6%
Laundry and Dry Cleaning	1.1	1.3	1.2	1.2	1.2	1.2
China, Glassware, Silver, and Linen	1.3	1.6	1.6	1.8	1.6	1.5
Contract Cleaning	0.4	0.3	0.5	0.8	0.3	0.5
All Other Expenses	8.1	7.5	6.8	5.9	8.1	6.9
Total Food and Beverage Expense	50.8%	53.2%	54.9%	52.4%	53.1%	52.7%
Food and Beverage Departmental Income	23.7%	22.1%	22.7%	27.5%	22.4%	24.2%

Source: *Trends in the Hotel Industry, USA Edition, 1989* (Houston, Texas: Pannell Kerr Forster, 1989), p. 49.

often become more motivated to implement the property's profit plan and are less likely to blindly adhere to budget numbers which they feel are imposed on them.

As a Profit Plan

The operations budget is developed by projecting revenue, determining profit requirements, and estimating expenses for each month of the upcoming fiscal year. These monthly plans are then combined to form the operations budget for the year.

Many food service businesses re-forecast expected results of operations and revise operations budgets as they progress through the budget year. This re-forecasting is necessary only when actual results begin to vary significantly from the operations budget due to changes that occur after the budget has been prepared.

Projecting Revenue. Revenue is projected by forecasting food and beverage sales for the budget period. Sales histories and past monthly income statements are the basic sources of information that managers use to project revenue. However, a number of other factors must also be taken into consideration. For example, new competition, planned street improvements, and other activities over which the operation has little or no control may affect future sales levels. Also, general economic and social conditions such as predicted increases in inflation or changing lifestyles within the community may also affect the food service operation in the upcoming year. In addition, sales promotion plans of the operation, remodeling, and other activities scheduled for the upcoming year may affect revenue projections for the budget period.

Determining Profit Requirements. If you were to ask commercial food service managers how much profit they wanted their operations to generate, answers might include: "As much as possible"; "At least as much as last year's"; or, "As much as my competition is making." These answers indicate a passive approach to determining profit requirements. Most passive approaches view profits as "left-overs." That is, profit is seen as whatever is left after expenses have been subtracted from revenue.

A more active approach to determining profit requirements reverses the passive view and subtracts profit requirements from projected revenue to arrive at allowable expense levels. This approach ensures that the operations budget seriously takes into account the expectations of owners and investors who provide the financial support necessary for the food service operation to remain in business.

Many not-for-profit institutional food service operations must generate income in excess of direct operating expenses to pay their share of overhead, equipment, and other costs. This excess of income over direct expenses is often referred to as a "surplus." The managers of an institutional food service operation should factor the required surplus into the operations budget, just as commercial food service managers factor profit requirements into their operations budgets.

Estimating Expense Levels. Many expenses are directly related to sales volume and will vary as sales volume changes. For example, food costs and beverage costs increase as sales increase because more food and beverage products must be purchased. These types of expenses can be estimated by comparing past expenses with projected sales levels. Other types of expenses do not fluctuate with sales volume and, therefore, are much easier to estimate. These expenses, often referred to as fixed costs, include rent, depreciation, insurance, license fees, etc.

As a Control Tool

Developing a thorough operations budget reminds managers of the extent to which they are responsible for meeting revenue, profit, and expense goals. The operations budget helps pinpoint responsibility and encourages managers to use the budget as a control tool.

Exhibit 13.3 Sample Monthly Report Format

CURRENT PERIOD			Line Item	YEAR-TO-DATE		
Actual	Budget	Variance		Actual	Budget	Variance

The process of budgetary control identifies and analyzes significant variances between budgeted figures and actual results of operations. Variance analysis may indicate that additional investigation by management is required to determine the exact causes of significant variances. Once these causes have been identified, management is able to take whatever actions are necessary.

In order for budgets to be used effectively for control purposes, reports are generally prepared on a monthly basis. These reports are useful only when they are timely and relevant. Reports issued weeks after the end of an accounting period are too late to allow managers to investigate significant variances, determine causes, and take necessary corrective actions. Relevant reports include only the revenue and expense items for which the food service manager is responsible. From a control perspective, for example, it may not be helpful to include fixed costs as items on a monthly budget report because these costs are fixed and food service managers are generally unable to make decisions or take actions to affect these types of costs.

Reports should include sufficient detail to allow the food service manager to make reasonable judgments regarding variances from the budget plan. Almost all budgeted revenue and expense items on the report will differ from actual results of operations. Figures describing the actual results of operations that can be compared with budgeted amounts are obtained from monthly income statements. Differences are to be expected because no budgeting process is perfect. Simply because a variance exists does not mean that management should analyze it and take corrective actions. Only significant variances require management analysis and action.

With assistance from the operation's controller, top management should provide food service managers with criteria by which to determine significant variances. When such criteria are expressed in terms of dollars or percentages, the format of the monthly reports should include dollar and percentage variance columns so managers can easily identify which variances are significant. Exhibit 13.3 illustrates a sample monthly report format. However, each food service operation should design its monthly report format to meet its own particular needs and requirements.[5]

The Income Statement

The income statement of a food service operation provides important financial information regarding the results of operations for a stated period of time. The time period may be one month or longer, but does not exceed one business year.[6]

Financial information reported on income statements is developed through a bookkeeping process. As business transactions occur, bookkeeping entries are made in the appropriate accounts. At the end of the month, trial balances and various types of adjusting entries are made to ensure that account balances accurately reflect the activity that occurred during the month.

Since the income statement reveals the results of operations for a period of time, it's an important measure of the effectiveness and efficiency of management. A later section of the chapter will examine common ratios used to evaluate management's effectiveness. Many of the figures needed to calculate important ratios come directly from the income statement.

Restaurant Income Statement

The income statement for a restaurant operation summarizes the sales, cost of sales, and gross profit generated by the sale of food and beverages. Exhibit 13.4 presents a sample summary income statement of the fictional Brandywine Restaurant for the month of January.

Note that the income statement also lists amounts for controllable expenses. As the name of this category implies, controllable expenses refer to costs that are generally within the control of one or more of the managers of the food service operation. As mentioned earlier, items listed as occupation costs are sometimes referred to as fixed costs or fixed expenses. This group of costs is generally not controllable by the food service management team.

Most restaurant operations prepare supporting schedules for the summary income statement in order to provide detailed information about major line items. For example, the Brandywine Restaurant may prepare a supporting schedule detailing food sales for the month of January. Depending on management's information needs, the supporting schedule could document food sales by meal period (breakfast, lunch, dinner) and/or by location (dining room, lounge, take-out counter, banquet room, etc.). The total food sales shown on the supporting schedule would represent the same total food sales amount that appears on the summary income statement for food sales ($533,250).

Hotel F&B Department Income Statement

The income statement for a hotel is a consolidation of the income and expenses reported on separate departmental statements. It also includes other items that are not of a departmental nature. For example, income taxes are not allocated to any specific department. Exhibit 13.5 presents a year-end summary income statement for the fictional Hotel DORO.

Since the income statement is generally the first major financial statement to be prepared, it is designated Schedule A. All schedules that support the income statement are assigned the prefix A and a sequence number. "A2" (second line of

Exhibit 13.4 Sample Summary Income Statement—Restaurant

Brandywine Restaurant
Income Statement
Month Ended January 31, 19XX

Sales	Amount ($)	Percent
Food	533,250	71.9
Beverages	208,500	28.1
Total Food and Beverage Sales	741,750	100.0
Cost of Sales		
Food	217,033	40.7
Beverages	58,172	27.9
Total Cost of Sales	275,205	37.1
Gross Profit		
Food	316,217	59.3
Beverages	150,328	72.1
Total Gross Profit	466,545	62.9
Other Income	8,250	1.1
Total Income	474,795	64.0
Controllable Expenses		
Payroll	203,981	27.5
Employee Benefits	35,604	4.8
Direct Operating Expenses	48,214	6.5
Music and Entertainment	6,676	0.9
Advertising and Promotion	14,093	1.9
Utilities	18,544	2.5
Administrative and General	40,055	5.4
Repairs and Maintenance	12,610	1.7
Total Controllable Expenses	379,777	51.2
Profit Before Occupation Costs	95,018	12.8
Occupation Costs		
Rent, Property Taxes and Insurance	35,604	4.8
Interest	6,676	0.9
Depreciation	17,060	2.3
Other Additions and Deductions	(2,967)	(0.4)
	56,373	7.6
Net Income Before Tax	38,645	5.2

the "Schedule" column in Exhibit 13.5) refers to Schedule A2—the year-end food and beverage department income statement presented in Exhibit 13.6.

Note that Exhibit 13.6 presents detailed information that is only summarized on the "Food and Beverage" line of the consolidated hotel income statement. Most hotel accounting systems combine food and beverage operations into one operating department because of joint costs. However, separate information is presented on

Exhibit 13.5 Sample Summary Income Statement—Hotel

Hotel DORO, Inc.
Statement of Income
For the year ended December 31, 19X2   **Schedule A**

	Schedule	Net Revenue	Cost of Sales	Payroll and Related Expenses	Other Expenses	Income (Loss)
OPERATED DEPARTMENTS						
Rooms	A1	$ 897,500		$143,140	$ 62,099	$692,261
Food and Beverage	A2	524,570	$178,310	204,180	54,703	87,377
Telephone	A3	51,140	60,044	17,132	1,587	(27,623)
Other Operated Departments	A4	63,000	10,347	33,276	6,731	12,646
Rentals and Other Income	A5	61,283				61,283
Total Operated Departments		1,597,493	248,701	397,728	125,120	825,944
UNDISTRIBUTED EXPENSES						
Administrative and General	A6			97,632	66,549	164,181
Marketing	A7			35,825	32,043	67,868
Property Operation and Maintenance	A8			36,917	24,637	61,554
Energy Costs	A9				47,312	47,312
Total Undistributed Expenses				170,374	170,541	340,915
INCOME BEFORE FIXED CHARGES		$1,597,493	$248,701	$568,102	$295,661	$485,029
FIXED CHARGES						
Rent	A10					28,500
Property Taxes	A10					45,324
Insurance	A10					6,914
Interest	A10					192,153
Depreciation and Amortization	A10					146,000
Total Fixed Charges						418,891
INCOME BEFORE INCOME TAXES AND GAIN ON SALE OF PROPERTY						66,138
Gain on Sale of Property						10,500
INCOME BEFORE INCOME TAXES						76,638
Income Taxes						16,094
NET INCOME						$ 60,544

Source: Raymond Cote, *Understanding Hospitality Accounting II,* 2d ed. (East Lansing, Mich.: Educational Institute of the American Hotel & Motel Association, 1991), p. 112.

sales and cost of sales for food and for beverages to allow analyses of the gross profit margins for each of these operational areas.

Note that in Exhibit 13.6, the cost of food and beverages consumed is reduced by the cost of meals provided to employees of the hotel. Generally, each department of the hotel is charged for its share of employee meal expenses.

Minor revenue accounts not specifically related to food and beverage sales are combined in a single line item called "Other Revenue." This line item may include

Exhibit 13.6 Food and Beverage Income Statement—Hotel DORO

	Food	Beverage	Total
Hotel DORO, Inc. **Food and Beverage Department Income Statement** **For the year ended December 31, 19X2**			Schedule A2
REVENUE	$360,000	$160,000	$520,000
ALLOWANCES	1,700	130	1,830
NET REVENUE	358,300	159,870	518,170
COST OF FOOD AND BEVERAGE SALES			
Cost of Food and Beverage Consumed	144,400	40,510	184,910
Less Cost of Employees' Meals	9,200		9,200
Net Cost of Food and Beverage Sales	135,200	40,510	175,710
OTHER INCOME			
Other Revenue			6,400
Other Cost of Sales			2,600
Net Other Income			3,800
GROSS PROFIT			346,260
EXPENSES			
Salaries and Wages	177,214		
Employee Benefits	26,966		
Total Payroll and Related Expenses		204,180	
Other Expenses			
China, Glassware, and Silver	7,779		
Contract Cleaning	3,630		
Kitchen Fuel	2,074		
Laundry and Dry Cleaning	5,182		
Licenses	800		
Music and Entertainment	16,594		
Operating Supplies	11,409		
Uniforms	2,568		
Other Operating Expenses	4,667		
Total Other Expenses		54,703	
TOTAL EXPENSES			258,883
DEPARTMENTAL INCOME (LOSS)			$ 87,377

Source: Raymond Cote, *Understanding Hospitality Accounting II,* 2d ed. (East Lansing, Mich.: Educational Institute of the American Hotel & Motel Association, 1991), p. 104.

revenue from the sale of cigarettes, cigars, gum, and candy, and from cover charges and meeting room rentals.

Payroll expenses associated with chefs, cooks, servers, bartenders, cashiers, dishwashers, and other food and beverage personnel are charged to the food and beverage department. Also, note that kitchen fuel—the gas and electricity used in the kitchen for cooking—is charged to the food and beverage department. Music and entertainment provided for the benefit of food and beverage guests is also charged as an expense to this department.[7]

The Balance Sheet

A balance sheet reports the financial position of a food service operation by showing the assets, liabilities, and equity on a given date. Understanding how this statement is used to reveal the financial position of a business is the key to understanding the logic behind the sequence of categories that appear on the statement. The major categories that appear on the balance sheet are:

- Assets

- Liabilities

- Equity

Simply stated, assets represent anything a business owns that has commercial or exchange value; liabilities represent the claims of outsiders (such as creditors) on assets; and equity represents the claims of owners on assets. On every balance sheet, the total assets must always agree (that is, balance) with the total of the liabilities and equity sections. Therefore, the very format of the balance sheet reflects the fundamental accounting equation:

$$\text{Assets} \quad = \quad \text{Liabilities} \quad + \quad \text{Equity}$$

Exhibit 13.7 presents a sample year-end balance sheet for the fictional Deb's Steakhouse. The following sections briefly describe the major line items of the "ASSETS" and "LIABILITIES" sections of the balance sheet. The "OWNER'S EQUITY" section of a balance sheet varies in relation to the type of business organization: a sole proprietorship, a partnership, or a corporation.[8]

Assets

Assets are arranged on the balance sheet according to their current or non-current status. Current assets can be defined as those assets that are convertible to cash within twelve months of the balance sheet date. All other items in the "ASSETS" section are classified as non-current assets.

Current assets are usually listed in the order of their liquidity, that is, the ease with which they can be converted to cash. The line item listed as "Cash" includes cash in house banks, cash in checking and savings accounts, and certificates of deposit. "Accounts Receivable" include all amounts due from guests on open charge accounts. "Inventories" include merchandise held for resale, such as food provisions and beverage stock, and also include operating supplies. "Prepaid Expenses" may include prepaid interest, rent, taxes, and service contracts.

The "PROPERTY AND EQUIPMENT" section of the balance sheet lists non-current assets. As indicated in Exhibit 13.7, the costs for building and for furniture and equipment are decreased by amounts shown under the heading "Accumulated Depreciation." Depreciation spreads the cost of an asset over the term of its useful life.

Exhibit 13.7 Balance Sheet—Deb's Steakhouse

Deb's Steakhouse
Balance Sheet
December 31, 19X2

ASSETS

CURRENT ASSETS

Cash	$34,000	
Accounts Receivable	4,000	
Inventories	5,000	
Prepaid Expenses	2,000	
Total Current Assets		$ 45,000

PROPERTY AND EQUIPMENT

	Cost	Accumulated Depreciation	
Land	$ 30,000		
Building	60,000	$ 15,000	
Furniture and Equipment	52,000	25,000	
China, Glassware, Silver	8,000		
Total	150,000	40,000	110,000

OTHER ASSETS

Security Deposits	1,500	
Preopening Expenses	2,500	
Total Other Assets		4,000

TOTAL ASSETS | | | $ 159,000

LIABILITIES

CURRENT LIABILITIES

Accounts Payable	$11,000	
Sales Tax Payable	1,000	
Accrued Expenses	9,000	
Current Portion of Long-Term Debt	6,000	
Total Current Liabilities		$ 27,000

LONG-TERM LIABILITIES

Mortgage Payable	40,000	
Less Current Portion of Long-Term Debt	6,000	
Net Long-Term Liabilities		34,000

TOTAL LIABILITIES | | | 61,000

OWNER'S EQUITY

Capital, Deb Barry—December 31, 19X2	98,000
TOTAL LIABILITIES AND OWNER'S EQUITY	$ 159,000

Source: Raymond Cote, *Understanding Hospitality Accounting I*, 3d ed. (East Lansing, Mich.: Educational Institute of the American Hotel & Motel Association, 1995), p. 76.

The "OTHER ASSETS" section of the balance sheet includes assets that do not apply to other line items. For example, "Security Deposits" include funds deposited with public utility companies and other funds used for similar types of deposits.

Liabilities

Liabilities are also arranged on the balance sheet according to their current or non-current status. Current liabilities are obligations that will require an outlay of cash within twelve months of the balance sheet date. Non-current liabilities are often referred to as long-term liabilities, or, simply, long-term debt.

The "Total Current Liabilities" line alerts the restaurant operator to cash requirements of the operation and is often compared with the total figure for current assets. A major line item of interest to food service managers is "Accounts Payable," which shows the total of unpaid invoices due to creditors from whom the operation receives merchandise or services in the ordinary course of business.

Ratio Analysis

A ratio gives a mathematical relationship between two figures and is computed by dividing one figure by the other figure. Ratios generate new information. Ratios and ratio analysis help make the numbers on financial statements or operations reports more meaningful, informative, and useful.

In order to be useful as indicators or measurements of the success or well-being of a food service operation, the computed ratios must be compared against some standard. There are basically three different standards that are used to evaluate the ratios computed for a given operation: ratios from a past period, industry averages, and budgeted ratios.

Comparing present ratios with corresponding ratios calculated for past accounting periods sometimes reveals significant changes that management should look into. For example, if the monthly food cost percentage is significantly higher than for prior months, managers may need to investigate the cause(s) for the increase and take appropriate corrective action.

Industry averages provide another useful standard against which to compare ratios. After calculating the return on investment for their food service operation, investors may want to compare this with the average return on investment for similar food service operations. By comparing their operation's return on investment to the national average, investors can get an indication of the ability of their operation's management to use resources effectively to generate profits for investors.

Ratios are best compared against planned ratio goals. For example, in order to more effectively control the cost of labor, management may project a goal for the current year's labor cost percentage (discussed later in this chapter) that is slightly lower than the previous year's level. The expectation of a lower labor cost percentage may reflect management's efforts to improve scheduling procedures, increase productivity, or control other factors related to the cost of labor. By comparing the actual labor cost percentage with the budgeted percentage, management is able to assess its success toward controlling labor costs.

Different evaluations may result from comparing ratios against these different standards. For example, a food cost of 33% for the current period may compare favorably with the prior year's ratio of 34% and with an industry average of 36%, but may be judged unfavorably when compared with the operation's planned goal of 32%. Therefore, care must be taken when evaluating the results of operations using ratio analysis.

Ratios are generally classified by the type of information that they provide. Five common ratio groups are as follows:

- Liquidity

- Solvency

- Activity

- Profitability

- Operating

A full discussion of ratios is beyond the scope of this book. What follows are general introductions to the ratios included in these five ratio groups.[9]

Liquidity Ratios

Liquidity ratios reveal the ability of a food service operation to meet its short-term obligations. The most common liquidity ratio is the current ratio, which is the ratio of total current assets to total current liabilities. Using figures from Exhibit 13.7, the current ratio for Deb's Steakhouse can be calculated as follows:

$$\text{Current Ratio} = \frac{\text{Current Assets}}{\text{Current Liabilities}}$$

$$= \frac{\$45,000}{\$27,000}$$

$$= \underline{1.67} \text{ or } 1.67 \text{ to } 1$$

This result means that for every $1 of current liabilities, Deb's Steakhouse has $1.67 of current assets. Thus, there is a cushion of $.67 for every dollar of current debt.

Owners and stockholders normally prefer a low current ratio to a high one, because they view most current assets as less productive than investments in non-current assets. Creditors normally prefer a relatively high current ratio, as this provides assurance that they will receive timely payments. Managers are caught in the middle, trying to satisfy both owners and creditors while, at the same time, maintaining sufficient liquidity to ensure the smooth operation of the food service business.

Solvency Ratios

Solvency ratios measure the extent to which the food service operation has been financed by debt. If an operation carries a lot of debt, its ability to meet its long-term obligations may be questionable. A food service operation is solvent when its assets exceed its liabilities. The most common ratio of the solvency group is called the solvency ratio, which is total assets divided by total liabilities. Using figures from Exhibit 13.7, the solvency ratio for Deb's Steakhouse is determined as follows:

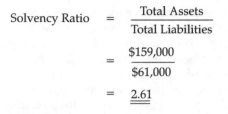

$$\text{Solvency Ratio} = \frac{\text{Total Assets}}{\text{Total Liabilities}}$$

$$= \frac{\$159,000}{\$61,000}$$

$$= \underline{\underline{2.61}}$$

This result shows that Deb's Steakhouse has $2.61 of assets for each $1 of liabilities, or a cushion of $1.61. As with the current ratio, owners and stockholders normally prefer a low solvency ratio to a high one. Creditors, on the other hand, prefer a high solvency ratio, as it provides a greater cushion should the food service business experience financial losses. Managers are again caught in the middle, trying to satisfy both owners and creditors.

Activity Ratios

Activity ratios reflect management's ability to use the assets of the food service operation. Managers are entrusted with inventory, fixed assets, and other resources to generate earnings for owners while providing products and services to guests. One important activity ratio for food service operations is inventory turnover.

The inventory turnover ratio shows how quickly the inventory is being used. Generally, the quicker the inventory turnover the better, because inventory can be expensive to maintain. Maintenance costs include storage space, freezers, insurance, personnel expense, recordkeeping and, of course, the cost of opportunities lost because the money tied up in inventory is unavailable for other uses.

Food inventory turnover is calculated by dividing the cost of food used by the average food inventory. The average food inventory is computed by adding the inventory at the beginning of a period to the inventory at the end of the period and dividing by two. Assume that, during a particular month, Deb's Steakhouse recorded the following data: a beginning food inventory of $5,000; an ending food inventory of $6,000; and a cost of food sales of $18,975. Inventory turnover for that month can be calculated as follows:

$$\text{Average Food Inventory} = \frac{\text{Beginning + Ending Inventory}}{2}$$

$$= \frac{\$5,000 + \$6,000}{2}$$

$$= \underline{\underline{\$5,500}}$$

$$\text{Food Inventory Turnover} = \frac{\text{Cost of Food Sales}}{\text{Average Inventory}}$$

$$= \frac{\$18,975}{\$5,500}$$

$$= \underline{\underline{\$3.45}}$$

This means that food inventory for the month turned over 3.45 times.

The speed of food inventory turnover generally depends on the type of food service operation. A fast-food operation generally experiences a much faster food inventory turnover than does a fine dining restaurant. In fact, a fast-food restaurant may have a food inventory turnover in excess of 200 times for a year.

Although a high food inventory turnover may be desired because it means that the food service operation is able to run with a relatively small investment in inventory, too high a turnover may indicate possible stockout problems. Failure to provide desired items to guests may not only immediately result in disappointed guests, but may also result in reduced business if the problem persists. Too low an inventory turnover may suggest that food is overstocked, and, in addition to the costs of maintaining the inventory, the cost of spoilage may become a problem.

An inventory turnover for beverage supplies should generally be calculated separately from food supplies. A beverage inventory turnover is calculated similarly to the food inventory turnover. Some food service operations calculate beverage turnovers separately for different types of beverages sold.

Profitability Ratios

Profitability ratios show management's overall effectiveness as measured by returns on sales and investments. A common profitability ratio is profit margin, which measures management's ability to generate profits on sales.

Profit margin is determined by dividing the net income by total revenue. Net income is the income remaining after all expenses have been deducted from revenue. Using figures from Exhibit 13.8, the profit margin for Deb's Steakhouse can be determined as follows:

$$\text{Profit Margin} = \frac{\text{Net Income}}{\text{Total Revenue}}$$

$$= \frac{\$37,000}{\$170,000}$$

$$= \underline{.2176} \text{ or } 21.76\%$$

If the profit margin is lower than expected, then expenses and other areas should be reviewed. Poor pricing strategies and low sales volume could be contributing factors to a low profit margin.

Operating Ratios

Operating ratios assist managers in analyzing the operations of a food service business. Many operating ratios relate expenses to revenue and are useful for control purposes. For example, an actual food cost percentage is calculated and compared with the budgeted food cost percentage to evaluate the overall control of food costs. Any significant deviation is investigated to determine causes for the variation between actual costs and budgeted costs. Exhibit 13.9 suggests operating ratios useful to food service managers. The following sections examine only a few of the more commonly calculated operating ratios.

Exhibit 13.8 Income Statement—Deb's Steakhouse

Deb's Steakhouse
Statement of Income
For the Year Ended December 31, 19X2

REVENUE

Food Sales	$120,000	
Liquor Sales	50,000	
Total Revenue		$170,000

COST OF SALES

Food	42,000	
Liquor	11,000	
Total Cost of Sales		53,000

GROSS PROFIT | | 117,000

OPERATING EXPENSES

Salaries and Wages	36,000	
Employee Benefits	6,900	
China, Glassware, and Silverware	300	
Kitchen Fuel	900	
Laundry and Dry Cleaning	2,100	
Credit Card Fees	1,500	
Operating Supplies	5,000	
Advertising	2,000	
Utilities	3,800	
Repairs and Maintenance	1,900	
Total Operating Expenses		60,400

INCOME BEFORE FIXED CHARGES | | 56,600

FIXED CHARGES

Rent	6,000	
Property Taxes	1,500	
Insurance	3,600	
Interest Expense	3,000	
Depreciation	5,500	
Total Fixed Charges		19,600

NET INCOME | | $ 37,000

Source: Raymond Cote, *Understanding Hospitality Accounting I*, 3d ed. (East Lansing, Mich.: Educational Institute of the American Hotel & Motel Association, 1995), p. 68.

Food Cost Percentage. The food cost percentage is an important food service ratio that compares the cost of food sold with food sales. Most food service managers rely heavily on this ratio for determining whether food costs are reasonable. Using

Exhibit 13.9 Common Operating Ratios

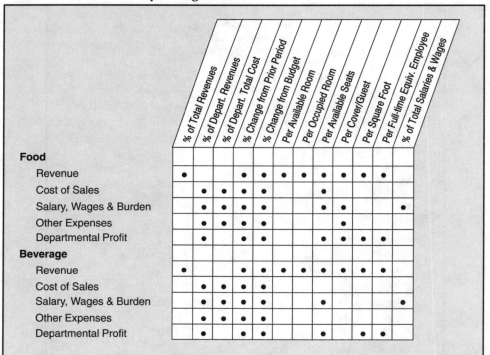

	% of Total Revenues	% of Depart. Revenues	% of Depart. Total Cost	% Change from Prior Period	% Change from Budget	Per Available Room	Per Occupied Room	Per Available Seats	Per Cover/Guest	Per Square Foot	Per Full-time Equiv. Employee	% of Total Salaries & Wages
Food												
Revenue	•			•	•	•	•	•	•	•	•	
Cost of Sales		•	•	•	•		•					
Salary, Wages & Burden		•	•	•	•			•	•			•
Other Expenses		•	•	•	•				•			
Departmental Profit		•		•	•			•	•	•	•	
Beverage												
Revenue	•			•	•	•	•	•	•	•	•	
Cost of Sales		•	•	•	•							
Salary, Wages & Burden		•	•	•	•			•				•
Other Expenses		•	•	•	•							
Departmental Profit		•		•	•			•		•	•	

Source: R. M. (Max) Gaunt and George R. Conrade, "How to Analyze Financial Statements," *Lodging*, February 1983, p. 47.

figures from Exhibit 13.8, the food cost percentage for Deb's Steakhouse can be determined as follows:

$$\text{Food Cost Percentage} = \frac{\text{Cost of Food Sold}}{\text{Food Sales}}$$

$$= \frac{\$42,000}{\$120,000}$$

$$= \underline{.35} \text{ or } 35\%$$

This result means that of every $1 of food sales, $.35 goes toward covering the costs associated with purchasing, transporting, delivering, and storing food. The food cost percentage figure is best compared with the food cost percentage that was budgeted for the period. A significant difference in either direction should be investigated by management. Managers should be just as concerned about a food cost percentage that is significantly lower than the budgeted goal as they are about a food cost percentage that exceeds budgeted standards. A lower food cost percentage may indicate that the quality of food served is lower than desired, or that smaller portions are being served than are specified in standard recipes. A higher food cost percentage than the budgeted standard may be due to poor portion control, excessive food costs, theft, waste, spoilage, or a host of other factors.

Beverage Cost Percentage. The beverage cost percentage results from dividing the cost of beverages sold by beverage sales. Using figures from Exhibit 13.8, the beverage cost percentage for Deb's Steakhouse can be determined as follows:

$$\text{Beverage Cost Percentage} = \frac{\text{Cost of Beverages Sold}}{\text{Beverage Sales}}$$

$$= \frac{\$11,000}{\$50,000}$$

$$= .22 \text{ or } 22\%$$

This result shows that of every $1 of beverage sales, $.22 goes toward covering the costs associated with purchasing, transporting, delivering, and storing beverages. As with the food cost percentage ratio, this ratio is best compared to the budgeted standard for beverage costs for that specific time period. Some food service operations also calculate a beverage cost percentage by type of beverage sold and by beverage outlet.

Labor Cost Percentage. In many food service operations, labor is one of the largest expenses. Labor expense includes salaries, wages, bonuses, payroll taxes, and fringe benefits. A general labor cost percentage is determined by dividing total labor costs by total revenue. Using the salaries and wages figure ($36,000) and the employee benefits figure ($6,900) from Deb's Steakhouse (as shown in Exhibit 13.8), the labor cost percentage can be calculated as follows:

$$\text{Labor Cost Percentage} = \frac{\text{Labor Costs}}{\text{Total Revenue}}$$

$$= \frac{\$36,000 + \$6,900}{\$170,000}$$

$$= \frac{\$42,900}{\$170,000}$$

$$= .25 \text{ or } 25\%$$

This result indicates that of every $1 of food and beverage sales, $.25 goes toward covering the cost of labor required to generate the food and beverage sales. As with the food cost percentage ratio, this ratio is best compared with the budgeted standard for that particular time period. Some food service operations may calculate labor costs by type of labor or by type of food and beverage outlet (dining room, lounge, banquet room, etc.).

Average Food Service Check. This ratio is determined by dividing the revenue generated during a meal period by the number of guests served. If Deb's Steakhouse generated $300 of revenue from food and beverage sales during a meal period and served 95 guests, the average food service check is calculated as follows:

$$\text{Average Food Service Check} = \frac{\text{Total Food Revenue}}{\text{Number of Guests Served}}$$

$$= \frac{\$300}{95}$$

$$= \underline{\$3.16}$$

Check averages are often calculated for different dining areas and/or for various meal periods. In addition, managers often separately track the average beverage service check for their operations.

Seat Turnover. Seat turnover is the number of times that a given seat in a sit-down dining area is occupied during a meal period. This ratio is determined by dividing the number of guests served during a meal period by the number of seats available. If during a meal period, Deb's Steakhouse served 95 guests with 38 available seats, then the seat turnover can be calculated as follows:

$$\text{Seat Turnover} = \frac{\text{Number of Guests Served}}{\text{Number of Available Seats}}$$

$$= \frac{95}{38}$$

$$= \underline{2.5} \text{ times}$$

This result indicates that each seat available was occupied 2.5 times during the meal period. As the seat turnover rate increases, more guests are served during a meal period and more sales revenue should be generated.

Food Service Payroll Accounting

Payroll is a significant expense for almost all food service operations. Labor costs are a major concern of food service managers and usually are the first area looked at when costs need to be cut. However, cutting labor costs may prove self-defeating, since most food service operations are highly service-intensive. For example, a reduction in staff may produce poor service, which may lead to guest dissatisfaction, lost business, and a bad reputation.

Food service managers responsible for personnel functions and/or payroll preparation should be knowledgeable about the most current employment and payroll laws and regulations—federal, state, and, in some cases, local.[10] It's possible for federal and state payroll regulations to differ on the same issue. In this event, as a general rule, the employer must apply those standards, federal or state, that are the most beneficial to the employee. The issue is further complicated by contract law, such as union-negotiated rights. Contract rights prevail over federal and state laws if their provisions are more beneficial to the employee.

Maintaining a current knowledge of these laws is a never-ending effort. Significant changes may occur regarding minimum wages, income tax rates, Social Security taxes, and employment rights. These changes are regulated by both federal and state governments. In addition, certain cities have income tax withholding laws. Violations of payroll laws or labor regulations may bring civil and/or criminal penalties. Managers should contact the operation's attorney on a periodic basis for current information on employment and payroll laws.

The following sections examine fundamental aspects of food service payroll accounting. Managers should know about the impact the Fair Labor Standards Act and the tip reporting requirements established by the Tax Equity and Fiscal Responsibility Act of 1982 have had on food and beverage operations. These sections will include a discussion of the special nature of payroll accounting for tipped employees.

The Fair Labor Standards Act

The Fair Labor Standards Act (FLSA), commonly known as the federal wage and hour law, covers such areas as equal pay for equal work, child labor, recordkeeping requirements, minimum wage rate, and conditions defining overtime pay. The FLSA applies to most food service operations. However, certain small businesses with exceptionally low sales volumes may be exempt.

Food service managers must keep up with changing rules and regulations connected with the FLSA. For example, effective April 1, 1990, the minimum hourly rate increased from $3.35 per hour to $3.80 per hour. In addition, effective April 1, 1991, the minimum hourly rate is $4.25 per hour.

The FLSA also requires that all food service employees covered by this act be paid at the rate of at least one and one-half times their regular hourly rate for all hours worked in excess of 40 hours per week. The FLSA makes no provisions for rest periods or coffee breaks. It also makes no provisions for vacation, holiday, severance, or sick pay. Furthermore, the FLSA does not require extra pay for work on Saturdays or Sundays.

For example, a food service employer is not required to pay employees one and one half times their regular pay for any weekend or holiday hours worked during a week if the total hours worked do not exceed 40. Also, if an employee works 40 hours in a three-day workweek, the employee is not entitled to overtime pay according to FLSA provisions. However, custom, union contracts, and many states have established overtime provisions that are more generous to employees. In these situations, the FLSA provisions do not apply.

As suggested earlier, states may have legislation that contradicts standards established by the FLSA. In cases where state and federal laws differ, the law offering the greater benefit to the employee prevails. For example, state laws may set a minimum wage rate that is greater than that set by federal law, and this higher minimum wage rate would prevail. State laws may also contain provisions to regulate overtime pay, employee meals and lodging, tip reporting, uniforms, and more.

Payroll Accounting for Tipped Employees

Preparing the payroll for tipped employees is complex because tipped employees earn wages from two sources: the employer they work for and the guests they serve. A tip is considered payment by a guest to a hospitality employee for services rendered and must be included as part of the gross income reported by the employee on his or her personal income tax return. For purposes of determining tip income, tips include cash tips and tips recorded on credit card vouchers and distributed to the employee.

If an employee splits tips among other employees, only the portion which the employee retains is included in his or her gross income.

All income earned by an employee, whether received as wages or as tips, is taxable and subject to both federal and state income tax withholding provisions. Some food service operations may add service charges to guests' billings. These service charges are distributed to servers and other customarily tipped employees. A service charge is not considered a tip. Such charges are defined as wages by the Internal Revenue Service (IRS) and are treated the same as other wages for purposes of tax withholding requirements.

The Tax Equity and Fiscal Responsibility Act of 1982 (TEFRA) established regulations affecting food and beverage operations with respect to tip reporting requirements. The intent of the regulation is for all tipped employees to report tips of at least 8% of the gross receipts of the food service operation.

The 8% tip regulation does not apply to every food and beverage establishment. For example, cafeteria and fast-food operations are exempt from the 8% tip regulation. "Cafeteria operations" are defined as food and beverage establishments that are primarily self-service and in which the total cost of food and/or beverages selected by a guest is paid to a cashier (or is stated on a guest check) before the guest is seated. "Fast-food operations" are defined as food and beverage establishments where guests order, pick up, and pay for their orders at a counter or window and then consume the items at another location, either on or off the premises. In addition to cafeteria and fast-food operations, food and beverage establishments are exempt from the 8% tip regulation when at least 95% of their gross receipts include a service charge of 10% or more. As pointed out previously, service charges are not considered tips. Service charges are defined as wages by the IRS and are taxed the same as other wages.

The 8% tip regulation defines "gross receipts" as all receipts (both cash and charge sales) received for providing food and/or beverages. However, according to the 8% tip regulation, the following are typically *not* considered part of an operation's gross receipts because tipping is not customary for these services:

- Complimentary hors d'oeuvres served at a bar
- Complimentary dessert served to a regular patron
- Carry-out sales
- Services to which a 10% (or more) charge is added

An exception applies to gambling casinos. In casinos, the retail value of complimentary food and/or beverages served to guests is considered to be part of gross receipts because tipping is customary for this service.

If the total tips reported by employees fail to equal 8% of gross receipts for the period, the deficiency is called a tip shortfall. This shortfall must be allocated to appropriate employees.

Exhibit 13.10 Sample Employee Report of Daily Sales and Tips

Employee Report of Daily Sales and Tips

Business _____   Week Ending _____/_____/_____

(Month/Day/Year)

Employee _____

	Date	Date	Date	Date	Date	Date	Date	
Enter day of the month								Grand Total
	Mon.	Tues.	Wed.	Thurs.	Fri.	Sat.	Sun.	
SALES 1. Total sales to patrons								
2. Charge sales in								
TIPS 1. Total cash and charge tips								
2. Total charge tips in								
Total hours worked								

Check shift worked: ☐ Days   ☐ Evenings   ☐ Split

Source: Raymond Cote, *Understanding Hospitality Accounting II,* 2d ed. (East Lansing, Mich.: Educational Institute of the American Hotel & Motel Association, 1991), p. 283.

When a shortfall is allocated, the employer is required to provide each directly tipped employee with an informational statement showing the tips reported by the employee and the tips that should have been reported. "Directly tipped employees" are those who receive tips directly from guests. Examples of directly tipped employees are hosts, servers, and bartenders. "Indirectly tipped employees" are employees who do not normally receive tips directly from guests. These employees include buspersons, service bartenders, and cooks. These employees do not have to help make up the shortfall.

An employer does not have to provide employees with tip allocation statements when the total tips reported for a period are greater than 8% of the gross receipts for that period. For example, assume that a large food and beverage establishment records gross receipts of $100,000 for a particular period. If the actual tips reported by employees total more than $8,000 ($100,000 × 8%), the employer does not have to provide employees with tip allocation statements.

Employees should maintain adequate records to substantiate the total amount of tips included in income. If possible, the employee should keep a daily record of his or her sales, cash tips, charge tips, and hours worked. To facilitate recordkeeping, a business may provide the employee with a multi-purpose form similar to the one shown in Exhibit 13.10.

Minimum Wage Tip Credit

Provisions of the FLSA establish conditions that allow employers to apply a tip credit toward the minimum wage of tipped employees. This tip credit effectively lowers the gross wages payable by the employer because the tips may be treated as supplemental wages.

On April 1, 1990, the FLSA tip credit increased to 45% of the minimum wage amount of $3.80 per hour. This results in a maximum allowable tip credit of $1.71 per hour ($3.80 × 45% = $1.71). Effective April 1, 1991, the FLSA minimum hourly wage rate increases to $4.25 per hour, and the tip credit increases to 50%. This results in a maximum allowable tip credit of $2.125 per hour ($4.25 × 50% = $2.125). An employer may not round the hourly tip credit to $2.13 because this would cause the tip credit to exceed 50% of the $4.25 hourly wage rate.

Using the FLSA Formula to Compute the Tip Credit. The following example illustrates how the gross wages payable by the employer are calculated when the actual tips received by an employee are greater than the maximum FLSA tip credit. Assume that, in April, 1991, an employee has worked 40 hours and the employer has chosen to use the allowable tip credit against the minimum wage. The employee reports tips from all sources amounting to $98. The maximum FLSA tip credit is $85 (40 hours × $2.125 per hour = $85). The gross wages payable by the employer are calculated as follows:

Gross wages (minimum wage: 40 hours × $4.25 per hour)		$170.00
Less the lower of:		
Maximum FLSA tip credit (40 hours × $2.125)	85.00	
Actual tips received	98.00	
Allowable tip credit		85.00
Gross wages payable by the employer		$ 85.00

Using Actual Tips Received to Compute the Tip Credit. If an employee's tips are less than the FLSA maximum allowable tip credit, the employer may not use the FLSA formula to compute a tip credit. Instead, the actual tips received by the employee are used as the tip credit. This ensures that the employee does not earn less than the minimum hourly wage from the combined payments of the employer (in the form of wages) and guests (in the form of tips).

Assume that, in April, 1991, an employee has worked 40 hours and the employer has chosen to use the allowable tip credit against the minimum wage. The employee reports tips from all sources amounting to $70. The maximum FLSA tip credit is again $85. The gross wages payable by the employer are calculated as follows:

Gross wages (minimum wage: 40 hours × $4.25 per hour)		$170.00
Less the lower of:		
Maximum FLSA tip credit (40 hours × $2.125)	85.00	
Actual tips received	70.00	
Allowable tip credit		70.00
Gross wages payable by the employer		$100.00

Endnotes

1. *Uniform System of Accounts for Hotels,* 8th rev. ed. (New York: Hotel Association of New York City, 1986), p. vi.

2. *Uniform System of Accounts for Restaurants,* 5th rev. ed. (Washington, D.C.: National Restaurant Association, 1983), p. 13.

3. *Uniform System of Accounts and Expense Dictionary for Small Hotels, Motels, and Motor Hotels,* 4th rev. ed. (East Lansing, Mich.: Educational Institute of the American Hotel & Motel Association, 1987).

4. For more information on operations budgets for food and beverage operations, see Jack D. Ninemeier, *Planning and Control for Food and Beverage Operations,* 3d ed. (East Lansing, Mich.: Educational Institute of the American Hotel & Motel Association, 1991).

5. The budget process is discussed in more detail in Raymond S. Schmidgall, *Hospitality Industry Managerial Accounting,* 3d ed. (East Lansing, Mich.: Educational Institute of the American Hotel & Motel Association, 1995).

6. For a more complete discussion of income statements, see Raymond Cote, *Understanding Hospitality Accounting I,* 3d ed. (East Lansing, Mich.: Educational Institute of the American Hotel & Motel Association, 1995), and Raymond Cote, *Understanding Hospitality Accounting II,* 2d ed. (East Lansing, Mich.: Educational Institute of the American Hotel & Motel Association, 1991).

7. For more information on an income statement for a hotel food and beverage department, see Schmidgall, *Managerial Accounting.*

8. For a fuller explanation of the equity section of the balance sheet, see Cote, *Hospitality Accounting I* and *Hospitality Accounting II.*

9. For more information on ratios, see Schmidgall, *Managerial Accounting.*

10. Employment and payroll laws and regulations are discussed in more detail in Jack P. Jefferies, *Understanding Hospitality Law,* 3d ed. (East Lansing, Mich.: Educational Institute of the American Hotel & Motel Association, 1995).

Key Terms

average food service check
balance sheet
beverage cost percentage
current ratio
eight percent tip regulation
Fair Labor Standards Act
food cost percentage
income statement

inventory turnover
labor cost percentage
minimum wage tip credit
operations budget
profit margin
seat turnover
solvency ratio
uniform system of accounts

Discussion Questions

1. How do food service managers benefit from adopting the uniform system of accounts appropriate for their operation?

2. How does active profit planning differ from passive profit planning?

3. How is the operations budget used as a control tool?

4. Why is the income statement a measure of the effectiveness of food service managers?

5. What do the assets, liabilities, and equity sections of a balance sheet represent?

6. What standards can be used to evaluate the ratios computed for a food service operation?

7. Why would creditors of a food service operation prefer that the operation's balance sheet indicate relatively high current and solvency ratios?

8. What are some factors that could contribute to a high food cost percentage?

9. Why must tipped employees keep a daily record of sales and tips?

10. How does the Fair Labor Standards Act's minimum wage tip credit affect the gross wages payable by a food service employer to tipped employees?

Chapter Outline

Computer Basics
    Electronic Data Processing
ECR/POS Technology
    Order Entry Devices
        Keyboards
        Touch-Screen Terminals
        Magnetic Strip Readers
        Hand-Held Server Terminals
    Display Units
    Output Devices
        Guest Check Printers
        Work Station Printers
        Receipt Printers
        Journal Printers
Automated Beverage Control Systems
    Order Entry Device
        Dispensing Unit Preset Buttons
        Keyboard Units
    Delivery Network
    Dispensing Units
        Touch-Bar Faucet
        Console Faucet
        Hose and Gun Device
        Mini-Tower Pedestal
        Bundled Tower Unit

This chapter was written and contributed by Michael L. Kasavana, Ph.D., Professor, School of Hotel, Restaurant and Institutional Management, Michigan State University, East Lansing, Michigan.

14

Food Service Automation— Hardware

Food service managers are constantly challenged to find new ways to increase sales while controlling and reducing costs. A major stumbling block for many managers is the lack of detailed, timely information about their operations. Timely information is needed in order to measure current effectiveness and to plan business strategies. The cost of manually collecting detailed information is often prohibitive. However, a food service computer system can provide timely information that managers can use to plan more efficient and effective service and enhance their control over the food service operation.

Food service computer systems use specific hardware components and a wide variety of software application programs. The hardware components and software programs vary considerably depending upon the type of food service operation, the kinds of meals offered, and the degree of autonomy given to food service managers within the particular structure of the business (independent, franchise, or chain).

Food service computer systems rely on electronic cash register (ECR) and point-of-sale (POS) technology. This chapter examines the basic hardware components of this technology.[1] Hardware components described include cashier terminals, precheck terminals, input devices, display units, and output devices. These components are used to process service area transactions and to capture data which are stored and later processed into timely reports for management. (Chapter 15 examines software programs and the types of reports that can be generated for management.)

This chapter also includes a section on automated beverage control systems. A brief discussion of typical system components focuses on order entry devices, delivery networks, and dispensing units.

Computer Basics

Every business collects and analyzes data about its operations. While all businesses use some type of information system, a computerized system enables managers to collect and analyze data much more easily. A computer is a managerial tool capable of processing large quantities of data much more quickly and accurately than any other data processing method. Computers can perform arithmetic operations such as addition, subtraction, multiplication, and division, and can perform logical functions as well, such as ranking, sorting, and assembling—all at great speed. In addition, computers are capable of storing and retrieving tremendous amounts of information, thereby allowing managers to exercise control over procedures that might otherwise be overlooked.

A food service computer system streamlines the process of collecting and recording data and expands the ways in which information is organized and reported. In addition, automation enables management to speed up the process by which useful information is made available to decision-makers.

How much does a food service manager need to know about a computer to operate one? About as much as a cook needs to know about microwave technology in order to use a microwave oven!

To use a microwave oven, a cook simply sets the proper controls and presses the start button. Microwaves are applied to food and the timer signals the completion of the process. This takes place regardless of the cook's knowledge of microwave engineering. However, if the cook has some understanding of microwave technology in addition to basic kitchen skills, he or she can use the microwave oven more effectively.

Similarly, in order to use a computer, a food service manager does not need to learn the intricacies of electronic circuitry etched on silicon chips. The manager simply needs to learn how to instruct the computer to carry out the desired functions. However, basic knowledge about how a computer system operates will better equip a manager to use a computer as an effective tool in managing information needs. Such knowledge also enables food service managers to select computer systems that best meet the information needs of their operations, or to expand the data processing functions of their present computer systems.

A basic knowledge of computer jargon (often termed "computerese") can also be extremely helpful in identifying the functions desired from a computer system and in understanding the functioning of the system itself. We will define many common computer terms throughout this and the next chapter.

Electronic Data Processing

Steps to process data are basically the same regardless of whether a manual or a computerized system is used. The manual conversion of data into information is accomplished through a cycle of events identified as input, processing, and output (see Exhibit 14.1). For example, standard food recipes can be seen as data processing techniques that food service operations have used for a long time to convert raw ingredients into finished menu items. Viewed from the perspective of the data processing cycle, ingredients and their quantities are the inputs to recipe production; following the recipe's instructions is the processing by which the desired output (the number of standard portions) is produced.

The speed, accuracy, and efficiency required for an effective information system are often best achieved through electronic data processing. The difference between manual data processing and electronic data processing lies in the automation of the process and the addition of a memory unit. Exhibit 14.2 contains a simplified diagram of an electronic data processing cycle.

Electronic data processing employs a computer system. The automation of input, processing, and output within the basic data processing cycle results in faster

Exhibit 14.1 The Data Processing Cycle

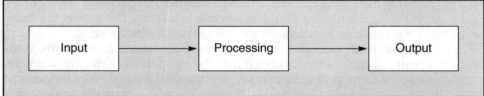

Exhibit 14.2 The Electronic Data Processing Cycle

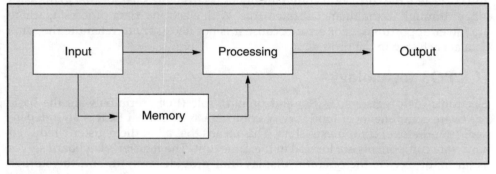

and more efficient operation. Also, the addition of a memory unit allows for the storage of data and/or instructions for more reliable and thorough processing.

The primary function of all information systems, including computerized systems, is to transform data into timely, accurate, and useful information. Electronic data processing achieves this objective by reducing turnaround time, streamlining output, and minimizing the handling of data.

Turnaround time refers to the time that elapses between data input and information output. An efficiently designed data processing system provides food service managers with rapid access to the information they need in order to make timely and effective decisions.

A frequent criticism of electronic data processing is that computer systems produce large volumes of irrelevant information. This criticism is misdirected. If a computer system overwhelms management with reams of useless information, it is not the fault of the computer—it is the fault of the computer system design. An efficiently designed electronic data processing system streamlines output. Streamlining the output of a computer means generating only those reports that are of real use to those who request them.

Reducing the number of times that data must be handled enhances both the speed and the accuracy of data processing tasks. Consider the process of manually calculating daily sales totals in a food service operation. The total amount on each guest check is first recorded in a sales journal by meal period. The amounts are then totaled and may be carried over to a sales ledger. Amounts recorded in the sales ledger are then totaled for all of the day's meal periods to arrive at a total daily sales amount. During each of these steps it is possible to make any number of mistakes such as recording the wrong number, writing a number's digits in the wrong order (transposing them), calculating a total incorrectly, and so on. The greater the number of times data must be handled, the greater the possibility for error.

In a computerized data processing system, guest check amounts are computed internally as each order is entered into the computer system. The amounts can then be accessed by programs that prepare the sales journal, sales ledger, and eventually the restaurant's financial statements. Therefore, once the amount of a guest check is entered correctly, all subsequent sales reports will be mathematically correct. If the amount is initially entered incorrectly, but the mistake is identified and corrected, the correction automatically flows from the sales journal to the sales ledger through to the financial statements. With electronic data processing, there are fewer opportunities for error because it is not necessary to rehandle the same data at each step in the process.

ECR/POS Technology

Electronic cash registers (ECRs) and point-of-sale (POS) terminals are the basic hardware components of food service computer systems. An ECR is an independent (stand-alone) computer system. This means that all of the register's required hardware components are located in the same unit. The register's keyboard serves as an input device, the operator display unit provides output, and the storage (memory) unit and central processor are located within the terminal housing. Therefore, an ECR is a complete computer that need not be connected to any other device in order to operate.

A POS terminal, on the other hand, contains its own input/output units and may even possess a small storage (memory) capacity but does not contain its own central processing unit. In order for POS transactions to be processed, the terminal must be interfaced (connected) to a central processing unit which is located outside of the terminal's housing. Since the central processing unit is the most expensive component of a computer system, many food service properties reduce the cost of automation by interfacing several POS terminals to one large central processing unit.

Since ECR/POS devices are generally sold as modular units, everything but the basic terminal is considered optional equipment. The cash drawer is no exception. Management may choose to not have a cash drawer at all, or have up to four cash drawers connected to a single register. Multiple cash drawers may enhance management's cash control system when several cashiers work at the same register during the same shift. Each cashier can be assigned a separate cash drawer so that, at the end of the shift, cash drawer receipts can be individually reconciled.

A terminal without a cash drawer is commonly referred to as a precheck terminal. Precheck terminals are used to enter orders, not to settle accounts. For example, a server can use a precheck terminal located in the dining room to relay orders to the appropriate kitchen and bar production areas, but generally cannot use this device for guest check settlement. An ECR/POS device with a cash drawer is commonly referred to as a cashier terminal. This device can normally handle both prechecking and cashiering functions.

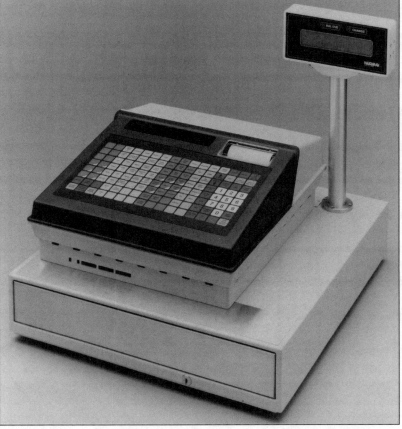

ECR with internal receipt printer and customer display unit. (Courtesy of Norand Corporation, Cedar Rapids, Iowa)

In addition to ECRs and/or POS terminals, food service computer systems generally require additional hardware components, such as:

- Order entry devices
- Display units
- Output devices

Order Entry Devices

Order entry devices include keyboards, touch-screen terminals, magnetic strip readers, and hand-held terminals.

Keyboards. The most common order entry device is the keyboard. Two primary types of keyboard surfaces are micro-motion and reed style. The micro-motion design is characterized by a flat, spill resistant mask. Reed styling, on the other hand, involves raised key construction. Both keyboard designs are usually capable of supporting interchangeable menu boards.

Exhibit 14.3 Sample Menu Keyboard

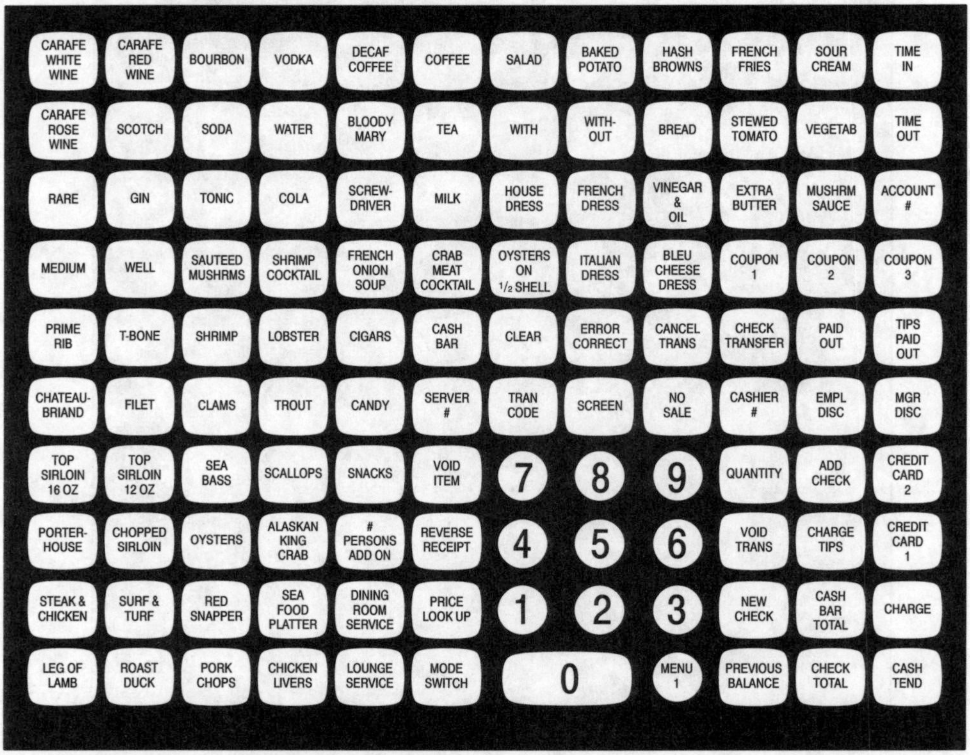

Source: Validec, Inc., San Carlos, California.

A menu board overlays the keyboard surface and identifies the function performed by each key during a specific meal period. Exhibit 14.3 presents a sample menu board for a micro-motion keyboard design. Different types of keyboard keys identified by a menu board include:

- Preset keys
- Price look-up keys
- Modifier keys
- Function keys
- Settlement keys
- Numeric keypad

Preset keys. A preset key is programmed to access the price, descriptor, department code, tax, and inventory status for a specific menu item. Automatic menu pricing makes faster guest service possible and eliminates price and tax errors by servers during busy meal periods. The term "descriptor" refers to the abbreviated description of a menu item, such as "SHRMPCKT" for shrimp cocktail or "PRIME" for prime rib. A department code refers to the menu category to which the preset item belongs. Typical department codes are appetizer, entrée, dessert, etc.

Once a preset key is pressed, a description of the item and its price are retrieved from the system's memory and appear on the operator's display unit. This data may also be relayed (along with preparation instructions) to the appropriate production station or printed on a guest check. In addition, the sales represented by this transaction are retained for revenue reporting and for tracking inventory levels. Sales data of individual items are important for guest check totaling as well as for producing management reports.

Price look-up keys. Since terminals generally have a limited number of preset keys, price look-up keys are used to supplement preset keys. Price look-up keys operate similarly to preset keys, except that they require the user to identify a menu item by its reference code number (up to five digits) rather than by its name or descriptor. For example, if a server wants to record the sale of a cheeseburger and there is no preset key for that item, the server would need to enter the code number for cheeseburgers (706, for example) and press the price look-up key. Once activated, price look-up keys perform the same functions as preset keys.

Modifier keys. Modifier keys allow servers to relay preparation instructions (such as rare, medium, or well-done for a steak) to remote work station printers or video display screens located in food production areas. Typically, a server enters the item ordered and then presses the appropriate preparation modifier.

Modifier keys can also be used to legitimately alter menu item prices. For example, modifier keys may be useful to a restaurant that sells house wine by the carafe and half-carafe. Instead of tying up two preset keys (one for carafe, the other for half-carafe), a single preset key can be designated for house wine by the carafe and a modifier key can be programmed as a half-portion modifier. When a half-carafe is sold, the server simply presses both the carafe preset key and half-portion modifier key to register a half-carafe sale. The system adds the price of a half-carafe to its running total of wine revenues. In addition, the system adjusts its perpetual inventory records accordingly.

Function keys. While preset and price look-up keys are used for order entry, function keys assist the operator in processing transactions. Sample function keys are: clear, discount, void, and no-sale. These keys are important for error correction (clear and void), legitimate price alteration (discount), and proper cash handling (no-sale).

Settlement keys. Settlement keys are used to record the methods by which accounts are settled: cash, credit card, house account, charge transfer to the guest's folio (in a hotel), or other payment method.

Numeric keypad. The set of keys making up the numeric keypad are used to ring up menu items by price, access price look-up data by menu item code number, access open guest check accounts by serial number, and perform other data entry operations. For example, if the register or terminal is used to record and store payroll data, the numeric keypad can be used to enter employee identification numbers as employees begin and end their workshifts. The numeric keypad may also be used to enter report codes which initiate the production of management reports.

Touch-Screen Terminals. Touch-screen terminals simplify data entry procedures and may be used in place of traditional keyboards. A special microprocessor within the terminal is programmed to display data on areas of the screen that are sensitive to touch. Touching one of the sensitized areas produces an electronic charge, which is translated into signals processed by the terminal in much the same way that a terminal would process signals from a conventional keyboard.

Magnetic Strip Readers. A magnetic strip reader is a device that connects to a cashier terminal. These devices do not replace keyboards or touch-screen terminals. Instead, they extend the capabilities of these components.

Magnetic strip readers are capable of collecting data stored on a magnetized film strip typically located on the back of a credit card or house account card. Rather than requiring special processing, credit card transactions can be handled directly with the ECR/POS system.

Hand-Held Server Terminals. Hand-held server terminals are remote order entry devices. Remote order entry devices may revolutionize ECR/POS technology and could eventually replace traditional server order pads and precheck terminals.

Hand-held server terminals, also referred to as portable server terminals, perform most of the functions of a precheck terminal and enable servers to enter orders at tableside. This technology can be a major advantage for large establishments with long distances between server stations and outdoor dining areas, or very busy lounges where it is difficult to reach a precheck terminal. In any establishment, service may be faster because servers do not have to wait in line to use a precheck terminal during peak business periods. In some cases, appetizers and drinks may be ready to serve just seconds after a server has finished entering the orders and has left the table.

A two-way communications capability allows a server to communicate special instructions to production areas—"no salt" or "medium rare," for example—when keying in the order. Production employees can also communicate with the server. For example, they can immediately alert a server if an item is out of stock. Typically, when an order is ready for pickup, a production employee can alert the server via a signal sent to the server's hand-held terminal.

Since all items must be entered through the server's hand-held unit, the common problem of coffee and/or desserts being inadvertently left off guest checks can be reduced. In addition, some units enable managers to monitor service through their own hand-held devices.

Display Units

In addition to an order entry device, ECRs and POS terminals contain an operator display unit (a monitor) enabling the user to review and edit entries. An operator display unit enables the user to check transactions in progress and to respond to prompts necessary for carrying out various system procedures.

Some ECRs and POS terminals with cash drawers may also support a customer display unit. In food service operations where guests view settlement transactions, serious consideration should be given to the use of a customer display unit.

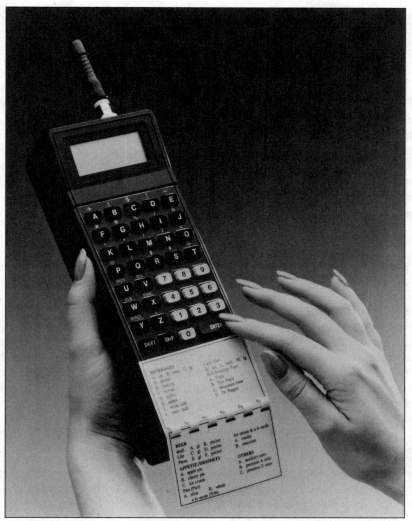

Hand-held server terminal. (Courtesy of Norand Corporation, Cedar Rapids, Iowa)

Output Devices

Output devices include guest check, work station, receipt, and journal printers.

Guest Check Printers. Guest check printers are standard ECR/POS output devices. Sophisticated guest check printers have automatic form number reader capability which facilitates order entry procedures. Instead of accessing a guest check by the server manually inputting a guest check's serial number, a bar code imprinted on the guest check presents the check's serial number in a machine readable format. The server simply slips the guest check into the terminal's automatic form number reader unit, and the bar code provides rapid access to the correct guest check account.

Overprinting items and amounts on guest checks is a problem with some printers. Usually, servers must manually align the printer's ribbon with the next blank printing line on the guest check. If the alignment is not correct, the guest check appears disorganized and messy with items and amounts printed over one another or with large gaps between lines of print.

Printers with automatic slip feed capability prevent overprinting by retaining the number of the last line printed for each open guest check. The server simply aligns the top edge of the guest check with the top edge of the printer's slot and the terminal automatically moves the check to the next available printing line and prints the order entry data. Since guest checks are placed within the printer's slot the same way every time, servers may spend less time fussing with the guest check and more time meeting the needs of their guests.

Exhibit 14.4 presents a sample guest check printed by a device equipped with both automatic form number reader and slip feed capability.

Work Station Printers. Work station printers are usually placed at kitchen preparation areas and service bars. As orders are entered at precheck or cashier terminals, they are sent to a designated remote work station printer to initiate production. Exhibit 14.5 presents printouts produced by remote work station printers. The printouts correspond to items printed on the sample guest check illustrated in Exhibit 14.4. This communication system enables servers to spend more time meeting the needs of their guests while significantly reducing traffic in kitchen and bar areas.

If the need for hard copy output in production areas is not critical to an operation's internal control system, video display units (kitchen monitors) may be viable alternatives to work station printers. Since these units are able to display several orders on a single screen, kitchen employees do not have to handle numerous pieces of paper. An accompanying cursor control keypad enables kitchen employees to easily review previously submitted orders.

Receipt Printers. Receipt printers produce hard copy on thin, narrow register tape. Although the usefulness of receipt printers is somewhat limited, these devices may help control the production of menu items that are not prepared in departments receiving orders through work station printers.

For example, when servers prepare desserts for their guests and the pantry area is not equipped with a work station printer, desserts could be served without ever being entered into the POS system. When this happens, it is also possible that desserts could be served without ever being posted to guest checks. This situation can be avoided by using a receipt printer. Servers preparing desserts can be required to deliver a receipt tape to the dessert pantry area as proof that the desserts are properly posted to guest checks for eventual settlement. This procedure enhances management's internal control by ensuring that a record of every menu item served is stored somewhere in the computer system.

Journal Printers. These output devices produce a continuous detailed record of all transactions entered anywhere in the system. Journal printers are usually located in a secure area remote from service and production areas. Hard copy is produced

Exhibit 14.4 Sample Guest Check

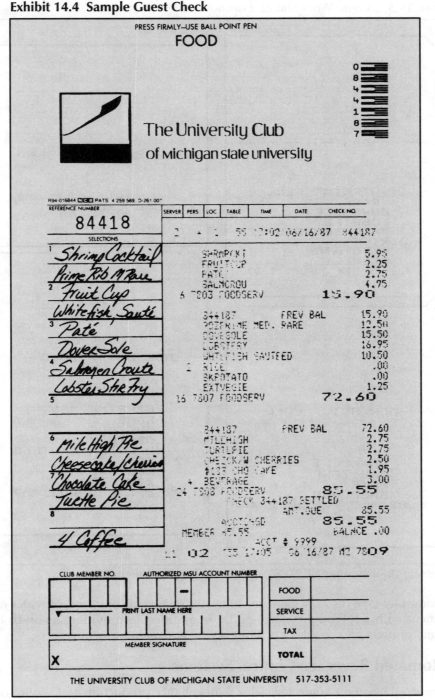

Exhibit 14.5 Sample Work Station Printouts

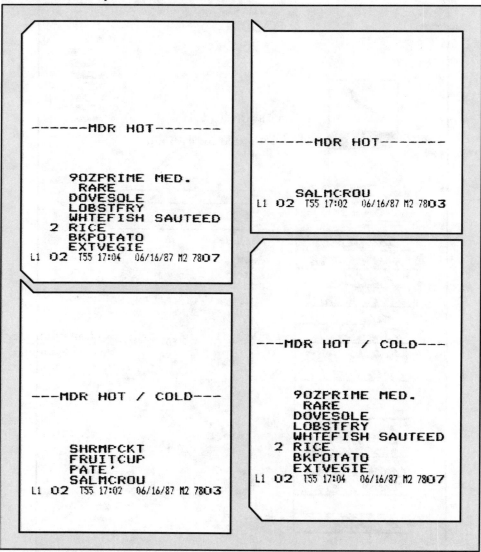

```
------MDR HOT--------


      9OZPRIME MED.
       RARE
      DOVESOLE
      LOBSTFRY
      WHTEFISH SAUTEED
    2 RICE
      BKPOTATO
      EXTVEGIE
L1  O2  T55 17:04   06/16/87 M2 7807
```

```
------MDR HOT-------


      SALMCROU
L1  O2  T55 17:02   06/16/87 M2 7803
```

```
---MDR HOT / COLD---



      SHRMPCKT
      FRUITCUP
      PATE'
      SALMCROU
L1  O2  T55 17:02   06/16/87 M2 7803
```

```
---MDR HOT / COLD---

      9OZPRIME MED.
       RARE
      DOVESOLE
      LOBSTFRY
      WHTEFISH SAUTEED
    2 RICE
      BKPOTATO
      EXTVEGIE
L1  O2  T55 17:04   06/16/87 M2 7807
```

Courtesy of The University Club, Michigan State University, East Lansing, Michigan

on computer tape (usually there are 20 to 40 columns of copy) and provides management with a thorough system audit. In addition to providing an audit trail, journal printers are capable of printing a variety of management reports.

Automated Beverage Control Systems

Automated beverage control systems may enhance production and service capabilities while improving accounting and operational controls. A beverage control unit is the brain of an automated system. This control unit is generally located close to a beverage storage area and is primarily responsible for regulating all essential mechanisms within the system. The unit communicates requests from order entry terminals to the system's delivery network and directs the flow of beverages from a storage area to a dispensing unit.

Automated beverage control systems may employ different types of sensing devices that increase operational controls within the system. Three common sensing devices are glass sensors, guest check sensors, and empty bottle sensors. A glass sensor is an electronic mechanism located in a bar dispensing unit that will not permit liquid to flow from the dispensing unit unless there is a glass positioned below the dispensing head to catch the liquid. Guest check sensors prevent the system from fulfilling beverage orders unless they are first recorded on a guest check. When a server or bartender places a beverage order whose ingredients are out of stock, an empty bottle sensor relays a signal to the order entry device.

Sophisticated systems are able to record data input through order entry devices, transport beverage ingredients through a controlled delivery network, dispense ingredients for ordered items, and track important service and sales data which can be used to produce various reports for use by management.

Components of an automated beverage control system include an order entry device, a delivery network, and dispensing units.

Order Entry Device

In an automated beverage control system, the primary function of an order entry device is to initiate activities involved with recording, producing, and pricing beverage items requested by guests. There are two basic order entry devices: a group of preset buttons located on a dispensing unit, and keyboard units.

Dispensing-Unit Preset Buttons. A group of preset buttons on a dispensing unit is the most popular order entry device. These devices may result in lower system costs because the dispensing unit serves as both an order taker and a delivery unit. However, since dispensing units may only support up to 16 preset buttons, the number of beverage items under the control of the automated beverage system is limited.

Keyboard Units. Keyboard units function similarly to precheck terminals; beverage dispensing is performed by a separate piece of hardware. Since they support a full range of keys (including preset keys, price look-up keys, and modifier keys), keyboard units place a large number of beverage items under the control of the automated system. Keyboard units are most effective when equipped with a guest check printer that has an automatic form number reader and automatic slip feed capabilities.

Delivery Network

An automated beverage control system relies on a delivery network to transport beverage item ingredients from storage areas to dispensing units. Exhibit 14.6 provides an overview of one kind of delivery network. The delivery network must be a closed system capable of regulating temperature and pressure conditions at various

Exhibit 14.6 Delivery Network of an Automated Beverage Control System

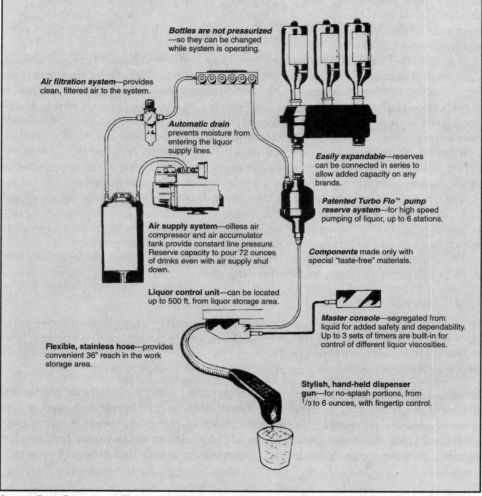

Bottles are not pressurized —so they can be changed while system is operating.

Air filtration system—provides clean, filtered air to the system.

Automatic drain prevents moisture from entering the liquor supply lines.

Easily expandable—reserves can be connected in series to allow added capacity on any brands.

Patented Turbo Flo™ pump reserve system—for high speed pumping of liquor, up to 6 stations.

Air supply system—oilless air compressor and air accumulator tank provide constant line pressure. Reserve capacity to pour 72 ounces of drinks even with air supply shut down.

Components made only with special "taste-free" materials.

Liquor control unit—can be located up to 500 ft. from liquor storage area.

Master console—segregated from liquid for added safety and dependability. Up to 3 sets of timers are built-in for control of different liquor viscosities.

Flexible, stainless hose—provides convenient 36" reach in the work storage area.

Stylish, hand-held dispenser gun—for no-splash portions, from 1/3 to 6 ounces, with fingertip control.

Source: Berg Company, a division of DEC International, Inc., Madison, Wisconsin.

locations and stages of delivery. To maintain proper temperature conditions, the delivery network typically employs a cooling sub-system that controls such mechanisms as cold plates, cold boxes, and/or cold storage rooms.

Most automated beverage control systems are able to deliver beverage ingredients by controlling pressure sources such as gravity, compressed air, carbon dioxide, and nitrous oxide. Gravity and compressed air are used for delivering liquor, nitrogen or nitrous oxide for wine, compressed air for beer, and a carbon dioxide regulator for post-mixes. A post-mix soft drink dispenser places syrup and carbonated water together at the dispenser instead of storing, transporting, and distributing the soft drink as a finished product.

The particular pressure source selected to transport a specific ingredient is a function of its effect on the taste and wholesomeness of the finished beverage item. For example, if carbon dioxide were attached to a wine dispenser, the wine would become carbonated and spoiled; if compressed air were hooked up to a post-mix soft drink dispenser, the finished beverage item would not have any carbonation. Pressure sources not only affect the quality of finished beverage items, but may also affect the timing flow of mixture, portion size, and desired foaming.

Almost any type of liquor and accompanying liquor ingredient can be stored, transported, and dispensed by an automated beverage control system. Portion sizes of liquor can be controlled with remarkable accuracy. Typically, systems can be calibrated to maintain portion sizes ranging from one-half ounce to three and one-half ounces.

Dispensing Units

Once beverage item ingredients are removed from storage and transported by the delivery network to production areas, they are ready to be dispensed. Automated beverage control systems may be configured with a variety of dispensing units. Common dispensing units include:

- Touch-bar faucet
- Console faucet
- Hose and gun device
- Mini-tower pedestal
- Bundled tower unit

Touch-Bar Faucet. A touch-bar faucet can be located under the bar, behind the bar, on top of an ice machine, or on a pedestal stand. These devices may not have the versatility, flexibility, or expandability of other dispensing units. Typically, touch-bar faucets are dedicated to only a single beverage type and are preset for one specific portion size output per push on the bar lever. A double shot of bourbon, therefore, may require the bartender to push twice on the bar lever.

Console Faucet. Console faucet dispensing units are similar to touch-bar faucet devices in that they can be located in almost any part of the bar area. In addition, these units may be located up to 300 feet from beverage storage areas. Unlike touch-bar faucet devices, console faucet units are able to dispense various beverages in a number of portion sizes. Using buttons located above the faucet unit, a bartender can trigger up to four different portion sizes from the same faucet head. An optional feature of this kind of dispensing device is a double-hose faucet unit that can transport large quantities of liquids in short amounts of time.

Hose and Gun Device. The hose and gun device has traditionally been a popular dispensing unit. Control buttons on the handle of the gun can be connected by hoses to liquors, carbonated beverages, water, and/or wine tanks. These types of dispensers can be installed anywhere along the bar and are frequently included as standard dispensing equipment on portable bars and at service bar locations. Depressing a control button normally produces a premeasured flow of the desired beverage. The number of beverage items under the control of a hose and gun dispensing unit is limited to the number of control buttons the device supports. Some newer units offer the bartender up to 16 buttons for product dispensing.

Mini-Tower Pedestal. The mini-tower pedestal dispensing unit combines the portion-size capabilities of console faucet units with the button selection technique of hose and gun devices. In addition, the mini-tower concept offers increased control of bar operations. In order for a beverage to be dispensed, the mini-tower unit requires that a button be pressed and a glass sensing device requires that a glass be placed directly under the dispensing head. This automated dispensing unit has been popular for dispensing beverage items that need no additional ingredients prior to service, such as wine, beer, and call brand liquors. A mini-tower unit can also be located on a wall, ice machine, or pedestal base in the bar area.

Bundled Tower Unit. The most sophisticated and flexible dispensing unit is the bundled tower unit, also referred to as a tube tower unit. The bundled tower unit is designed to dispense a variety of beverage items. Beverage orders must be entered on a separate piece of hardware, not on the tower unit. Bundled tower units may support in excess of 110 beverage products and contain a glass-sensing element. Each liquor has its own line to the tower unit and a variety of pressurized systems can be used to enhance delivery from storage areas. While other units sequentially dispense beverage item ingredients, the bundled tower unit simultaneously dispenses all ingredients required for a specific beverage item—bar servers merely garnish the finished product. This dispensing unit can be located up to 300 feet from beverage storage areas.

Endnotes

1. Detailed information on computer hardware is contained in Michael L. Kasavana and John J. Cahill, *Managing Computers in the Hospitality Industry*, 2d ed. (East Lansing, Mich.: Educational Institute of the American Hotel & Motel Association, 1992).

Key Terms

automatic form number reader
automatic slip feed
beverage control unit
bundled tower dispensing unit
console faucet dispensing unit
delivery network
empty bottle sensor
function keys
glass sensor
guest check printer
journal printer

kitchen monitor
menu board
mini-tower pedestal dispensing unit
modifier keys
precheck terminal
preset key
price look-up key
receipt printer
touch-bar faucet dispensing unit
work station printer

Discussion Questions

1. What are the three phases of the data processing cycle? What are the functions performed in each phase?

2. How does electronic data processing differ from data processing?

3. What is the difference between an electronic cash register (ECR) and a point-of-sale (POS) terminal?

4. What is the function of a menu board?

5. How do preset keys differ from price look-up keys?

6. What functions are performed by modifier and numeric keys?

7. What are two important features available for guest check printers?

8. Within an ECR/POS system, what functions are performed by work station printers? by receipt printers?

9. What are the basic components of an automated beverage control system?

10. What are five common automated beverage dispensing units and their distinguishing features?

Chapter Outline

This chapter was written and contributed by Michael L. Kasavana, Ph.D., Professor, School of Hotel, Restaurant and Institutional Management, Michigan State University, East Lansing, Michigan.

15

Food Service Automation—
Software

THE HARDWARE OF any computer system does nothing by itself. In order for hardware components to operate there must be a set of software programs that direct the system in what to do, how to do it, and when to do it. Electronic cash register (ECR) and point-of-sale (POS) software not only direct internal system operations, but also maintain files and produce management reports. The first sections of this chapter examine the types of data stored in major ECR/POS files and the kinds of reports that can be prepared for use by management.

While sophisticated ECR/POS systems maintain important data regarding service-related activities, specialized software has been developed to facilitate management-related back-of-the-house activities. These software programs are generally designed for microcomputers (personal computers) which are typically located in management offices. In larger food service operations, specialized software may run on minicomputers, which are more powerful than microcomputers.

This chapter examines specialized back-of-the-house software programs related to recipe management, menu management, sales analysis, inventory management, and general food service accounting. Many other software programs have been developed to facilitate specialized management activities, such as sales forecasting, employee scheduling, operations budgeting, and capital budgeting.[1]

A fully integrated food service computer system connects ECR/POS technology with management's microcomputers. This connection, referred to as an interface, enables specialized management software programs to access and process data maintained by ECR/POS system files. By reducing the number of times that data must be handled, fully integrated food service computer systems increase the speed and the accuracy of data processing tasks.[2]

ECR/POS Software

The major files stored and maintained by sophisticated ECR/POS systems include: a menu item file, an open check file, a labor master file, and limited inventory files. The following sections briefly examine the types of data stored by these ECR/POS files and the kinds of information contained in some of the more significant reports that can be printed by the system on standard register tape.

Types of ECR/POS Files

Menu Item File. A menu item file contains data for all meal periods and menu items sold. Important data maintained by this file may include the menu item's identification number, description, recipe code number, and selling price. This file also stores historical information on the actual number of items sold. This data can be accessed by management or by sophisticated forecasting programs to project future sales and to help schedule needed personnel.

Open Check File. The open check file maintains current data for all open guest checks. This file is accessed to monitor items on a particular guest check, to add items to a guest check after the initial order has been entered, and to close the guest check at the time of settlement. Data contained in an open check file can usually be printed at any time.

Labor Master File. The labor master file contains one record for each employee and maintains data required to produce labor reports for management. Each record in the labor master file may accumulate the following data on an employee: employee name, employee number, social security number, job codes, hours worked, total hourly wages, wages declared, credits for employee meals, number of guests served per meal period, and gross sales per meal period. Some ECR/POS systems are unable to compute net pay figures for each employee because of restricted processing ability and limited internal memory capacity.

Inventory Files. The inventory files maintained by some ECR/POS systems may not meet all the needs of most food service operations. Some systems are incapable of tracking the same item as it passes through the purchasing, issuing, and production control points. Purchase units (case, drum, etc.) commonly differ from storeroom inventory or issue units (#10 can, gallon, etc.), which, in turn, differ from standard recipe units (ounces, teaspoons, cups, etc.). Some ECR/POS systems are unable to support the number of conversion tables that are necessary to track menu items through ingredient purchase, storage, and use.

ECR/POS Management Reports

ECR/POS systems may access data contained in several files to produce consolidated reports for use by management. While the kinds of reports produced vary in relation to the type of ECR/POS system operating at a property, significant reports include an open check report, a server productivity report, a daily labor report, and a daily revenue report.

Exhibit 15.1 presents a sample open check report. This report lists all guest checks that have not been settled. The report may list items such as the serial number of a guest check, server number, the time the guest check was opened, the elapsed time since the guest check was opened, the number of guests, the table number, and the amount currently owed. Some ECR/POS systems enable management to require that individual server check-out reports be printed before servers leave the property at the end of their shifts. This printout ensures that all checks assigned to servers have been properly settled. If not, the open check report is used to list the guest checks for which the server is held accountable.

When property procedures require servers to close each guest check at the time guests settle their accounts, accurate server productivity reports can be produced. Daily productivity reports may be generated for each server and cashier in

Exhibit 15.1 Sample Open Check Report

```
              SMITH'S RESTAURANT   1050

                                            14:25

                 OPEN CHECKS REPORT

  CHECK    TIME     EMPLOYEE NAME        AMOUNT
  041232   12:51    B LANGFORD           134.53
  041891   13:10    R NIMS                89.68
  024593   13:28    J JACKSON             45.90
     •
     •
  006793   13:45    C HILL                34.78
  012225   14:21    K BARNHILL            67.14

                                            14:25
```

Source: International Business Machines Corporation, White Plains, New York.

Exhibit 15.2 Sample Server Productivity Report

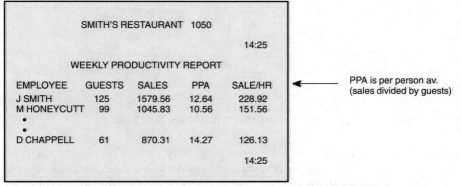

```
              SMITH'S RESTAURANT   1050

                                            14:25

              WEEKLY PRODUCTIVITY REPORT

  EMPLOYEE     GUESTS   SALES    PPA    SALE/HR
  J SMITH        125    1579.56  12.64   228.92
  M HONEYCUTT     99    1045.83  10.56   151.56
     •
     •
  D CHAPPELL      61     870.31  14.27   126.13

                                            14:25
```

PPA is per person av.
(sales divided by guests)

Source: International Business Machines Corporation, White Plains, New York.

terms of guest count, total sales, and average sales. In addition, a weekly productivity report may be generated, showing the average sales amount per guest for each server. Exhibit 15.2 shows a sample server productivity report.

Although some ECR/POS systems are unable to compute the net pay for employees, data accumulated by the labor master file can be accessed to produce a number of labor reports. Exhibit 15.3 illustrates a sample daily labor report. This report lists an employee's job code, employee number, the hours worked, gross wages, and declared wages (tips).

ECR/POS systems may access data contained in several files to produce a daily revenue report, such as the one shown in Exhibit 15.4. Data contained in this report may be used to determine sales trends, identify product needs, and monitor advertising and sales promotional efforts.

Some ECR/POS systems produce a sales analysis report. This report enables management to measure the sales performance of individual menu items by department or product category within certain time intervals. These time intervals

Exhibit 15.3 Sample Daily Labor Report

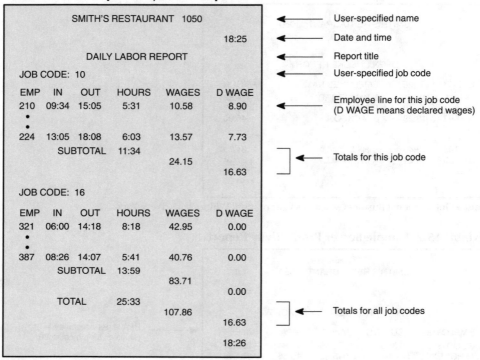

							User-specified name
SMITH'S RESTAURANT 1050						←	
					18:25	←	Date and time
	DAILY LABOR REPORT					←	Report title
JOB CODE: 10						←	User-specified job code
EMP	IN	OUT	HOURS	WAGES	D WAGE		
210	09:34	15:05	5:31	10.58	8.90	←	Employee line for this job code (D WAGE means declared wages)
•							
•							
224	13:05	18:08	6:03	13.57	7.73		
	SUBTOTAL		11:34				
				24.15		←	Totals for this job code
					16.63		
JOB CODE: 16							
EMP	IN	OUT	HOURS	WAGES	D WAGE		
321	06:00	14:18	8:18	42.95	0.00		
•							
•							
387	08:26	14:07	5:41	40.76	0.00		
	SUBTOTAL		13:59				
				83.71			
					0.00		
	TOTAL		25:33				
				107.86		←	Totals for all job codes
					16.63		
					18:26		

Source: International Business Machines Corporation, White Plains, New York.

are commonly referred to as day parts. Day parts may vary in relation to the type of food service operation. Fast-food restaurants may desire sales analysis reports segmented by 15-minute intervals, table service restaurants by the hour, and institutional food service operations by meal period.

Back-of-the-House Software

Recipe Management Software

Recipe management software maintains two of the most important files used by an integrated food service computer system: an ingredient file and a standard recipe file. Most other management software programs must be able to access data contained within these files in order to produce special reports for management.

Ingredient File. An ingredient file contains important data on each purchased ingredient. Ingredient file data generally include ingredient code numbers and descriptions, as well as each ingredient's:

- Purchase unit and cost per purchase unit
- Issue unit and cost per issue unit
- Recipe unit and cost per recipe unit

Exhibit 15.4 Sample Daily Revenue Report

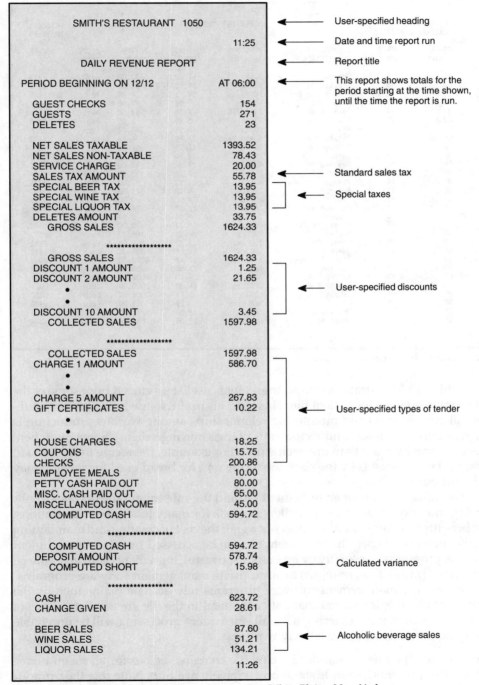

SMITH'S RESTAURANT 1050		← User-specified heading
	11:25	← Date and time report run
DAILY REVENUE REPORT		← Report title
PERIOD BEGINNING ON 12/12	AT 06:00	← This report shows totals for the period starting at the time shown, until the time the report is run.
GUEST CHECKS	154	
GUESTS	271	
DELETES	23	
NET SALES TAXABLE	1393.52	
NET SALES NON-TAXABLE	78.43	
SERVICE CHARGE	20.00	
SALES TAX AMOUNT	55.78	← Standard sales tax
SPECIAL BEER TAX	13.95	
SPECIAL WINE TAX	13.95	← Special taxes
SPECIAL LIQUOR TAX	13.95	
DELETES AMOUNT	33.75	
GROSS SALES	1624.33	
******************		
GROSS SALES	1624.33	
DISCOUNT 1 AMOUNT	1.25	
DISCOUNT 2 AMOUNT	21.65	
•		← User-specified discounts
•		
DISCOUNT 10 AMOUNT	3.45	
COLLECTED SALES	1597.98	
******************		
COLLECTED SALES	1597.98	
CHARGE 1 AMOUNT	586.70	
•		
•		
CHARGE 5 AMOUNT	267.83	
GIFT CERTIFICATES	10.22	← User-specified types of tender
•		
•		
HOUSE CHARGES	18.25	
COUPONS	15.75	
CHECKS	200.86	
EMPLOYEE MEALS	10.00	
PETTY CASH PAID OUT	80.00	
MISC. CASH PAID OUT	65.00	
MISCELLANEOUS INCOME	45.00	
COMPUTED CASH	594.72	
******************		
COMPUTED CASH	594.72	
DEPOSIT AMOUNT	578.74	
COMPUTED SHORT	15.98	← Calculated variance
******************		
CASH	623.72	
CHANGE GIVEN	28.61	
BEER SALES	87.60	
WINE SALES	51.21	← Alcoholic beverage sales
LIQUOR SALES	134.21	
	11:26	

Source: International Business Machines Corporation, White Plains, New York.

Exhibit 15.5 Sample Ingredient Cost List

```
01  - CHICKEN DELICIOUS, INC.             INGREDIENT COST LIST                    SA1222
001 - CHICKEN DELICIOUS #1                                                        10.35.19

    EXPENSE      INGRED.    INGREDIENT        PURCHASE    PURCHASE    RECIPE    RECIPE    RECIPE
    CATAGORY     NUMBER     DESCRIPTION         UNIT        COST      YIELD     UNIT      COST
      01            1       Chicken           Case         51.00      32.00    Head      1.5937
      02           41       Shortening        50 lb        19.12      50.00    1b         .3824
      03           42       Milk & Egg Dip    24 lb/cs     28.51      24.00    1b        1.1879
      03           43       Fine Salt         80 lb         7.98      80.00    1b         .0097
      03           44       Seasoning         24 1b/10     61.38      24.00    Pkts      2.5575
      03           45       Flour             25 lb         3.89       1.00    Bag       3.8900
      04            2       Roll              80/cs         6.76     180.00    Each       .0375
      05            3       Potato Mix        6 #10 Cans   31.88      34.80    1b         .9160
      06           49       Cabbage           50 lb        11.75      50.00    1b         .2350
      06           50       Onions            1b            1.70      50.00    1b         .0340
      06           52       Mayonnaise        4 Gal.       17.81      40.00    Gal.       .4452
      06           53       Salad Oil         4 Gal.       16.43      32.00    Pint       .5134
      06           54       Vinegar           4 Gal.       11.92      32.00    Pint       .3725
      06           55       Sugar             25 lb         8.98      25.00    1b         .3592
      06           56       Salt              80 lb         4.90      80.00    1b         .0612
      07            6       Gravy Mix         24 1b/cs     16.07      24.00    1b         .6695
      07           65       Pepper            1 1b          4.41       1.00    1b        4.4100
      07           66       Margarine Qtrs    30 lb        11.22      30.00    1b         .3740
      09           12       Bucket            100 cs       20.72     100.00    Each       .2072
      09           15       Dinner Box        250 cs       13.32     250.00    Each       .0532
      09           16       Snack Box         300 cs       12.54     300.00    Each       .0418
      09           17       Plastic Forks     6000 cs      37.47    6000.00    Each       .0062
      09           19       Napkins           6000 cs      31.68    6000.00    Each       .0052
      09           28       3.5 oz cup        2000 cs      29.10    2000.00    Each       .0145
      09           29       3.5 oz lid        2000 cs      14.20    2000.00    Each       .0071
      09           69       Labels            1000 cs       2.71    1000.00    Each       .0027
      10           75       Milk              1/2 Pint       .19       1.00    Each       .1900
      15           21       Chicken Livers    Case         72.00      72.00    1/2 1b    1.0000
      15           22       Breading          25 lb        25.00     650.00    1 Cup      .0384
```

Source: Tridata, Inc., Atlanta, Georgia.

Exhibit 15.5 illustrates a sample ingredient cost list produced from some of the data contained in an ingredient file. This report is useful for detailing unit expenditures at current costs and monitoring relationships among various product units (such as purchase, issue, and recipe units of the same ingredient). Some ingredient files may specify more than one recipe unit. For example, the recipe unit for bread used for French toast is by the slice; the recipe unit for bread used for stuffing may be by the ounce.

The initial creation of an ingredient file and the subsequent file updates (daily, weekly, monthly, etc.) is often a challenging task for many food service operations. The benefits of an ingredient file may outweigh the cost of creating and maintaining the file, however. When the ingredient file can be accessed by other management software programs (especially by inventory software), ingredient data can easily be transferred (rather than re-input) to appropriate management software programs.

Since other management software programs rely on data maintained by the ingredient file, it is important that data contained in the file are accurate. If errors are made when initially entering data, all subsequent processing will be unreliable and system reports will be relatively worthless.

Standard Recipe File. A standard recipe file contains recipes for all menu items. Exhibit 15.6 presents a sample standard recipe file printout. Note that the printout includes a "high warning flag" (near the bottom of the "Price/Oz" column). This

Exhibit 15.6 Sample Recipe File Printout

```
Item Name: New York Steak Dinner    Code: 4    Category: Dnnr = 2
============================================================
No.    Ingredient      Code      Price/Oz      Meas.    Lrg. Units    Sml. Units    Extension
============================================================
0    New York Strip      2        $0.2484        1       0.0 Pnds       8.0 Ozs      $1.9872
1    Russet Potatoes     1        $0.0125        1       0.0 Pnds       9.0 Ozs      $0.1125
2    Butter Chips       1D        $0.1375        1       0.0 Pnds       2.0 Ozs      $0.2750
3    Salad Batch        2R        $0.0247        1       0.0 Pnds       6.0 Ozs      $0.1482
4                        0        $0.0000        1       0.0 Pnds       0.0 Ozs      $0.0000
5                        0        $0.0000        1       0.0 Pnds       0.0 Ozs      $0.0000
6                        0        $0.0000        1       0.0 Pnds       0.0 Ozs      $0.0000
7                        0        $0.0000        1       0.0 Pnds       0.0 Ozs      $0.0000
8                        0        $0.0000        1       0.0 Pnds       0.0 Ozs      $0.0000
9                        0        $0.0000        1       0.0 Pnds       0.0 Ozs      $0.0000

Selling Price:  $8.95                      Yield: 100%      Total Food Extension:    $2.5228
Total Ozs.  25.0                        Cost/Oz.:  $0.1189   +   Misc. Food Cost:    $0.0000
Base Recipe Code:  3 Dinner Set Up                         + Cost of Base Recipe:   $0.4500
Food Cst % =          $2.9728 x 100/        $8.95    =33.2%   =  Total Food Cost:    $2.9728
                              High Warning Flag Set At:  35%    Labor or Non-Food:   $0.0000
Profit = Selling Price - Total Cost =                   $5.98    =     Total Cost:    $2.9728
                      * ENTER <1> TO MODIFY FILE. <2> TO EXIT *
```

Source: Advanced Analytical Computer Systems, Tarzana, California.

feature signals when changes in ingredient costs increase the food cost percent of a standard recipe beyond a predetermined level designated by management.

Some recipe management software programs provide space within standard recipe records for preparation instructions (also referred to as assembly instructions) which are typically found on standard recipe cards. This can be a useful feature when the number of portions yielded by a particular standard recipe needs to be expanded or contracted to accommodate forecasted needs. For example, if a standard recipe is designed to yield 100 portions but 530 portions are needed, it may be possible (depending on the particular menu item) to instruct the system to proportionately adjust the ingredient quantities. A recipe for 530 portions can be printed that includes preparation information, thus providing a complete plan for the new recipe's production.

Few restaurants purchase all menu item ingredients in ready-to-use or pre-portioned form. Some ingredients are made on the premises. This means that the ingredients within a standard recipe record may be either inventory items or references to other recipe files. Recipes that are included as ingredients within a standard recipe record are called sub-recipes.

Including sub-recipes as ingredients for a particular standard recipe is called chaining recipes. Chaining recipes enables the food service computer system to maintain a single record for a particular menu item that includes a number of sub-recipes. When ingredient costs change, recipe management software programs must be capable of automatically updating not only the costs of standard recipes, but also the costs of sub-recipes that are used as ingredients.

Menu Management Software

Most food service software programs sort and index data into timely, factual reports for management. Menu management software goes a step further and helps managers plan menus, price menu items, and evaluate menus by answering such questions as:

- What is the most profitable price to assign a menu item?

- At what price level and mix of sales does a food service operation maximize its profits?

- Which current menu items require repricing, retention, replacement, or repositioning on the menu?

- How should daily specials and new items be priced?

- How can the success of a menu change be evaluated?

The following sections examine two types of menu management software: precosting/postcosting software and menu engineering software.

Precosting/Postcosting Software. Precosting analysis enables management to determine a menu's profitability before actual production and service. Projections of cost of sales figures enable management to review and adjust operations before an actual service period begins. For example, if precosting analysis finds projected costs to be outside an acceptable range, management may consider raising prices, decreasing portion sizes, altering accompaniments, or substituting menu items.

Although the managers of most food service operations with non-automated systems have access to the necessary data for precosting calculations, few manually perform the analysis because it can be time-consuming. Computer-based precosting programs significantly streamline the analysis by accessing appropriate data from the ingredient file, recipe file, and other files to precost a menu within minutes.

Postcosting analysis differs from precosting analysis in that postcosting is based on actual sales, not forecasted sales. Postcosting software conducts a special type of sales analysis that multiplies the number of menu items sold by standard recipe costs to determine a potential food cost amount for a completed meal period.

Menu Engineering Software. Menu engineering software processes menu mix (MM) and contribution margin (CM) data for each menu item. The resulting information enables managers to evaluate possible changes to a menu's current mix of menu items and to make sound pricing decisions. A full discussion of menu engineering is beyond the scope of this text.[3] This section presents only a broad overview of the menu engineering concept.

Menu mix relates the sales of a particular menu item to the total number of menu items sold. A menu mix percentage is calculated by dividing the number sold of a specific menu item by the total number of all menu items sold. Each item on the menu is then categorized as either high or low in popularity.

The contribution margin of a menu item is calculated by subtracting its food costs from its selling price. An item's contribution margin is categorized as either high or low by comparing it with the average contribution margin of all items on the menu. Exhibit 15.7 illustrates a menu mix analysis report. Note that the report produces the following classifications:

- Menu items high in both menu mix and contribution margin are classified as stars (winners).

Exhibit 15.7 Menu Mix Analysis

Menu Mix Analysis							
Item Name	MM Count	% MM Share	Group Rank	% CM Share	Contr. Margin	Group Rank	Menu Class
Fried Shrimp	210	7.00	HIGH	6.73	3.10	LOW	PLOWHORSE
Fried Chicken	420	14.00	HIGH	11.89	2.74	LOW	PLOWHORSE
Chopped Sirloin	90	3.00	LOW	2.37	2.55	LOW	<< DOG >>
Prime Rib	600	20.00	HIGH	18.60	3.00	LOW	PLOWHORSE
King Prime Rib	60	2.00	LOW	2.67	4.30	HIGH	?PUZZLE?
NY Strip Steak	360	12.00	HIGH	14.88	4.00	HIGH	**STAR**
Top Sirloin	510	17.00	HIGH	19.24	3.65	HIGH	**STAR**
Red Snapper	240	8.00	HIGH	7.44	3.00	LOW	PLOWHORSE
Lobster Tail	150	5.00	LOW	7.05	4.55	HIGH	?PUZZLE?
Tenderloin Tips	360	12.00	HIGH	9.12	2.45	LOW	PLOWHORSE

Source: Hospitality Financial Consultants, Inc., Okemos, Michigan.

- Menu items high in menu mix but low in contribution margin are classified as plowhorses (marginal).

- Menu items low in menu mix but high in contribution margin are classified as puzzles (potential).

- Menu items low in menu mix and low in contribution margin are classified as dogs (losers).

The software goes a step further and identifies practical approaches by which to re-engineer the next menu. For example, simple strategies would include: retain stars, reprice plowhorses, reposition puzzles on the menu, and remove dogs.

Sales Analysis Software

Sales analysis software typically merges service-related data maintained by the ECR/POS system with data maintained by recipe management software. The sales analysis software then processes this combined data into numerous reports that help management direct daily operations in such areas as:

- Menu planning
- Sales forecasting
- Menu item pricing
- Ingredient purchasing
- Inventory control
- Labor scheduling
- Payroll accounting

Exhibit 15.8   Assorted Sales Analysis Reports

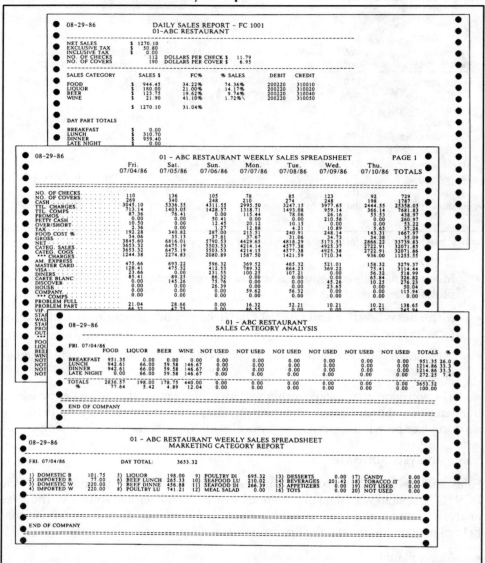

Source: Datachecker Systems, Inc., a subsidiary of National Semiconductor Corporation, Santa Clara, California.

A wide variety of sales reports can be produced. Also, reports are often tailored to the unique needs of a particular food service operation. Several kinds of reports are illustrated in Exhibit 15.8. Note that sales analysis software can print management reports on paper larger than the narrow tape used by most ECR/POS printers.

Inventory Management Software

From the point of view of food service managers, inventory software is perhaps the most important part of a fully integrated computer system. The most effective inventory programs track inventory items by unit and by cost. Conversion tables within the software program must be able to track ingredients (by unit and by cost) as they pass through purchasing, storing, and production control points.

For example, assume that an ingredient such as canned green beans is purchased, issued, and used in different units. When a shipment of the ingredient arrives, it should be easy to update the inventory record by simply entering the number of purchase units (cases of #10 cans) received. The computer system should then automatically convert this entry into issue units (#10 cans). Without this conversion capability, it would be necessary to manually calculate the number of units that will be stored and increase the inventory record accordingly. Similarly, at the end of a meal period, the system should be capable of updating inventory records by entering the standard recipe units that were used to prepare the menu items sold. If the food service computer system cannot convert issue units into recipe units, then these calculations must be performed manually.

Similarly, the system should also be able to track the costs associated with these various units. For example, assume that bottle ketchup is purchased by the case (24 twelve-ounce bottles), issued from the storeroom to the kitchen by the bottle, and used in recipes by the ounce. Given information regarding the purchase unit's net weight and cost, the system should be able to automatically extend costs for issue units and recipe units.

In order to arrive at these costs through manual calculations, an employee would first compute the price-per-ounce of the purchase unit. This is done by converting 18 pounds of ketchup (24 twelve-ounce bottles) to 288 ounces and then dividing $20.40 (the price per case) by 288 ounces to arrive at the recipe unit cost of $.07 per ounce. Multiplying $.07 by 12 ounces yields the issue unit cost (per bottle) of $.85. Performing these calculations manually for every inventory item can be a tedious, error-prone, time-consuming process. A fully integrated food service computer system can perform these calculations in fractions of a second.

Another concern is how usage is tracked by inventory software—by unit, by cost, or by both unit and cost. A system that tracks items by unit may be able to report changes in stock levels, but may not be able to provide financial data necessary for food costing. On the other hand, a system that tracks items primarily by product cost may not facilitate spot-checks of items in storage, or maintain perpetual inventory data. The most effective inventory programs are those that track items in terms of both unit and cost. Exhibit 15.9 illustrates a sample inventory usage report that details usage in both units and dollar amounts.

General Accounting Software

Food service computer systems vary in the number of general accounting software programs they provide. Four major back-of-the-house software programs relate to fundamental accounting tasks within the areas of accounts receivable, accounts

Exhibit 15.9 Sample Inventory Usage Report

Fine Restaurant
THE FOOD–TRAK (r) SYSTEM
FOOD USE REPORT

Name of Food (1)	Inv Unit	Actual Usage (Units)	Ideal Usage (Units)	VARIANCE in Units	VARIANCE in Dollars	% Sales	Usage Ratio	Days Left (2)	Beginning Inv (Units)	Purchase in Inv Units	Ending Inv (Units)	Cost per Inv Unit	Inventory Ending Value (3)	Index
Group: 1> MEATS														
BACON	LB	158.00	111.27	46.73	$85.	0.1.	1.4	12.4	100.00	150.00	92.00	$1.820	$167.44	F00212
CANADIAN-B	LB	61.30	65.25	-3.95	-$13.	-0.0	0.9	0.0	0.00	61.30	0.00	$3.190	$0.00	F00256
CANADIAN B	LB	11.50	0.00	11.50	$42.	0.1	0.0	0.0	28.00	15.50	32.00	$3.650	$116.80	F00193
CHIC LIVER	LB	351.50	120.75	230.75	$355.	0.4	2.9	8.9	327.50	96.00	72.00	$1.540	$110.88	F00200
CORN BEEF	LB	46.00	0.00	46.00	$78.	0.1	0.0	0.0	0.00	46.00	0.00	$1.690	$0.00	F00219
CUBESTEAK	LB	8.00	0.00	8.00	$18.	-0.0	0.0	0.0	4.00	10.00	6.00	$2.240	$13.44	F00198
HAM	LB	94.10	101.44	-7.34	-$19.	-0.0	0.9	7.6	56.80	88.80	51.50	$2.590	$133.38	F00213
HOT DOGS	LB	9.00	0.00	9.00	$18.	-0.0	0.0	0.0	5.00	10.00	6.00	$2.040	$12.24	F00196
LAMB	LB	1,155.50	1,304.84	-149.34	-$521.	-0.7	0.9	0.0	162.00	993.50	0.00	$3.490	$0.00	F00216
NEW YORK	LB	556.25	430.11	126.14	$851.	1.1	1.3	8.6	240.00	562.25	246.00	$6.750	$1,660.50	F00214
PORK LOIN	LB	50.50	0.00	50.50	$93.	0.1	0.0	0.0	0.00	57.50	7.00	$1.850	$12.95	F00188
PRIME RIB	LB	0.00	0.00	0.00	$0.	-0.0	0.0	0.0	0.00	0.00	0.00	$1.000	$0.00	F00279
SALAMI	LB	1.90	2.06	-0.16	-$2.	-0.0	0.9	54.5	4.00	5.40	7.50	$2.880	$21.60	F00222
SAUS LINKS	LB	29.00	30.00	-1.00	$30.	-0.0	1.0	31.5	32.00	60.00	63.00	$2.130	$134.19	F00201
SHOULDER	LB	20.00	0.00	20.00	$30.	0.0	0.0	0.0	0.00	20.00	0.00	$1.490	$0.00	F00215
TENDER	LB	707.20	758.98	-51.78	-$243.	-0.3	0.9	4.8	329.00	620.20	242.00	$4.690	$1,134.98	F00218
TOP ROUND	LB	14.00	15.96	-1.96	-$5.	0.0	0.9	22.6	38.00	0.00	24.00	$2.580	$61.92	F00194
TOP SIRLOIN	LB	485.65	540.40	-54.75	-$192.	-0.2	0.9	4.6	154.75	497.90	167.00	$3.500	$584.50	F00217
VEAL	LB	0.00	0.00	0.00	$0.	0.0	0.0	0.0	0.00	0.00	0.00	$2.440	$0.00	F00197
BROCHETTE	EACH	-6.00	-6.00	0.00	$0.	0.0	1.0	15.0	0.00	0.00	6.00	$5.005	$30.03	S00024
COOK CRN B	LB	8.00	7.00	1.00	$2.	0.0	1.1	17.1	16.00	0.00	8.00	$2.253	$18.03	S00030
CB HASH	LB	148.75	24.00	124.75	$284.	0.4	6.2	15.0	172.75	0.00	24.00	$2.277	$54.64	S00026
GRAHAM CC	LB	-16.00	-16.00	0.00	$0.	0.0	1.0	0.0	0.00	0.00	0.00	$12.272	$0.00	S00076
GRND BEEF	LB	0.00	0.00	0.00	$4.	0.0	1.0	39.4	26.00	0.00	42.00	$7.662	$321.79	S00022
HAM 1.5 OZ	EACH	15.00	0.00	15.00	$0.	0.0	1.0	0.0	23.00	0.00	8.00	$0.243	$1.94	S00088
HAM 3 OZ	EACH	-3.00	-3.00	0.00	$1.	0.0	1.0	15.0	0.00	0.00	3.00	$0.486	$1.46	S00089
LAMB–TRIM	LB	46.00	46.00	0.00	$0.	0.0	1.0	46.6	189.00	0.00	143.00	$7.852	$1,122.91	S00019
LUNCH LAMB	LB	0.00	0.00	0.00	$0.	0.0	1.0	0.0	0.00	0.00	0.00	$7.852	$0.00	S00018
MEATLOAF	LB	0.00	0.00	0.00	$0.	0.0	0.0	0.0	0.00	0.00	0.00	$4.714	$0.00	S00023
NY – TRIM	LB	-19.50	-19.50	0.00	$0.	0.0	1.0	52.3	48.50	0.00	68.00	$9.000	$612.00	S00017
PRIME COOK	LB	17.00	0.00	17.00	$23.	0.0	1.0	0.0	17.00	0.00	0.00	$1.333	$0.00	S00097
RB 1.5 OZ 3	EACH	0.00	0.00	0.00	$0.	0.0	0.0	37.5	6.00	0.00	10.00	$0.310	$3.10	S00025
STROG MEAT	LB	-30.00	-30.00	0.00	$0.	0.0	1.0	0.0	62.00	0.00	21.00	$0.000	$0.00	S00091
TEND – TRIM	LB	-4.00	-4.00	0.00	$0.	0.0	1.0	46.0	0.00	0.00	92.00	$7.147	$657.49	S00021
TOP SIR–TM	LB	-13.25	-13.25	0.00	$0.	0.0	1.0	53.2	33.75	0.00	47.00	$6.667	$313.33	S00020
TURK 1.5 OZ	EACH	-6.00	-6.00	0.00	$0.	0.0	1.0	45.0	12.00	0.00	18.00	$0.245	$4.42	S00092
TURK 3 OZ	EACH	0.00	0.00	0.00	$0.	0.0	0.0	0.0	0.00	0.00	0.00	$0.491	$0.00	S00093
Group Total:		$14,563.85	$13,675.16		$889.	1.1				$13,216.91			$7,305.96	
Group: 2> SEAFOOD														
COD	LB	8.00	0.00	8.00	$16.	0.0	0.0	0.0	25.00	0.00	17.00	$1.980	$33.66	F00189
Group Total:		8.00	0.00	8.00	$16.	0.0	0.0	0.0	25.00	0.00	17.00	$1.980	$33.66	

Prepared MON 10/24/83 FOOD–TRAK is a Registered Trademark Copyright (c) 1983 – System Concepts Inc. – All Rights Reserved

Source: System Concepts, Inc., Scottsdale, Arizona.

payable, payroll accounting, and financial reporting. These programs are examined in the following sections.[4]

Accounts Receivable Software. The term "accounts receivable" refers to obligations owed to the property from sales made on credit. Accounts receivable software typically performs the following functions:

- Maintains account balances

- Processes billings

- Monitors collection activities

- Generates aging of accounts receivable reports

- Produces an audit report indicating all accounts receivable transactions

Accounts receivable software generally maintains a guest master file. This file typically contains guest data and billing information such as the number of days elapsed between payments and the invoice to which the last payment applied. Many accounts receivable programs also maintain an accounts aging file, containing data that may be formatted into a variety of reports. For example, an aging of accounts receivable report segments each account in the accounts aging file according to the date the charge originated.

Accounts Payable Software. The term "accounts payable" refers to liabilities incurred for food, supplies, equipment, or other goods and services purchased on account. An accounts payable program maintains a supplier master file, an invoice register file, a check register file, and typically performs the following functions:

- Posts supplier invoices

- Monitors supplier payment discount periods

- Determines amounts due

- Produces checks for payment

- Facilitates the reconciliation of cleared checks

An important report produced by accounts payable software is the cash requirements report. This report lists all invoices selected for payment and the corresponding cash requirement totals. Exhibit 15.10 presents a sample cash requirements report.

Payroll Accounting Software. The labor-intensive nature of food service operations makes payroll accounting an important part of an integrated food service computer system. Payroll accounting software streamlines payroll accounting tasks and is generally able to handle the complexities involved in properly processing time and attendance records, unique employee benefits, pay rates, withholdings, deductions, and required payroll reports. Payroll accounting software typically performs the following functions:

Exhibit 15.10 Sample Cash Requirements Report

```
                              ACCOUNTS PAYABLE
                             ABC RESTAURANT INC.
     Date: 10/01/86                                                    Page:  1
                          CASH REQUIREMENTS REPORT
                            PAY DATE OF 10/15/86
==============================================================================
  Voucher  Invoice                    Due   Amount    Memo    Discount  Payment
  Number   Number    Description      Date   Due     Amount   Amount    Amount     Balance
==============================================================================

       4  -  GEORGIA POWER
      12  1598632   Power           072886  1227.59    0.00     0.00    1227.59     0.00
                                            -------   ------   ------   -------    -----
                                            1227.59    0.00     0.00    1227.59     0.00
      10  -  DUNN SUPPLIERS
       1  15966     Paper Straws    071586   100.23    0.00     0.00     100.23     0.00
                                            -------   ------   ------   -------    -----
                                             100.23    0.00     0.00     100.23     0.00

  200000  -  McCORMICK FOOD SERVICES
      10  12563     MISC. FOOD      071586   326.55    0.00     0.00     326.55     0.00
                                            -------   ------   ------   -------    -----
                                             326.55    0.00     0.00     326.55     0.00
==============================================================================



                    DISBURSEMENT DETAIL BY COMPANY
                    ------------------------------

   COMPANY    VENDOR    VOUCHER   DISBURSEMENT AMOUNT   DISCOUNTS TAKEN   NET DISBURSEMENT
   -------    ------    -------   ------------------    --------------    ----------------
      01         4        12            1227.59              0.00             1227.59
      01        10         1             100.23              0.00              100.23
      01      200000      10             326.55              0.00              326.55
                                   ------------------    --------------    ----------------
```

Source: Datachecker Systems, Inc., a subsidiary of National Semiconductor Corporation, Santa Clara, California.

- Maintains an employee master file
- Calculates gross and net pay for salaried and hourly employees
- Produces paychecks
- Prepares payroll tax registers and reports

In restaurant operations, a single employee may work at different tasks over a number of workshifts; each task may call for a separate pay rate. Therefore, payroll accounting software must be flexible enough to meet all the demands placed on it with a minimum of actual programming changes. It must be capable of handling job codes, employee meals, uniform credits, tips, taxes, and other data which may affect the net pay of employees.

Financial Reporting Software. Financial reporting software (also referred to as general ledger software) is structured by the food service operation's chart of accounts that lists financial statement accounts and their account numbers. The software maintains account balances, prepares trial balances, computes financial and operating ratios, and produces financial statements and a variety of reports for management's use.

Generally, financial reporting software is capable of tracking accounts receivable, accounts payable, cash, and adjusting entries. However, in order to track these areas, the financial reporting software must have access to account balances maintained by other back-of-the-house software programs. With a fully integrated food service computer system, daily file updates ensure that the balances held in the financial reporting files are current.

Endnotes

1. For more information about software programs for the hospitality industry, see *PC Applications for the Hospitality Industry* (East Lansing, Mich.: Educational Institute of the American Hotel & Motel Association, 1988). Software program.

2. Detailed information on computer software is contained in Michael L. Kasavana and John J. Cahill, *Managing Computers in the Hospitality Industry,* 2d ed. (East Lansing, Mich.: Educational Institute of the American Hotel & Motel Association, 1992).

3. Menu engineering is discussed in more detail in Jack D. Ninemeier, *Planning and Control for Food and Beverage Operations,* 3d ed. (East Lansing, Mich.: Educational Institute of the American Hotel & Motel Association, 1991). Menu engineering is also the subject of *Menu Management Exercise* (East Lansing, Mich.: Educational Institute of the American Hotel & Motel Association, 1989). Software program.

4. *Ledger Software* is an interactive software program that introduces students to computerized schedules, income statements, balance sheets, statements of equity, financial ratios, and more. Available from the Educational Institute, P.O. Box 1240, East Lansing, MI 48826.

Key Terms

chaining recipes
ingredient file
issue unit
labor master file
menu engineering software
menu item file
menu mix

open check file
postcosting
precosting
purchase unit
recipe unit
standard recipe file

Discussion Questions

1. What types of data are stored by the major files maintained by ECR/POS systems?

2. Why is it important that specialized software programs be able to access data stored in ECR/POS systems?

3. Why is an accurate ingredient file of recipe management important to food service operations with integrated software systems?

4. What purpose does a "high warning flag" serve in a standard recipe file of menu management software?

5. What is meant by "chaining recipes"?

6. What is the difference between precosting and postcosting software?

7. What are the variables by which menu engineering software analyzes the profitability of menu items?

8. How can differences among purchase units, issue units, and standard recipe units complicate the design of inventory software programs for food service operations?

9. What are some of the typical functions performed by accounts payable software programs?

10. What special demands may food service operations make on the design of payroll accounting software programs?

Glossary

A

AESTHETIC BALANCE
In menu planning, the degree to which meals have been constructed with an eye to the colors, textures, and flavors of foods.

À LA CARTE MENU
A menu in which food and beverage items are listed and priced separately.

ALCOHOLIC BEVERAGE MENU
A menu which lists cocktails, wines, and other alcoholic beverages an operation offers to guests. Alcoholic beverages can be listed on a separate menu or included on the regular menu. Restaurants with a large selection of wines may have a separate wine list. Many beverage menus also include no- or low-alcohol drinks.

ALLOWABLE FOOD COST
A budgeted food cost determined by subtracting non-food expenses and profit requirements from forecasted food sales.

ARTWORK
In menu planning, artwork includes drawings, photographs, decorative patterns, borders, etc., that are included on the menu to attract interest, highlight menu copy, or reinforce the operation's image.

AUTOMATIC FORM NUMBER READER
A feature of a guest check printer that facilitates order entry procedures. Instead of a server manually inputting a guest check's serial number to access the account, a bar code imprinted on the guest check enables the machine to "read" the serial number.

AUTOMATIC SLIP FEED
A feature of a guest check printer that prevents overprinting of items and amounts on guest checks.

AVERAGE FOOD SERVICE CHECK
A ratio comparing the revenue generated during a meal period to the number of guests served during that same period; calculated by dividing total food revenue by the number of guests served.

B

BALANCE SHEET
A financial statement giving the account balances for assets, liabilities, and equity on a given date.

BANQUET MENU

A banquet menu is usually a table d'hôte menu—a set meal with few, if any, choices. Banquet meals tend to be elaborate.

BASIC FOUR FOOD GROUPS PLAN

An eating plan that classifies foods required for good health into four groups— milk and other dairy products, meat, fruits and vegetables, and grains—with recommended portions and servings from each group that should be consumed daily. The plan provides the basics for a daily meal plan that meets the nutritional needs of most healthy people.

BEVERAGE CONTROL UNIT

Part of an automated beverage control system, located close to a beverage storage area and primarily responsible for regulating all essential mechanisms within the system.

BEVERAGE COST PERCENTAGE

A ratio comparing the cost of beverages sold to beverage sales; calculated by dividing the cost of beverages sold by beverage sales.

BROILER

Food service equipment that cooks with radiant heat from above or below the food.

BUDGETED FOOD COST PERCENTAGE

A tool used in the profit pricing method; determined by dividing allowable food costs by forecasted food sales. The resulting percentage is divided into an item's standard food cost to arrive at a selling price.

BUFFET SERVICE

Traditional buffet service involves arranging food on platters that are then placed on large serving tables. Sometimes each course is placed on a separate table.

BUNDLED TOWER DISPENSING UNIT

A machine in an automated beverage control system designed to dispense a variety of beverage items. Also referred to as a tube tower unit.

BUSINESS BALANCE

In menu planning, the balance between food costs, menu prices, the popularity of items, and other financial and marketing considerations.

C

CAFETERIA SERVICE

A type of service in which guests pass through serving lines and receive food items from service staff. "Scramble" cafeteria layouts reduce long serving lines by providing separate serving stations for different types of food.

CALIFORNIA MENU

A menu that offers breakfast, lunch, and dinner items on one menu, with all the items available at any time of the day.

CALL BRAND

A specific beverage brand that guests request by name when they place an order.

CALORIE

A measure of the energy contained in food. Technically, it is the amount of heat needed to raise the temperature of 1 kilogram of water 1°C.

CARBOHYDRATES

Basic nutrients that are the main source of fuel for body processes such as digestion and respiration. They also help maintain proper body temperature and eliminate the need for the body to use protein as an energy source.

CHAINING RECIPES

Including sub-recipes as ingredients for a particular standard recipe. This enables the food service computer system to maintain a single record for a particular menu item that includes a number of sub-recipes.

CHAIN RESTAURANT

A restaurant that is part of a multi-unit organization. Chain restaurants often share the same menu, purchase supplies and equipment cooperatively, and follow operating procedures that have been standardized for every restaurant in the chain.

CHEMICAL POISONING

Occurs when toxic substances contaminate foods or beverages.

CHILDREN'S MENU

A menu for children featuring simple, nutritious food served in small portions. Children's menus are usually designed to entertain the child; they may fold into hats or masks, be shaped like animals, or have word games, stories, or mazes printed on them.

CHOLESTEROL

A fatty substance found in the human body and in foods derived from animal products. It has been linked to heart disease.

COMMERCIAL FOOD SERVICE OPERATION

An operation that sells food and beverages for profit. Independent, chain, and franchise properties are all commercial food service operations.

CONSOLE FAUCET DISPENSING UNIT

A machine in one kind of automated beverage control system that is able to dispense various beverages in a number of portion sizes. It can be located up to 300 feet away from beverage storage areas. Using buttons located above the unit, a bartender can trigger up to four different portion sizes from the same faucet head.

CONTRIBUTION MARGIN
The menu item's selling price minus the item's standard food cost.

CONTROLLING
The management task of measuring actual results with expected results, as in measuring actual sales against expected or budgeted sales. Controlling also refers to safeguarding the operation's property and income.

COORDINATING
The management task of assigning work and organizing people and resources to achieve the operation's objectives.

CUISINE
A particular style or manner of preparing or cooking food.

CURRENT RATIO
Ratio of total current assets to total current liabilities, calculated by dividing current assets by current liabilities.

CYCLE MENU
A menu that changes every day for a certain period of days, then the cycle begins again; a cycle menu is really a series of different menus. Cycle menus are designed to provide variety for guests who eat at an operation frequently—or even daily.

D

DEEP FRYER
Food service equipment that cooks food by submerging it in hot fat.

DELIVERY INVOICE
A supplier's bill indicating the products that were delivered, their quantities and prices, and the total amount owed to the supplier.

DELIVERY NETWORK
Part of an automated beverage control unit that transports beverage item ingredients from storage areas to dispensing units.

DESCRIPTIVE COPY
Menu copy devoted to describing menu items. The purpose of descriptive copy is to inform guests about the menu item and increase sales.

DESSERT MENU
A separate menu designed to remind guests of the dessert items listed on the regular menu. It may also list desserts not listed on the regular menu and include dessert specials. Upscale restaurants may include after-dinner wines, cordials, brandies, and liqueurs on the dessert menu.

DINNER COST

The standard food cost for items combined to form dinners or other meals that are priced and sold as one menu selection.

DIRECTING

The management task of supervising, scheduling, and disciplining employees. Supervising includes such things as training and motivating employees.

DOORKNOB MENU

A type of room service menu that a housekeeper can leave in the guestroom. A doorknob menu lists a limited number of breakfast items and times that the meal can be served. Guests select what they want to eat and the time they want the food delivered, then hang the menu outside the door on the doorknob. The menus are collected and the orders are prepared and sent to the rooms at the indicated times.

DRAM SHOP ACTS

Legislation establishing third-party liability for accidents involving intoxicated drivers. Such laws often hold that bartenders, servers, and owners can be jointly held liable if they unlawfully sell alcoholic beverages to a minor or an intoxicated person who then causes injury to others.

DRY-HEAT COOKING

Cooking methods that require hot air or hot fat.

E

EIGHT PERCENT TIP REGULATION

A federal regulation established by the Tax Equity and Fiscal Responsibility Act of 1982 requiring all tipped employees to report tips of at least eight percent of a food service's gross receipts.

ELASTICITY OF DEMAND

A term economists use to describe how demand responds to price changes.

EMBOSS

Embossing involves stamping an image in relief—either positive (raised) or negative (recessed)—on a surface such as a page in a menu.

EMPTY BOTTLE SENSOR

Optional part of an automated beverage control unit that relays a signal to the order entry device when a server places a beverage order calling for ingredients that are out of stock.

EMULSION

A mixture of two ordinarily unmixable liquids. Unstable emulsions (such as oil and vinegar) separate when left standing; stable emulsions (like mayonnaise) do not separate.

ETHNIC MENU
Menu featuring a particular cuisine—Chinese, Mexican, Italian, etc.

EVALUATING
The management task of: (1) reviewing the operation's progress toward overall organizational goals, (2) measuring employee performance, and (3) assessing the effectiveness of training programs.

EXTERNAL OR PERSONAL SELLING
A marketing technique that involves hiring salespeople to generate leads and make personal sales calls outside of the food service operation itself. External selling is uncommon in the food service industry.

F

FAIR LABOR STANDARDS ACT
Commonly known as the federal wage and hour law; covers such areas as equal pay for equal work, child labor, recordkeeping requirements, minimum wage, and conditions defining overtime pay.

FATS
Basic nutrients that serve as concentrated sources of heat and energy for the body.

FEASIBILITY STUDY
A form of market research that analyzes the possible site, relevant demographic statistics, probable competitors, and projected financial success of a proposed food service operation.

FIBER
The indigestible cell walls of plants.

FIRST-IN, FIRST-OUT (FIFO)
A system of rotating and issuing stored food under which items that have been in storage longest are used first.

FIXED MENU
A menu which is used for several months or longer before it is changed. Daily specials may be offered, but a set list of items forms the basic menu.

FLAT ORGANIZATION
An organization with very few personnel levels—sometimes only one.

FOIL STAMPING
Foil stamping involves applying a thin foil film onto a surface such as paper. The foil may be artwork or copy.

FOOD COST PERCENTAGE

A ratio comparing the cost of food sold to food sales; calculated by dividing the cost of food sold by food sales.

FOOD GRADING

The process of analyzing food relative to specific, defined standards in order to assess its quality. Food grading is optional.

FOOD INFECTION

A type of foodborne illness caused by bacteria and viruses in food that are consumed with the food and later reproduce inside the body. With food infection, it is the germs themselves—not the toxins they produce—that cause the illness.

FOOD INSPECTION

An official examination of food to ensure wholesomeness. Inspection of certain foods is required by law.

FOOD POISONING

Occurs when germs get into food and produce toxic waste products. With food poisoning, it is the toxin—not the germs themselves—that produces the illness.

FOOD SERVER STATION

A certain section or number of tables in the dining room for which a server is responsible.

FOOD TEMPERATURE DANGER ZONE

A temperature zone between 41°F (5°C) and 140°F (60°C) in which many kinds of harmful germs multiply rapidly.

FORMAT

In menu planning, the shape, size, and general makeup of the menu.

FRANCHISE

A special type of chain operation. The franchisee (the owner of the franchise property) pays fees to use the name, building design, and business methods of the franchisor (the franchise company). The franchisee must agree to maintain the franchisor's business and quality standards.

FRUIT

The matured ovary of a plant, including the seeds and adjacent parts. It is the reproductive body of the seed plant. Fruits are high in carbohydrates and water and are excellent sources of vitamins and minerals.

FUNCTION KEYS

Part of an ECR/POS system terminal; function keys assist the user in processing transactions. They are important for error correction (clear and void), legitimate price alteration (discount), and proper cash handling (no-sale).

G

GARNISH
(1) Decorative edible items used to ornament or enhance the eye appeal of another food item. (2) To add such a decorative item to food.

GLASS SENSOR
An electronic mechanism located in a bar dispensing unit that will not allow liquid to flow from the dispensing unit unless there is a glass positioned below the dispensing head.

GUEST CHECK PRINTER
A sophisticated printer that may be equipped with an automatic form number reader and/or automatic slip feed capabilities.

GUEST COMMENT CARD
A short questionnaire that typically contains only a few questions. Guest comment cards are filled out by guests and used by food service managers to define current markets and to improve the operation.

GUEST SURVEY
A questionnaire completed by guests and used by food service managers to define current markets and to improve the operation. Managers may talk guests through the survey or leave it with them to fill out. Questionnaires may be long, and some questions may require detailed answers.

H

HEADING
In menu planning, headings are the menu's major heads, subheads, and names of menu items. Major heads usually identify meal courses—"Appetizers," "Entrées," etc., while subheads indicate categories within the major head. Subheads for the major head "Entrées" may be "Steaks," "Seafood," etc.

HOMOGENIZATION
A process that breaks up fat particles so they will remain suspended.

HOSPITALITY
The cordial reception of guests.

HOUSE BRAND
Beverage brand served when the guest does not request a special brand.

I

INCOME STATEMENT
A financial statement that provides information regarding the results of operations, including revenue, expenses, and profit for a stated period of time.

INDEPENDENT

An operation owned by an owner or owners with one or more properties that have no chain relationship—menus may not be identical among properties, food purchase specifications may differ, operating procedures are varied, etc.

INGREDIENT FILE

Contains important data on each purchased ingredient, such as ingredient code number, description, purchase unit, purchase unit cost, issue unit, issue unit cost, and recipe unit cost.

INSTITUTIONAL FOOD SERVICE OPERATION

An operation in an institution such as a business, hospital, or school. Traditionally, institutional food service operations have focused on nutrition and other non-economic factors; today, as costs mount, there is a need to manage institutional food service operations as professional businesses.

INTERNAL MERCHANDISING

The use of in-house promotional materials such as posters, table tent cards, wine displays, and dessert carts to promote additional sales.

INTERNAL SELLING

Specific sales activities of employees in conjunction with an internal merchandising program to promote additional sales and guest satisfaction.

INTOXICATION (LEGAL DEFINITION)

While this varies from state to state, in many states intoxication is defined as a blood-alcohol concentration (BAC) .10 gram or higher of alcohol per 100 milliliters of blood.

INVENTORY

The amount of food, beverages, and other supplies on hand.

INVENTORY TURNOVER

A ratio showing how quickly an operation's inventory is moving from storage to productive use; calculated by dividing the cost of products used by the average product inventory.

ISSUING

The distribution of food and beverages from the storeroom to authorized individuals who requisition these items.

J–K

JOURNAL PRINTER

An output device of an ECR/POS system that produces a continuous detailed record of all transactions entered anywhere in the system.

KITCHEN MONITOR
A video display unit capable of showing several orders on a single screen.

L

LABOR COST PERCENTAGE
A ratio comparing the labor expense to the total revenue generated; calculated by dividing labor costs by total revenue.

LABOR MASTER FILE
Contains one record for each employee, usually with the following data: employee name, employee number, social security number, job codes, hours worked, total hourly wages, wages declared, credits for employee meals, number of guests served per meal period, and gross sales per meal period.

LAMINATE
To seal in thin sheets of plastic.

LAYOUT
In menu planning, a rough sketch or plan of a menu's copy and artwork to show what the finished menu should look like.

LEAVENING
Incorporating gases into a baked product to increase the product's volume and make it lighter.

LINE MANAGER
A manager with decision-making authority within the organization.

M

MANAGEMENT
Involves using what you've got—resources—to do what you want to do—attain organizational objectives. "Getting work done through other people" is another popular definition of management.

MARINADE
A seasoned liquid, usually containing vegetable or olive oil and an acid such as wine, vinegar, or fruit juice. Herbs, spices, or vegetables are often added for flavoring.

MARKETING PLAN
A business plan that translates ongoing market research into strategies and tactics. Creating a marketing plan involves selecting target markets, determining marketing objectives, creating action plans to meet those objectives, and monitoring and evaluating those plans to measure their success and help set new objectives.

MENU BOARD

A keyboard overlay for an ECR/POS system terminal that identifies the function performed by each key during a specific meal period.

MENU ENGINEERING SOFTWARE

Menu management software that helps managers evaluate possible changes in a menu's current offerings and make sound pricing decisions.

MENU ITEM FILE

Contains data for all meal periods and menu items sold, including identification number, description, recipe code number, selling price, ingredient quantities for inventory reporting, and sales totals.

MENU MIX

Relates the sales of a menu item to the total number of menu items sold.

MINERALS

Basic nutrients that serve as tissue building materials and body regulators.

MINIMUM WAGE TIP CREDIT

A credit allowed employers by the Fair Labor Standards Act. Employers can apply a tip credit toward the minimum wage of some tipped employees.

MINI-TOWER PEDESTAL DISPENSING UNIT

A machine that combines the button selection technique of hose and gun devices with the portion size capabilities of console faucet units. Part of one kind of automated beverage control system.

MISE EN PLACE

A French term meaning "to put everything in place."

MODIFIER KEYS

Part of an ECR/POS system keyboard used in combination with preset and price look-up keys to detail preparation instructions for food production areas; also used to alter prices based on designated portion sizes.

MOIST-HEAT COOKING

Cooking methods that require water or another liquid.

N

NEGLIGENCE

Failure to exercise the care that a reasonably prudent person would exercise under like or similar circumstances.

NUTRITION

The science of food.

NUTRITIONAL BALANCE
In menu planning, the degree to which the menu offers a variety of foods in the four basic food groups. This is more important for institutional operations than commercial operations, although commercial operations should take care that the components of a well-balanced meal are available from among the menu items they offer.

O

OCCUPATIONAL SAFETY AND HEALTH ADMINISTRATION (OSHA)
An agency of the United States Department of Labor created to help make working conditions safer for employees.

OPEN CHECK FILE
Maintains current data for all open guest checks; is accessed to monitor items on a particular guest check, add items to a guest check after initial order entry, and close a guest check at the time of settlement.

OPERATIONS BUDGET
Management's detailed plans for generating revenue, determining profit requirements, and estimating expenses for the food service operation.

ORGANIZATION CHART
A diagram that shows the relationships among various employee positions in an operation.

ORGANIZING
The management activity that attempts to best assemble and use limited human resources to attain organizational objectives. It involves establishing the flow of authority and communication among people.

OVEN
Food service equipment which cooks food in a heated chamber. Examples include range, deck, roasting, convection, rotary, microwave, infrared, and recon ovens.

P

PAGE PROOF
A copy of a menu page as it will look when printed, provided by a typesetter.

PASTEURIZATION
A process of controlled heating that destroys bacteria in milk and other food products.

PLANNING
The management task of creating goals, objectives, and programs of action to reach those goals and objectives. It should be done before undertaking other management tasks.

PORTION COST

The standard food cost for an item that is sold as a single menu selection. The portion cost indicates the cost incurred by preparing one portion of the menu item according to its standard recipe.

POSTCOSTING

A special type of sales analysis that multiplies the number of menu items sold by standard recipe costs to determine a potential food cost amount for a completed meal period.

POTENTIALLY HAZARDOUS FOOD

Non-acidic, high-protein food (such as meat, fish, poultry, eggs, and milk) that is most susceptible to germ growth.

PRECHECK TERMINAL

An ECR/POS system terminal without a cash drawer; used to enter orders but not to settle accounts.

PRECOSTING

A special type of sales analysis that projects cost of sales figures, enabling managers to review and adjust operations before an actual service or meal period begins.

PRESET KEY

Part of an ECR/POS system keyboard programmed to maintain the price, description, department, tax, and inventory status of a designated menu item.

PRICE LOOK-UP KEY

Part of an ECR/POS system keyboard that operates like a preset key except that it requires the user to identify a menu item by its reference code number.

PROFIT MARGIN

An overall measure of management's ability to generate sales and control expenses; calculated by dividing net income by total revenue.

PROFIT PRICING

A pricing method that ensures that profit requirements and non-food expenses are factored into the pricing decision.

PROTEINS

Basic nutrients made of building blocks called amino acids. During digestion, proteins are broken down into separate amino acids which are then rearranged by the body to build required tissues. Complete protein foods supply essential amino acids in amounts which closely approximate the body's protein requirements.

PUBLIC BAR

A bar where bartenders prepare alcoholic beverages and serve them directly to guests or food servers. Guests can order and pick up their own beverages at public bars.

PUBLICITY

Free media coverage of a food service operation, its staff, or special property events.

PUBLIC RELATIONS

The process of communicating favorable information about a food service operation to the public in order to create a positive impression.

PURCHASE ORDER

An order for food or other supplies prepared by an operation's purchasing staff and submitted to suppliers.

PURCHASE RECORD

A detailed record of all incoming shipments from suppliers, typically used by small food service operations.

PURCHASE REQUISITION

Form used by storeroom personnel to alert the purchasing department that products need to be re-ordered from suppliers. The form specifies the products that are needed, how many are needed, and how soon they are needed.

PURCHASE SPECIFICATIONS

A detailed description of the quality, size, weight, and other characteristics desired for a particular item.

R

RANGE

Food service equipment with a flat cooking surface used to fry, grill, sauté, etc. Two basic types of ranges are solid-top and open-top.

REACH-IN OR ROLL-IN REFRIGERATOR

Small refrigerated unit used to store food products at point-of-use in production areas or in server or guest areas. May be used for central storage at small operations.

RECEIPT PRINTER

A printing device that produces hard copy on narrow register tape.

RECOMMENDED DIETARY ALLOWANCES (RDAs)

The amounts of essential nutrients that experts believe adequate for the nutritional needs of most healthy people.

REQUEST-FOR-CREDIT MEMO

A form filled out by the property's receiving clerk that lists products that were on the supplier's invoice but were not delivered or were returned because of damage or other reasons. This memo should be signed by the delivery person and attached to the supplier's invoice.

REQUISITION

A written order used by production personnel identifying the type, amount, and value of items needed from storage.

ROOM SERVICE MENU

A menu offered by lodging properties that serve food to guests in the guestroom, suite, cabin, etc. Room service menus usually offer a limited number of items because it is difficult to maintain food quality while transporting the food to the guest.

S

SEAT TURNOVER

A ratio indicating the number of times that a given seat in a sit-down dining area is occupied during a meal period; calculated by dividing the number of guests served by the number of available seats.

SENIOR CITIZEN'S MENU

A menu that seeks to accommodate seniors and their special health needs by offering items low in calories, sodium, fat, or cholesterol.

SERVICE BAR

A bar where service bartenders prepare alcoholic beverages for food servers, who then present them to guests in the dining room. Guests typically do not order or pick up their own beverages at service bars.

SIDEWORK

Setup and cleanup work that must be done before and after dining rooms are opened. Examples include restocking server supply stations, filling salt-and-pepper shakers, etc.

SODIUM

A mineral used to season and preserve food.

SOLVENCY RATIO

A measure of the extent to which an operation is financed by debt and is able to meet its long-term obligations; calculated by dividing total assets by total liabilities.

STAFFING

The management activity of recruiting and hiring applicants.

STAFF MANAGER

A manager who serves in an advisory or special capacity to the line managers. His or her primary role is to help line managers in other departments make decisions by providing them with information and expert analysis.

STANDARD FOOD COST

The ideal food cost that managers should expect when a menu item is prepared according to its standard recipe.

STANDARD RECIPE

A formula for producing a food or beverage item specifying ingredients, the required quantity of each ingredient, preparation procedures, portion size and portioning equipment, garnish, and any other information necessary to prepare the item.

STANDARD RECIPE FILE

Contains recipes for all menu items. Important data maintained by this file include: recipe code number, recipe name, ingredients, preparation instructions, number of portions, portion size, cost of ingredients, menu selling price, and food cost percentage.

STEAM-COOKING EQUIPMENT

Food service equipment, such as steam-jacketed kettles and compartment steamers, that cooks food by the direct or indirect application of steam.

SUGGESTIVE SELLING

Techniques used to encourage guests to buy certain menu items with the objectives of increasing sales of the most profitable items and increasing the check average.

SUPPLEMENTAL MERCHANDISING COPY

Menu copy devoted to subjects other than the menu items. Supplemental merchandising copy includes basic restaurant information as well as copy designed to entertain.

T

TABLE D'HÔTE MENU

A menu that offers a complete meal for one price. Sometimes two or more complete meals are offered on the menu, each with its own price. Meals on table d'hôte menus are set by the menu planner and guests are given few, if any, choices.

TABLE SERVICE

A type of service in which guests are seated at a table and food servers wait on them. Four basic styles of table service are American, English, French, and Russian.

TAKE-OUT MENU

A menu that offers food to guests who want to pick up the food at the restaurant and consume it elsewhere.

TILTING BRAISING PAN

Flat-bottomed cooking equipment that can be used as a kettle, griddle, fry pan, steamer, oven, or warmer/server. The bottom of an electric tilting braising pan is a heavy stainless steel plate heated by an electric element. Tilting braising pans can reduce the total cooking time of many food products by as much as 25%.

TOUCH-BAR FAUCET DISPENSING UNIT

Part of an automated beverage control unit, typically dedicated to a single beverage type and preset for one specific portion size output per push on the bar lever.

TRAFFIC PATTERN OR WORK FLOW

The pathways employees form as they go about their work. Good design and layout seek to minimize employee backtracking, intersections where several employee paths cross, and other traffic pattern problems.

TRUTH-IN-MENU LAWS

Laws that seek to protect guests by prohibiting inaccurate claims on the menu in such areas as freshness, geographical origin, and food preparation techniques.

U–V

UNIFORM SYSTEM OF ACCOUNTS

A manual (usually produced for a specific segment of the hospitality industry) which defines accounts for various types and sizes of operations, generally provides standardized financial statement formats, explains individual accounts, and provides sample bookkeeping documents.

VEGETABLE

Any plant grown for an edible part other than the ovary, which is classified as fruit.

VEGETABLE FRUIT

A vegetable (such as tomatoes) technically classified as a fruit because it contains the ovary of the plant.

VITAMINS

Basic nutrients that promote growth, help digest foods, prevent certain diseases, and perform a number of other important functions for health and well-being.

W

WHITE SPACE

The areas of a menu not covered with words or artwork.

WORK STATION

A place in which one employee works or where one menu item is made.

WORK STATION PRINTER

A printing device usually placed in kitchen preparation areas and service bar locations.

Index